THE THEOLOGY OF VOCATIONS

THE
THEOLOGY
OF
VOCATIONS

CHARLES A. SCHLECK, C.S.C.

THE BRUCE PUBLISHING COMPANY
MILWAUKEE

IMPRIMI POTEST:

Howard J. Kenna, C.S.C.
Provincial Superior

NIHIL OBSTAT:

John A. Schulien, S.T.D.
Censor librorum

IMPRIMATUR:

✠ William E. Cousins
Archbishop of Milwaukee
September 11, 1962

Library of Congress Catalog Card Number: 62–20960

© 1963 The Bruce Publishing Company
MADE IN THE UNITED STATES OF AMERICA

To the Seat of Wisdom

as a sign

of

filial gratitude

Preface

THE present work was undertaken at the request of many students whom I had the pleasure of teaching at the Summer School of Theology at the University of Notre Dame. The course, which is substantially contained in the present book, was inserted in the theological curriculum as an elective intended primarily for those engaged in the recruitment and formation of young religious and for those teaching the course on the "states of life" in their respective schools.

As the reader passes from page to page, he will quickly discover the many lacunae and inadequacies of the various treatments. This is due to several factors. First, the work is intended to be merely a survey course covering the main states of life that lie open to the Christian. Consequently, it is not meant to be exhaustive or complete, nor a masterpiece contributing the last word. It is, rather, intended to meet a rather pressing need, to inaugurate a series of subsequent similar works, better, more thorough and accurate, by writers much better qualified than the present author. I must confess that my own field is dogmatic theology, especially sacramental. Another factor accounting partially for the inadequacies to be found herein stems from the lack of time and ability to concentrate on the subject matter itself. This, I know, is a rather common problem with American authors. The major portion of the work was done in haste, after a full year of teaching usually five or six tracts in dogmatic theology, and during the time itself, at which the course was being taught.

Notwithstanding these admitted limitations, I have with some trepidation decided to place it before the public. I know that many will wish I had not. Perhaps the reason pushing me to do so has a biblical foundation: "I tell you even if he will not bestir himself to grant it out of friendship, he will certainly get up for shame's sake and give his friend (all he has)" (Lk. 11:8).

There is one section that will certainly call for intense criticism — that on marriage. To mellow this just a trifle, I would advise the reader that the writer has just finished a special volume entitled *The Sacrament of*

Matrimony: A Dogmatic Study which will shortly appear through the kindness of the same publishing firm. It was in view of this (of the larger sale of this coming work, I might add!) and of the length of the present volume that I have given this important subject rather short shrift. Then too, the subject has already been the precise and special objective of a plethora of recent works.

In conclusion I would like to thank Father Roland Simonitsch, C.S.C., and Father Robert Pelton, C.S.C., former and present heads of the Department of Theology at the University of Notre Dame, for having "invited" me to give the course. Most of all I would express my deep gratitude to the many Sisters whose veils will have to hide them in anonymity, without whose insistence, cooperation, and, above all, prayers, the present work would never have been published. A word of thanks also to a humble housewife and mother, Mrs. Larusso, of Jordan, Minn., for typing the final manuscript. Lastly, a word of thanks in advance to the many critics who will furnish me with many suggestions to attempt, perhaps, a future ascent to the Omega Point!

Washington, D. C.
September 1962

Contents

Contents

THE THEOLOGY OF VOCATIONS

Introduction

WHEN a particular problem arises in a society it immediately causes a rather detailed study and examination of the entire subject of which it is a part. For it is only by such a study that all the issues involved can be perceived. In fact we can say that such a situation or occurrence is often providential since it forces us to reexamine with more than usual precision "attics and cellars" that have never been gone into. Striking examples of such situations have occurred throughout the ages of the Church in regard to the various dogmas of our Faith. The more problematical any one of them became the more did it force the best minds of the Church to turn their attention on it, and to bring into the light and clarity of our common vision the precise teaching of Christ. Thus, for example, in our own day the science of Mariology has witnessed much progress both by way of organization or systematization as well as by way of penetration into Mary's destiny and role in the Church. Much of our former rhetoric has been replaced by reflection, our legend by history, our sentimentality by virility, and exuberance by discretion.[1] While most of the essentials of Mariology are already contained in the New Testament with their preparations or foreshadowings in the Old, still it was necessary that much time should elapse between the Church's foundation and her subsequent understanding of the place and importance of the Virgin Mother of God.

It seems to me that a similar phenomenon has occurred in regard to the problem of "vocations." In the past fifteen years or so a renewed interest and study has taken place in this regard. Several reasons, no doubt, are responsible for this. There is the well-known fact that psychology has made us very much aware of the importance of *orientating a person on the path of life mapped out for him or her by God.* Before every human being there stands a kind of picture of that which he wishes to or should become. He will not be satisfied or fully at peace until the idea shown in that picture has been realized.[2] Another reason that might be given is

---

[1] Cf. *The Virgin Mary*, Jean Guitton (New York: Kenedy, 1952), Chap. 1, p. 10.
[2] Cf. *The Psychology of Asceticism*, J. Lindworsky, S.J. (Baltimore: Carroll Press, 1950), p. 15.

the so-called *shortage of vocations*. This has done much to "stir the embers" making us investigate the various factors which might be responsible for the plight in which we find ourselves. And finally, just as *attacks against the sacredness of marriage* have forced us to once again reexamine the institution called into question, so, too, attacks *against vocations to the higher walks of life*, especially virginity, have constrained us to reexamine these institutions. As was true in the case of marriage so too in the case of these, results have been attained and are being attained which serve to bring out the riches which Divine Providence has incorporated into these realities.

The present work does not intend or pretend to study the problem of "vocations" from all the elements which in one way or another enter into it. Each of them is the object of a special science or discipline: the sociological elements, that of the study of sociology; the psychological elements, that of psychology; and the theological elements, that of theology. As the title of the work clearly indicates, it is the intent of this book to investigate the problem of "vocation" from a *theological* viewpoint, attempting to consider at least the more important of the theological factors involved. It is hoped that such a study will provide those engaged in one way or another in vocational work, or those interested in the problem of vocations with the basic ideas essential to their needs or quest. Before entering upon the study proper, however, it would be best for us to recall some of the preliminary ideas which will serve to clarify the title of the work and indicate its place in the over-all picture of theology.

A Theology . . .

The purpose of all intellectual endeavor is to bring us a little closer to the understanding of God, not perhaps directly, but at least indirectly. The simple reason for this is that all knowledge and truth is ultimately derived from Him who is First Truth so that in knowing the truth which is the object of any intellectual discipline, we are led to a fuller understanding and knowledge of God Himself. It was this which prompted the famous dictum of the Apostle Paul: "The knowledge of God is clear to their minds; God himself made it clear to them. From the foundations of the world men have caught sight of his invisible nature, his eternal power, and his divineness as they are known through his creatures."[3] In a sense we can say that because all things created are "sacramental" or significative, reflecting something of God their Creator, or since every

---

[3] Rom. 1:19–20.

effect gives us some knowledge of its cause, the attainment of any truth gives us some knowledge of God.

If such be true of all study, it is especially true of theology whose very object is God Himself, not seen or known through created realities, but known through revelation. The theologian attempts to avail himself of the sources of revelation, Scripture and Tradition. Indeed he must return to them constantly, since it is his duty in presenting Sacred Doctrine to indicate whether and how the teachings of the living authority of the Church are found there, either explicitly or implicitly.[4] But neither theology nor the theologian can stop there. The science of which he is an expositor demands that he push on by a constant and ever deepening attempt to analyze *rationally* by the use of an elaborated philosophy the *content* of revealed truth. It is by reason of the very nature of his science that the theologian attempts to *organize* a presentation of the subject which he is to unfold. He takes the terms, concepts, and statements of Scripture and Tradition in which God has made Himself known to men and then elaborates them into an organic intellectual construction or whole. This is done according to a logical order in which the mutual relationships and proportions between the various things concerned receive as clear a presentation as possible.

From this it should be clear that the scope of any work in theology is very definitely limited. It embraces only one of the elements included in a famous dictum of St. Augustine: "*Veritas pateat, veritas placeat, veritas moveat.*" Only the first lies *directly* within the scope of scholastic theology — to make the truth evident. The other two are outside its proper scope, even though a theologian will, at times, and *should* indicate the connection which doctrine has with life. Otherwise a "divorce" could very easily occur between the two. While theology must be rooted in Scripture and Tradition, indeed, takes them as its sources and foundations, it does not pretend to usurp their place or substitute itself for them. It attempts, rather, to *show* how and if the doctrine being discussed is contained in the sources, and if it is, "in the same sense in which it has been defined."[5] Then by a rational presentation of the mystery or truth being discussed, it attempts to embody in human language the response which faith makes to this revelation, so that the depth of the mystery contained in it is made more clear to the human mind.[6]

The wisdom which is theology does not claim to exhaust the meaning

---

[4] Cf. *Humani Generis*, Pius XII, *AAS* 42 (1950), 568.

[5] *Inter Gravissimas*, Pius IX, October 26, 1870.

[6] Cf. "Theology and the Bible," by C. Kearns, O.P., in *The Word of Life* (Dublin: M. H. Gill and Son, Ltd., 1959), pp. 103–111.

of Revelation. Rather, it essentially recognizes in its deep humility that the power of faith and charity and the Gifts of the Holy Ghost perfecting these, wisdom, understanding, and knowledge, have a far greater capacity for penetrating into its mystery than the most acute and subtle rational analysis could ever hope to effect.[7]

As we have mentioned or rather hinted at, although there is no direct connection between theology and grace and virtue, still there is an indirect connection between them, one that is much more intimate than that existing between all other inferior sciences or branches of learning and grace. *Cognitio gignit amorem* — "Knowledge begets or gives rise to love"; for the more thoroughly we know something the more we are attracted by it, if we find it to be good and true. Thus the intellectual knowledge of God should serve to give us a greater affective knowledge of Him. This, however, is not due so much to the theological method as it is to the teacher. It is he alone who must keep his gaze fixed constantly on the ultimate goal of the life of man — intimate union with God. In order to realize his contribution to this goal, the theologian must bring to his presentation a deep spirit of piety, so that, like Aquinas, while he brings to the intellect the light of knowledge, he also increases at the same time in the will the flame of virtue. No theological method, regardless of how perfect it be, if it find wanting in the teacher the virtues of purity, detachment from the goods of the world, humility, a love for prayer, and for God, will ever bridge the gap existing between doctrine and life. If these be found, it is very likely that the two principal effects which Pius XI taught should be obtained from theological study will be realized: an all-embracing love for God and a great desire for the things of eternity.[8]

... of Vocations

As we have just seen, theology is "faith seeking to understand" and this applies completely to our present study.[9] THE THEOLOGY OF VOCATIONS is an attempt to arrive at an understanding of vocation both in its general aspects and in its particular incarnations. It is not a biblical theology, nor a patristic theology of the problem of vocation, nor one which deals merely with the teaching of the magisterium of the Church on this question. Rather, its purpose is to utilize all these sources, particularly the last mentioned, organizing them into a schema or logical sequence so that the present-day teaching of both the magisterium of the Church

---

[7] Cf. *Life of the Spirit*, editorial, March, 1958, p. 388.

[8] Cf. encyclical, *Studiorum Ducem*, AAS 15 (1923), 310–311.

[9] Cf. St. Augustine, *In Joan. Evan.*, tract, 29, 6, PL 35, 1630; *De Trinitate*, 8, 5, 8, PL 42, 952.

and of her theologians might be presented as clearly as possible. In view of this end — clarity and fullness of treatment — some of the more attractive and interesting considerations will not be taken up, such as an historical approach to the entire question. It is not the intention of the author to deny the very important value of such considerations. But it seemed best to sacrifice these values in view of the end sought. Moreover, these questions have often been discussed by much more competent authors than the present writer.[10]

It is the intent of this book to consider from a theological viewpoint the notions of vocation, both in a general way and then as we see it realized in various individuals or, rather, groups of individuals which make up our society. Thus we intend to take up the vocation of those to whom God has granted certain charisms, that of those who pertain to the active and contemplative life, that of those who belong to the states of perfection, and finally that of those who pertain to that division often called the secular states. One of these last-mentioned states — matrimony — will not be discussed in detail, not, certainly, from any lack of affection for this way of life on the part of the author, but, owing to the fact of an already superfluous number of excellent and thorough works on this state or vocation.

The Theology of Vocations in Its Relation to the Whole of Theology

In order to provide a better grasp of the reason for the present study and in order to place it correctly in the logical sequence of the various theological tracts, it might be best to indicate its position in the systematic presentation of God's teaching to men. In the opening part of his theological treatise, St. Thomas divides the study of theology as follows:

I. The *First Part* treats of God, His Essence, the Distinction of Persons in the Godhead, and whatever concerns the Procession of Creatures from Him.

II. The *Second Part* considers the movement of men back to God; for although they proceed from God in the act of creation still it is with a view to making their way back to their Source who is to be the constant object of their knowledge and love.

---

[10] Cf. *Christian Spirituality*, Pierre Pourrat, S.S. (Westminster, Md.: Newman Press, 1953 ff.), 4 vols.; *Western Monasticism*, Dom C. Butler, O.S.B.; The Religious Life Series, esp. the vols. on *Vocation, Poverty, Obedience, Chastity, Communal Life*, and *Apostolic Life* (London: Blackfriars, 1952 ff.); *The First Spiritual Writers*, F. Cayre, A.A., F&F Book (London: Burns and Oates, 1959); *Post Reformation Spiritual Writers*, Louis Cognet, F&F Book (Burns and Oates, 1959); *Religious Orders of Men*, Jean Canu, F&F Book (Burns and Oates, 1960).

III. The *Third Part* studies the Incarnation and Redemption or the Mystery of Christ in Himself and in His continued activity through the Sacraments, which have been aptly called the "remnants of the Incarnation."

In this very general division of theology, the study which we are about to undertake lies in the second main division — the so-called Second Part of the *Summa* of the Angelic Doctor, which considers man's return to God. In this division Thomas' concern is to show how man made according to the image and likeness of God and elevated to the pursuit of a supernatural goal can attain that destiny through his own powers of action supernaturalized or divinized by the principle of grace.[11] After treating of the entire grace-life both in general and in particular diffused, as it is, throughout the essence of the soul and its powers, he proceeds to show how this life can be exercised by a Christian, or how a Christian can make his way back to God in one of several ways. Today and for some time now, this treatment has been and is called the *states of life*. It is precisely in regard to this last area that the present study will center its attention.

While all the tracts in theology are mutually related if not directly, at least indirectly, there are some which have a more intimate relation with each other than they do with others. In the present study this is also true as we shall now point out.

On the One God and God the Creator

As we shall see more and more clearly as we proceed through the book, vocation is a singling out of an individual by God for divine service to be exercised in and through some walk of life. It is the author of the Book of Ecclesiasticus who has so concretely and simply indicated this:

> Some he would assign high dignity; others should be lost in the common rabble of days. So it is that all men are built of the same clay. Son of Adam is son of earth, yet the Lord in the plentitude of his wisdom has marked them off from one another, not giving the same destiny to each. There are those he has blessed with high station; there are those he has set apart and claimed for himself; there are those he has put under a ban and turned them into humble folk, or degraded from their former distinction. Clay we are in the potter's hands; it is for him who made us to dispose of us; clay is what potter wills it to be and we are in our maker's hands to be dealt with at his pleasure.[12]

Or perhaps, we might point to the Lord's description of the vocation of the Apostles: "You have not chosen me, but I have chosen you that

---

[11] Cf. I–II, Q. 109, Introduction.
[12] Ecclus. 33:10–14.

you might go forth and bear fruit, and that your fruit should remain."[13] In both of these passages we are clearly given to understand that the manner in which we serve God is something that is *determined* by *Him*; for we have not chosen Him, but, rather, He has chosen us. The inspired writers in both of these instances seem to love to dwell on this action of determination on the part of God, howsoever we might wish to clarify this notion in theology.

It is because of this determination that the whole problem of vocation is intimately connected with the treatise on God, the One God and God the Creator. Vocation pertains or belongs somehow or other to *providence* and to *predestination*, God's election from all eternity. And this — God's election of any given individual — pertains to, or is the result of, His *dilection*, His infinite love which creates and infuses different communications of His goodness into creatures. In fact, we shall see that it seems that the whole of the theology of vocations is founded upon some of the fundamental doctrines which are discussed in the tract on the One God and God the Creator, especially that of God's free and gratuitous love in regard to creatures. It is St. Thomas who gives us a hint as to the *fundamental theological principle* involved in the mystery of vocation:

> God loves all existing things. For these insofar as they exist are good since the very being of a thing is itself a good. Now, we have shown above[14] that God's will is the cause of all things. It must needs be, then, that a thing has some being or any kind of good, only inasmuch as it is willed by God. To every existing thing, God wills some good. Hence *since to love anything is nothing else than to will good to that thing*, it is clear that God loves everything that exists. Yet His love is not like ours. Because since our will is not the cause of goodness in things but is moved by it as by its object, our love whereby we will good to anything is not the cause of this goodness, but conversely its goodness, whether real or imaginary, calls forth our love by which we will it to preserve the good it has and receive besides the good it does not have, and to this end we direct our actions. *The love of God, on the other hand, infuses and creates goodness in things.* . . .
>
> Since to love a thing is to will it good, something may be said to be loved more or less in a twofold way. In one way on the part of the act of the will itself which is more or less intense. God does not love things more than others in this way, because He loves all things by an act of the will that is one, simple, and always the same. In another way, on the part of the good itself that a person wills for the one he loves. In this way we are to love that being more than another for whom we will a greater good, even though our will is not more intense. In this way we must needs say that God loves some things more than others. For since God's love is the cause of goodness in things no one thing would be better than another if God did not will greater good for one than for another.[15]

---

[13] Jn. 15:16.   [14] Q. 19, a. 4.   [15] I, Q. 20, aa. 2–3.

In these two articles we are presented with the basis of a theology of vocations. To love anything is to will that thing some good. In God's case such a willing is not prompted by any good that He discovers in the thing loved. Rather, it is the cause of the good found in the creature. Moreover, He is said to love some creatures more than others in accordance with the good that He communicates or infuses into them. In proportion to the perfection of the gifts which He has given to creatures God is said to love some more than others. Thus, for example, those who may have received greater natural gifts of beauty or intellect can be said to be loved by God more than others less favored on these accounts. Likewise, in the order of grace some can be said to be loved more by God than others in proportion to the intensity of grace they may have received from God.

Perhaps an example might serve to illustrate this teaching. God is said to have loved Christ not only more than He loves the whole human race, but more than He loves the entire created universe. The reason is because He has willed for Him a greater good in giving Him a name that is above all names; for it is by God's will alone that the man Christ is true God.

From this it seems that we are logically to conclude that the mystery of vocation like all the other mysteries of the Christian life can be reduced to the above fundamental relationship of God with His creatures — a relationship of love.

Another aspect of vocation that links it up with this tract is the manner in which this singling out takes place. It is the teaching of some theologians that God in His governance over the universe employs spiritual creatures to carry out His plan. In reference to man these creatures, the angels, are said to illuminate us, to instruct us, and to carry the messages of God to man and the prayers of man to God. God has no need of such help. It is merely that He has established an order of operation in which He uses these creatures as His instruments or ministers.[16] Since vocation is a singling out of a creature by God, it seems that we can rightly conclude that this is done through the intermediary of an angel, whether we are aware of this or not. This angel or messenger awaits our consent or our refusal and carries our answer back to God. Consequently, an individual's vocation is a kind of a miniature Annunciation, but one which is most often hidden and invisible to the majority of persons. It is usually known only by conjecture arrived at after reflection and the taking of counsel.

---

[16] Cf. Tob. 5:17 ff.; Dan. 8:16; 9:21; Lk. 1:11, 19, 26, 27; Acts 8:26; 10:3 ff.; cf. also St. Bernard, In Ps. Qui Habitat, Sermo 12, nos. 4–7, PL 183, 232–234.

In the case of a vocation to one of the higher ways of life, we might say that God sends this messenger who speaks to us in a kind of a *special* way. Or we might say, following St. Thomas' interpretation of our Lord's meeting with Mary Magdalen after the Resurrection: He sends this messenger to address us by our first name thereby indicating His special love for us beyond others.[17]

Grace

Another tract closely connected with the theology of vocation is that of grace. For granted that one of the elements involved in vocation is an inspiration or divine motion given by God to the soul, we are also given to understand that this mystery also is to be studied in the light of our knowledge of grace. It is not something that pertains to or can be measured by things belonging to the natural order. Rather, it is a reality that pertains to the realm of those things which lie far beyond all of man's natural powers and exigencies. It is supernatural in its origin, its nature, and its destiny.[18]

This notion — the intimate connection between vocation and the supernatural or the order of grace — can never be forgotten. Those called by God to help discern, foster, or form vocations causing them to grow and bring forth fruit can never lose sight of this fact. They are working in an order of realities that is proper to God alone. The leading part in vocation always belongs to Him. Indeed we might say that He occupies the whole stage; for in a field those who plant and water merely carry out the conditions necessary for growth. The growth itself, however, can only proceed from some life-giving force. In this case, because the life pertains to the order of grace, it can come only from God Himself, the Master of all such life. We are fields of Christ's tilling and structures of God's designs.[19] While a vocation is a "dialogue," if you will, its most active part comes from God. His designs precede man's reaction since the divine plan is *always ahead* of us.[20]

While the activity of this grace of vocation will always remain in the ultimate analysis mysterious since it pertains to an order that surpasses perfect knowledge, still the presence of this grace in God's plan is real and admits of study. For grace even though it implies obscurity also implies objectivity and real existence as both the Old and the New Testa-

---

17 Cf. *Commen. in Joannem* (Rome: Marietti, 1952), p. 465.
18 Cf. "The Teaching of the Church on Vocations to the Priesthood and Religious life," by John F. Sweeney, S.J., in NCEA Annual Meeting, *Proceedings*, 1959, p. 369.
19 Cf. 1 Cor. 3:5 ff.
20 Cf. F. Suarez, *Our Lady the Virgin* (Dublin: Scepter, 1959), pp. 24–25.

ments so clearly indicate. We have, for example, God's singling out of the chosen people, and among them certain ones — an Abraham, a Joseph, a Samuel, a David, an Esther, a Judith, an Isaias, a Jeremias — to accomplish certain designs that He willed in order to manifest His love, His mercy, and His justice.

The Mystical Body

The study of this problem should also give us a deeper insight into and love for the mystery of the Mystical Body of Christ, the Church. For if it is true that the Church shows before men a remarkable beauty, it is so only because of vocation, which we might call the "touch" of the Master Artist who is constantly completing the attractiveness of His Spouse. It is St. Paul who has so wonderfully described this action in his Epistle to the Ephesians:

> But to each one of us grace was given according to the measure of Christ's bestowal. Thus Scripture says: "Ascending on high he led away captives he gave gifts to man" . . . and he himself gave some men as apostles, and some as prophets, others again as Evangelists, and others as pastors and teachers in order to perfect the saints for a work of the ministry, building up the Body of Christ until we all attain to the unity of Faith and the deep knowledge of the Son of God, to perfect manhood, to the mature measure of the fullness of Christ. . . . We are to practice the truth in love and so grow up in all things in him who is the Head, Christ. For from him the whole body (being closely joined and knit together through every joint of the system according to the functioning in due measure of each single part) derives its increase to the building up of Israel itself in love.[21]

The Church is truly the Queen spoken of so often in Sacred Scripture who is circumdata varietate — "surrounded about with variety." It is brilliantly displayed by the teaching of the Apostles, the confession of martyrs, the purity of virgins, and the sorrow of penitents. It was because of this close connection between vocation and the various organs of the Mystical Body that St. Thomas in treating of the states of life wrote:

> The difference of states and duties in the Church has reference to the perfection of the Church. For even as in the order of nature and natural things perfection which in God is simple and uniform is not to be found in the created universe except in a multiform manner, so too, the fullness of grace which is centered in Christ as Head flows forth to His members in various ways for the perfecting of the Body of the Church. This is the meaning of the words of the Apostle Paul [in the passage just quoted]. . . .
> Thirdly, this difference in variety pertains to the dignity and beauty of the Church which consists in a certain order. . . . Hence the Apostle says[22]

[21] Eph. 4:8–13.
[22] 2 Tim. 2:20.

that in a large house there are not only vessels of gold and silver, but also of wood and of earth.[23]

Conclusion

Vocation, because it is an effect of a special grace from God and because every grace demands some kind of communication from Him, brings with it something of God Himself to the creature. For every communication is also an assimilation, such that the one communicating life to another does so after a determinate manner. In proportion as God communicates His graces to creatures He assimilates them to Himself more or less according to the measure which He communicates. This communication, as we shall see throughout our study, consists in some modification of the grace-life that we possess.

Seeing this role of man in God's plan of re-creation and redemption, our spirit of faith, humility, and gratitude, our spirit of docility and trust should be deepened. And with the deepening of these particular qualities certainly the Spirit of God Himself will lend a hand in uniting to our theological wisdom regarding the problem of vocation, that Wisdom which comes only from the Holy Ghost activating His Gifts so that we may have a *loving insight* into this mystery as well as an intellectual one. This should not be too difficult; for, as we have seen, this mystery is so wonderfully bound up with the mystery of God's love for man.

While it is true that an intellectual understanding of vocation is most important, we must beware lest it be the final termination of our study. To separate the intellectual knowledge of the theology of vocation from an affective knowledge of it would be to do an injustice to our endeavor. For the former should serve to dispose us for the latter. With prayer, especially to the Holy Ghost, and a more faithful practice of the spirit of detachment so essential for any close union with and understanding of divine things we should arrive at a deeper appreciation of our life of grace, especially as this is manifested in and through the activity or exercise of the virtue of religion. For it is this virtue and its two acts, the internal act of devotion and the external act of sacrifice, that form the basis of the theology of the grace of vocation. It seems that so far as vocation is concerned, this virtue is modified by the divine activity, the end result being that the one affected is meant to be in God's designs an incarnation of the virtue of religion. The priestly character and the vows of religion make of our lives a *sacrificium laudis*, a sacrifice of praise as the Secret Prayer

---

[23] II–II, Q. 183, a. 2; cf. also the Apostolic Constitution of Pius XII on Secular Institutes, *Provida Mater Ecclesia*, Eng. transl. in *Apostolic Sanctity in the World*, ed. J. Haley, C.S.C. (Notre Dame, Ind.: U. of Notre Dame Press, 1957), p. 127 ff. and Bouscaren-O'Connor, *Canon Law Digest*, III, p. 135 ff.

for the feast of St. Catherine of Siena has it, "fragrant with the internal and external odor of chastity" which seems to attract and ravish the eye of God.

May God grant that all who peruse this study may be brought just a little more close to Him; that they may become, in fact as well as in theory, that part of creation which is the more illustrious portion of the flock of Christ. May they become that part of creation which is elevated above the rest (the mountains and the hills of the liturgy) which receives through God's mercy the first dew falling from heaven, of which the liturgy of Pentecost speaks. For it is this that will render the work and life of those whom God has called by His special love to a life of service most fruitful in regard to their own sanctification and that of countless other souls. Finally, may this study be some incentive to our realizing more fully and actually the assertion of the author of the Book of Proverbs: "The path and footsteps of the just are as a splendid light that grows unto the perfect day," which is, as we know, the day of eternity in Christ.[24]

---

[24] Prov. 4:18.

CHAPTER ONE

Vocation in General

THE reality which we call vocation is not a new discovery. It is a fact which has occurred since the creation of the world; a fact which is continuing now and will continue until God's eternal plan for our universe is brought to a conclusion. It was for this reason that the inspired writer of the very first book of the Bible taught that God created the world and all that was in it, that He brought order and beauty and splendor out of the initial chaos which then existed. There was no intention on his part to transmit to the reader the creation-event as it actually happened. His purpose was to indicate symbolically certain fundamental truths of creation. Among these was the assertion that from the very beginning of creation all things were subjected to the orderings and direction of Divine Providence. Moreover, in a very special manner he conveys by means of a popular narrative easily understandable by the audience for whom he wrote, the careful workings of this Providence in regard to man. He teaches that man was constituted in a state of intimacy with God, given the gift of immortality, destined to a life of intimate union with God. He presents us with the fact of man's fall and with God's intervention in his life by way of a promise to send to the human race a Redeemer who would be responsible for the restoration of man's pristine privileges in one way or another.

Nature of Vocation in General

As the story or "history" of the human race unfolds in Revelation, the intervention of God, or the determination or election of God, His dilection of a people and of individuals within that people is more and more clearly brought out. The Jewish nation as a whole is called God's elect and is an object of vocation.[1] Likewise certain individuals pertaining to this nation were selected by God for special missions. We have Abraham,[2]

[1] Cf. Exod. 19:3–5.　　　[2] Cf. Gen. 12:1–3.

Moses,[3] David,[4] Samuel,[5] Esther, Judith, John the Baptist, and others. In the New Testament we find the Apostles chosen by God to be the pillars of His new Church. This in turn — the new Israel — the new chosen people as well as each individual member of this people is also the object of God's special love or predilection.[6] We might say that Sacred Scripture in almost all of the accounts which it gives of God's having chosen a nation or an individual for some mission or work, seems to bring before our minds the *severity* with which God enjoined these determinations on His creatures. The story of Saul, who usurped the right of the priest to offer sacrifice;[7] the story of Core and his faction, who were destroyed for having attempted to perform rites which God Himself wished to reserve to the priesthood;[8] these and other accounts convey the fact that God has had throughout the history of mankind a very special interest and intervention in reference to the affairs of men.

In the biblical accounts of vocation we find that sometimes the purpose of the vocation is made known to the one called; at other times it is not. Abraham, for example, was not immediately given a full picture of his own vocation.[9] On the other hand, Moses and Gideon were told the purpose of their missions — the deliverance of Israel from its enemies. Likewise when Saul and David were called the object of their mission was indicated to them — to be kings of the chosen people.[10] The prophets also were given a definite mission — the communication of the word of God to Israel.[11] This same element can also be noted in the New Testament accounts of certain vocations, as, for example, in the case of the Apostles, of Paul, etc. And when there is question of the Christians, the object of their calling is also rather clearly specified, at least in a general way. They were to be a kingdom of priests and a holy nation.[12]

From the various passages dealing with these vocations we discover that in most cases the call or the invitation or designation is made known to the individual *through a direct address of God*. This was true with Abraham, Moses, Gideon, Samuel, Isaias, Jeremias, Ezechiel, Amos, and others. In some cases this vocation or mission was made known through others, through angels, as in the case of Mary; through Christ, as in the case of the Apostles; or in the Old Testament, for example, through the prophets.

[3] Cf. Exod. 3:1–4; 17.
[4] Cf. 1 Kings 16:13.
[5] Cf. 1 Kings 3 ff.
[6] Cf. Rom. 8:29–30; Gal. 1:6–15; 1 Cor. 1:26–30.
[7] Cf. 1 Kings 13.
[8] Cf. Num. 15:1 ff.
[9] Cf. Gen. 12:1–3.
[10] Cf. Ps. 89:20–38; 1 Sam. 9:15–16.
[11] Cf. Is. 6; Jer. 1:4–10.
[12] Cf. 1 Pet. 2:9.

Sometimes this call was made known by means of a command[13] and at other times by means of an invitation.[14] At any rate, it seems that a biblical vocation to some office or duty which accomplishes the work of God is not conceived as authentic unless there exists *some sign* that God wishes this person to undertake the office or mission.

It is interesting to note that these vocations, whether indicated in the Old or the New Testament, seem to include a number of elements. Thus, for example, the call often includes a *renunciation* of something. Abraham, as a result of his call, had to renounce his country and his relatives[15] and this for a mission, which, as we mentioned above, was not indicated to him. In the New Testament this renunciation becomes more and more explicit since a vocation in the Christian dispensation is intimately connected with the mystery of the Cross of our Lord. Some would have to abandon their homes, their work, their families.[16] They were warned that they would suffer persecution and be universally hated.[17] In fact, this element of renunciation is so proper to the Christian vocation that our Lord constantly referred to it throughout the course of His public life. Moreover, Luke makes special mention of this element when speaking of our Lord's invitation to the rich young man.[18] In order to follow Christ our Lord made specific mention of the necessity of one's showing a love for Him that was greater than that for one's family.[19]

If we investigate the call of Jesus to His Apostles and followers, we note that one of the things He seems to have specifically insisted on was *renunciation of riches*. He forbade His disciples to take money on their journey; He was sad when the rich young man turned away and decided not to follow Him.

Another element that seems to be indicated is that the person called will receive for his fidelity to it some kind of reward, both in this life, where he is promised intimate union with God (the union of friendship), and especially in the next, where he is promised to have a throne from which he can sit in judgment over the twelve tribes of Israel. While Christ very definitely held up a picture of vocation which indicated a negative element — the Cross and renunciation of whatever the "world" in the Johannine sense held up as desirable and good — still it also included a positive element, one which we are beginning to realize more and more in our modern presentation of vocation. Jesus did not demand

---

[13] E.g., Paul.
[14] E.g., Moses, Amos, Jeremias.
[15] Cf. Gen. 12:2.
[16] Cf. Mt. 4:18–22 and parallel passages.

[17] Cf. Mt. 10:22.
[18] Cf. Lk. 9:57–62.
[19] Cf. Mt. 10:37–38.

a total commitment offering nothing in return. No, what a person would gain in making this gift or donation was something very positive; but only the one who possessed a *deep faith* or a *living and a loving response* to the call would be able to grasp this. One of the special rewards which He mentioned to His disciples was that they would be associated in the work of God in a most wonderful manner, such that they would be called His friends. As their response to this call developed and deepened, they would experience this closeness to God, not perhaps, in the external factors of life, but deep within the depths of their soul. They would become more and more convinced that they were the *ambassadors of Christ*[20] and the *fragrance of God*.[21]

But the element which appears perhaps most frequently is the *promise and the assurance of divine protection and assistance* guaranteeing the success of the mission entrusted — according to God's way of judging success. The Lord is said to have blessed Abraham and those who would bless him. He greeted Gideon with assurance that He was with him in the undertaking. It was the hand of the Lord who held David firm in his task, the arm of the Lord that strengthened him. Again it was the Lord who upheld His servant Jeremias and made his face as hard as flint. This assurance is indicated in a most striking manner whenever the object of the call shied away from it under the plea that he was not capable of the task.[22] For this purpose He often gave them peculiar gifts to accomplish their mission, making the mouth of Isaias like a sharp sword[23] and giving him a tongue for teaching.[24] To Paul He gave the power necessary to accomplish his office.[25]

This assurance was especially given against persecution which was often promised or foretold to those whom God called. Jesus, for example, assured His Apostles that they would be persecuted and yet that He would be with them in that hour, for it would be His Spirit who would give them words to speak at that time.[26] From all these texts it is quite clear that the Word of God in speaking of vocations seems to imply that God does not call one to an office without endowing him with the external and internal gifts necessary to accomplish it.

From what we have seen above, a biblical analysis of vocation would yield the following results: (1) it is directed toward a particular task or office or mission; (2) it is made known through a divine revelation; (3) it includes an assurance and promise of divine protection and assistance

---

20 Cf. 2 Cor. 5:20.
21 Cf. 2 Cor. 2:15–17.
22 Moses, Exod. 4:1 ff.; Jer. 1:6–9.
23 Cf. Isa. 49:2.

24 Cf. Isa. 50:4.
25 Cf. 2 Cor. 3:4–6; 4:7.
26 Cf. Mt. 10:19–20.

necessary for its accomplishment; (4) it includes the possibility, indeed, the promise at times, of persecution or opposition of some kind or other; (5) it includes above all a total commitment that demands renunciation especially of wealth; (6) it is rewarding and assures one who is faithful to it of intimate association with the work of God here below and of eternal life in the world to come.

Today we find these same elements still present in any Christian analysis of vocation, even though not in exactly the same way as during the years in which God's message was revealed to man. The Old and New Testament view of vocation or election to the chosen people or to the Church is still very much present today in Christian thought. The one Christian vocation can be fulfilled by some in the lay state, by others in the clerical state, by some in religion, by others in the state of matrimony. Today just as in biblical times we have, first of all, a vocation to the chosen people and then, in addition, to some way of life in and through which this basic and fundamental vocation might be the more easily realized. This additional vocation is not really different from the first; it is merely a means of enabling us to fulfill the first. Yet because it implies some kind of permanence, it is called a *state of life*.

Moreover, it remains true today no less than in biblical times that a vocation is always a *call to some mission or office*. For the Church of the New Testament, the Church of today, has as many if not more missions and offices to fulfill than did the Church of the Old Law and the Church of the Apostles. And for this mission certain qualifications are necessary. Otherwise the work of the Church could not be carried on successfully. The admission of unsuitable candidates to some office or mission would only lead to disaster affecting not only the individual, but also in some way the society itself of which they are a part. It would hinder not only the individual's fulfillment of his or her destiny, but also that of the society, at least to some extent.

The *method*, however, in which this call is made to the individual is not exactly the same. Vocation through a direct communication of God to the individual is very rare today, although such vocations will undoubtedly occur until the Church reaches her final achievement. While the communication of vocation is from God and must be from Him, still He has left it to the Church to determine the genuinity of this communication. She does not have a free hand in this determination, however. For her mission exercised through her official ministers is not to give a vocation or infuse a vocation into some person. It is and will always remain to *declare* that a vocation is present or not present, has been given or has not been given. This she does in accordance with certain norms which are called "the signs of vocation." It is for this reason that time and time again the Roman Pontiffs have insisted that vocation is not merely a question of human or natural making. Consequently, while authorities are dealing with vocations and must pronounce upon them in accordance with the rules of prudence, they may never forget that they are dealing with something that is supernatural and not merely natural. They must remind themselves often, even constantly (I do not say, obsessively) that many in the history of the Church were, according to mere human calculations, unfit candidates for some work or mission. This was also true of many biblical characters who were called by God to perform some special mission. Yet, just as God called them and prepared them in a special way for their mission, so too does He even now at times, and will continue to do so, in order to confound the wise and the strong with the foolish and the weak.

Lastly, today just as before the Christian vocation demands a *total commitment* made according to the possibilities of the mode of life in question, one according to the married state, another according to the clerical state, another according to the religious state, one in the cloister, another in the world. This total commitment will always demand *renunciation*, one that is proper to the state in question. It is this idea that at times seems to be absent or neglected in our presentation of vocation today, whether it be that of marriage, or that of the religious life, or even to the Christian life as such. For comparing our present-day literature on vocations to the higher states of life, for example, with the literature of the Gospels treating of the same subject one cannot help but feel that there is at least a change of emphasis if not in concept in regard to Christ's understanding of the call of God. I wonder whether or not Christ would make the same change if He were living in our own time?[27]

Division of Vocation

Considering vocation in a general way, it seems that we can say both from revelation and its theological elaboration that it admits of two divisions, the second of which is capable of further subdivision.

In the natural order the vocation of every human being is the manifestation of God's goodness and perfections to the degree and extent in which God has communicated them to him. This is what Scripture seems to imply when it states that God has made all things for Himself.[28] Every creature comes into being as a kind of witness to or testimony of the

---

[27] Cf. *Scriptural Approach to Vocations*, J. L. McKenzie, S.J., *NCEA Bulletin*, 1959, pp. 377–381.

[28] Cf. Prov. 16:4.

goodness of God. Thus the *greatness* of every creature, its being brought out of nothing into something is a living witness to the divine Omnipotence. The *beauty* of every creature is a living witness to the divine Wisdom which reaches from end to end ordering all things mightily and sweetly. By reason of his creatureliness every man has a vocation to manifest God's glory and His goodness, and this he would do even had he not been raised to the supernatural order.

Indeed, St. Thomas in his consideration of the final goal or end of creation goes even further than this in his declaration. He states that the perfection of every creature is realized when it reaches or achieves that assimilation or likeness to God for which He has destined it. Since the perfection of every creature is its vocation, then the vocation of every creature is to realize this assimilation as perfectly as possible. This thought of the Angelic Doctor seems to lie at the very heart of any attempt to understand the mystery of human vocation. In his treatment of God as the final cause of all creatures he writes:

> Every agent acts for an end. . . . Now the end of the agent and that of the patient as such is the same, but in a different way respectively. For the impression which the agent intends to produce and which the patient intends to receive are one and the same. Since it does not belong to the First Agent who is Agent only and not patient to act for the acquisition of some end, He intends only to communicate His perfections which are His goodness. Every creature, however, intends to acquire its own perfection which is the likeness of the divine perfection and goodness. Therefore the divine goodness is the end of all things.[29] . . . All things desire God as their end in desiring any particular good whether this desire be intellectual or sensible or natural, i.e., without knowledge; for nothing is good and desirable except inasmuch as it participates in the likeness of God.[30]

---

[29] I, Q. 44, a. 4, c.

[30] *Ibid.*, ad. 3. Later on in his treatment, St. Thomas could write that even in the natural order man can be said to have been made according to the image and likeness of God the Trinity, not in the same way, of course, as He is said to have been made according to the image and likeness of the Trinity in the order of grace, however:

"As we have seen, the distinction of the divine Persons is only according to origin, or rather, according to the relations of origin. Now, the mode of origin is not the same in all things, but in each thing is adapted to its nature . . . Hence it is manifest that the distinction of the divine Persons is suitable to the divine nature. Therefore to be made according to the image and likeness of God by imitation of the divine nature does not exclude being the image of God by the representation of the divine Persons, but rather, one follows upon the other. We must therefore say that in man exists the image of God both as regards the divine nature and as regards the Trinity of Persons; for in God himself there is one nature in Three Persons" (I, Q. 93, a. 5, c.).

"Every effect in some degree represents its cause but diversely. . . . Some effects represent only the causality of the cause, but not its form, as smoke represents fire. . . . Other effects represent the cause in terms of likeness of its form, as fire generated represents fire generating, and as the statue of Mercury represents Mercury. Now the processions of the divine Persons are referred to the acts of the intellect and the will. For

Coming to the *supernatural* order of grace we would expect this natural vocation not to be opposed to that to which one is called in this new order, but, rather, perfected by this new call. Grace perfects and builds upon and works according to the nature in which it is received. Consequently, in this order man's mission or vocation would still be to be assimilated or likened to God the Trinity, and indeed in a much more marvelous manner than would have been his lot had he not been elevated. According to the teaching of Revelation the end of man is eternal life, which is the knowledge and love of the divine Essence and Persons. Or we might say it is the possession of the divine Persons such that we see them just as they are, not through a mirror or a glass or in a dark manner, but face to face. Eternal life consists in knowledge of God upon which there follows the act of eternal love proper to the blessed in the one immobile instant of eternity.[31]

This was to be obtained through the living of the Christian life of grace which is an inchoation of the life of glory. Man's vocation as a wayfarer in the supernatural order is to the life of grace lived as perfectly as possible, not in a static manner, but in a constantly growing manner, such that the Trinity of Persons become more and more the object of our knowledge and love. This is brought about by our growing fidelity to the commandments of God. For it is Christ Himself who promised us that the more faithfully we would keep His commandments the more would He and His Father (and the Holy Ghost) come to make Their abode with us.[32] From the intensification of this mutual cohabitation there was to come about even to the very last instant of life a growing understanding of God and a growing love for Him, a growing assimilation to Father, Son, and Holy Ghost. If we consider the whole of Revelation, we would see that this was to take place especially through the intensification of the theological virtues — Faith, Hope, and Charity, exercised not always directly, but sometimes indirectly as inspiring or strongly yet sweetly moving the person to the exercise of other virtues.[33]

In God's designs the basic vocation of every man coming into the world is this Christian life which is a kind of a Trinification, or the reproduction in our soul-life of the life of the Trinity of Persons. This

---

the Son proceeds as the Word of the intellect and the Holy Ghost proceeds as the Love of the will. Therefore in rational creatures which possess intellect and will, there is found the representation of the Trinity by way of image inasmuch as there is found in them a word conceived in the intellect and love proceeding in the will" (I, Q. 45, a. 7).

[31] Cf. 1 Cor. 13:12. For a longer treatment, cf. the work of the author, *The Theology of Spiritual Guidance*, U. of Notre Dame Press, mimeographed notes, 1956, p. 18 ff.

[32] Cf. Jn. 14:21–23.

[33] Cf. 1 Cor. 13:4 ff.

vocation man is not free to reject. For if he rejects it or in some way fails to attain it, he has failed to attain the vocation to which he is destined by his Creator. It is this fundamental vocation of the Christian which is so frequently spoken of by the Apostles in their writings. Paul, for example, calls it the "vocation of the Lord," that is, a call to embrace and to live the life that has been set up or established and merited for us by Christ.[34]

This basic or fundamental Christian vocation can be lived and fulfilled in many different ways. It can be fulfilled in the married state or in the state of virginity, as the Apostle so clearly points out.[35] It can be fulfilled, as we have seen in the Introduction, by preaching, teaching, almsgiving, prophecy, etc.,[36] or by what we might call particular or special vocations within the framework of the Christian vocation itself. There are many ways in which we could approach the study of these vocations, all of which have their advantages and disadvantages. But only some of these approaches will be indicated as well as the one we shall follow in this work.

Suarez, for example, divided the Christian life into two categories or divisions: (1) the common Christian life, which includes all those not mentioned in the next category, and (2) the state of perfection. Consequently, for this theologian, the first category would include marriage, virginity in the world, and the single state insofar as this can be called a vocation. The second category would include the religious life, the episcopate, and in a certain sense, as we shall see later, the priesthood. By this division the author does not at all intend to deny that those who are found in the first category cannot and do not perform works of supererogation, or that they are incapable of growing in spiritual perfection with the assistance of God's grace. He calls these "common" because they do not bind one by a special obligation to works of supererogation and because they do not afford them any special means for that purpose. The state of perfection, on the other hand, lays upon its members obligations to perform such works and affords them the special means or at least affords them more means to practice these works. In the state of perfection there is greater security from the enemies that would lead away from perfection, and a mode of life that is more perfectly geared to attain it.

---

[34] Cf. 1 Cor. 1:26; Eph. 4:1; Phil. 3:14; 2 Thess. 1:11; Heb. 3:1. Peter also refers to this vocation, calling the faithful "a chosen race, a royal priesthood, a consecrated people, a people God means to have for himself, a people that was once not God's people but now is" (1 Pet. 2:9–10; 2 Pet. 1:10).

[35] Cf. 1 Cor. 7; cf. also Mt. 19.

[36] Cf. Eph. 4:4–7 ff.

Another author, Fr. Salmon, O.P., in his work on vocation[37] gives a slightly different division. The following is a schematic presentation of it:

1. Divine worship which he calls the *basic vocation* imposed on us as a result of our creation.
2. The order of grace or the supernatural order which he considers to be the privilege and obligation of all men.
3. The supernatural perfection of charity which is also of obligation for all men. This vocation can be realized in and through various states of life, stable modes of living, which imply some obligation with respect to evangelical perfection. He lists the following states:
    a) The ordinary state of the simple Christian
    b) The state of perfect chastity
    c) The religious state
    d) The sacerdotal state
    e) Christian marriage

While each of the preceding divisions has elements of value, at present because of recent developments in the legislation of the Church especially regarding secular institutes, the following division is the one commonly followed by theologians:

1. The States of Perfection:
    a) Secular institutes
    b) Religious communities of the common life which have public vows whether these be solemn or simple. To these can be likened societies of the common life without any vows at all or with only private vows.
    c) The Episcopate
2. The "secular" states:
    a) The priesthood[38]
    b) Consecrated or dedicated chastity lived in the world
    c) Christian marriage

Even this division, however, seems to neglect several considerations or aspects of what is included in the reality which we call vocation. St. Thomas, for example, in his treatment of the states of life considered first of all the various charismatic gifts which marked the early Church in a special way, and which even today are found diffused throughout it. Afterward he took up the active and the contemplative lives. It seems somewhat regrettable that today for the most part these considerations are omitted from many treatments of the states of life. Yet by their very definition the charismatic gifts are *special*, that is, not given to all the

---

[37] *La Vocation*, La Sarte, Huy.

[38] The author wishes to note here in presenting this division that there is some question of the place which the priesthood ought to occupy in it. Up to the present the place indicated is that given to it by the majority of theologians. A fuller treatment of this problem will be taken up later on when treating of the episcopate and the priesthood.

members of the Church, but only to some for a definite purpose within the community. Moreover, the omission of a treatment of the active and contemplative lives such as these are considered in Thomistic tradition almost necessarily obscures the problem of whether or not true Christian contemplation is something that is reserved to those few whom God calls to the strictly contemplative life of the cloister.

Because of this the following division of the particular or special vocations within the Christian vocation itself seems to be more adequate. And it is in accordance with this division that the study of vocation given in this book will proceed:

Chapter   II. The Charismata
Chapter III. The Active and the Contemplative Lives
Chapter IV. The States of Perfection
            Secular Institutes
            Religious Communities of Public Vows (and Societies of
               the Common Life)
            The Episcopate
Chapter   V. Other Forms of the Life of Christian Perfection
            The Priesthood
            Consecrated Virginity
            Christian Marriage

Finally, in order to complete our treatment it would be best to take up the question of why the religious vocation, unlike the Priesthood and Matrimony, is not marked by a sacramental ceremony. It would seem that the religious life, superior to and more excellent, as it is, than the state of Matrimony, ought to have been elevated to the dignity of a sacrament. The fact is clear: It has not been so elevated. But the reason for this is not clear. Consequently, it is a field that is open to speculation on the part of theologians to see whether or not there might be some reasons of fittingness involved in this plan established by God.

CHAPTER TWO

The Charismata

IN THE beginning of his treatment of the charismatic gifts St. Thomas points out that one of the historical actualities which differentiated Christians in the early Church was the presence or absence in individuals of one or more of these gifts. They were given not for the sanctification of the individual as is true of habitual or sanctifying grace, but for the good of the community in which the individual lived. While it is true that a theology of these gifts which God has given to His Church was not completely and scientifically presented until the time of the scholastic theologians, still their existence was universally recognized and accepted by the faithful. Moreover, it was accepted and felt by all that such gifts would, in some way or other, never be entirely absent from the Church throughout the course of her entire existence.[1] For this reason, then, as well as for the historical reason of their importance in the early Church it would be wise for us to treat of them, not exhaustively, of course, but sufficiently to understand and appreciate them.

The basic Scripture passage in which these gifts are presented to us is found in St. Paul's first Epistle to the Corinthians[2] even though they are spoken of elsewhere.[3] The reason for this seems to be that although these gifts were distributed throughout the other Churches during this period,[4] still they were present in the Church of Corinth to such an extent that their presence was having a detrimental effect on the doctrine which Paul had preached to the members, namely, their intimate union with one another as members of the one Body of Christ. The widespread diffusion of these gifts was threatening the collective life of the Church which was one of the favorite themes of Paul. Consequently, in his letter

---

[1] Cf. *Mystici Corporis*, AAS 35 (1943), 200.
[2] Cf. Chaps. 12–14.
[3] E.g., Rom. 12:3–8; Eph. 4:7–16; 1 Pet. 4:10–11.
[4] E.g., Acts 2:1–13; 5:12; 6:10; 9:31.

to the Corinthians, Paul thought it necessary to point out to them the true value which they were to place on these gifts, finally contrasting them with charity which, in the hymn that followed, stands out as the real core and essence of the perfection of our life in Christ. For our purposes it seems enough to consider first the *nature* of the Charismata, and second their *division*.

The Nature of the Charismata

This question or problem was first introduced scientifically only in the twelfth and thirteenth centuries under the Scholastics. For the theologians at that time began to question whether or not each of these gifts consituted some special grace of the Spirit in the *active sense*, i.e., whether in and through each of these gifts, the Spirit gave Himself to the subject as is true in the communication of sanctifying or habitual grace. From the scriptural accounts of these gifts the Scholastics for the most part felt that by reason of their lack of inner consistency and by their connection with the Christian society or community rather than with the individual himself, they were not something habitual in the strict sense of the word. Nonetheless they concluded that they did pertain to the concept of "grace," but on a lower plane than the gift of sanctifying grace itself. For this reason theologians called them *gratiae gratis datae*, graces that were gratuitously given by God which did not, like habitual grace,[5] make one pleasing to Him. The general opinion of the Scholastics has been well stated by St. Thomas:

> The higher the good to which a virtue is ordered the more excellent is the virtue. Now the end is always greater than the means. But sanctifying grace directs man immediately to a union with his last end, whereas gratuitous graces (*gratiae gratis datae*) direct man to what is preparatory for the end. For this reason sanctifying grace is nobler than gratuitous grace. For this latter is ordered to the Common good of the Church, or to the ecclesiastical order, while sanctifying grace is ordered to the separate common good which is God. . . . Gratuitous grace cannot cause another to be united with God since this is had only through sanctifying grace. However, it can cause certain dispositions for it.[6]

We might define the charismatic gifts as "those special gifts or graces of God which pertain in some way or other to the supernatural order and which are for the most part actual and transient, and given for the common good of the Church rather than for the personal good of the individual which is God Himself." These gifts are still present in the

---

[5] *Gratia gratum faciens.*
[6] I–II, Q. 111, a. 5 c, and response.

Church today although we are not as aware of them as were the early Christians. The Church still has, from time to time, her great preachers and teachers and spiritual directors. Consequently, we can say that all these gifts become incarnated from time to time, especially when the Church has need of them. Their constant presence in the Church, sometimes evident sometimes hidden, acts as a continued reminder to all of the solicitude of Christ for His Spouse, sending her His Spirit to build up the progeny which is the family of God.

Division of the Charismatic Gifts

In a rather beautiful though terse article the Angelic Doctor presents us with the fundamental division of the gratuitous or charismatic gifts enumerated by St. Paul in the passage mentioned. He writes:

> . . . a gratuitous grace is ordered to this, namely, that a man may help another to be led to God. Now, no man can help in this by moving interiorly (for this belongs to God alone), but only exteriorly by teaching or persuading. Hence gratuitous grace embraces whatever a man needs in order to instruct another in divine things which are above reason. Now, for this three things are required. First, a man must possess the fullness of knowledge of divine things so that he is able to teach others. Secondly, he must be able to confirm or prove what he says otherwise his words will have no weight. Thirdly, he must be capable of presenting fittingly to his hearers what he knows.[7]

He then proceeds to indicate the following division of the gifts as they are found in St. Paul:

1. Those which give the fullness of knowledge of divine things, such that one is able to teach them well

Faith, or certitude regarding those invisible notions which are the principles of Catholic Doctrine.

The Word of Wisdom, which refers to knowledge of divine things. The teacher must know the principal conclusions of the science which he knows by means of the First Cause.

The Word of Knowledge: this gift illustrates the divine realities known with the aid of examples and effects taken from the realm of secondary causes. This is, of course, a knowledge of human things — what we might call the "knack of hitting upon the right comparison" to show some hidden or obscure truth more clearly.

---

[7] I–II, Q. 111, a. 4.

2. Those which confirm divine revelation

By works

- *The Gift of Healing:* the teacher, for example, who by restoring bodily health would confirm his teaching.

- *The Gift of Miracles:* this is sometimes given merely *to manifest the divine* power (e.g., the preserving of the Eucharistic species over a period of two or three hundred years; or the liquefaction of blood that has been shed by a martyr).

By knowledge

- *The Gift of Prophecy:* some receive this gift — that of knowing what God alone can know in the way of future contingents — to enable them to prove their teachings.

- *The Discernment of Spirits:* some as we know from reading the lives of the saints received this gift even to the extent of being able to read the secrets of the heart.

3. Those which assist one in *preaching or presenting* to an audience what he knows

- *The Gift of Tongues:* this particular gift enables one to grasp and know the idiom through which he communicates his teaching.

- *The Gift of Interpretation of Speech:* this gift enables one to understand the sense of what is said.

From this schema it can be seen that the charismatic gifts are divided into three categories: (1) those which pertain to knowledge; (2) those which pertain to locution or speech; (3) those which pertain to work or operation. Each of these might be briefly discussed.

SECTION 1. THE CHARISMATA WHICH PERTAIN TO KNOWLEDGE

In his treatment of the charismata which pertain to knowledge St. Thomas discusses them under the single general heading of *prophecy*. This he considers from the viewpoint of its nature, its mode, its divisions.

The Nature of Prophecy

Prophecy requires two things: (a) that the mind of one be elevated to perceive divine things and (b) that the mind so elevated *actually* perceive them. The first of these he calls *inspiration* (slightly different from the modern usage of the word) and the second *revelation* (also slightly different from modern usage). Of these two elements the second is the more important since it is here that we find the consummation of prophecy. Only upon its presence is the veil of obscurity and ignorance removed — and this is necessary for knowledge.

Prophecy requires a certain intelligible light exceeding the natural light of our reason. This light is *transient*, however, and on this score differs from the light of reason as well as from the light of faith and that of glory. Each time one prophesies he receives the light of prophecy anew, giving him *actually*, that is, after the manner of a transient help, something that is divine. However, even though this illumination does not remain, there does remain a kind of *aptitude* to be enlightened again in somewhat the way in which a mind and heart that has once been aroused to fervor is more easily recalled to its former devotion and promptitude in the service of God, should it fall from this fervor for one reason or another.

According to St. Thomas prophecy *properly speaking* centers around future events, although less properly it can also embrace those present happenings which take place at a distance from the seer. An example of this latter would be the incident recorded in 4 Kings 5:26, where the prophet Eliseus knew what his disciple Ghiezi was doing even though he was quite some distance from him.

The mind of the prophet can be instructed by God either by way of an *express revelation* or by way of a kind of *mysterious instinct* to which the human mind is subjected without knowing it. The former type of instruction carries with it a *certainty* about what is known through revelation; the latter does not. Moreover, in the latter case the one to whom God is making the revelation does not know that God is working in his mind and is unable to distinguish whether his thoughts are conceived by divine motion or by his own spirit.

There is nothing false connected with genuine prophetical knowledge. The reason for this is that the same knowledge should exist in the one teaching and in the one taught; since in this case the one teaching is God who can neither deceive nor be deceived, the knowledge which the prophet receives from Him cannot be false. However, on this score we must be careful. For the divine foreknowledge has reference to future events in one of two ways: (1) either as they are in themselves inasmuch as it sees them in their presentiality if we may use the word; and (2) in their causes, since God also sees the order of the causes in relation to their effects. Although future contingents in themselves are determined in the mind of God, yet in their causes they are not so determined that they cannot come about otherwise. In the divine intellect this twofold knowledge of things — in themselves and in their causes — is always united even though they are not united in prophetical revelation, since God does not always give a prophet the knowledge of the event as perfectly as He Himself knows it. Striking examples of these different kinds of revelation can be seen in our Lord's prophecy concerning the destruction of the city of Jerusalem centering around the event itself,[8] and Jonas' prophecy to the people of Ninive which centered around the causes since the event, as we know, never really did occur according to the story.[9] The impression of the divine foreknowledge is imprinted upon the mind of the prophet such that he either knows the actual event or the order of the causes which would ultimately lead up to the event. If the impression or the illumination is of the second kind, then it can happen that the event never actually occurs because the order of the causes has been changed. It is in virtue of this that theologians are accustomed to speak of the efficacious and conditional decrees of God. The uncertainty of the event is not on the part of God but rather on that of man. Whatever comes about has been decreed by God (efficaciously) and whatever does not come about has not been decreed by God, or, decreed by Him, but only conditionally or inefficaciously.

This difference is somewhat difficult to understand. But perhaps the following figure might help to clarify it. We might imagine the sequence of created events as a sort of a Bayeux tapestry and we in time walking close beside it. The only event before us is that which occurs in the present; the others are only remembered or expected. The gaze of eternity, however, or the gaze of God and the Blessed is that of a spectator far enough away to be able to take in the whole of the thing at once

---

[8] Cf. Mt. 24.   [9] Jonas 3.

(*tota simul*). Or again we might liken it to the different views of one and the same countryside which are had by one from the valley and from the top of a mountain. In the former instance he sees things piecemeal, whereas in the latter instance he sees all of them together in one glance. The knowledge of God, unlike that of man, is more rightly thought of as the knowledge of a never fading instant, rather than a foreknowledge of the things to come. That is why it is better for us to speak of Providence, rather than of Pre-vidence or Foreknowledge.[10]

From all this we can conclude that prophecy can be defined as "knowledge supernaturally given to one concerning truths which exceed the powers of his nature for the good of the community."[11] The truths themselves which are given in the revelation made to a prophet can be either supernatural in themselves or natural. The manner in which they are acquired, however, must always be supernatural. Thus they can be said to be always supernatural *quoad modum* (or *extrinsically* supernatural) and sometimes supernatural *quoad substantiam* (or *intrinsically* supernatural) in addition.

The Cause of Prophecy

While prophecy exceeds the natural capacity of any person at any time — at least so far as its mode of acquisition is concerned — God can and does make use of certain *natural aptitudes* of the one to whom He grants the revelations. A person, for example, who is detached from material things is much more apt or suited to receive the influx of spiritual things as well as the subtle movements of the imagination which occur through the impression of natural causes. On the other hand, one who is constantly occupied with sensible things is not so capable (naturally speaking) of perceiving such things. St. Thomas, for example, was fond of using the expression in regard to mortification: *Qui infectus est amore mundi, non potest gustare divina* — "One who is infected with the love of the world cannot taste the things of God."

By this we are not to understand that a natural disposition is *required* for one to be capable of receiving these illuminations or revelations. God is in no way dependent on natural dispositions for producing His spiritual effects. Nor is the state of grace necessary for one to receive this or any other charism. They do not pertain to the will, but rather to one of the other faculties of man; moreover, they are given not for the good of the individual but for the good of the Church. In many instances the persons

---

[10] Cf. *L'Idée de Création*, Sertillanges, O.P. (Paris: Aubier, 1945), p. 161 ff.

[11] "La Somme Théologique," éd. de Revue des Jeunes, *La Prophétie*, P. Synave, O.P., and P. Benoit, O.P., p. 270.

to whom God granted these favors were not always the best, simply speaking.[12]

While it is true that prophetical knowledge is given to a human being by God, still He can employ other creatures to transmit this revelation, as, for example, the angels. This is very much in keeping with the workings of divine Wisdom who does all things according to order. Order demands, however, that the lowest things should be directed by those things which occupy a midway place and these in turn by those who occupy a higher place. Man, who is the lowest of the intellectual creatures, is fittingly directed or illuminated by the angels in his encounters with God. In fact this seems to be a rather frequent happening in regard to the supernatural economy established by God. Scripture, for example, seems to imply that the angels act as intermediaries in our encounters with God, even perhaps with respect to our vocation.[13]

It is perfectly possible for the devil to imitate the work of the good angels to a certain extent. For by reason of the keenness of his intellect he is able to conjecture much more accurately regarding future or contingent events than is man. While such a conjecture might appear to be supernatural to man, still it is a phenomenon completely natural to the angelic nature. There are three differences between the "prophecy" which is of divine origin and that which is of diabolic origin: (1) divine prophecy extends to all that is known by God alone; diabolical prophecy takes in only that which is known by the angelic intellect; (2) divine prophecy implies an illumination of the intelligence; diabolic prophecy cannot give this; (3) prophecy which is of divine origin cannot be false; that originating from the devil sometimes contains errors.[14]

Manner in Which Prophetical Knowledge Is Communicated

The prophets or those to whom God makes these revelations are not granted a share in the Beatific Vision. They do not see the truth in the

---

[12] E.g., Isaias, Jeremias. Cf. also the *Life of St. Theresa*, Chap. 13, Peers, I, pp. 81–82; *Way of Perfection*, Chap. 5, Peers, II, p. 24 ff., for parallel situations.

[13] Cf. *The Angels and their Mission*, Jean Danielou, S.J. (Westminster, Md.: Newman, 1957); *What is an Angel?* Pie-Raymond Regamey, O.P., F&F Book (London: Burns and Oates, 1959).

[14] A phenomenon parallel to what has just been discussed occurs today in mystical experience. It was because of the similarity of operation occurring in regard to extraordinary favors that the mystics constantly urged that they be submitted to the judgment of a competent person and that even then, when they had been authenticated, the individual receiving them should never judge his spiritual progress in their light. Cf. *Way of Perfection*, Chap. 4, Peers, II, p. 20; esp. *Interior Castle*, Mansion VI, Chap. 3, Peers, II, pp. 279–290; Chap. 8, pp. 310–312. Cf. also *Ascent of Mt. Carmel*, Bk. 2, Chaps. 22–32, Peers, I, pp. 172–210 passim.

Divine Essence. This is reserved for the Blessed alone. Rather, in the case of prophetical knowledge a *divine light* is infused into the mind enabling the seer to *pass judgment* on the ideas (species) which are either infused directly by God or acquired in some way from sensible things. This light is *created* and plays upon either newly impressed species or ideas or old ones previously acquired, but now divinely arranged or coordinated, or merely presented but to be prophetically significant of something. When something is presented to the seer's mind by means of sensible ideas or species — whether these be divinely formed (the burning bush seen by Moses or the writing shown to Daniel) or otherwise produced but to be prophetically significant (some of the "signs" in St. John) — no rapture or ecstasy or alienation from the senses is required. Nor is such required when there is question of the prophet's being illuminated by infused species (today this is called by the mystics an *intellectual vision*). The only time rapture or ecstasy is required is when prophetical knowledge is communicated through images experienced in the imagination and not derived from sense experience, at least directly (today the mystics call this an *imaginary vision*). Sometimes this rapture is complete; at other times it is not complete. For prophetical knowledge in the *most proper sense* of this expression the person moved by God must be aware of what is taking place. If this is not true (as in the case of the soldiers casting lots for the garment of Christ, and of Caiphas) he is not said to possess the charism of prophecy in the strict sense.[15]

The process of prophetical revelation has a parallel in regard to mystical phenomena and experience. Indeed, we might say that it is here that many of the charisms mentioned by Paul and indicated above find their constant historical reincarnation so to speak. St. Teresa and St. John of the Cross have given a remarkable treatment of these *gratiae gratis datae* in their various writings.[16]

The Division of Prophecy

There are several ways in which prophetical knowledge could be divided. There is, for example, the division given by St. Thomas in the II–II, Q. 174, a twofold division which can be expanded to a threefold one. The following is a schematic presentation of it:

---

[15] For a much longer treatment of this, cf. "La Somme Théologique," *La Prophétie*, p. 247 ff.

[16] Cf. *Interior Castle*, Mansion VI, Chaps. 4–5; *Life*, Chaps. 20, 24, 33; for a complete index to these passages, cf. Peers ed. of her works, Vol. III, p. 392. Cf. also St. John of the Cross, *Ascent of Mt. Carmel*, Bk. 2, Chap. 17 ff., Peers, I, pp. 130–134; 187–194.

Prophecy of Denunciation ⎰ This refers to the prediction of an event known in its causes. Often it is conditional, depending upon whether or not the causes actually come about. The prediction of Jonas to the people of Ninive was of this kind.

Prophecy of Foreknowledge ⎰ *Prophecy of Predestination:* when the thing comes about but is accomplished by God Himself. This always regards a good.

Prophecy of Foreknowledge (in the strict sense) : when the event actually takes place, but through secondary causes acting freely. It may be either good or evil.

Another division that could be given, and one which is very much in keeping with the division of visions given by the mystics, would originate from the *medium* through which something is known — whether it be through some vision of the senses or through an imaginary vision, or through an intellectual vision. Of these types, the most perfect is the last mentioned since it approaches nearer to the vision of the Blessed who see truth in the Divine Essence. When this is employed by God it indicates that the mind of the seer is of a high caliber. Something similar occurs in regard to natural knowledge. Some students can grasp abstract thought without needing examples taken from sense knowledge to assist them.

It is the teaching of St. Thomas that even though intellectual visions are the most perfect still one is said to be more properly a prophet who receives his knowledge through an imaginary vision. The reason he gives is that the visions of those who are still on earth should normally include something of obscurity and remoteness from pure intelligible truth. It is interesting to note that St. Teresa in her evaluation of the three types of visions follows the same order as Thomas, thereby indicating, it seems, a very close parallel between the prophetical revelation or the charism of prophecy of Thomas and the visions of mystical experience.[17]

---

[17] Cf. *Interior Castle*, Mansion VI, Chap. 5, Peers, II, p. 295 ff.; Chap. 8, p. 309 ff. It is worthwhile noting that no new *public* revelation has been made to the Church since the death of the last Apostle. What has been given since that time down throughout the ages of the Church's history are *private* revelations, some of which have received the Church's approval and some of which have not, even though she may not have rejected them. These private revelations are usually helpful for the direction of human actions or morals. It seems that we would be correct in saying that no genuine revelation is made today which does not have in mind the good of the Church as a whole, either because it helps to direct human action or morals, or because it confirms

Section 2. The Charismata Which Pertain to Locution or Speech

Under this category of charisms we find two mentioned by the Apostle: (1) the Gift of Tongues and (2) the Gift of the Words of Wisdom and Knowledge. The reception of these constituted a kind of special vocation in the early Church and even today. For there are still some who are teachers, some who are preachers, etc.

The Gift of Tongues

We might note that this gift gave St. Paul more trouble than the others. As we find it in the members of the Church of Corinth it referred to an ecstatic condition in which articulate or inarticulate utterances were voiced whose *general* character could be understood, but not particular (e.g., prayer and thanksgiving). The gift does *not* refer to the ability to speak in foreign tongues, nor does it indicate an ability to speak some magical jargon which no one could understand. Because of the *love of display* on the part of the people who had this gift and because of the *similarity* it had to certain "gifts" found in contemporary pagan religions, Paul was most solicitous to see to it that it was properly controlled and governed.[18]

When Sacred Scripture speaks of the Apostles and their possession of tongues, there may be question of their actually having spoken and understood the languages of the people to whom they were speaking. However, it may also merely indicate that they were understood by all the persons present because they knew the language of the Apostles or because of some kind of divine intervention.[19]

For all its striking quality the Gift of Tongues is not as excellent as

---

some teaching or doctrine of the Church already revealed, or because it does both. The appearance of our Blessed Mother at La Salette was given for the direction of human actions. For the people of that particular section of France were falling off in the practice of their religious duties. The apparition of Mary to St. Bernadette at Lourdes occurred most especially it seems for the confirmation of a doctrine that had just been defined shortly before — the Dogma of the Immaculate Conception. The repercussions of this doctrine in the field of human actions is not to be denied of course. Again the appearance of the Sacred Heart to St. Margaret Mary seems to have been given both for the confirmation of the doctrine of the genuine human love of Christ for mankind, as well as for the direction of human acts or for the improvement of morals.

[18] Cf. *A Catholic Commentary on Holy Scripture* (New York: Thomas Nelson and Sons, 1953), pp. 789–790.

[19] Cf. *The Mystery of the Church*, Y. Congar, O.P. (London: Chapman, 1960), p. 48; *Catholicism*, H. de Lubac, S.J. (New York: Longmans, Green, 1950), Chap. 2.

that of Prophecy. For the knowledge of truth is much more excellent than its diffusion. Moreover, the Gift of Prophecy seems to have been more useful for the Church, since it is much more profitable to her that one be able to explain and interpret what he says, than merely to say it. Moreover, with respect to those outside the Church it is more important that they be convinced of revelation than that they hear someone speaking in a rather strange way.

The Gift of the Words of Wisdom and Knowledge

Today we might call this the "Gift of Preaching or Teaching." It refers to that particular power or charism by which one has control over an audience. This efficaciousness admits of three extensions. It can extend (1) to the mind, illuminating it through instruction; or (2) to the affections such that they willingly and eagerly listen to the word of God; thus one's words would have not only illuminating force, but also the power of unction; or (3) to daily life or action. In this last case, the preaching or the teaching would sway the audience making them desire to put it into practice.

It is to be noted, as St. Thomas points out, that during the history of the Church this gift has been given not only to men but also to women. These latter, however, had to use it privately or in familiar conversation, never in public or in any official magisterial capacity. He gives three reasons for this: (1) in the Church they are to be subject to men; (2) such a position might easily incite men's minds to lust; (3) they are not perfect in wisdom or even so perfect as to be able to be entrusted with public teaching.[20]

Just how true these reasons would be today might be questioned, since the place and role of women in society and in the Church has changed somewhat. However, it does not seem to have been the intention of the saint to deny them opportunity for teaching as such, but only for teaching officially, as representing the magisterium of the Church. Consequently, while it is true that orders and congregations of religious women established for the purpose of teaching youth were not the rule in his day as it is now, it does not seem that he would forbid them exercise of this role today![21]

Thomas is also very careful to point out that as far as the Beatific

---

[20] II–II, Q. 177, a. 2.

[21] Moreover, we ought to note that wherever and whenever the woman does engage in teaching she does so after her own manner, that is, with a maternal purpose forming not only minds, but to a large extent hearts and wills as well. Perhaps this idea could be more developed here but I have done this elsewhere (cf. Review for Religious, January, 1961).

Vision is concerned the woman will not be at any disadvantage, for if she has loved much on earth her reward in heaven will be equal in intensity to the measure of that love. While the man in the society of the Church is usually entrusted with the so-called "spotlight" roles, it might just happen that in the society of the Blessed the roles may be reversed. For what is required there is not so much knowledge, but love, and in this department the woman seems to be better qualified than the man. The created person who occupies the highest place in the Beatific Vision is, as we know, a woman.

In conclusion we might cite a passage from St. Thomas himself concerning the position of the woman in the mystery of the Redemption:

> A woman is not allowed to teach publicly in Church, but she may be permitted to give familiar or private instruction. As Ambrose says[22] a woman is sent to those of her own household but not to the people to bear witness to the Resurrection. Christ, however, appeared to a woman first so that as she was the first to bring the source of death to man she might also be the first to announce the dawn of Christ's glorious Resurrection. Hence Cyril says[23] woman who formerly was the minister of death is the first to see and proclaim the adorable mystery of the Resurrection. Womankind has procured through this action absolution from ignominy and the removal of her curse.
>
> Hereby it is shown so far as the state of glory is concerned that the woman shall suffer no harm or loss. For if they are inflamed with greater charity they shall attain greater glory for the divine Vision; because the women whose love for our Lord was more persistent — so much so that when even the disciples withdrew from the sepulchre they did not depart — were the first to see Him rising in glory.[24]

SECTION 3. THE CHARISMATA WHICH PERTAIN TO WORK OR OPERATION

Under this heading are listed the charisms of healing and the working of miracles. Because the gift of healing is a particular kind of miracle St. Thomas rightly treats of them together. These particular gifts were given by the Spirit to the various members of the Church so that the teaching of the Church might have some confirmation when it was presented to the outsiders. Just as our Lord, in His own lifetime, confirmed His teaching often enough by working miracles, so too did He

---

[22] Comm. on Luke, 24/24, PL 15, 1845.
[23] Comm. on John, 20/17, PG 74, 697.
[24] III, Q. 55, a. 1, ad 3.

grant a similar charism to certain members of the society He had founded, and for the same purpose — to confirm its authenticity, to make its teaching credible. Because it is natural or normal for man to arrive at intelligible truth through sensible things, the presence of these gifts in the Church is most reasonable. While they may be continually present in the Church they do not remain in any individual permanently so that he can use them almost at will, like one or other of the virtues. Their use always depends upon a transient communication of a divine power to an individual given for the purpose mentioned above.

St. Paul mentions the gift of healing separately from that of miracles because through this operation a special benefit was given to an individual person in addition to its bringing him or a group to the knowledge of God. Since this is not true of all miraculous power — that the individual be benefited — the Apostle mentions this gift apart from the other miraculous powers given to men.

It is perfectly possible for one not in the state of grace to perform a miracle, at least according to the teaching of many theologians. The reason for this is that miracles are worked either for the confirmation of some truth that has been preached, or as a proof of the holiness of the one working the miracle. While only the good can work a miracle in confirmation of their own holiness, the wicked also can work one in confirmation of revealed truth. However, it seems more fitting that God would use someone renowned for holiness for such a work more often than a sinner.

We should not forget that there are certain things which can be brought about by diabolical intervention which, although beyond the natural power of man, are not beyond the natural power of the fallen angels. That is why we must always be careful in regard to "strange" occurrences that happen in the realm of occult phenomena.

Conclusion

Terminating our study of the charismata which give a certain "vocation" in the Church, we should note that they are never opposed to one another. Rather, they complement one another. There is a common finality for which they are given, and this is attained only when each one is faithful to the gift which he has or may have received from God. Among these gifts there is one that is most important for those engaged in vocational work: the *discernment of spirits*. It holds a place analogous to that of prudence in the order of the virtues, and to the Gift of Counsel among the Gifts of the Holy Ghost. It is also helpful for the one who is called, since it permits him in advance to determine the course of action to be followed among the many which exist in the Mystical Body. More-over, it enables him to place his entire life under the control and guidance of the Holy Spirit.

The *authenticity* of these various charisms can be recognized especially by the *docility* of the one possessing them to the Holy Ghost, by his respect for authority, and by a lively feeling or desire to bring about the common good to which the exercise of these gifts is always subordinated.

One who has received one or other of these gifts has a vocation or mission in the Church. Yet this mission must be exercised according to the norms and the good of the entire society and not independently of these. Although we have insisted that the charisms are not essentially connected with holiness of life still most often they are entrusted to those who are very close to God. It was from observation that the Angelic Doctor could write:

> When the virtue of charity is intensified, then by the same reason of charity the subject receives or obtains the conferring of a new effect of grace, such as the gift of miracles or any other spiritual gift of this kind.[25]

---

[25] III Sent. dist. 20, q. 5, a. 1, sol. 2.

CHAPTER THREE

The Active and Contemplative Lives

THE importance and relevance of a thorough consideration of the active and contemplative lives does not have to be proved. It is something which almost spontaneously makes itself felt in the minds and hearts of those who are truly seeking God, especially if they are compelled to do so outside the framework of the canonical contemplative life. On the one hand, they are aware of the call of God: "Leave thy country behind thee, thy kinsfolk and thy father's home and come away into a land I will show thee."[1] On the other hand, there is the fact of an increased activity and work, a growing demand for the services of those who have dedicated their lives to the answering of this call of God. As a result of this apparent "pulling in opposite directions" the very real fact of growing tensions, questionings, doubts, and discouragements can be readily noticed especially among those who are truly "seeking the Lord."

Solutions to the problem have been proposed, not all of which are completely satisfactory or in keeping with the constant teaching of the Church concerning the necessity of combining exercises of the contemplative life with those of the active. Some have spoken of a "spirituality of action" which, though not necessarily contradictory, has often been presented as though it were a spirituality which either excluded or neglected, not by desire but by constraint, contemplative activity. Such a spirituality in the last analysis would be un-Christian. No Pope has ever taught that one must give himself to the active apostolate in order to become perfect. Rather, the constant papal warnings voiced again and again to religious superiors and subjects engaged in the apostolate has always been to protect and encourage frequent and daily withdrawal from the world at least for a time. In fact we can lay down as a general rule that there is one point in common for all seeking theological perfection or the life of contemplation to which all are called and this point will always remain common, as

---

[1] Gen. 12:1.

Pius XII has pointed out: "whoever selects evangelical perfection as his goal must necessarily withdraw and separate himself from this world. Externally, of course, this is to be done in accordance with one's God-given vocation. Internally, it is to be done without limitation."[2] It is the teaching of the Church that one cannot speak of a spiritual formation that can be realized exclusively through external activity. Recollection in God, some prayer life, and the other practices of the ascetical life traditional at all times in the history of the Church are essential. Activity is not life; rather it presupposes life, an interior life that is frequently nourished by conversation with God.

The problem is before us, and yet many of the solutions which have been proposed have not sufficiently answered it. We might, therefore, legitimately ask ourselves the question: Why? Any answer to this question would have to follow a solution whose basic principle has already been given by the Pope just mentioned. Almost at the very beginning of one of the addresses referred to[3] he mentioned: "How many misunderstandings, mental blocks, and erroneous judgments would be avoided if when speaking of the contemplative life one took the trouble of recalling the doctrine of the Angelic Doctor whose main points we have just given."[4] It seems that much of the difficulty lies in a misunderstanding of the principles involved in the two lives which sum up the whole of human activity. For this reason it would be well for us to treat these principles which have to form the basis of any and every particular solution that might prove to be practical for an individual or for a group of persons living a common life. Before doing this, however, it would be best for us to review some of the background involved in the actual presentation of the question by St. Thomas.

The treatise on the active and contemplative lives is placed toward the end of the Angelic Doctor's moral theology or considerations on human behavior in general. It is only after having studied those things which are common to all human conditions of life — the last end, human acts, the passions, habits, virtues and vices — that he turns his attention to those various ways or states or pursuits of life in which these can be exercised.

While the gospel story of Martha and Mary is often used as a kind of basis upon which to make the distinction between the two lives, the real foundation is to be sought elsewhere — in classical Greek thought.

---

[2] Instruct. to Religious Superiors, Haud Mediocri, February 11, 1958; The Pope Speaks, 5 (1959), 204; cf. also The Contemplative Life, Cédant volontiers, July 18, 1958; Menti Nostrae, September 23, 1950.

[3] The Contemplative Life.

[4] Cf. The Pope Speaks, 5 (1959), 63–64.

According to this tradition the life of a man was presented through the intermediary of two pictures, as it were. There was the life of the man of action, of one who mingles in the affairs of the world, the hustle and bustle of ordinary family life, of one who engaged in the earning of a livelihood and all that goes with it. And there was the life of the wise man, the intellectual, if you will, or the contemplative, who leads a life that is free from all material cares, who is able to leisurely and peacefully consider truths and rise from this consideration to Him who is beyond them, the One whom we call God. In short, we might say that Greek thought conceived of two kinds of lives — that of the man of action and that of the man of contemplation.

These notions regarding the division of human life into active and contemplative were taken over by the early Fathers of the Church. We find them in the writings of St. Clement of Alexandria, and of Origen who is the first to interpret the biblical episode of Martha and Mary in the light of this division which is Hellenic in origin and terminology. Following Origen we have some of the greatest of the Fathers following this classical division — St. Gregory the Great, St. Augustine. Consequently, its continued presence through the writers of the Middle Ages — St. Bernard, for example, and the Scholastics of these years, should not be wondered at. Moreover, the divisions were not adopted without some modifications, as we would expect, modifications which will be made clear in due time.

Some authors, however, felt that this "Aristotelian" idea of the division of life was somewhat foreign to that presented to us in the Gospels. They felt that this division such as it was presented in Greek thought was somewhat selfish or self-centered. It seems to picture to us one who seeks to contemplate God by flight from the world and the evasion of the entire sensible order. On the other hand they said, the spirituality of the Gospels seems to be an active spirituality, one that was to be exercised through external activity in which we would demonstrate our love for God in and through service rendered to our neighbor.[5]

Such a view does not seem to be entirely correct. Otherwise the Church would never have approved and expressed her admiration for forms of life which would be in some sense foreign to or outside the directives of evangelical thought. Nor would the Fathers of the Church have expressed their great admiration for this way of the Christian Life called contemplative, that is, one which busied itself with the things of God. This division of the Christian life into active and contemplative is not

---

[5] Cf. A. J. Festugière, L'Enfant d'Agrigente, 2 ed. (Paris: ed. du Cerf, 1950), Chap. 7; Hausherr, "Les grands courants de la Spiritualité orientale," Orientalia Christiana Periodica (1935), 114–138.

something merely borrowed and taken over from Greek thought. It was something already mentioned in the Gospels, in the episode of Martha and Mary: "Martha, Martha, how many cares and troubles thou hast! But only one thing is necessary; and Mary has chosen for herself the best part of all, that which shall never be taken away from her."[6] How wise such a division of life is, how very much in keeping with the very purpose of Christianity can be seen from even a superficial analysis of the goal or the end of the Christian life. This, as we know, consists in the perfection of charity which has two acts: the love of God directly and the love of God manifested in and through our love for our neighbor. Just as human activity can be divided into an active and a contemplative life, so, too, divine-human activity could be similarly divided.

As we shall see in the course of our study the observation made by St. Augustine in the *City of God* still presents us with the best solution to the problem of the harmonization of the two lives. He wrote in the nineteenth chapter of the nineteenth book:

> Or take the three modes of life — the contemplative, the active and the contemplative-active. One can live the life of faith in any of these three and get to heaven. What is not something merely arbitrary is that he love truth and do what charity demands. No man must be so committed to contemplation as to give no thought to his neighbor's needs, nor so absorbed in action as to dispense with contemplation.
>
> The attraction of leisure ought not to be empty-headed inactivity, but the quest or discovery of truth, both for his own progress and for the purpose of sharing ungrudgingly with others. Nor should the man of action love worldly position or power (for all is vanity under the sun) but only what can be properly and usefully accomplished by means of such position and power, in the sense which I have already explained, of contributing to the eternal salvation of those committed to one's care. . . .
>
> In the same way no man is forbidden to pursue knowledge of truth for that is the purpose of legitimate leisure. But it is the ambition for the position of dignity which is necessary for government that is unbecoming, although of course dignity itself and its use are not wrong in themselves. Thus it is the love of study that seeks a holy leisure; and only the compulsion of charity that shoulders necessary activity. If no such burden is placed on one's shoulders time should be passed in study and contemplation. But once the burden is on the back it should be carried since charity so demands. Even so, however, no one should give up entirely his delight in learning, for the sweetness he once knew may be lost and the burden he bears overwhelm him.[7]

This advice and solution to an age-old problem will also be ours from an analysis of the principles involved in the theology of the two lives. This St. Thomas divides into four considerations: (1) the Division of

6 Lk. 10:38.   7 *PL* 41, 647.

Life into Active and Contemplative; (2) the Contemplative Life; (3) the Active Life; and (4) a Comparison between the two. It is in this order that we shall take up our study.

Section 1. The Division of Life Into Active and Contemplative

In Thomistic thought which, as we have seen, rests on the tradition of both the Greek philosophers and the early Fathers of the Church, human activity or life from one point of view is divided into active and contemplative. This division is not at all an arbitrary one. It is, rather, established on that activity which is *most properly* or specifically *human*, namely, that of the intellect, which as we know is either practical or speculative depending upon whether one engages in external activity or the search for truth. Every living thing gives proof of its "life" by that operation which is most proper to it and to which it is most inclined. Since the proper life of man is the life or the activity of the intellect, the life of every human being would be determined in accordance with the end toward which he directs the activity of his mind. Experience teaches us that among men there are some who develop their intellect for purposes of exterior activities which vary with epoch, nationality, and environment. These are said to lead the *active life*. It is the life of a man who uses his practical intellect for the greater portion of the day engaging in civic affairs or in business or in one or other of the professions. There are others, however, who develop their intellects for purposes of study and the contemplation of truth. These are said to lead the *contemplative life*. It is the life of one who spends his time predominantly in search of or in quest for truth and knowledge.

In Thomas' thought we ought to note that even though human activity is divided in accordance with the activity of the intellect, there is an essential connection between the predominant occupation of one's intellect and his will, a connection which is often lost sight of in the study of this problem. Thomas is very careful to point out that the "life" of every man is that in which he takes his *delight*. Thus even though there be question of an intellectual operation it is one which brings with it a certain amount of delight or pleasure. Normally speaking, therefore, the man of affairs engages in exterior activity with and for others, *because he takes a certain delight* in this. The contemplative, on the other hand, engages in contemplation because he derives from this a certain pleasure even though this may not be of the sensible order.[8]

---

[8] II–II, Q. 179, a. 1.

This particular division of life into active and contemplative seems to be adequate since it is based on a *predominance* of contemplation or action in one individual. While we might speak of a "mixed life," one which involves both contemplation and action, still strictly speaking one is said to live the contemplative life when he is engaged in contemplation or the use of the speculative intellect, and the active when he is engaged in exterior activity. This "mixed life" is a combination of extremes and is *virtually* contained in them as the tepid is contained in the hot and the cold, and the gray in the white and the black. The deeper the *balance* of action and of contemplation the more perfectly mixed is the life in question.

This division given by Thomas can be readily seen in the natural order of things. The "philosopher" or the intellectual is usually one who devotes himself for the greater portion of his life to the study or the contemplation of truth. The practical man of affairs, on the other hand, is one who devotes the greater part of his life or day to affairs or works of an external nature such as were mentioned above.

But the division is also acceptable *within a Christian framework or setting*, that is, in reference to charity which is the bond of perfection. The division then can also be made in reference to the love of God and the love of neighbor, which are essentially implied in this setting. The reason for this is rather simple. The active and contemplative division of life is not based on a distinction of *ultimate* ends necessarily; it can be based on a distinction or difference of proximate ends of human activity. This is most evident certainly in the application of this division to the Christian life. For the ultimate end of this life in a very special way is the glory of God, through our union with Him either through charity if there be question of the present life, or through glory or consummated charity if there be question of the life to come. But the immediate or the proximate ends or means as far as the last end is concerned can be different, and such they are in our present consideration. For the immediate end of the active life is the expression of charity or our love for God and for our neighbor in the service of our neighbor. The immediate end of the contemplative life is the expression of our love for God and for our neighbor too, in the direct service of God. In strict theological language we would say that in the case of the Christian both the one living the active life and the one living the contemplative life would have the same *finis operantis*, the perfection of charity, even though they would have diverse *fines operis*, or frameworks of life, by which this perfection would be achieved.[9]

---

9 Cf. III Sent. dist. 36, a. 3, ad 5.

Consequently, there are those within the framework of the Mystical Body who find their delight in the contemplation of divine truths and spend the major portion of their time in such a pursuit. And there are those who find and take their delight in works of charity toward their neighbor, such as nursing, or caring for orphans or the aged and sick. And there are still others who attempt to live a rather even balance of the two activities. Such a life, active, or contemplative, or mixed, can be lived within some *canonical* form of life established or at least approved by the Church in some official manner, or it can be lived in some private form, such as was almost universally true in the earliest days of the Church.[10]

These last two principles are of the utmost importance in determining and guiding vocations to the religious life and the priesthood. For the various institutions or orders merely provide a *canonical framework* or *organization* of life wherein one or other of these ways of life can be followed more easily and more securely. Depending upon the individual's temperament and other qualifications he will arrive at the perfection of charity and fulfill his mission in life toward the Mystical Body by living one of these divisions of life whether inside or outside some canonical framework established for this purpose. Thus one or other of these ways of life could be led in the priesthood, in the religious life, in a secular institute, in the life of dedicated virginity lived in the world, and in the married state, for not even these last mentioned are exempt from living one or other of these basic divisions of human life.[11] That is why St. Francis de Sales very pointedly remarked that "it is an error or rather a heresy to say that devotion [the perfection of charity, in his language] is incompatible with the life of a soldier, a tradesman, a prince, or a married woman. . . . Wherever we are we may and we should aspire to a perfect life."[12]

Section 2.   The Contemplative Life

The expression "the contemplative life" has two meanings, related to be sure, but nonetheless distinct. It has an *objective* meaning in which case it refers to a canonical form of life approved by the Church. This we

---

[10] Cf. Apostolic Constitution, *Sponsa Christi*, tr. Daughters of St. Paul (Apostolate of the Press, 1955), pp. 11–15.

[11] Cf. *Sponsa Christi*, Statutes, Art. 2, para. 2; and especially, *The Contemplative Life*, Cédant volontiers, July 18, 1958. *The Pope Speaks*, 5 (1959), 61–81.

[12] Cf. *Introduction to a Devout Life*, Part I, Chap. 3; also *Spiritual Conferences*, 13, Spirit of the Rules; and *Christians in the World*, Jacques Leclercq (New York: Sheed and Ward, 1961), p. 170 ff.

find, for example, among the Trappists, the Trappistines, the Carthusians, the Cloistered Carmelites, the Poor Clares, Benedictines, Second Order Dominicans, Ursulines, and others. Understood in this sense, the contemplative life refers to an organized mode of living in which the whole of life and every activity can easily and effectively be penetrated by Him who is sought. It is a life whose whole framework is orientated in a special way toward the acquisition of habitual interior contemplation. Such a mode of life does not allow for as much activity as does the life of the so-called active religious communities or orders, or even as much as that of the mixed orders.

The expression also has another meaning — subjective — in which case it refers to that interior life of an individual which is characterized by the habitual presence of contemplation. This type of contemplative life can be lived anywhere theoretically at least, in any vocation, and is even compatible with a most active sort of life. We might point out that historically considering the problem of the contemplative life, the expression vita contemplativa as we find it used in the early Church writers and even by St. Bernard and St. Thomas practically always signifies the second meaning just given. For them this life was to be found especially in preachers and pastors of souls, rather than merely or even specifically in those who left the world for the desert or the cloister or for some form of retired life.[13] It is this second sense, the sense used by the great writers of antiquity, that we are now about to consider.

Nature of the Contemplative Life

First of all those who devote themselves primarily and principally (not necessarily exclusively) to the contemplation of or pursuit after truth are said to live the contemplative life. While it is very true that the essential act involved in contemplation, the moment in which the mind intuitively or contuitively, as it were, "sees" or passes beyond all barriers preventing an open gaze or a simple gaze at truth is only of very short duration, still the whole effort involved in searching for this and in preparing for this event pertains to the contemplative life. When there is question of the Christian contemplative life, the whole of one's effort is directed to and finds its ultimate perfection only in the contemplation of or the simple gaze at divine Truth which is the supreme beatitude or happiness of the human mind.

Even though this life is, formally speaking, a life of the intellect both in its preparatory operations and activity and in its possessing or express-

---

[13] Cf. Western Monasticism, Dom Cuthbert Butler, O.S.B. (New York: Dutton, 1922), p. 290 ff.

ing operation, still it is not at all entirely divorced from the affective makeup of man. There is, indeed, a very definite sense in which it can be said to pertain to the will or to the rational affective life of man, and this essentially. This is most pronounced in the case of mystical contemplation, but is not absent from the contemplation of the philosopher or from that of the theologian. This relation of the will to the intellect in contemplation is *twofold*. The will moves the intellect to contemplate, and it enjoys or rejoices in the Truth or the One contemplated.

Causally speaking contemplation is said to be in the will or the affections either by reason of the *love of concupiscence* or by reason of the *love of friendship*, or by reason of both. That is to say that a person is moved to consider or gaze upon an object of knowledge out of love for the thing known (love of friendship), or he is moved to consider it out of his love for the action of knowing (love of concupiscence), or he is moved out of love for both. In Christian contemplation both of these motivating forces are usually present, even though the former predominates for the most part. For one who gives himself over to the contemplative life does so out of love for God primarily but also for the legitimate and ordered delight which follows upon the possession of the vision of divine truth — such as this can be had here on earth. He is said to engage in this life because of his desire to see God whom he loves with the love of friendship and because of his desire (again, ordered, of course) to find his perfection or his happiness in this action. St. Gregory the Great was one of the first to bring out this causal connection between charity and contemplation, or between the activity of the will and that of the intellect. He writes in his *Homilies on Ezechiel*: "The contemplative life tramples on all cares and longs to see the face of its Creator. Thus, it is out of the love of God that one is fired or inflamed by the desire to contemplate His beauty."[14]

Terminatively speaking, however, contemplation can be said to exist in the will because once the person has attained the object desired, once the intellect gazes on the object longed for, the will takes a certain delight or complacency or relish in the possession of the object. In this way, then, the love of God which is placed at the beginning of contemplation, acting as its impelling motive, is also found at its end; for contemplation culminates in the joy and rest and delight which the will experiences or feels when the intellect possesses the object desired or sought after or loved.

Experience also points out that as long as the object possessed and loved is not fully known, as long as there remain in it hidden "attics and cellars" so to speak, which have not been investigated, the one loving

---

[14] *Hom. 2 in Ezech., PL* 76, 953.

is pushed on to a greater desire to know more by a kind of a holy curiosity. This tendency is something of rather common experience. We see it forming the basis for continued research in the case of the physical sciences. We see it forming the basis for continued growth in the love of two persons for each other. But we see it very marked when the object loved is not finite but infinite, presenting to the lover an inexhaustible font or source of knowledge and love. This is what we are faced with in Christian contemplation whose object is God Himself. So long as the object is not fully known this mutual interactivity on the part of the will and the intellect can and should take place. The will moves the intellect to seek the object, and then from the presence of the object in the intellect with all of its still unexplored riches, it presses the intellect on in quest of an ever greater knowledge of the thing loved. It is only when the object is fully known or when it cannot be known any more fully for one reason or another, that the will rests and is content with the knowledge possessed.

The principle involved here is most important for it lies at the core of a happy and fruitful vocation. It is the fundamental reason why the Church has constantly insisted upon a balanced life, that together with whatever active apostolate a religious community or a priest engages in, some time must be spent daily in the consideration of divine things or in the exercises of the interior life. So many "lost vocations" or what are sometimes called "temporary vocations" could have been saved or preserved if the persons or, perhaps, their superiors had been aware of this principle — the mutual interactivity of action and contemplation which is not something merely arbitrary but absolutely necessary for a theological contemplative life to grow and to flower and to produce its effects within the Church. It is hardly any wonder that our Lord warned His disciples: "You ought always to pray and never to faint";[15] or that the sovereign pontiffs have constantly pointed out the unique force of contemplative prayer. We would do well to ponder the words of Pius XII on this score. "It must be stated without a reservation that no other means has the unique force and efficacy of meditation and that as a consequence its daily practice can in no wise be substituted for."[16] "The Primacy of meditation and of contemplation of God and divine truth is above all other means of perfection: it is above all practices, it is above all forms of organization and federations — this is what We want to emphasize and support with Our authority."[17]

---

[15] Lk. 18:1.

[16] *Menti Nostrae, AAS* 42 (1950), 638.

[17] *The Contemplative Life,* July 18, 1958, *The Pope Speaks,* 5 (1959), 66.

The Relationship of the Moral Virtues to Contemplation

A second most important consideration in any treatment of the contemplative life and one often completely overlooked today is the relationship of the moral virtues to contemplation. In fact, it seems that we would not be far wrong in saying that from a failure to understand or to recall this relationship, many persons living in the world, or in so-called active or apostolic religious societies, have not made the progress they ought to in their respective vocations.

The exercise of the moral virtues — Justice, Fortitude, and Temperance, with all their potential parts or satellite virtues such as Religion, Obedience, Piety, Patience, Chastity, Humility — do not pertain *essentially* to the contemplative life. This is clear from the following considerations. First of all, these virtues reside in the *appetitive* faculties of man either in the will itself or in the irascible and concupiscible faculties considering these as having some relation to the will. The contemplative life, however, consists in the exercise of the intellect. Second, the contemplation of truth is a kind of knowing which in itself has little influence on the moral virtues which deal with the inclination to external action. Their exercise requires not merely knowledge but a certain tendency or inclination in the faculty to enable it to elicit its proper actions with some facility and in conformity with right reason. Lastly, the moral virtues pertain to the exercises of another life especially, the active life, not so much in the direct contemplation and prayer to God, as in service to our neighbor.

Even though the moral virtues do not pertain to the contemplative life *essentially*, they can and do pertain to it *dispositively*. For the act of contemplation in which the contemplative life essentially consists requires the control of the passions which could so easily prevent or hinder its exercise. The passions easily tend to withdraw the soul's movement toward intelligible things, and direct it to sensible things. The moral virtues exist to offset this, doing so by curbing or directing the passions and by quelling the disturbances which arise from outward occupations. By causing a certain freedom from the impetuosity of passion or emotion they are said to bring about a kind of peace to the soul and thereby dispose one for contemplation. It is because the moral virtues bring our "house to rest" as John of the Cross says[18] or because they effect a certain balanced or proportioned movement in our faculties, that a true beauty can be found in them and in their exercise.

Beauty by reason of its excellence is to be found essentially and by

---

[18] *Ascent of Mt. Carmel*, Bk. I, Chap. 15, Peers, I, p. 62.

right in the contemplative life. The reason for this is rather simple. Beauty consists in a certain clarity and proper proportion. Both of these, however, are found in the intellect whose activity forms the characteristic mark of the contemplative life. But even though this is true, beauty can also be said to exist by participation in the moral virtues and in their exercise. For these can be said to share in the ordering of reason since they exist only because of reason's having impressed its directive or guiding force upon the faculties in which they exist. An application of this assertion would serve to clarify it. St. Thomas mentions that in a very special way we find beauty in the virtue of temperance which represses or brings under control those desires which would prevent the light of reason from exercising its control over our lower nature. By bringing this proportion or balance or beauty into our lower nature this virtue overcomes any lack of harmony existing between the lower nature and reason and reduces the former to the service of the latter. That is why St. Thomas so frequently throughout his theology mentions that the virtue of chastity — particularly that of virginity (which is perpetual chastity practiced by intention rather than by force of circumstances) — serves in a special way to dispose one for contemplation since indulgence in carnal pleasure more than anything else tends to draw the mind away from the contemplation of divine things to sensible things. This is the reason, he remarks, why when God calls one by common grace He does not demand that they forego an earthly marriage, but when He calls them by a special grace (to contemplation he says) then He demands that they forego the "wine of the marriage feast."[19]

While this observation of St. Thomas already serves to bridge the gap existing between the active and the contemplative lives, at least partially, there is another which narrows it down even more. There is a sense — and Cajetan points it out in his commentary on this question — in which the moral virtues can be said to dispose one *directly* for contemplation. The explanation given is most convincing. He says that they *directly* dispose one for the increase of charity and charity is the very cause of contemplation itself. I believe that this assertion on the part of the great Thomistic commentator is based on a teaching found elsewhere in St. Thomas where he treats of the growth of the supernatural virtues. It is well worth quoting at least in part:

> The comparative greatness of the virtues can be understood in two ways. First, as referring to their specific nature, and in this way there is no doubt that in a man one virtue is greater than another, for example, charity than faith and hope. Secondly, it may be taken as referring to the degree of

19 Cf. "Exposition on the Prologue of St. Jerome to the Gospel of St. John," *Commen. in Joannem*, Marietti ed., 1952, p. 5.

participation by the subject, according as a virtue becomes intense or weak in its subject. In this sense all the virtues in one man are equal *with an equality of proportion* insofar as their increase in man is equal. Thus the fingers are unequal in size but equal in proportion, since they grow in proportion to one another.[20]

This particular teaching of the Angelic Doctor on the proportionate equality of growth in regard to all the supernatural virtues is very illuminating. It seems to the present writer that it holds the key to the problem which we mentioned above — the possible existence of harmony between action and contemplation. In fact the solution seems to be so simple that perhaps it has been somewhat overlooked by those in search of it. The virtues grow proportionately in such a way that when one person grows in one virtue, e.g., humility, or patience, or obedience, or chastity, he is at the same time growing proportionately in all the other virtues too. The intensification of any one virtue brings along in its wake a *proportionate* intensification of all the others. We might attempt to make a practical application of this principle to our problem.

Let us take the case of a religious engaged in a rather active apostolate, such as nursing, or taking care of the aged, or elementary teaching. During the course of the day, the exercise of a countless number of moral virtues is usually required — patience, humility, obedience, chastity, and others. In the exercise of the particular virtue required at any given moment the religious increases *not only* the virtue being exercised, but also *all* the virtues which form the spiritual physiognomy of the Christian. This increase is given immediately or in due time as St. Thomas teaches, depending upon whether the person has elicited an act that is of greater intensity than the habit or virtue in question or not.[21] Whenever the habitus of *any* virtue is increased, the habitus of all the others are *simultaneously* increased.

This increase affects the virtue of charity also which, as we have pointed out, is the *cause* of contemplation. It seems that we are logically to conclude that a person who grows in any virtue grows in the virtue of charity at the same time, and growing in charity, becomes more apt for the act of contemplation. Too often religious or lay persons pursuing their own respective vocations seem to forget this truth. They feel that they are automatically excluded from contemplation because the very nature of their work demands that they be with the "sons of men" for the greater portion of their day. The truth of the matter is far otherwise. For *in the exercise of the virtues proper to their vocation* they are also disposing themselves for or actually realizing an increase in the virtue of charity which is the cause of contemplation, and the measure of its intensity.

---

[20] I–II, Q. 66, a. 2, c.   [21] Cf. II–II, Q. 24, a. 6.

Consequently, it should be true that when God gives them the opportunity for the exercises proper to the contemplative life, e.g., mental prayer or spiritual reading, they should find themselves becoming more and more disposed for the act of contemplation itself. This is merely a simple gaze or a quick insight into some truth or mystery of our faith. Indeed it could very well happen that they would be more habitually disposed for contemplation than another living the canonical contemplative life or a private contemplative life, if they have been more generous in the practice of the virtues proper to it.

This rather abstract presentation of a very deeply spiritual truth and reality has been very clearly asserted by the Doctor of Mysticism St. John of the Cross. He writes:

> The fact is that while faith has become ever more deeply rooted and infused into the soul by means of that emptiness and darkness and detachment from all things, or spiritual poverty, all of which may be spoken of as one and the same thing, at the same time charity has become rooted and infused into the soul ever more deeply also. Wherefore the more the soul desires obscurity and annihilation with respect to all outward or inward things that it is capable of receiving the more is it infused by faith and consequently, by love and hope, since all these three theological virtues go together.[22]

While the saint limits himself here to the theological virtues, still there is no reason to think that this same phenomenon is not also true in regard to the infused moral virtues as St. Thomas explicitly teaches.

There is one important point we should make note of. The contemplation of an active religious is often different from that of the contemplative, not in essence to be sure, but in subject matter and surrounding circumstances. The contemplation of the active religious often centers around the *moral virtues* such as they are seen in the life of Christ and the saints. For it is with these virtues that he is so often occupied. It might very well happen that a religious engaged in nursing or teaching may receive a *sudden insight* into the patience of Christ or His sufferings on the cross at the very moment that he or she is engaged in the exercise of the apostolate to those members in whom He continues His Passion. The priest in the confessional, for example, if he has very faithfully fulfilled his ministry, may be granted to *suddenly experience* in his own person something of the patience of Christ, or something of the fatigue Christ endured for the salvation of the world — something we might almost say of the very Passion of Christ itself. For this reason such a person is said to

---

[22] *Ascent of Mt. Carmel*, Vol. I, p. 180. From *The Complete Works of St. John of the Cross*, tr. and ed. by E. Allison Peers from the critical edition of P. Silverio de Santa Teresa, C.D. Pub. in three vols. by Sheed and Ward, Inc., New York.

enter just a little more deeply and often very suddenly, just when he or she least expects it, into some understanding of one of the mysteries of our faith; this is true and genuine contemplation. Indeed, very often — and the Saint of Lisieux is our witness to this — a soul receives lightning-like insights when it is engaged in exterior work, rather than when it is enjoying the peace and quiet of contemplation. There is the story of the Little Flower who had to endure the constant jangling of a rosary by another Sister during the period of mental prayer. During such periods her prayer consisted of one constant effort to control her annoyance at this distraction. On another occasion in her autobiography she speaks of the physical drowsiness which she so often experienced after the reception of Holy Communion. Just at those times when we would think a contemplative such as she was enjoying the highest type of prayer and union with God, the exact opposite was true. But it is she herself who tells us that because of the efforts she made at these times, later on during the course of the day during her work she would often receive sudden insights into some aspect of one or other of the mysteries of our faith. The same phenomenon can and often does happen in the lives of those who are engaged in a life that would have to be classified as "active."

For this reason we should always insist in the formation or the instruction of those who may be called by God to the active life that their possibility for enjoying what authors call "contemplation" or what we might rather call a deeper understanding of a mystery of faith, depends largely upon the degree of their fidelity to the exercise of the virtues *proper to their own vocation*, not to the virtues proper to the life of a contemplative order. While it is true that we do not often see this in the hustle and bustle of the day, still the actuality of this fact seems to be beyond dispute. For if the assertion of the Angelic Doctor is true, then there is a contemplation which is proper to the active religious, in this sense, that the active religious will more probably receive his or her insights into one or other of the mysteries of Redemption such as these involve the practice or exercise of the *moral virtues*. It is in this way that we can say that the active life or the exercise of the moral virtues should not only dispose one for contemplation, but at times be the *very occasion for it*, for contemplative insights into some aspect of the Christian Mystery.

These virtuous acts tend to purify the soul reducing it more and more to God and to His ordination, ridding it of the selfishness which prevents it from seeing God, and disposing it for the divine activity. The active religious would do well rather than complain about the lack of time for prayer and for reflection, to practice the virtues that are asked of him in the particular vocation or even obedience which has been received from God. For in proportion as he practices these virtues in that same proportion will he dispose himself for contemplation. *Pati divina* is one of the phrases which often occurs in the writings of the mystics and likewise in that of the theologians who speak about the activity of the Holy Ghost in the soul — to *suffer* the divine action, to *endure* it, to *accept* it with love, regardless of how nonspiritual it might appear to be and perhaps is in itself — this is the sign and measure of one's deep faith and love. And we know that these are the virtues which lie at the root of all contemplative thought or insight. When God calls us to a certain way of life, then our perfection, that perfection willed for us by God, consists not in "pining" away for some other form of life or some idea that is perhaps more ephemeral than real, but rather, in the perfect living of the life to which we are called, to the perfect exercise of the virtues that are demanded in that life. The reward — let us leave that to God. But we may be sure that this practice will lead us to true contemplation and that even during our life here on earth — unless God shall have reserved this for us in the next life.

Father de Caussade writes on this point:

> We are not told that these holy persons (Joseph and Mary) sought the holiness of circumstances, but rather holiness in all circumstances. We must conclude that there is no special path which is the most perfect (for *all* individuals), but that in general, the most perfect path lies in submission to the order of God in the accomplishment of our exterior duties as well as in the interior dispositions of our being. In everything we should say "*Dominus est*" "it is the Lord" and in all circumstances we should find a gift from God.[23]

Again he says in another place: "Should the divine will withdraw us from the act of contemplation in order to hear confessions etc., and this even for a long time, that very duty forms Jesus Christ in the depths of our hearts, and all the sweetness of contemplation at that time would but destroy Him."[24]

For those whom God has called to a life which demands the absorption of the mind in one or other of the works of the exterior apostolate there must be an approach like this to the sanctification of such works. They cannot constantly interrupt their work in order to apply themselves actually to the thought of God. Consequently, their orientation to Him must be *virtual*, one which can, however, easily be actualized at the proper time. The very simple thought of the Apostle Paul will always be true:

---

[23] *Abandonment to Divine Providence*, 3 Eng. ed. (St. Louis: B. Herder, 1921), pp. 20, 22, 25.
[24] *Ibid.*, p. 13.

"For those who love God all things work together unto good." The temptations of one's life, even those that are most humiliating, are permitted for the good of the soul, to lead it to a deeper and more firm practice of some virtue and to a deeper possession of the virtue of charity which is the very cause of contemplation itself.

Genesis of Contemplation

The contemplative life has one act in which it is finally completed, namely, the contemplation of truth. Yet since man's nature is not like that of the angel's, that is, that he grasp truth by simple apprehension without needing any method of discourse, he arrives at this act through other acts which lie either in the reception of principles, from which one proceeds to contemplation, or in the deduction from principles of the truth one intends to contemplate, or penetrate. This is true not only of that contemplation which might be called philosophical, but also of that which is Christian, that which occurs through the action of the Holy Spirit in the soul, working through His own gifts, especially those of wisdom, knowledge, and understanding, or working through a certain connaturality which is set up between the soul and divine truth, through the presence of charity which unites man to God.

It is for this reason that we find in all communities rules concerning spiritual reading, conferences, retreats — monthly and annual — mental prayer, particular examen, office, etc., those acts so to speak, which assist the individual to arrive at a deeper understanding of or contemplation of divine truth. We might give the following genesis of the act of contemplation:

1. The receiving of principles:
    a) Through the *hearing* of sermons, conferences, retreats, etc.
    b) Through *reading*, particularly the reading of Sacred Scripture; for as St. Thomas mentions in his commentary on the Gospel of St. John: "It is Sacred Scripture which is the instrument by which we can draw out of the well, living water springing up unto life everlasting. Through the depth of the well, we are to understand the profundity of Sacred Scripture and of divine wisdom. The ladle through which it is drawn is prayer."[25] St. Teresa herself mentions that she found more food for thought in the Gospels than in the most carefully planned books imaginable.[26]
    c) Through *prayer*.
2. The deduction from the principles received through these channels was to be arrived at:
    a) Through *meditation*.

---

[25] *Commen. in Joannem*, Chap. 4, lect. 2, n. 582, Marietti ed., 1952, p. 111.
[26] Cf. *Way of Perfection*, Chap. 21, Peers, II, p. 90.

   b) Through *speculation*, which is, perhaps, even though not the same
      as meditation, closely allied to it, at least insofar as both are said
      to be *discursive*.
   c) Through *consideration* and *thought* or *reflection*. This likewise ac-
      cording to St. Bernard is merely a species of meditation.
3. Contemplation with the subsequent admiration, which is the simple act
   of gazing on the truth (and when there is question of Christian contemplation, with love) : "*Gustate et videte quam suavis est Dominus.*"[27]

Object of Contemplation

We have seen that the contemplative life as understood in a Christian
context consists in the contemplation or the "simple apprehension" of the
truth. The truth in question is not *any* truth whatsoever — at least, if we
consider the principal act of the contemplative life — but rather, of *divine
truth*, because the contemplative considers contemplation to be the end
of the whole human life. This can be possessed in one of two ways. (a)
Imperfectly, when there is question of that contemplation which occurs
through a glass and in a dark manner.[28] Through this contemplation of
divine truth one possesses a certain inchoation or beginning of happiness,
one which begins now in the present life and will be continued in the
life to come. This is the contemplation which we have through faith
illuminated by the gifts of understanding and wisdom. (b) *Perfectly*, when
there is question of that contemplation which will be had in the Beatific
Vision where we shall see God face to face.

---

[27] Conrad Pepler, O.P., in seeking an answer to some of the problems facing religious
today wrote some years ago: "Liturgy must be made a part of the religious life instead
of being as too often is the case, an accidental addition. . . . Liturgical prayer . . . must
be made sufficiently practical to lie within the capacities of the average community, in
such a way that it would always be considered a privilege to attend. . . .
   "Again the mortifications and penances of modern religious should be full-blooded
and rigorous, but they should be as far as possible, directly related to this divine work,
the *Opus Dei*, in its widest sense (that is, they must be in conformity with the work
and the apostolate of the community in question). . . .
   "Here also the true doctrine of the correct relation between Christian action and
contemplation could be of considerable assistance when applied to the communal work
undertaken by religious. Work in which the moral virtues are principally applied should
in any case tend towards contemplation whatever that work may be. . . .
   "Many remedies could be suggested in this sphere, but in particular that of contemplative study of the Divine Word in the Scriptures and the Fathers of the Church
would seem most imperative for all religious . . . the insistence upon the *lectio divina*
— divine reading — upon the worship and work of God would demand a slowing down
of the present pace of the lives of most religious men and women. Such a 'rallentando'
presents, perhaps, the most serious problem today, and until that is solved it remains
unlikely that the modern religious will regain complete balance of liturgical and
ascetical principles involved in their lives and institutions." Cf. *Cross and Crown*,
1952, pp. 235–236, a summary of an article which first appeared in *Life of the Spirit*,
Blackfriars, London, January, 1952.
[28] Cf. 1 Cor. 13:12.

However, from another point of view, contemplation can have as its object God's effects. These too can be said to pertain to contemplation in a kind of dispositive manner since they dispose us for the contemplation of God. Thus St. Paul wrote: "For the invisible things of God . . . are clearly seen being understood by the things that are made."[29] It is for this reason that St. Augustine lays down a rule that is most helpful for those who might be engaged in the pursuit of knowledge which is considered to be profane or secular of its very nature: "In the study of creatures we must not exercise any empty curiosity, but should make them the stepping-stone to higher things imperishable and everlasting."[30] To treat this thought adequately would involve going into the whole of the theology of creation which considers all things that exist either as vestiges or images of God the Trinity, or as things which reflect the perfections of the God who created them for His own glory and to receive a share or communication in His own goodness.

In addition to these things which might lead us to God we also have the fact that even the sins of a person can lead him to the thought of God, at least indirectly. Thus the more we arrive at the understanding of our own nothingness before God the more do we understand His greatness. We might say that one of the supreme acts of contemplation, if not *the* supreme act, is a striking insight and immovable conviction of the basic truth of creation — that man has been brought out of nothing into being, or that man is not, while God alone is.

From these foregoing considerations we might conclude that there are four things which pertain to the contemplative life: (1) the *moral virtues*, disposing us for it; (2) those actions which *lead to contemplation* — such as hearing, reading, and prayer; (3) the *contemplation of divine effects* as well as the *consideration of one's sins*; (4) the *contemplation of divine truth itself*, in which the act of contemplation is found.

The saints have always maintained that *in via* it is not possible for us directly to see the Divine Essence, at least, in any permanent way.[31]

---

[29] Rom. 1:20. [30] *De Vera Religione*, 29, PL 34, 145.

[31] We might note here that some of the saints, e.g., St. Thomas himself, held that Moses and St. Paul saw the Essence of God in this life, but only in a transitory or fleeting way. This occurred, he teaches, when they were in a state of rapture, midway between the present state and the life to come. Cf. the present article, and Q. 174, a 4. St. Gregory, however, mentions that no one living in this mortal life reaches such a height of contemplation as to fix his eyes on the ray of boundless light. Cf. *Hom.* 2 in Ezech., PL 76, 956. St. Augustine seems to leave this possibility open, for he says: "No one seeing God lives this mortal life wherein the bodily senses have their play, and unless in some way he depart this life, whether by going out of the body altogether, or by withdrawing from his carnal senses, he is not caught up into that vision." *De Gen. ad Litteram*, 12, 27, PL 34, 477. This is also the position of St. John of the Cross, cf. *Spiritual Canticle*, Stanza the First, Peers, II, pp. 31–32.

According to St. Thomas, indeed, the only one who possessed the view of the Essence of God in this life in a permanent way was Christ Himself who was Comprehensor as well as Viator. When the mystics speak of their having seen God, or the Trinity of Persons, they mean that they have received from God some type of extraordinary favor which we mentioned above, either an imaginary vision or an intellectual vision, such that God enlightens them on some mystery, e.g., the Trinity. This He does by giving them some kind of species or thought-idea which imperfectly expresses something of the mystery in question.

Because of this we find St. Thomas writing:

> In the present state of life human contemplation is impossible without phantasms because it is connatural to man to see the intelligible species in the phantasms. The knowledge of our intellect, however, does not rest in the phantasms themselves, but sees in them the purity of the intelligible truth; this is true not only with respect to natural knowledge but also with respect to that which we receive through revelation.[32]

The Act of Contemplation

Contemplation is not pure repose (for this is merely a condition for it, namely, the leisure that is needed for us to engage in such a practice). It is, rather, an activity of the spirit. Consequently, we are not to see in it a movement of search or of acquisition, but rather an activity of possession in which we simply enjoy what we possess. The act of contemplation is a simple gaze or glance which comes at the end of our investigation or search. Thus an intellectual preparation is normally presupposed for any kind of contemplation, but once one arrives there, at the terminus of the activity, then he possesses the object in one simple lightninglike vision, imitating the simplicity of God in His own knowledge. In the natural order of things something similar occurs in the case of poetic inspiration, which is a sudden or quick perception of or insight into something of the order of nature. In the case of supernatural contemplation the "insight" is due to what is called gratia operans, a sudden movement or activity of the Holy Ghost in the soul which takes place without the active cooperation of the soul, not, however, without its passive cooperation or its consent to this activity. When there is question of poetic inspiration, on the other hand, we have a movement of or an activity in the mind which is due to what we call a motio operans, a quick illumination of the purely natural order, which illuminates one's perspective of a given idea or scene or event.

In Christian contemplation it is love or charity that moves us toward

---

[32] II–II, Q. 180, a. 5, ad 2.

the object which is in some way related to God. That is why St. Thomas insists so much on charity being both the *cause* and the *end* of our quest. However, we ought to note that love does not merely move us to search for the object loved in the case of Christian contemplation, *but it passes into the condition of the object loved.* In view of this fact, a certain knowledge of the object arises from the very fact that we are united to it through love. We call this a "connatural" knowledge, or a knowledge possessed through connaturality; it is a kind of instinctive knowledge if you will, arising from our union with it. In agreement with St. Gregory the Great, St. Thomas speaks of love as being a kind of knowledge because of this phenomenon: "*Amor est notitia.*"[33]

St. Gregory describes contemplation as a struggle in which the mind disengages itself from the things of the world, and fixes its attention wholly on spiritual things. Thereby it raises itself above itself and mounts up to a momentary perception of the unencompassed Light, as through a crack in a wall; then, exhausted by its effort and blinded by the vision of the Light, it sinks back wearied to its normal state, to recuperate its spiritual strength by exercising the works of the active life until in due time it can again brace itself for another act of contemplation.[34]

Contemplation seems to be, according to these authors, a kind of a foretaste of heavenly joy. It implies delight, first by reason of its being an operation of man and man delights in performing those operations which are proper to him; and *second*, by reason of its object, God. This "delight" is described by St. Thomas in the following manner:

> Although the contemplative life consists essentially in an act of the intellect it has its beginning in the appetite, since it is through charity that one is urged to the contemplation of God. And since the end corresponds to the beginning, it follows that the term and the end of the contemplative life have their existence in the affections since one delights in seeing the object loved; this very delight in the object arouses a still greater love for it. Hence Gregory says: "When we see one whom we love we are so aflame as to love him more."[35] This is the ultimate perfection of the contemplative life, namely, that the divine truth be not only seen but also loved.[36]

By a person's having to struggle rather laboriously to arrive at the possession of this object, he loves it all the more once he arrives at it even though this be only for a moment. The saints, for example, have insisted that temptation and even strong temptation is compatible with one's attaining to contemplation. In their eyes it is granted not only to those who

---

[33] Comm. in Joannem, Chap. 15, lect. 3, Marietti ed., 1952.
[34] Cf. Hom. 2 in Ezech., PL 76, 955.
[35] Cf. ibid., 954.
[36] II–II, Q. 180, a. 7, ad.1.

do not experience such a combat, but even to those who are put to the test, or who undergo, at times at least, rather severe temptation of one kind or another. Thus St. Paul seems to have experienced this when he spoke of the "good that I would, that I do not, but the evil that I would not that I do." St. Gregory clearly confirms the testimony of Paul: "It often happens that the spirit raises the mind up to things that are above and afterwards the flesh assails it with importunate temptations and when the mind is drawn to the contemplation of heavenly things it is beaten back by the images presented to it, those that are illicit. For the sting of the flesh suddenly wounds him whom holy contemplation was carrying outside of the flesh."[37]

The effects of the act of contemplation are self-knowledge, or a knowledge of our own nothingness, a greater knowledge of God's grandeur, humility, fervor, and love, the lessening of concupiscence. Temptations in a sense might be considered "effects" also, for it often happens as Gregory pointed out that one who is carried away in contemplation most often is harried by temptation lest he be puffed up in mind. For it is common experience that if contemplation should so raise the mind that temptation was lacking or absent, it would fall into pride.[38]

The Signs of a Contemplative Vocation

In trying to discern a vocation, as we shall see at much greater length later on, there are certain signs by which one can with some degree of certitude detect or make some conjecture as to its presence. Thus a vocation to a contemplative community is usually given to someone who in some way manifests the characteristic marks of such a vocation. Generally speaking these are often perceived in a kind of contemplative temperament, if we may use this purposely vague expression. We should note, however, that this temperament is not always immediately evident; often it lies rather hidden in a person's character. It is for this reason that very often those least suspected of possessing anything like the qualifications required for the contemplative life actually have a call to such a way of life. Even though they do not possess an externally placid temperament

---

[37] Moralia, Bk. 10, Chap. 14, PL 75, 937.

[38] Cf. Hom. 2 in Ezech., PL 76, 954. We might note that the mystics speak also of an arid contemplation, one which usually occurs during the periods known as the Dark Nights of the Senses and the Spirit. If delight is present at these times, it is usually not perceived.

Such an act of contemplation here below is not of long duration. This is due to the weakness of our human nature which is not as yet elevated to possess the light of glory. St. Teresa mentions that if we have it at all, it is usually of short duration. Cf. Interior Castle, Mansion 5, Chap. 1, Peers, II, p. 251.

or one that is almost passive this does not at all militate against their possessing the qualities that are needed for such a vocation. In fact this very thing, this placid and passive temperament, this desire to remain aloof from all people may be merely a kind of selfishness, or some external effect of a deep and hidden pride, or a feeling of inferiority, or some similar defect. Hence, the fact that one seems to be the life of the party and "mixes easily" with other people, possesses outstanding qualities of leadership and learning does not mean that he is not qualified for the contemplative life or that he should necessarily be urged to enter an active community. Vocation is God's decision which the individual comes to understand and detect under the help of God's grace; it is this grace which, if it be efficacious, determines the will or makes it firm in its desire to embrace this or that mode of life. There are, however, certain signs which seem to be essential for a contemplative vocation.

Very basically we might say that a contemplative vocation demands a very strong faith. This will include a faith in the transcendence of God, His sovereign rights, His unsearchable love for creatures. Another way of phrasing this disposition for a contemplative vocation is "a deep and strong desire for the Absolute." There is no hope that one will be able to stand the lack of the tangible so prevalent in the contemplative vocation, unless there be an exceptionally strong faith, unless one feels called by God "to work in the dark," so to speak, not only for one's own salvation, but also for that of others. A vocation to the contemplative life does not consist in one's despising action, but rather, in one's going beyond it, for he or she sees a broader picture than does the active, seeing that human effort has little efficacy of itself even though God does make use of it. A person called to the contemplative life in some way or other is caught up in the conviction that the principal share in the whole work of redemption belongs not to action, but rather to love; and it is this reason that motivates his seeking admission to the cloister. Thus we might say that in the spiritual order there are two signs of a contemplative vocation: (1) the sense of what is due to God, and (2) the sense of the limitations of the creature.

To these spiritual criteria we might also note several natural ones that help to determine the presence or the absence of a contemplative vocation, or a contemplative temperament. First of all — well-balanced nerves; these are required more in the cloister than they are anywhere else perhaps. A temperamental balance is the only sure natural safeguard for one's ability to endure the special difficulties which are encountered in the atmosphere of a contemplative community. The long hours of silence and of occupation with things that are not too absorbing leave the mind and memory and the imagination much time to work. These allow for much introspection which, in the case of one who lacks well-balanced nerves, very often ends up with some sort of neurosis or emotional or functional disorder. It is for this reason that those who are in charge of contemplative communities have mentioned that it takes practically the whole of one's period of temporary probation — the novitiate and the years of temporary vows — and sometimes much longer to determine with some degree of accuracy the temperamental balance of an individual.

Added to this requirement there must also be the *presence of sound judgment,* or sufficient qualities of mind and will. This is usually called "common sense." For in the things of the spirit, especially where one has by vocation the calling to seek throughout the greater part of the day the things of God in a kind of an abstract sort of way, sound judgment is most essential. Deception in the ways of prayer is one of the easiest things possible. And it is the presence of sound judgment that will help to avoid the pitfalls to which the contemplative life is singularly subjected.[39]

In many communities that are cloistered and still have some sort of work to do that requires special ability, as is true of some cloistered Benedictine and Dominican communities, the presence of those qualities which are special and proper to the type of contemplative life involved are also required. Someone has said that they have had in their convents persons who have gone on saying their morning and night prayers out of little books of devotion without paying the slightest attention to the offices of prime and compline which were recited in choir.

When one applies for admission or asks advice concerning such a vocation, the person being asked should inquire into the genesis of the vocation, its history, and the reasons why the applicant feels called to a contemplative order. The frankness of the answers should be carefully noted, and the simplicity with which the story comes out. Special care should be taken concerning the reading of the one seeking advice, for often it happens that from the reading of the mystics one feels that he or she is called to the contemplative life. Thus, for eqample, in our day, many after having read one or several of Thomas Merton's books have felt that they were meant for the Trappist life, only upon being interviewed to go away very much convinced that they did not have a vocation to such a life.

A certain amount of testing should be done even before one is admitted to a novitiate. For it sometimes happens when all the testing is done in the novitiate, the person who perhaps never should have even been

---

[39] Cf. *Way of Perfection,* Chap. 17, Peers, II, pp. 69–76.

allowed this far, comes out of the experience broken and something of a misfit for some time afterward. To avoid this their course in the world should be followed: How do they conduct themselves in the midst of secular preoccupations and work? How do they receive the sacraments? With what frequency, even despite exterior difficulties? Some authors are of the opinion that it is the proper course to subject a contemplative vocation to testing in the world, asking young persons to continue their education there, keeping track of development in the intellectual, social, and spiritual spheres. What is most important is that one have a regular confessor who knows the life to which the person aspires and can give the proper help in disposing one for it.

Above all, here, in the case of the contemplative vocation as well as in that of the active, the words of Pius XI are most important:

> Be severe. These might be hard words, but they are prompted by love, for true love, love worthy of our Lord's friends, can be satisfied with nothing short of the truth . . . we are not alluding merely to severity in general, that is, of discipline, but first and foremost in accepting postulants. If anyone tells you that there is too much severity even now, we authorize you to reply that the Pope wants it that way, because he clearly sees the need of it (for the length of his pontificate has allowed him to acquire wide experience in this field). Indeed, if the religious life is to be kept in all its splendor there must be severity, particularly with regard to vocations because although divine grace helps nature, still it does not destroy it.[40]

Within the cloister, the ultimate criterion which contemplative orders count on is what they term *expansiveness*. This is nothing else than the ability of the person to adapt himself or herself to the way of life proper to the community, which, of course, is the ultimate criterion of all communities whether they be active or contemplative. This is quite compatible with temptation against, and even some dislike for the life, so long as it does not destroy the conviction of the person's "being in the right place."

One other help to the discernment of a contemplative vocation (and it is also just as true for discerning any religious or priestly vocation), is that the counselor must be a person of prayer. Recognizing and fostering vocation is not like giving guidance about the choice of a profession. If a director is not a man of prayer, even though in other respects he may be the best possible psychologist, he will do a great deal of harm in this field. Though he must use all the natural means of investigation in his power, in the last resort only he who prays will be capable of discovering and guiding those who pray. Thank God that even then when a mistake may

---

[40] An address of the Holy Father to the Very Reverend Father Donatus de Wello, Minister General of the Capuchins. Quoted in *Vocation*, Religious Life Series, II (Westminster, Md.: The Newman Press, 1952), pp. 63–64.

have been made, it will be *felix culpa*; for even though reason would say that such and such a person should never have belonged to such and such an order, still he will render that order immense good, and sanctify himself in it.[41]

Section 3.   The Active Life

In opening this treatment of the active and the contemplative lives, we mentioned that the two are distinguished from each other by reason of the *predominance* of one's activity, whether it be in the consideration of truth, or whether it be in the pursuit of exterior activity or, let us say, in the exercise of the moral virtues, in the love of one's neighbor. Not that the contemplative life does not demand the exercise of the moral virtues, but it does not demand their exercise in the same way, and, as it were, as a vocation, as the active life does. For a call to an active community demands the exercise of the moral virtues as a vocation, as the means to perfection. Thus we might say that the contemplative life allows a more frequent exercise of the theological virtues not merely as commanding virtues or those which are behind the scenes, but rather as eliciting virtues, those which play the title or leading role. In the active life, however, the theological virtues are indeed present, but as commanding virtues giving vitality and direction to the moral virtues, which play the principal role. To see this adequately certain points might be briefly discussed.

The Object of the Active Life

We have already said that the active life differs from the contemplative in occupation, inasmuch as each has a different immediate object. The occupation of the contemplative life is the consideration of truth, or in the case of Christian contemplation, the consideration of divine truth through the exercises of the interior life of prayer. The occupation of the active life is external work or action. As we know, however, it is the *moral* virtues that are directed to action or operation. From this it follows that the moral virtues pertain essentially to the active life, and that the happiness of the active life will depend upon the perfection in which one performs the actions of those moral virtues which are demanded by the occupation in which such a person is engaged. Not that there is any intention of saying that the active life consists *exclusively* or solely in the

---

[41] Cf. *Vocation*, Religious Life Series, Chap. 4: "The Recognition of a Contemplative Vocation," François de St. Marie, O.C.D., p. 48 ff. Cf. also *Way of Perfection*, Chaps. 13–14, Peers, II, p. 53 ff. Also, *Constitutions*, Peers, III, pp. 224–225.

exercise of the moral virtues, but rather that it consists principally in the exercise of these virtues. For this reason we know that exercises of the contemplative life, such as mental prayer, the examination of conscience, spiritual reading, and retreats are essential to all active communities.

However, even these moral virtues can, in a sense, pertain to the contemplative life, that is insofar as the person exercising them does so in order to dispose himself for the contemplative life or contemplation whenever this is given by God. For this reason, the works of the active life, insofar as they are ordered or intended by the person performing them to dispose himself for this life can be said to pertain to the contemplative life. The nurse in a hospital or the teacher in the classroom, can by properly using the moral virtues which he or she may be called upon to exercise in the course of the day, dispose himself or herself for a very profitable period of mental prayer. The fact that these works enable him or her to see the suffering of people at first hand, the difficulties and temptations of life, which are after all a share in the passion of Christ, can or does serve to make one penetrate deeply into the passion and death of Christ. Under this method of facing our active works they would become not so much distractions from the life of prayer, as acts disposing one for it, and at times the very occasion for truly contemplative prayer. From this viewpoint, then, even the exercise of the moral virtues and the active life can belong to the contemplative life. Something like this can also be seen, for example, in the case of the virtues. For wherever we find one virtue ordered to another virtue it somehow becomes that virtue. In the case of a religious, for example, the exercise of obedience becomes an act of the virtue of religion, or worship, an act of sacrifice and devotion, in the service of God. The same is true of the virtues pertaining to the other vows.

The basis for this conclusion lies in the distinction between the finis operis and the finis operantis. From the viewpoint of the act or work itself (ex parte operis) it pertains to the active life, but from the viewpoint of the one performing the work or the action (ex parte operantis) it is the work of the contemplative life, or rather one which in some way pertains to it or is included under it. Thus in the case of the saints engaged for the greater part of their lives in active works, St. Camillus de Lellis, St. Vincent de Paul, St. Pius X, the Curé of Ars, all the works which they performed, although in one sense works of the active life, became works of the contemplative life by reason of the intention and the constant effort of the individual to make them contribute to their understanding of the mysteries of God, particularly of the mystery of the Mystical Body of Christ. These works were not merely distractions in their lives, a good change, or a good diversion, but rather works by which they disposed both themselves and others for the contemplative life, which is more perfect than merely to dispose oneself for the contemplative life, as we shall see at greater length later on. The generous service of God in and through the works of the active life in the case of one who is called by God to lead that life, regardless of how material or secular they sometimes seem to be and are, as for example the administration of some material work of a community, can bring to the individual the peace and the cleanness of heart, which are so necessary for greater union with God. When these actions are performed out of a great love for God, they dispose for charity and the vision of God to be given either in this life (and to some extent at least) or in the life to come.[42]

Why is it, one may ask, that so few of those engaged in the active life seem to enjoy the favors of contemplation? The objection needs clarification. First of all it would have to be shown conclusively that this is true. Moreover, even though the statement were correct, the fact would be due not to their being engaged in the active life, but rather to their not having ordered their active life to creating within them a deeper desire for God and a deeper love for Him and for the mercy which He has shown us. Seeing misery in its various forms, spiritual and corporal, should lead us to a deeper understanding of sin, of our own nothingness, of a greater need for God, etc., all of which should be, as it were, profounder insights into the mysteries of our salvation. Perhaps it is because religious engaged in the active life have not ordered their activity in this way, in a deeply supernatural way, they have not deepened themselves in their union with God, nor disposed themselves to receive the graces of contemplation, not of that extraordinary kind which consists in or is accompanied by visions and revelations and what we have called above the charismata, but in that kind which consists in a deeper vision, a far more

---

[42] This basic division or distinction between the *finis operis* and the *finis operantis* ought to have been more clearly pointed out in the excellent article by Father Plé, "Apostolic Action as a School of Perfection," in *Apostolic Life*, Chap. 8, Blackfriars, London, 1958. It is true that there is a unity between contemplation and action, but this has to be more precisely determined, so that the *objective* dignity of the two lives can be clearly seen. The ideas mentioned here and later on in some of the practical suggestions will make it clear that Dom Chautard's observation concerning the danger involved in the apostolic activity is correct. It certainly is not his intention to say that apostolic activity is in no way a means of grace and union with God, or that it can only be sanctified by times of prayer. He is taking man as he is constituted, living under the present economy of a sin-laden world that hates the very thought of silence and stillness. While I do believe that there is such a thing as a spirituality of action, still this has to be explained in accordance with the distinction between the virtues of the active life and those of the contemplative life, both of which, *in their own proper way*, can lead us to the perfection of love.

penetrating vision of the aspects of the various mysteries connected with the life of grace. This is brought about by a naturalism, or practical naturalism, which seems to underlie so much of their activity. Or it might be brought about from a failure to guard themselves against the influences of secularism and materialism or, let us say, the worldly attitude which so easily can creep into a life in which often perhaps the tenor of recreations, conversations, and social meetings cannot be classed under those exercises of the moral virtues which dispose one for the graces of the interior life. The courage necessary to put everything into every action is found in a very few persons; that is why we have so few canonized saints. Heroicity of virtue is a rare thing even in religious communities.

The Role of Prudence in the Active Life

From what we have seen there flows another truth, that for the perfect living of the active life the virtue of prudence is most essential. For it is this virtue which directs one in the performance of action, since it is "right reason about things to be done." Thus the knowledge of prudence is directed to the works of the moral virtues and belongs directly to the active life. When a person is occupied constantly with external things, he sees less of intelligible things or those things which we would call the objects of the speculative intellect. Nevertheless the external occupations of the active life enable one to see more clearly in judging what is to be done — which function belongs to prudence — both on account of experience, and on account of the mind's attention to these things. For it is only when the mind is attentive to something that it takes on all its forcefulness in regard to this thing.

This role of prudence stems from its relationship to the moral virtues. For prudence is a virtue perfecting the practical intellect which governs our moral life. Its function is to direct the exercise of the moral virtues and to a certain extent even the intellectual virtues. It is the habitus of deciding correctly just what act or acts will attain the goal of moral virtue. Consequently, its work is not merely to know what ought to be done in a given case, but in actually prescribing and commanding that it be done here and now. Because it moves our powers to act morally, correctly, it supposes the righteousness of the appetite or the help of the moral virtues. It presupposes, then, that one's will is good and that it is actively tending toward good. This latter, however, is the work of the moral virtues of justice, fortitude, and temperance, and of the satellite virtues, so to speak, which pertain to these cardinal virtues. Consequently, there is a mutual relationship between prudence and the other moral virtues. The function of the former is to direct the actions of these virtues to their goal and the proper goal of the latter is to act in conformity with right reason. It is the function of the moral virtues to find and to appoint their own goal but it is the work of prudence to decide how they shall attain the goal, by means of what action or actions.

Teaching and the Active Life

Because the consideration or the study of truth pertains to the contemplative life a person might wonder just where the work of teaching would have to be placed. For it is true that teaching does demand study and the search after truth, at least after some truth which should lead us ultimately to the Supreme Truth from which all truth derives. St. Gregory, however, has mentioned that the active life is to give bread to the hungry and to teach the ignorant the words of wisdom.[43]

Teaching, however, may pertain to either life, the active or the contemplative. For teaching has two objects: the matter or the truth which is taught, and the communication of this truth. Regarding the matter taught, if this truth is one in which the person takes delight and is not at least principally ordained toward action, then teaching pertains to the contemplative life. Thus, for example, the study of philosophy is considered at times to belong to the contemplative life and likewise the study of theology, particularly the study of speculative theology. If, however, the truth considered directs one in action, such that one conceives a truth inwardly *so as to be directed in action*, then teaching pertains to the active life. If we consider the other object of teaching, however, the communication of truth through speech and writing, then all teaching pertains to the active life, for it is an external action. On this score we should note, however, that there is a kind of teaching that can be given to others and yet does not extend beyond the limits of the contemplative life. It is that which is ordained to the knowledge of truth alone. That teaching however, which is ordered to persuade others to living a good life (and this is called preaching rather than teaching), pertains to the active life. Yet St. Thomas very surreptitiously adds in this place that he who gives himself up to the labor of preaching, sees less (contemplates less) and yet yields more good, or brings more good into being "*minus videt et amplius parit.*"[44]

Consequently, teaching according as it is the exercise of knowledge and the perfection of the one teaching pertains to the contemplative life, but it pertains to the active life according as through it there is intended the good of another.

---

[43] Cf. *Hom. in Ezechielem,* II, *PL* 76, 953.
[44] Cf. *III Sent.,* dist. 35, Q. 1, a. 3, qcl, 1, ad 2m.

SECTION 4. THE COMPARISON OF THE ACTIVE LIFE WITH THE CONTEMPLATIVE LIFE

Perhaps a treatment of this question seems almost out of place insofar as the answer seems to have already been given, at least so far as the excellence of the one over the other goes. Both philosophically speaking and theologically speaking the contemplative life is more excellent than the active life, for in both cases the object of the former is more noble or more excellent than the object of the latter. Moreover, our Lord Himself has mentioned that Mary, who signifies the contemplative life, has chosen the better part whereas Martha, although perhaps not having chosen the worse part, has chosen one that is less excellent than that chosen by Mary.

Such a solution to the problem of comparing the two, however, is evidently just a little too easy. For the very work of Christ Himself, at least for a few years of His life, was one of action, that is, of preaching the word of God. Moreover, His first disciples were chosen for this same work, since the faith would be made known normally through the medium of preaching. The active life, then, would seem to be not only essential and a part of the over-all structure of our Christian religion, but it seems to have actually occupied in some way a place of excellence.

For this reason the following notions concerning the two lives will be of some help to our understanding the relation between the two, for at times those who belong to the one life do not understand the problems and the use and the role which the other has in the Church of God. Therefore a presentation of certain principles will help to see the importance of both of these lives within the Christian life itself.

Absolute Comparison

Absolutely speaking, the contemplative life is more excellent than the active life and this, according to St. Thomas, is true for eight reasons.

1. The contemplative life belongs to man according to that which is most excellent in him, i.e., the intellect. For it is an operation of the intellect with respect to divine truth. And a little knowledge of God is much more excellent than a far more extensive knowledge of His creatures.

2. The contemplative life can be *more continuous*, although of course not in its highest degree, i.e., as regards the highest degree of contemplation. For this reason Mary is pictured as sitting at our Lord's feet, at rest, therefore, as though this were her uninterrupted activity.

3. The contemplative life is *more delightful* than the active. This can be shown from Martha's having been troubled while Mary was, as it were,

as St. Augustine says, at a feast.[45] On this point we must be careful, however, for while this is true, nevertheless the trials of the contemplative life are much more difficult than those of the active. Thus St. Teresa remarks:

> I know about both types of lives and I am well aware that the trials of the contemplative life are intolerable; and they are of such a kind that were God not to feed them (Contemplatives) with consolations, they could not be borne. It is clear, then, that since God leads those whom He most loves by way of trials, the more He loves them, the greater will be their trials; and there is no reason to suppose that He hates Contemplatives, since with His own mouth He praises them and calls them friends. . . . I think when those who lead an active life occasionally see Contemplatives receiving consolations, they suppose that they never experience anything else. But I assure you that they might not be able to endure their sufferings for as long as a day.[46]

4. In the contemplative life a person is *more sufficient* since he needs fewer things for that purpose. It was for this reason that our Lord chided Martha with being solicitous about many things.

5. The contemplative life is *loved more for its own sake*, while the active life is directed to something else. Thus it is written in the Book of the Psalms: "One thing have I asked of the Lord, this will I seek after that I may dwell in the house of the Lord all the days of my life, that I might see the delight of the Lord."[47]

6. Another reason for the excellence of the contemplative over the active life lies in the former's consisting *in leisure and rest*. It is what the scholastics have called a *vacatio*, a "vacation," or ceasing from activity, with the quiet, etc., which this implies.

7. The contemplative life is *more like the Divine Life, since it is about divine things*, whereas the active life is about human things and cares. As Augustine writes, "In the beginning was the Word, and to Him Mary was listening: the Word was made flesh: Him Martha was serving."[48]

8. The last reason given is something similar to the first, that the contemplative life is according to that which is most proper to man, namely the intellect; in the works of the active life, however, the lower powers common both to us and to brutes have their part to play.

To these reasons, St. Thomas adds another,

> Mary has chosen the better part which shall not be taken away from her. Augustine explains these words thus: "Not that thou hast chosen badly,

---

[45] Cf. *Sermon to the People*, Sermon 103, 4, *PL* 38, 615.

[46] *Way of Perfection*, Vol. II, p. 72 ff. From *The Complete Works of Saint Teresa*, tr. and ed. by E. Allison Peers from the critical edition of P. Silverio de Santa Teresa, C.D. Pub. in three vols. by Sheed and Ward, Inc., New York.

[47] Ps. 26:4.   [48] *Sermon 104*, 2, *PL* 38, 617.

but she hath chosen better. Why better? Listen. Because it shall not be taken away from her. But the burden of necessity shall at length be taken from thee; but the sweetness of truth is eternal."[49] For this reason, the contemplative life is said to make one more free. For it consists in a certain liberty of mind, since it thinks not of temporal things but rather of those that are eternal. The contemplative life since it is free in comparison with the active life commands the active life, prescribing at times certain works of the active life as dispositions for the contemplative life.[50]

It is by reason of the excellence of the contemplative over the active life that the saints have always insisted that one can never give up the contemplative life except for a time, that is, when the burden of charity demands that one expend himself in the service of others. Thus St. Thomas writes

> Sometimes a person is called away from the contemplative life to the works of the active life on account of some necessity of the present life, yet not so as to be compelled to forsake contemplation altogether. Hence Augustine writes: "The love of truth seeks a holy leisure, the demands of charity undertake an honest toil (the work namely of the active life). If no one imposes this burden upon us (that is the work for the salvation of our neighbor, or more properly the immediate needs of our neighbor), we must devote ourselves to the search for and the contemplation of truth, but if it be imposed upon us we must bear it, for charity demands it of us. Yet even then we must not altogether forsake the delights of truth lest we deprive ourselves of its sweetness and this burden overwhelm us."[51] It is clear, then, that when a person is called from the contemplative to the active life, this is done by way not of subtraction but by way of addition.[52]

Cajetan in his commentary on this article notes regarding this last assertion by St. Thomas, that the mixed work, which is proper to prelates, namely, to contemplate and to act or engage in activity, is more perfect than either the simple contemplative work or the simple active work. Whence the Lord did not say of Mary that she had chosen the best, but rather the better part. The contemplative part of life, then, is better than the active part. But, as we know, the whole is better than any of its parts, and this is proper to the state of prelates.[53] For this reason prelates (bishops) should not only be concerned with the active life, but they should excel in the contemplative life, for as St. Gregory says "a prelate or a pastor should be foremost in action, more uplifted than others in contemplation."[54]

---

[49] *Sermon 103*, 4, PL 38, 615.
[50] II–II, Q. 182, a. 1.
[51] *City of God*, Bk. 19, c. 19, PL 41, 647.
[52] *Loc. et op. cit.*
[53] Commentary on this article, Leonine ed.
[54] *Pastoral Care*, Part II, Chap. I, PL 77, 26.

Relative Comparison

Relatively speaking, however, and in particular cases one should prefer the active life on account of the needs of the present life. The saints have made much of this particular truth, and today writers are making even more of it, pointing out that under certain conditions in certain epochs, in certain localities, the active life and the works of this life may be more important than those of contemplation or the contemplative life, and under such conditions, if one's vocation allows, he must give up the "sweetness of the life of prayer" for that of action. This is the teaching of the greater Fathers of the Church, such as St. Gregory, St. Augustine, and the medievalists St. Bernard and St. Thomas, and while we would expect this to be the teaching of those who had to give themselves over to action in accordance with the demands of their vocation as SS. Augustine, Gregory the Great, and Thomas did, still we might not expect to find this the teaching of someone like St. Bernard, the abbot of a Cistercian monastery.

The Relative Merit of the Two Lives

Concerning the merit of the two lives, we must make a distinction similar to that made in regard to their relative excellence. The root of merit is charity, so that the greater act of charity merits the greater reward. Charity, however, consists not only in the love of God, but also in the love of neighbors. Of these two acts of the one charity, the love of God is of itself the more meritorious of the two. This stems from the fact that it is more important to love that which is goodness by essence rather than that which is goodness by participation. For we love our neighbor only insofar as he is capable of possessing God, of sharing in the goodness and the intimate life of God Himself. Whatever pertains more directly to the love of God is of its very nature more meritorious than that which pertains directly to the love of our neighbor, even though this latter be for the sake of God. The contemplative life, as we have seen, however, pertains directly and immediately to the love of God, whereas the active life is more directly concerned with the love of neighbor, because it is busy about much service as St. Luke mentions.[55] St. Gregory the Great and the other writers on these two lives have been unanimous in asserting this truth. Thus, St. Gregory writes, "The contemplative life surpasses in merit the active life, because the latter labors under the stress of present work [by reason of the necessity of assisting our neighbor] while the

---

[55] Cf. Lk. 10:40.

former with heartfelt relish has a foretaste of the coming rest [that is, the contemplation of God]."[56]

While *simply speaking* then, or as it were, abstracting from certain extenuating circumstances, or objectively considering the question, and all other things being equal, the contemplative life surpasses in merit the active life, still it may happen that a person engaged in the works of the active life merits more by these works than another does through the works of the contemplative life. Thus, through the excess of divine love a person may now and then suffer separation from the sweetness of divine contemplation for the time being, that God's will may be done and for the sake of His glory. Even St. Paul mentioned that for the sake of His brethren he would willingly be separated from the sight and the presence of Christ as seen in vision.[57] St. John Chrysostom, commenting on this statement, writes: "His mind was so steeped in the love of Christ, that although he desired above all to be with Christ, he despised even this because thus he pleased Christ."[58]

The greater sign of charity which is at the basis of all merit is shown when a person renounces whatever pertains to this life and delights to occupy himself entirely with divine contemplation, in accordance with the divine will. For this reason, then, we have to be most careful in interpreting the ideas being expressed today regarding the spirituality of action. For, in a sense, there is such a thing but it is reducible to the spirituality of the active and the contemplative lives, or of the active life as opposed to that of the contemplative life. As such it has already been time and again gone through and investigated by the great Fathers and theologians of the Church. St. Thomas very calmly wrote in answer to a similar objection raised in his own day, particularly with respect to the orders which were mendicant and allowed their subjects an active life in conjunction with the contemplative life:

A sacrifice is rendered to God spiritually when something is offered to Him: and of all men's goods, God especially accepts that of the human soul when it is offered to Him in sacrifice. Now a man ought to offer to God in the first place, his own soul, according to the teaching of the author of the Book of Ecclesiasticus,[59] "have pity on thy soul pleasing God"; in the second place, the souls of others according to the words of the Apocalypse,[60] "He that hears, let him say come." And the more closely a person unites his soul or another's to God, the more acceptable is his sacrifice to God: therefore it is more acceptable to God that one apply one's own soul and the souls of others to contemplation than to action. Consequently the

[56] *Hom. III in Ezech.*, PL 76, 80.
[57] Cf. Rom. 9:3.
[58] *De Compunctione*, I, PG 47, 405.
[59] Ecclus. 30:24.
[60] Apoc. 22:17.

statement that "no sacrifice is more acceptable to God than Zeal for souls" does not mean that the merit of the active life is preferable to the merit of the contemplative life but that it is more meritorious to offer to God one's own soul and the souls of others, than any other external gifts.[61]

SUMMARY AND COROLLARIES

We have been told that there are two poles or two elements of the spiritual life. The first is that of *self-discipline*, or the proper ordering of our passions which occurs through the exercise and the development or evolution of the moral virtues. This is essential, fundamental, and something that can never be dispensed with, not even when the soul may have reached a very high degree of union with God. However, we must not forget either, that this pole is a disposition for something more important, a material cause for the formal cause, the preparation of some matter to receive a form of some spirit. Thus this ordering of the passions or self-discipline, if you will, was meant to lead to something more important, and that is the second pole of the spiritual life — *that man should be with God.*

The Latin text so often quoted by these writers in speaking of the differences between these two lives uses the expression *optimum partem*, "the best part." In the Greek text, however, it is interesting to note that the word used is *agathen* — the "good part" — "Mary has chosen the good part." The sense of the word as it occurs in other similar passages is that Mary has chosen the *necessary* part, and that necessary part is remaining with God, at His feet drinking in His words which He addresses to the interior of the soul. The part of Mary, then, is necessary for all seeking to live the Christian life. It is not limited merely to an elite or select group. While it might be the shorter part of their lives, and for the majority of men it is, still it is always the one thing really necessary for the vitalizing of the spiritual life.

The very life of the Church depends upon its contemplatives and above all upon the degree of contemplative activity and spirit which pervades the Church. We might say, I believe in all truthfulness, that the diffusion of contemplative prayer throughout the entire Mystical Body will determine the growth of the Church, and it will act as a counteraction to the religious externalism and formalism which is growing so rapidly and which is in the long run the very death of the spiritual life. This contemplative prayer is not the exclusive privilege of those who have been called to the canonical contemplative communities or orders in the

---

[61] II-II, Q. 182, a. 2. ad 3m.

Church. It belongs by right to the whole Body of the Church, to both spires, we might say, rising over the edifice which we call the Church, and which reach upward in their search for God. In the present period of our existence, when we find in the Church much feverish activity, the neglect of contemplative prayer as an element of the normal life of the members of the Mystical Body is most dangerous to the growth and the diffusion of the life of grace.

> There is the danger [writes one author], a danger which is even more than a danger, for it is to some extent a reality, that multiple religious activities, not to speak of a life which is purely secular in its outlook and attitude, will make us forget the one thing which is necessary, the good part which Mary was given by Christ: that man has been created for a union with God that is so close that it has been described by St. Paul in terms of man and God being one spirit.[62]

Periods of violence have always been periods of deep spirituality. When the world is calm, souls, which ought to be God's alone, venture out into the world more calmly and freely. They take the calmness of the world for innocence and think that because it is peaceful, it has ceased to be worldly; and the odor of worldliness taints even the breath of the good man. When the world's face shows its passions, then piety shrinks back and becomes more concentrated on God. It grows less inclined to try to make the best of two worlds, and in withdrawing it grows deeper and wider.

The modern world presents such a picture and as such has reduced the possibility of a spiritual life and of an intellectual life, as Father Sertillanges, O.P., has mentioned in his work on this subject.[63] God, therefore, takes His own reaction as a result of this fact. Perhaps it is for this reason that so many of our vocations are turning to the contemplative life. Because this one thing necessary, which they somehow or other almost, as it were, by intuition feel the need of today in our world, is not being supplied by so many of our active communities many of these vocations are turning to the contemplative life. They are doing this not so much because they wish to dedicate themselves completely to such a life, at least when they enter, but because it is the only way in which they feel that they can get enough of this one thing necessary. So often we hear the thought expressed: "Well I want to do some work for the salvation of souls, or I would like to undertake something of the active apostolate, but I also want something of the contemplative life. If I

---

[62] Cf. *The Third Spiritual Alphabet*, Francisco de Osuna, Introduction by Fr. Cuthbert (Westminster, Md.: Newman, 1948), p. xxiv.

[63] Cf. *La Vie Intellectuelle*, Rev. des jeunes, Paris, 1934, p. 105.

cannot get this in an active community, then I am willing and would rather go the whole way." Such expressions are becoming more and more common today. Because perhaps we are not guaranteeing prospective subjects the opportunity to lead something of an interior life, together with at least the minimum conditions necessary for it, those expressly mentioned in the Rules or Constitutions, they are turning to the other extreme as a solution, a solution which is not always perfectly in keeping with their inmost desires. Both St. Gregory and St. Bernard as well as St. Thomas mention that the majority of persons are not constituted to lead a life that is completely contemplative. This they attribute both to their desire to communicate and to enter into the active ministry of the Incarnate Redeemer who Himself gave up the leisure of the life without flesh, and to the difficulty involved in the effort of continuous contemplation.[64]

---

[64] Thus, St. Gregory notes: "Everyone who is converted to the Lord desires the contemplative life, and longs for the rest of the everlasting country; but first it is necessary that in the night of the present life he work what good he can and exert himself in labor . . . for the contemplative life is lovely in the mind, but while it longs to rest in silence it does not generate sons by preaching; it sees but it does not bring forth, because while it loves the pursuit of its quiet, it is less inflamed in the gathering of others, and what it sees within it is unable to open out to others by preaching. But we must know that just as it is the right order to pass from the active to the contemplative, so usually, it is useful for the mind to turn back from the contemplative to the active, that by the very fact that the contemplative has inflamed the mind, the active may be more perfectly held. Therefore, the active life ought to pass us on to the contemplative and yet sometimes the contemplative, by that which we have inwardly seen with the mind, ought to turn us back to the active. Whoever reaps benefit by seeing spiritual things is bound by speaking to lay them before others. For he sees in order that he may announce who by the fact that he reaps benefit for himself, by preaching has a care also for the advance of his neighbor." — Hom. II in Ezech., PL 76, 954 ff.

There are many other very beautiful passages where the same thought occurs. It would be well for us to note them here. "Whosoever opens his mind in holy works has over and above to extend it to the secret pursuits of inward contemplation. For he is no perfect preacher who either from devotion to contemplation neglects works that ought to be done, or from urgency in business puts aside the duties of contemplation. It is hence that the Redeemer of mankind in the daytime exhibits His miracles in cities and spends the night in devotion to prayer upon the mountain, for the purpose that he may teach all perfect preachers that they should neither entirely leave the active life for the love of the speculative, nor wholly slight the joys of contemplation from excess in working; but in their quiet imbibe by contemplation what in enjoyment they may pour back to their neighbors by word of mouth. For by contemplation they rise to the love of God and by preaching they return back to the service of their neighbor. In the sight of our eternal judge our charity should be colored with the love of both God and our neighbor, that the converted soul may neither so delight in repose for the sake of the love of God as to put aside the care and service of his neighbor, nor busying itself for the love of our neighbor, extinguish the fire of his love for the Most High." — Hom. VI in Ezech., PL 76, 860.

"Pastors must always fear and take watchful heed lest while they are concerned with

St. Bernard seconds the thought of St. Gregory given here when he also writes that the active life is good, but the contemplative life is better, since the one will end with time while the latter, like charity itself, will continue for all eternity. Yet the highest life is the mixed, which he compares to Jacob's ladder whereon we ascend to God by contemplation and descend to men through the exercises of the active life. "For the monk indeed does well in keeping a watchful guard over himself. But he who labors for the good of the people performs a more excellent and more manly work, and if this cannot be done without some degree of 'iniquity' that is without some slight departure from strict regularity of life and conversation, we must bear in mind that charity covers a multitude of sins."[65] Thus St. Bernard and St. Gregory long before him felt that contemplation was ordained to the active life in some way, to the production of good, so that ensuing zeal for souls is not merely a process of needful repose and recuperation of the spiritual forces of the soul after long or short periods of contemplation, but it is positively the direct effect of the highest kind.

---

external cares they sink from their inward purpose. For generally speaking while the minds of rulers incautiously serve the ends of temporal solicitude, they grow cold in inward love; and being spent on things abroad they are not afraid to forget that they have undertaken the government of souls. The solicitude, therefore, which is bestowed upon their subjects exteriorly must needs be kept within certain bounds." — *Regula Pastoralis*, Part II, c. 7, PL 77, 41.

"We ought to bear in mind that when those are wanting who might fitly minister to the exterior needs of their neighbors those too who are full of spiritual gifts ought to condescend to their weakness and as far as they may with propriety be able to lend themselves with the condescension of charity to the earthly necessities of others. Nor should it weary the mind if its perception being over intent on the contemplation of spiritual things is sometimes as it were bent down diminished in managing the least concerns." — *Moralia*, Bk. 19, c. 25, PL 76, 126.

"Holy men who are obliged by the necessity of their employments to engage in outward ministrations are ever studiously betaking themselves to the secrets of their hearts; and there do they ascend to the height of most inward thought, while they put aside the tumults of temporal activities and at the summit of their contemplation search out the sentence of the divine Will. Hence it is that Moses frequently retires to the Tabernacle on doubtful points and there secretly consults God and learns what certain decisions to come to. For to leave the crowd and retire to the Tabernacle is to put aside the tumults of outward objects and enter into the secret recess of the mind. For the Lord is there consulted and we hear inwardly and in silence what we must do openly and without. This course good rulers daily do. And when they are aware they cannot settle doubtful points, they betake themselves to the secret recesses of their mind and what they first hear in silence, they afterwards make known to the world in their conduct. For in order that they may engage in outward employments without injury to themselves they constantly take care to withdraw to the secrets of their hearts. And they hear the voice of God while they withdraw themselves in the thoughts of their minds, from the influence of carnal things." — *Moralia*, Bk. 23, c. 20, PL 76, 273–274.

[65] *In Canticum*, Sermon 12, PL 183, 832.

In short, as Father Marie-Eugene mentions in his work on Carmelite spirituality: "The apostolate is not a work of supererogation. It is the normal sequel to contemplation and to contemplative love. To think only of intimate union with God is to be ignorant of the very nature of charity."[66]

In the Church, then, or in religion there are four elements: first, there is the external element of the Church, her sacraments and public worship; second, there is the intellectual element of doctrine and dogma and theology; third, there is the mystical element of will and emotion and personal religious experience; and, last, there is the element of service of others. A fully developed properly balanced religious life must be the result of an harmonious blending of these four elements, not one of which may be neglected except at the cost of a one-sided, distorted, enfeebled type of religion. In regard to the mystical element it is not something that is to be cultivated apart from the everyday duties of life. This comes about even in the most active of lives by the proper self-discipline which makes one overcome the difficulties which he will meet with in any life. A saint does not take from his environment half as much as he gives to it. In any case each life, the active or the contemplative, or one in which the two are supposed to be mixed, is a gift of grace. Yet we ought to realize that once we are called by God, and let us say that we are to live among our neighbors, one is by necessity, the other is by choice.

*   *   *   *

From these considerations of the two lives we might make the following practical observations:

1. In the direction or counseling of any vocation no attempt whatsoever should be made to belittle the contemplative vocation on the part of the active religious, neither should any such attempt to belittle the active vocation be made on the part of the contemplative religious. In fact it would be very helpful in any general course or interview on vocation where no choice has been made, and even in the formation of those, let us say, who have entered the institute of some religious community, to present one's own vocation in the perspective of the whole Church, to indicate the value and the use of other vocations as well as one's own, so that the one being informed will have a fairly good working idea of the place and value of each in the Church which is building itself up in love.

2. In our active communities, great care should be taken that the exercises of the interior life hold first place in the community. Thus the Popes have constantly come back to this idea, e.g., in their addresses to

---

[66] *I Want to See God* (Chicago: Fides, 1953), p. 336.

religious institutes and in their encyclicals and exhortations. Under no pretext of the good of souls should the exercises guaranteed by the Constitutions be omitted for any great length of time, for in omitting them the community would be doing its subjects an injustice and failing to accomplish its purpose for being in the Church. For the community itself must have, above all others, a deep faith in the providence of God, that as long as it is fulfilling its mission (and part of that mission is to pray, to lead the contemplative life, or to contribute to the apostolate of the Church through the exercises that pertain to the interior life) it is advancing the cause of the Church. The love of efficiency and of large-scale mass-production movements has come into the religious life from our secular life and can almost imperceptibly govern the policy of a community. When the subjects of an active community know and are convinced that they are being looked after more than the active works of the community, then there will always be a greater generosity and one more fervent and useful to the Church. A mother who gives birth to a child and then abandons it or fails to care for it, is not held in very high esteem in our society. The same is true of a religious community which would take a subject in and give it its initial formation and then fail to form the person until it arrives at a maturity sufficient for it to stand on its own feet. In the religious life, and especially in the modern world, because of the presence of the law of sin in our members and the ever increasing dangers, a formative vigilance should be kept on young subjects. Habits are not formed overnight; and because the habits that are opposed to the religious life and to a life of prayer and mortification are so prevalent today, it will demand perhaps a longer training and more gradual easing up of the exterior restrictions than ever before. One of the essential elements of the religious life, one which no adaptation can ever change, is that it is to a greater or less extent an *exire de saeculo*, a "going-out of the world." It is to a certain extent the admission on the part of the person that there are dangers in the world, dangers to one's salvation and to one's perfection. To deny the guarantees which a person seeks in asking for admission to a religious community would be not only an act of injustice against the individual and against the Church; it would, in a sense, be to shame the religious life and its very significance, and to blaspheme the mystery of Calvary.

3. The active religious life should be set forward as a challenge to arrive at the perfection of charity not through the exercises of the virtues proper to the contemplative life, at least for the major part of one's daily life, but rather through the exercise of the virtues proper to the active life, the moral virtues and those particularly which the religious may be called

upon to exercise in a given apostolate. Thus even in the same community these virtues will vary with the different apostolates. Some will have to realize it especially, though not exclusively, through the exercise of one virtue; others through the exercise of another. Religious in the years of their formation should be advised of this movement toward God, the movement *proper to their vocation*. For their charity will grow not in proportion as they hanker after the exercise of virtues which are not proper to their vocation but only through their own "way to God." If the moral virtue is the same, nevertheless in different apostolates within a community it may have to be exercised in a slightly different way or with a different psychological orientation. Thus, the exercise of patience will not be the same for a teacher as it is for one who is engaged in the care of the sick, or the preparing of meals in a convent kitchen. When first going into their work the religious or young priests should be advised to consult their spiritual director and/or an experienced religious or priest, so that weeks and, often enough, years, of the religious life are not lost, because of a lack of proper orientation.

To insist upon this approach is to start one off properly, with a true theological understanding of the growth of charity. For the virtues grow proportionately as the fingers on the hand. As one supernatural virtue grows — whether it be humility, patience, obedience, chastity, or any other — so at the very same time do the others grow proportionately to the extent that the intrinsic facility to elicit their acts is ready to hand. Does not St. Paul say: "I may speak with every tongue that men and angels use; yet if I lack charity, I am no better than echoing bronze or the clash of cymbals. . . . Charity is patient, is kind; charity feels no envy; charity is never perverse or proud, never insolent; has no selfish aims, cannot be provoked, does not brood over an injury; takes no pleasure in wrongdoing but rejoices at the victory of truth; sustains, believes, hopes, endures to the last."[67]

4. The young religious should be advised that it is through an active life perfectly carried out that one passes to the freedom of the contemplative life. Such a person is able to pass from the active to the contemplative

---

[67] 1 Cor. 13:1 ff. St. Paul speaks here of the fact that charitable love of which we speak draws to itself all the other virtues making them as it were one of its own family. Hence though it is patience and fortitude that suffer all things, the text says that it is love which does so. We shall find in Holy Scripture that love appropriates the name of other virtues which shows that Christ has endowed them with wonderful dignity grafting them upon itself and so making them theological. Therefore, we call the just man's alms *charity* and say that chastity is pure *love*, meekness is benignant *love*, zeal is fervent *love*, because it is the office of charitable love to order all the virtues to their final end, that they may become theological through a kind of participation they receive in charity. *The Third Spiritual Alphabet*, 16th treatise, Chap. 2, p. 315.

life and yet not give up the former; so that he who has arrived at contemplation does not abandon the activity of good works whereby he is able to be of use to others. God often sends one who has passed from the active life to the contemplative back to the active and will keep him in alternation of the two. In such a soul who undertakes to live the vocation from day to day, everything, Father DeCaussade remarks, preaches efficaciously. God gives to their silence their self-forgetfulness, their repose, their detachment, their actions or activity a certain virtue which works in hearts without their even being conscious of it. Thus they often do not feel this virtue going out from them and even themselves do not consciously contribute to the fact.[68]

In a sense we might ask the question: What is the point of classifying the friends of God as active and contemplative? For the active are truly supernaturally active only in the measure of their prayer. A person may wear the habit of a Martha but he may be a Mary. For prayer is chiefly the taking of a direction; a man fixes his thoughts, words, mind, and heart, even his acts and gestures, and the most meaningless of them are given value by the Light to whom they are directed. We must admit, however, that this condition is always a privilege. It does not come for the wishing. It is bought and at a great price — perfect fidelity to the virtues of one's vocation. Man gives the little he can and God gives the rest.

The active life should not be placed before the youth of today or at any time merely as one which is given over to external actions or works, but rather, as quieting or putting in order the internal passions of the soul; in this light it is a help to the contemplative life or the interior life of the individual. St. Gregory says concerning this that "Those who wish to hold the fortress of contemplation should first of all train in the camp of action. After careful study they will learn whether they no longer wrong their neighbor; whether they bear with equanimity the wrongs their neighbors do them; whether their soul is neither overcome with joy in the presence of temporal goods, nor cast down with too great a sorrow when those goods are withdrawn (in this way they will learn to withdraw within themselves and when there, to explore spiritual things); whether or not they carry with them the shadows of corporal things, or if these follow them whether they can prudently drive them away."[69] It is during these periods of prayer and reflection, that one will learn how to direct oneself in action.

5. Even within our active communities it would be most wise to adapt,

---

[68] Cf. DeCaussade, S.J., *Abandonment to Divine Providence* (St. Louis: B. Herder, 1921), p. 61.

[69] *Morals*, 6/37, PL 75, 763.

when this is prudent and possible, the temperament of the individual to an obedience or to a certain work within the community. God intends the talents and aptitudes He sends to communities to be used not annihilated, even though He may permit this for some greater good.[70]

On this score, however, great prudence must be exercised, for the foundations of obedience could be weakened if everyone was given exactly what he felt was best for him. On the other hand, however, if a religious manifests throughout many years of the religious life a definite aptitude for a quieter work within the community, and has expressed some desire for it, it certainly might prove most profitable to the whole community if he or she were assigned to this work.

6. There is a certain type of merit, called satisfactory, which is more plentiful and abundant in the active life than in the contemplative insofar as the active life is more laborious, and labor has the effect of satisfaction.[71] This is what is called an *accidental* reward, which gives a kind of added joy or delight in the Beatific Vision. With regard to that merit which is called *essential*, or let us say, that merit which makes us see God with either more or less clarity in the Beatific Vision, the contemplative life is more meritorious. For in it one does not so readily pick up the "dust of the earth" as in the active life, that is, the attachment to creatures, and the commission of perhaps countless small faults, in dealing with other human beings.

7. It is the teaching of St. Gregory, St. Bernard, and St. Thomas that it should be from a greater charity that one omits or gives up the consolation of the interior life or the delight which it brings, to seek the glory of God in the conversion of others. The demands made by our neighbor on our time, our health, our patience, and other things can become and should become the purifying activity of God upon the soul, as He reduces it more and more to becoming identified with His own will. And we know that purifications which come from God, by no choice of ours, are more suited to bring us to the perfection of charity than those which we

---

[70] Thus St. Thomas remarks concerning the temperaments of individuals: "He that is prone to yield to his passions on account of his impulse to action is likewise more apt for the active life by reason of his restless spirit . . . there are some so restless that when they are free from labor, they labor all the more because the more leisure they have for thought, the worse interior turmoil they have to bear. Others, on the contrary, have a mind that is naturally pure and restful so that they are apt for contemplation and if they were to apply themselves wholly to action, this would be detrimental to them. . . . Consequently those who are more apt for the active life can prepare themselves for the contemplative by the practice of the active life; while those who are more apt for the contemplative life can take upon themselves the works of the active life so as to become yet more apt for contemplation." II–II, Q. 182, a. 4, ad 3m.

[71] *III Sent.*, dist. 35, Q. 1. a. 4, qcl. 2.

choose for ourselves. In the active life, perhaps, we encounter more of these passive purifications than in the contemplative, where the life is determined and set according to pattern. However, here we must be cautious. For these purifications center more around the moral virtues than the theological, which again implies an objective inferiority of the active life in comparison to the contemplative. The detachment from self which the active life demands can and should dispose us for an intimacy with God, and for an experience of this intimacy with God, of His presence in the soul; and contemplation consists in this.[72]

8. Finally, it must be emphasized that no one will ever be absolutely certain that he is living the perfectly balanced life.

Thus St. Bernard remarks:

> Even the holy man feels grave uncertainty between the claims of fruitful labor and those of restful contemplation; and yet although he is always occupied about good things, he always feels a sense of regret as if he had been doing that which is wrong, and from one moment to another entreats with groans to be shown the will of God. In these uncertainties the one and only remedy is prayer and frequent upliftings of the soul to God that He

[72] *Interior Castle*, Mansion VI, Chap. 8, Peers, II, p. 310. There she speaks of this as being accompanied by an extraordinary favor or charism, which we have called above an intellectual vision; but the substance of contemplation is the experience of God's activity, often His very presence in the soul. This same saint has remarked in one place: "The surest sign that we are keeping these two commandments (the love of God and the love of neighbor) is, I think, that we should really be loving our neighbor; for we cannot be sure if we are loving God, although we may have good reasons for believing that we are, but we can be quite sure that we are loving our neighbor. And be certain that the farther advanced you are in this, the greater love you will have for God; for so dearly does His majesty love us that He will reward our love for our neighbor by increasing the love which we bear to Himself, and that in a thousand ways; this I cannot doubt. When I see people very diligently trying to discover what kind of prayer they are experiencing and so completely wrapped up in their prayers that they seem afraid to stir, or to indulge in a moment's thought, lest they lose the slightest degree of tenderness and devotion which they have been feeling, I realize how little they understand of the road to the attainment of union (with God). They think that the whole thing consists in this. But no — what the Lord desires is works. If you see a sick person to whom you can give some help, never be affected by the fear that your devotion will suffer, but take pity on him; if he is in pain, you should feel pain too. But believe me, if you are lacking in this virtue (the love for neighbor) you have not attained to union with God. So, ask our Lord to give you this perfect love for your neighbor, and allow His Majesty to work, and if you use your best endeavors and strive after this in every way that you can, he will give you even more than you desire. You must do violence to your own will that your neighbor's will is done in everything, even though this may cause you to forego your own rights, and forget your own good in your concern for others." *Interior Castle*, Mansion V, Vol. II, pp. 261–263, *passim. Op. cit.*

Perhaps it was this same thought that made St. Philip Neri once exclaim that were he at the very gates of heaven and discovered that some sinner on earth had need of his ministry, he would turn his back on the heavenly court, and come down to minister to the needs of his brother.

would deign to make continually known to us what we ought to do and when, and how, and in what manner we should do it.[73]

Rather than determine just exactly where we are or whether we are in the right place, let us remember and insist that the apostolic vocation should be born directly of charity which human misery sets in motion. Perhaps it was this thought that led St. Thomas to attempt to sum up the whole of tradition's teaching concerning the two lives or the two aspects of charity in a rather clear passage of the Quodlibetals:

> It pertains to the perfection of a virtuous friendship that one for the sake of a friend should abstain sometimes from the delight which he takes in his presence, in order to occupy himself in his service. In accordance with this principle one is said to love another more who is willing to absent himself from him for him rather than refuse to give up his presence in order to serve him.
>
> Accordingly we can distinguish three grades of charity. . . . There are some who freely or without any great difficulty separate themselves from the occupation of divine contemplation in order to implicate themselves in secular affairs. In such we find little or no charity. There are others, however, who take such delight in the contemplation of divine things that they are unwilling to abandon this work even in order to be employed in God's service for procuring the salvation of their neighbor. And there are still others who ascend to such a height of charity that they forego the contemplation of divine things even though they take their special delight in it, that they might serve God in procuring the salvation of their neighbor. This perfection can be seen in the person of St. Paul. . . .
>
> Moreover, it is also proper to prelates and preachers and certain others, who work for the salvation of others. Whence these are signified through the angels on Jacob's ladder ascending through contemplation and descending through their solicitude for the salvation of their neighbor.[74]

Only under this motivation can we begin to understand the very mysterious words of the Book of Proverbs: "My delight was to be with the sons of men."[75]

---

[73] In Canticum, Sermon 57, PL 183, 1054. Even St. Thomas felt this conflict and resolved it by saying on the eve of assuming his duties as a teacher: "Salve me, Domine quoniam diminutae sunt veritates inter filios hominum." — "Save me, O Lord, for I must descend among the sons of men where truth is to be found only in small bits."

[74] Quaestio unica De Caritate, a. 11, ad 6.

[75] Prov. 8:31. St. Thomas remarks concerning the persons of St. Peter and St. John the one signifying the active life and the other the contemplative life: "These two types of men designate two categories of persons, those who give themselves up to contemplation and those who give themselves up to the obedience of the commandments. It happens generally that the contemplative is the first to arrive at the knowledge of the mysteries of Christ because of this docility, but does not enter into them because sometimes while the intellect always precedes, the affections do not always follow. The active person, however, by the insistence of his fervor and by his sedulousness, even though he may understand these mysteries more tardily, still enters into them more

In a very beautiful passage concerning the mystical or hidden evolution of the entire Church, Fr. John Arintero writes:

> Granted the perfect organic solidarity of the mystical body of the Church we shall see that in it as in the human body there is no reason why the members should envy one another but there is much reason why they should mutually aid and assist one another. Some have a noble position, others a hidden and humble one. But none can say to his companion, that he has no need of him. The eye needs the hands and the head the feet. Those who work always in silence and whose fruits are scarcely noticed are the most vital and active and are always influencing the community and the common good. For all the great mysteries of life are realized in silence and obscurity. For it is there that Christ speaks to the soul. The more a person devotes himself to his function, letting himself be molded by the impress of the Holy Ghost, the better they serve one another and the less they impede one another. The more they depend upon one another, the more solidarity they enjoy. It does not matter that one does the work and the other receives all the glory, for if all wish to be eyes, there will be no hearing or taste, nor life, nor fruits of life.[76]

Regarding the relative meritoriousness of the two lives, everything considered, perhaps the best answer has been given by the saints: it belongs

---

quickly." *Comm. on John*, Chap. 20, lect. 1, n. 2487, Marietti ed., 1952, p. 462. For this reason he says some have said that Peter loved Christ with promptitude and fervor; John, however, was more loved with regard to the marks of familiarity which Christ showed him, because of his youth and his purity. *Op. cit.*, Chap. 21, lect. 5, n. 2641, p. 488.

Much more simply has St. Teresa of Avila given her commentary on the two lives in a passage from her *Way of Perfection:* "Saint Martha was holy, but we are not told that she was a contemplative. What more do you want than to be able to grow to be like that blessed woman who was worthy to receive Christ our Lord so often in her house, and to prepare meals for Him. If she had been absorbed in prayer and devotion all the time as the Magdalen was, there would have been no one to prepare a meal for this divine guest. Religious who are called to the active life must not murmur at others who are very much absorbed in contemplation. Remember that there must be someone to look after the meals and count yourself happy in being able to serve like Martha. Reflect that true humility consists to a great extent in being ready for what the Lord desires to do with you. If contemplation and mental prayer, and vocal prayer, and tending the sick, and serving in the house and working at even the lowliest tasks are of service to the guest who comes to stay with us, what should it matter if we do one of these things rather than another. I do not mean that it is for us to say what we shall do, but that we must do our best in everything, for the choice is not ours, but the Lord's. Let the Lord of the house choose our office. For He is wise and powerful and knows what is fitting for you and for Himself as well. Be sure that if you do what lies in your power, and prepare yourself for high contemplation with the perfection mentioned aforehand, then if He does not grant it to you (and I think that He will not fail to do so, if you have true detachment and humility) it will be because He has laid this joy up for you so as to give it to you in heaven." *Way of Perfection*, Chap. 17, Peers, II, p. 71.

[76] *The Mystical Evolution in the Development and the Vitality of the Church*, I (St. Louis: B. Herder, 1951), pp. 475–476.

to God to weigh our merits, for according to the Book of Proverbs, the Lord alone is the One who weighs our spirits.[77] One thing we can be certain of is that the more a person wishes to understand the secrets of the divine wisdom, the greater must he try to approach our Lord. For the secrets of the divine wisdom are revealed especially to those who are united to God through love.[78]

---

[77] Cf. (Prov. 16:2).

[78] *Commentary on John*, Chap. 13, lect. 4, n. 1807, Marietti ed., 1952, p. 338.

CHAPTER FOUR

States of Perfection

AT THE beginning of our treatment we mentioned that the states of life could be divided up by a *per se* division, into the states of perfection and the "secular" states. In the present rather long chapter we will take up the first of these divisions. First we will treat the notion of "state of perfection" in general and then the various states of perfection in particular: the secular institutes, religious communities of public vows, (also very briefly, societies of the common life), and the episcopate.

SECTION 1. THE NOTION OF "STATE OF PERFECTION"

The Notion of "State" in Theology

In modern and current speech, many words are used interchangeably as practically synonymous for the same thing or notion. Yet when we examine them closely we find that they very often imply more than just a shade of difference in their precise and strict sense. We find this true to a degree with respect to our present investigation. For the words *office*, *function* and *state* are often used for one another. The word "office" usually, although not exclusively, applies to the work to be performed by a person as a result of his trade, profession, or position. The word "function," though often used for the word "office," has a much wider application. It can be used in reference to all living things, their organs and members, as well as to all created or manufactured things. Thus we have the office of judge, or teacher, or doctor, and we have the function of eating and drinking, nutrition, digestion, and so on. A "state," however, seems to denote something far more permanent, such as a *stable manner of living* or an *organized and definite type of existence*.

Thus the notion of state, properly speaking, denotes a kind of position according to which a thing is disposed with a certain immobility in a manner which is according to its nature. Whatever is easily changeable, or whatever is merely extrinsic to a person does not constitute a state of that person, such as, for example, that one is poor (this does not refer to one who has willed or has taken some kind of promise to be poor, but merely to one who finds himself in this situation), or that he be rich, or constituted in some dignity. A "state," rather, seems to imply an obligation which binds a person insofar as he is his own master or is subject to another. This subjection or freedom from subjection is something which arises from a cause that is firmly established, and that can be removed only with difficulty. We might say that the notion of "state" implies two things: stability, or constancy, and some obligation or freedom from obligation. We ought to note, however, that the permanency implied in the notion of state or constancy or stability, is one that is difficult to change, not impossible.[1]

Usually a state is assumed with some solemnity.[2] For example, when a boy came of age in the Roman Republic, he received the toga virilis as a sign of his entering manhood. Therefore, we might define the notion of state in the following way: "A stable and permanent manner of living arising from definite obligations (or freedom from obligations) officially assumed in a solemn act or rite."

The presence of different states in the society which interests us, the Church, arises from the inability of any one individual to fulfill all the various needs which she has. Something similar is true of the human body; it is impossible for any one member to perform the works necessitated by the complex structure of the entire body. Various cells and members are necessary for the perfect functioning of the whole. These different states and duties and grades in the Mystical Body follow from three aspects or approaches to the Church.

The difference of states follows from the perfection of the Church. For just as in natural things, perfection which in God is simple and uniform, is not found in the created universe except in a multiform and manifold way, so too the fullness of grace, which is centered in Christ as head, flows forth to His members in various ways, for the perfecting of His Body which is the Church. "For this reason He made some to be apostles, some prophets, others evangelists, others pastors and doctors, for the perfecting of the saints."[3]

[1] Cf. C. Dukehart, S.S., The State of Perfection and the Secular Priest (St. Meinrad, Ind.: Grail Press, 1952), p. 25; W. Humphrey, S.J., Elements of the Religious Life, 2 ed. (New York: Benziger, 1903), p. 1; Secular Institutes, S. Canals (Dublin: Scepter, 1959), p. 12 ff.
[2] Cf. II-II, Q. 183.   [3] Ephes. 4:11–12.

The difference of duties follows from the needs or actions which are necessary for the Church. A diversity of actions requires a diversity of men appointed for them in order that all things may be accomplished without delay or confusion. This is indicated in the Epistle of Paul to the Romans: "As in one body we have many members, but all the members have not the same office, so we being many are one in Christ."[4]

The difference of grades follows from the consideration of the beauty and the dignity of the Church. Each of these demands a certain order. Hence the Apostle says that "in a great house there are not only vessels of gold and silver, but also of wood and of clay."[5]

It was this last aspect of the Church of the Old Testament which caused the psalmist to write that it was "a queen surrounded about with variety." In the Church of the New Testament, this variety has not been lessened, but rather made more perfect, and thus we have the teaching of the Apostles, the confession of martyrs, the purity of virgins, and the sorrowing of penitents. The distinction of states and duties, far from being an obstacle to the unity of the Church, contributes to it; for the Church's unity results from the unity of faith, charity, and mutual service. For the whole body is compacted (by faith) and fitly joined together (in charity) by what every joint supplies and ministers to the whole by mutual service.

Applying this general notion of state to the supernatural order of things, it may be said that there are three states in reference to freedom from sin and the servitude of justice. In every human effort or work, St. Thomas mentions, we can distinguish a beginning, a middle, and a term. Consequently the state of spiritual servitude or freedom is differentiated according to this same division, so that we can speak of the state of beginners, that of proficients, and that of the perfect. This division refers to an interior state rather than to an exterior one, and is applicable to a Christian whatever exterior state or walk of life he may embrace under the direction of God. Since freedom from sin is the result of charity, the same division given here applies also to charity. It is from this that we have the usual expression "the three states or ages or ways" of the spiritual life, or as some have expressed it, "the foothills, the midway point, and the peak or summit."

The State of "Perfection"

In order to understand the term "state of perfection," it is most useful to recall briefly the meaning of the word "perfection." For without at least some understanding of the word, the phrase takes on too much of a merely

---

[4] Rom. 12:4–5.
[5] 2 Tim. 2:20.

technical meaning without too much understanding being connected with it.

Perfection in General

To treat this adequately for our present purpose it would seem that we should investigate four notions involved in the idea of perfection: (1) the *nature* of perfection, (2) the *possibility* of perfection, (3) the *totality* of perfection, (4) the *basic division* of the means by which perfection is arrived at. Each of these will become more clear as we go on.

Nature of Perfection

In the tract on the theological virtues we are shown that the most excellent of the virtues is charity by which man participates in the Holy Ghost. We are shown also that of all the virtues which are infused into the human soul, of all the gifts by which man participates in the life of God, charity alone is the virtue which will remain when the light of faith will give way to the light of glory and of vision. Faith will be exchanged, so to speak, for vision, hope for possession, but charity will not be exchanged for any other gift.

The perfection of the Christian life, therefore, would seem to lie in the virtue of charity. The theological reason given for this truth is rather cogent. In syllogistic form it would read like this:

A thing is said to be perfect insofar as it attains its proper end, which is its ultimate perfection.

It is charity, however, which unites us to our last end who is God, since he that abides in charity, abides in God and God in him. Only through this virtue do we know that God remains with us in a most special way. For the Holy Spirit is given to us through charity which is diffused in our hearts.

Therefore, the perfection of the Christian life, consists especially in love, or in charity, which is the love of God and the love of neighbor.[6]

Whatever other perfections there are in man, such as the perfection of the intellect, of certain skills, or the like, must be referred to and subordinated to the perfection of charity. Otherwise the person would be lacking in a virtue most proper to man, that is, the virtue of prudence, which dictates first and primarily that man must be directed and ordered toward his last end. In the present plan of God, all other perfections which can be had by man must be subordinated to the perfection of His love for God and for his neighbor. It is through charity that we find verified the

---

[6] Cf. II–II, Q. 184, a. 1.

words of Christ: "And we will come and make our abode with him,"[7] for through charity the Trinity of Persons dwells within us as in their temple.

The other virtues also pertain to Christian perfection, not accidentally, but *essentially*, although *secondarily*. Thus, when St. Thomas mentions that the perfection of the Christian life consists absolutely in charity and relatively in the other virtues, he does not mean to imply that these latter are merely adjuncts, as it were, that can easily be disposed of or dispensed with. The other supernatural virtues also pertain to Christian perfection and essentially, even though secondarily. Charity holds the first place among the virtues, but the fact that it is first does not dispense with the others. As charity grows so do all the other virtues. And charity depends upon grace. Thus in proportion as we grow in grace, in that same proportion do we also grow in the perfection of perfection which is charity. And as was mentioned above, in proportion as we grow in any one supernatural virtue, in that same proportion do we grow also in the virtue of charity and in all the virtues. For grace is not increased in a human being except through the performance of human acts, whether those acts be of the moral or the theological virtues. Thus, according to the teaching of St. Thomas, if one performs an act of the virtue of patience or of fortitude or of temperance, that is more fervent than the power of the habit of that virtue which he possesses at that time, due to the gift of an actual grace that is rather strong, then that individual increases *actually*, that is, at that moment in the virtue, in grace, and in all the other virtues, proportionately. If the act is not as strong as the habit of the virtue which the person possesses at that time, then he wins a reward to be given, according to the teaching of St. Thomas, at some future date, when he does make an act that is stronger than the habit which he possesses, even if this be only at the moment in which he enters into the vision of God.

Perhaps of all the truths of the Christian Faith this is one of the most consoling. The perfection of the Christian life does not lie in the perfection of some faculty, along the lines of which some have been given more opportunities than others, as would be true, for example, if it lay along the lines of the intellect. Rather it is given with respect to a faculty, which in some respects is blind, and which in some respects is the same in all of us. The penetration of the essence of God will depend upon the intensity of the light of glory which we shall receive at the moment of our entrance into the Beatific Vision. The perfection of the light of glory which we shall receive depends upon the intensity of charity which we possess at the instant in which we are admitted to the vision of God. "For where there

---

[7] Jn. 12:33.

is greater charity, we find a greater desire for the possession of the thing loved, and it is this desire which makes the one desiring apt and ready to receive the thing desired. Whence he who has more charity shall see God more perfectly, and shall be more happy."[8] It is charity or divine love which has a unitive force or a unifying force and which transforms the person loving into the object loved. This is the very purpose for the Christian life — that the individual might be transformed into the likeness of Him who is the Image of God.

Since charity is defined as friendship, its presence in the soul sets up a relation of intimacy with the three divine Persons. It is proper to those who are friends, however, to communicate or exchange secrets and the most cherished thoughts of their hearts. This occurs to the degree that the one person does not really communicate these thoughts to another being but rather to its other half. For it is proper to friends to be of one mind and one heart. The perfection of charity brings with it a perfection of understanding such that the two (or the four) persons involved in this friendship understand one another perfectly. There is no need of explanation, when there is certainty of one another's benevolence. Love is a kind of knowledge and the picture of the Godhead and His communication in creation comes out more clearly as the light comes into play to show up the various nuances of color, the lights and the shadows of God's plan. It is through the intensification of the love of friendship that we shall realize the promise Christ made to the disciples at the Last Supper, that "whatsoever I have learned in the bosom of the Father I have made known to you."[9] In and through the mission of the Holy Ghost who proceeds from the Father and from the Son, the Word breathing forth love, we know that the work of God shall be perfected and that these Persons will suggest and teach us the heights and the depths of the mysteries of God.[10]

Charity is the bond of perfection and, like a bond, permeates the entire structure, solidifying it, giving it its own strength and its own form, by impressing upon the whole structure its own spirit and vitality, insofar as it draws all the other virtues and their acts unto itself. Thus as our Lord Himself mentioned in the Gospel, only on condition that He be lifted up

---

[8] I, Q. 12, a. 6.

[9] Jn. 8:38.

[10] Thus St. Paul mentions: "That he may grant you from his glorious riches to be strengthened with power through his Spirit unto the progress of the inner man; and to have Christ dwelling through faith in your hearts, so that being rooted and grounded in love, you may be able to comprehend with all the saints what is the breadth, and length and height and depth, and to know Christ's love which surpasses knowledge in order that you may be filled unto all the fullness of God." Ephes. 3:16, 19.

could He draw all things unto Himself,[11] so the virtue of charity draws all the other virtues unto itself, giving them *something* of itself — the power of meriting eternal life. It is thus said to inform all other virtues insofar as it draws them to its own end which is to merit eternal life and union with God.[12]

Possibility of Perfection

In Scripture we often read that man is making a journey, that he is exiled from the Lord and is making his way back to the Lord, that during this time he can advance and proceed and grow up in love which is the bond of perfection. The virtue of charity seems to be such that it cannot be restricted within limits, but rather can grow until the perfect day, or the day of eternity; for it is through this virtue that man is moved toward God or moves toward Him, not by footsteps of the body but rather by those of the mind and heart. This is very clearly stated by St. Thomas:

> The charity of the wayfarer can increase. For we are called wayfarers by reason of our being on the way to God, who is our Last End or beatitude. On this way we draw near to God, who is approached not by steps of the body, but rather, by the affections of the mind; and this approach is the result of charity, since it unites man's mind to God. It pertains therefore to the very notion of the charity of a wayfarer that it can increase, for if it cannot, then all further advance along the way would cease. . . . Charity increases only by its subject, the human will, partaking more and more of charity, that is, by being reduced to its act, and more subject to its act. . . . It implies therefore a more deep rooting of itself in the soul, so that it has the ability to produce an act of more fervent love. . . . God, therefore, when He increases this charity in the soul, makes it have a greater hold on the soul, and He makes the likeness of the Holy Ghost to be more perfectly participated by the soul.[13]

A limit to the increase of a form may be fixed in one of three ways. First the *form itself* may have a definite or fixed limit and when this has been reached it cannot go any further without passing into some other form. Thus, for example, in colors we have gray, which can become either black or white, depending upon which way it moves or is altered or changed. Second, the *power of the agent producing the form* may be limited with regard to it. A small acorn can produce a giant oak, but it cannot produce a giant sequoia tree, or an elm, or a spruce. Third, a form can be limited by reason of the *subject receiving the form*. For whatever is received is received according to the capacity of the recipient.

---

[11] Cf. Jn. 3:14.
[12] Cf. *Quaestiones Disputatae, Q.* unica De Caritate, a. 3, *ad* 7m ad 6m, ad 9m, *ad* 18m.
[13] Cf. II–II, Q. 24, aa. 4 and 5.

The virtue or form of charity cannot reach its limit here on earth under any of these considerations. For the virtue of charity as such is a participation of the infinite charity which is the Holy Ghost. Second, God is the cause of charity, and we know that the power of God is not restricted except in regard to what is contradictory. And last, the subject, the soul of man, the will of man is not so restricted that it admits of only a certain amount or measure of charity, beyond which it cannot go. For whenever God increases charity in the soul, He gives it a corresponding ability to receive a further increase. Thus we read in the psalms: "I ran the way of thy commandments Lord when thou didst enlarge my heart."[14]

The Totality of Perfection

The word "perfection" denotes a certain totality, for when a thing is said to be perfect it has arrived at the ultimate of its ability, for the perfect is that which lacks nothing. Yet in this regard we have to proceed most cautiously. In reality there is a threefold totality possible with regard to charity.

The first is called an *absolute totality*, that is, when the person loving loves the object loved as perfectly as it can be loved. In the case of charity, since the object loved is God, it is more than evident that the only person capable of adequately loving Him is Himself. Absolute perfection, then, is something that belongs to God alone.

The second is also called an *absolute totality*; but in this case the absoluteness does not take into consideration the thing or the object loved but rather the power of the person loving, such that the *affective power of the person always tends actually to God* as much as it possibly can. This perfection of charity is not possible in this life but only in the Beatific Vision. Such totality of perfection is impossible for the rational creature or for a human person here on earth. One cannot be always actually tending to God. There are some occasions when he must, at least, take some sleep.

The third is called a *relative totality*, that is, one which does not exhaust either the lovableness of the object loved or the power of the one loving. This relative perfection can be of two kinds. It can refer to that charity or love of God which excludes from man's affections *all that is contrary to charity* such as mortal sin. This perfection of charity is *absolutely necessary* for charity to be in the soul. Or it can refer to that charity or love of God which removes from a person's affections not only that which is contrary to charity but also *whatever hinders or prevents the mind's affections from tending wholly to God*. This is the charity of the so-called "perfect" here

---

[14] Ps. 118:32.

on earth, and, as such, is not necessary for those who are either beginners or proficients. Even these perfect, however, are not exempt from the commission of daily venial sins. For "they offend in many things" venially because of the weakness of the present life. This perfection of charity falls under a precept as something *to be attained*, or to be striven for, not as something essential for the existence of any and all perfection.

This relative totality of love can be had with respect to our neighbor also, and just as, in the case of God, we find two ways in which this can be had here on earth, so, too, with respect to the secondary act of charity, the love of neighbor, we find that there are two ways in which we can be said to love him. This is rather succinctly indicated by St. Thomas:

> Now in the love of our neighbor as in the love of God we may observe a twofold perfection: one without which charity is impossible, and consisting in one's having in one's affections nothing which is contrary to the love of one's neighbor: and another without which it is possible to have charity. The latter perfection may be considered in three ways. First as to the extent of love through which a man loves not only his friends and acquaintances but also strangers and even his enemies; for as Augustine says "this is a mark of the perfect children of God."[15] — Secondly, as to the intensity of love which is shown by the things which man despises for his neighbor's sake, through his despising not only external goods for the sake of his neighbor, but also bodily hardships and even death, according to John: "Greater love than this no man hath, that a man lay down his life for his friends."[16] Thirdly, as to the effect of love, so that a man will surrender not only temporal but also spiritual goods and even himself for his neighbor's sake according to the words of the Apostle:[17] "But I most gladly will spend and be spent myself for your souls."[18]

The Means by Which We Arrive at Perfection

The present problem of the means by which we arrive at the perfection of the Christian life, arose out of the difficulties which presented themselves in several Scripture texts concerning the means that one must take in order to arrive at the perfection of charity. Some argued that our Lord made the observance of the counsels a necessary requirement for arriving at the perfection of the life of charity. Others felt that the observance of the commandments was sufficient to arrive at that degree of charity necessary to save one's soul, i.e., at one of the lower grades of perfection.

The solution to the problem lies in our manner of conceiving the word "perfection." For perfection is said to consist in a thing in one of two ways: either *essentially* or *accidentally and instrumentally*. We have already seen that the perfection of the Christian life consists in the

---

[15] *Enchiridion*, 73, PL 40, 266.   [17] 2 Cor. 12:15.
[16] Jn. 15:13.   [18] II–II, Q. 184, a. 2, ad 3.

virtue of charity, which is the love of God and the love of neighbor. Concerning this we have no choice, for we have received this as a command or precept from the Lord, both in the Old and in the New Testament: "Thou shalt love the Lord thy God with thy whole heart"[19] and "Thou shalt love thy neighbor as thyself."[20] The perfection of charity consists in man's loving God with his whole heart and his neighbor as himself. We are commanded to love God and our neighbor not only to a certain degree, but rather without limit. This is evident from the very words used by Scripture, for we are commanded to love God with our whole heart, and not according to any measure — and our neighbor as ourselves; and, as we know from our own experience, each person loves himself the most. Charity, then, is the end of the commandment. The end is not subject to measure, but only those things which are directed to an end are subject to measure, that is, the means. This we can see, for example, in the case of a physician. For the physician, if he is a good one, does not wish merely to heal his patient to such and such a degree but to restore him to perfect health. What he measures or limits is the amount of medicine necessary to bring this about. Thus the *essential means* of arriving at the perfection of charity, or the perfection of the Christian life is *the observance of the commandments*: "If you love me keep my commandments."[21]

While the essential means to Christian perfection are found in the observance of the commandments or precepts of God, there are other means which instrumentally help us to arrive at it. These are the counsels, those exercises or practices which have been suggested by the Lord Himself as leading to perfection. There is a difference between the manner in which these exercises lead to perfection and the manner in which the precepts, or the observance of the precepts, leads to perfection. For the latter remove the obstacles which are contrary to charity, that is, those things which are incompatible with the existence of charity or perfection in the soul.

On the other hand, the counsels of poverty, chastity, and obedience are directed to the removal of those things which would prevent us from exercising the *act of charity* or from *making acts of charity*, even though these things are not in themselves contrary to charity. Such would be marriage and occupation with worldly affairs, and the solicitude which we daily encounter with respect to our place of residence, work, and the like. Whatever things are not commanded but suggested by the Lord in some special counsel *can be done rightly and are done rightly when referred to the love of God and our neighbor for the sake of God.* Thus Cassian

---

[19] Deut. 6:5; cf. also Lk. 10:27.   [21] Jn. 14:21.
[20] Lev. 19:8; cf. also Lk. 10:27.

writes: "Fastings, watchings, meditating on the Scriptures, the loss of one's wealth — these are not perfection, but only means to it, since the school of perfection does not find its end in them, but achieves its end through them and uses them only insofar as they assist one to achieve it. They are the steps to charity.[22] The evangelical counsels, whether they be observed under vow or not, are *instrumental* means for the more perfect and the more secure and easy way of arriving at charity, that is, if we consider man's ascent from an *objective* point of view, and not merely subjectively. *Objectively* speaking, these counsels are the finest and most delicate instruments which divine and infinite Wisdom has conceived for enabling one to arrive at the perfection of charity or the perfection of the love of God and neighbor. Thus, in order to arrive at the higher degrees of charity especially, or of the higher degrees of perfection, the observance of the counsels is most helpful. However, one can fulfill the commandment of love merely by attaining the lowest degree of divine love which consists in not loving anything contrary to God or more than God or equal to Him.

From these considerations we can see there are two ways of looking at charity, just as there are two ways of looking at man, either at birth or later on when he has attained the fullness of manhood. Thus there is that perfection of charity by which we are *born* into the spiritual life and another at which we arrive *only through growth*. The only obstacle to the attainment of that perfection of charity necessary for salvation is, in the case of an adult, the presence of mortal sin. One becomes a transgressor of the law of God with respect to the two commandments through the commission of some mortal sin. Venial sin is perfectly compatible with all degrees of perfection or of charity, for through venial sin we do not become a transgressor of the law, *as that is understood here*. Venial sin serves to slow down the flight of the affections to God; it is a kind of "stopping-off place," a detour, which one makes in his journey to God; but one does not fall back, at least immediately, upon the commission of a venial sin, even though he may dispose himself to fall back.

The "State" of Perfection

In the preceding considerations our investigations centered around the notion of "perfection" in the expression "state of perfection." Here the emphasis is on the word "state." Just exactly what do we mean when we speak in ordinary parlance, by the *state of perfection?* We saw that the word "state" referred to some condition of freedom or servitude; and for

---

[22] *Coll.*, I, Chap. 7, *PL* 49, 490.

our study, with regard to the spiritual or supernatural order of things, we defined it as "a stable and permanent ordering of one's life or manner of living arising or freeing one from definite obligations officially assumed in a solemn act or rite." When we apply this general definition of state to the notion of perfection, the obvious definition of the latter would be "a stable and permanent manner of living arising from a definite obligation to those things which are of perfection." One is said to be in the state of perfection, not through his having the act of perfect love, or through having arrived at the perfection of charity, or the highest of the three degrees, but "through his having obligated himself in perpetuity (or temporarily today) and by means of a certain solemnity to those things that pertain to perfection."[23] Thus, for St. Thomas as well as for the majority of Thomistic theologians, the state of perfection spoken of in the language of the Church is something that is concerned with the external actions of a person and not the internal except insofar as these external actions are of course ordered to interior perfection. Thus the phrase "states of perfection" refers only to that perfection which can be judged in the external forum, that is, a perfection *coram Ecclesia*, a perfection in the eyes of the Church. While it is the right and the privilege of God alone to judge the interior perfection of a given individual, or his degree of charity, still it pertains to the Church to determine what a state of perfection is, as the term is now used in our present considerations. As we all know by experience, there are persons in the states of perfection who are not at all perfect in charity, whereas some others, not in the states of perfection, are perfect.

Other authors have given similar definitions of the state of perfection, but not exactly and precisely the same. John Gerson, for example, defined it as "a manner of living in which one is obliged to acquire or to exercise perfection."[24] This obligation, he says, may arise either from a vow or from some ecclesiastical office. Father Lehmkuhl, S.J., defines it as "predicated of those who profess publicly before the Church (which in some way approves the action) that which pertains to perfection."[25] And Father Humphrey, S.J., defines it as "a profession or manner of living which is stable and which has been instituted either for the acquiring or the exercising of a man's own individual perfection in the Christian Life."[26] And finally Dom Odon Lottin, O.S.B., defines it as a "state of life in

---

[23] II–II, Q. 184, a. 4.
[24] *De Consiliis*, Opera Omnia, II, 678.
[25] *Theologia Moralis*, 9 ed., I, 295, n. 487 (Freiburg im Br., 1898).
[26] *Op. cit.*, p. 8.

which one's whole person is solemnly and irrevocably engaged in the practice of perfect charity."[27]

The state of perfection, very briefly, is a position or condition in which a person voluntarily places himself not so much in order to deny himself certain things as to practice certain actions which will lead him to the perfection of divine charity. The exercise of these actions will at the same time imply a negation just as the exercise of any action does, for if a person has a particular liking for lying down and walking, he cannot do both of these at the same time. If he chooses to do one thing, he must necessarily give up the other. This is an ordinary fact of life. It is no less true of the states of perfection. If one wishes to give oneself over to the service of God *completely*, then there are certain things which, although not contradictory or incompatible with the *habitual* exercise of charity, nonetheless do hinder its *actual* exercise, at least to a great extent. Therefore in order to allow oneself to practice acts of charity more frequently, one voluntarily removes the obstacles opposed to them. This one does because he knows it is through *acts* that we either dispose ourselves for an increase of charity, or we merit the actual increase of this gift, or virtue. A "state" of perfection is an external arrangement of life which gives not only the opportunity but the *obligation* and the *means* to practice certain actions, those which are of perfection, that is, those which lead one more firmly and easily and quickly to the higher perfections of the virtue of charity. This was recently stated again in the *Annus Sacer* "While it is true that all Christians must ascend or climb this holy peak of Christian perfection," writes Pius XII, "still there are some who advance toward it by means of a journey or a way which is entirely proper to them and one that offers helps of a higher nature."[28]

SECTION 2. SECULAR INSTITUTES

Having seen the notion of the word "state" and that of "perfection," and the meaning of the phrase "state of perfection," we are now ready to take up each of those particular institutions which enjoy a place or position in such a concept. We have already mentioned that an institution enters into the category of these states of perfection in the event that it receives an ecclesiastical judgment or pronouncement giving it such status. Positing this condition, we can say that there are today in the Church the

---

[27] "Doctrine de Saint Thomas sur l'état religieux," in *La Vie Spirituelle*, 7 (Jan. 1923), 390.
[28] *Annus Sacer*, AAS 43 (1951), 28.

following states of perfection (*acquirendae*) to be acquired, or the states by which we tend to arrive at perfection: secular institutes; religious communities which make profession of the vows of poverty, chastity, and obedience, explicitly taken or implied in the profession of obedience; and societies of common life. Added to this, *theologians* commonly teach that the episcopate also is to be considered a state of perfection, not a state in which a person tends to perfection, but rather one in which perfection is exercised or imparted or given or administered. This state of perfection, they teach, is higher or more excellent than that of any of the others mentioned. With this as a short introduction, we shall see the theology and, to the extent that this is needed, the canon law concerning the first of these states of perfection — the secular institutes.

In the Apostolic Constitution *Provida Mater Ecclesia*, issued by Pope Pius XII, a new state of perfection was established in the Church. In this particular document the Holy Father mentioned the development of institutions which offer to persons or to members of the Church a manner of life which was especially orientated to the perfection of charity. He writes: "the Church, ever faithful to Christ her Spouse, and true to Herself, under the guidance of the Holy Spirit, with continuous and unhesitating progress up to the establishment of the present Code of Canon Law, gradually developed the discipline of the state of perfection."[29] In the evolution of the life of the Church, religious institutes of both solemn and simple vows were considered to belong to the canonical states of perfection. Along with them the Church also recognized "as in a fairly complete sense equivalent to the canonical state of perfection, certain societies of great value to herself and frequently also to the state, which although they lack some of the requirements which are necessary for the complete state of perfection, such as public vows, yet in other respects which are regarded as essentials of the life of perfection, bear a close similarity to religious institutes and are almost necessarily connected with them."[30]

A year later this same Holy Father wrote of these new institutes:

> The Holy Spirit who ceaselessly re-creates and renews the face of the earth, constantly desolated and defiled as it is with so many and such great evils, has called to Himself by a great and special grace many beloved sons and daughters whom we lovingly bless in the Lord, to the end that being united and organized in Secular Institutes, they may be the salt of the earth — of that world of which they are not, yet in which by the will of God they must remain — the unfailing salt which, ever renewed by the

---

[29] *Provida Mater Ecclesia*, AAS 39 (1947), 115; for Engl. trans. cf. J. Haley, C.S.C., *Apostolic Sanctity in the World* (Notre Dame, Ind.: U. of Notre Dame Press, 1957), p. 128 or *Canon Law Digest*, III, p. 135.

[30] *Provida Mater Ecclesia*, AAS 39 (1947), 117; tr., Haley, op. cit., pp. 129–130.

grace of vocation, does not lose its savor; the light of the world, which shines in the darkness and is not extinguished; the small but potent leaven which always and everywhere active, mingling with every class of persons from the lowest to the highest, strives by example and in every way to reach and to transfuse them individually and collectively until the whole mass is so permeated that it is all leavened in Christ.[31]

Secular institutes, even though their members live in the world, by reason of the full dedicated life to God and to souls which they profess with the approval of the Church and by reason of the internal inter-diocesan and universal hierarchical organization which they have in vary-ing degrees, are according to the Apostolic Constitution "Provida Mater Ecclesia" rightly and properly numbered among the states of perfection which are juridically constituted and recognized by the Church.[32] This was later also explicitly stated in a decree of the Sacred Congregation of Religious.[33]

Nature or Definition of Secular Institutes

In speaking of the societies which he was establishing in the states of perfection in the Apostolic Constitution, Provida Mater, the Holy Father mentioned that they were

associations which in their internal constitution, in the hierarchial order of their government, in the full dedication unlimited by any other ties, which they require of their members strictly so-called, in their profession of the evangelical counsels, and, finally, in their manner of exercising the ministry and the apostolate, bear a closer essential resemblance to the canonical states of perfection and especially to the societies without public vows . . . even though they do not practice the religious life in common, but make use of other external forms.[34]

In the First Article of the Special Law of Secular Institutes, following immediately upon the above paragraph, a secular institute was defined as "a society, whether clerical or lay, whose members, in order to attain Christian perfection and to exercise a full apostolate, profess the evangeli-cal counsels in the world."[35] Thus we might say that the specific elements of such a society are its apostolic purpose, the secular state, the practice in the world of the evangelical counsels.[36]

---

[31] Primo Feliciter, AAS 40 (1948), 283; tr., Haley, op. cit., pp. 139–140.

[32] AAS 40 (1948), 85–86; Haley, op. cit., pp. 141–142.

[33] AAS 40 (1948), 296; cf. Haley, op. cit., p. 147.

[34] AAS 39 (1947), 117–118; cf. Haley, op. cit., p. 130.

[35] Provida Mater, Lex Peculiaris, Art. I, AAS 39 (147), 120; cf. Haley, op. cit., p. 133. Cf. also "The Nature of Secular Institutes in the Light of Papal Documents," Patrick Clancy, O.P., in Apostolic Sanctity in the World, Haley, p. 93 ff.

[36] Cf. Secular Institutes, J. Perrin, O.P. (New York: P. J. Kenedy and Sons, 1960), p. 52.

Purpose of the Secular Institutes

In the course of the years, particularly more recent years, many of the religious orders and congregations have realized that they were unable to get into many of the environments of modern-day life which more than ever before are in need of Christianization. Their dress, their mode of life, etc., forbid their entrance into many places and forms of the Apostolate. Yet their spirit, the spirit of complete detachment from the things of the world, *total* dedication to God, is something which these environments and places must feel if they are to be won back to Christ.

They were unable to accomplish this, however, to as large an extent as was wished. For even though they gave their spirit to the Third Orders, still the element of total dedication such as can be had through living the three evangelical counsels, was not a necessary element for admission or membership in these "orders." Something else had to be found. And this was accomplished through the appearance of the secular institutes. This purpose has been very clearly set down by Pius himself:

> The prosperous growth of these Institutes has shown with increasing clarity in how many ways they can be turned to the effective service of the Church and of souls. For living seriously the life of perfection at all times and in all places; for embracing such a life in many cases where the canonical religious life was either impossible or not appropriate; for the thorough Christian renovation of families, professions, and civil societies through an intimate and daily contact with a life perfectly and entirely dedicated to holiness; for exercising a varied apostolate and ministry in places, times, and circumstances, forbidden or inaccessible to priests and religious — for all these purposes, the Institutes can easily be used and adapted.[37]

If we were to attempt to define the idea "secular state," we would find it most difficult. It is easier felt than defined. A description, however, would probably include the following elements. It would exclude everything in manner, or dress or housing, which would differentiate it from that of the "decent Christian on the street." Just like others, members of secular institutes earn their living at various trades and professions (including the priesthood if we wish to classify that here as a profession). It would include the natural ties with family, relatives, friends, associates, and neighbors. It would seem to include the idea that no material or even moral enclosure or cloister except that needed to preserve the love they have promised to Christ causes their separation from the world.

All these elements and more are included in the term "secular state." The presence *in the world* of these persons appears as so essential that it imposes its own pattern and method on the life of complete dedication

---

[37] *Provida Mater*, AAS 39 (1947), 118; tr. Haley, *op. cit.*, p. 131.

which they have promised as well as on the specific apostolate which they have undertaken. They are to find their holiness in their daily living and mingling with the people of the world, because it is here where they are to find the specific actual vocational graces required for holiness. By their entrance into such a way of life they are assured, if they are truly called to it, that God's grace is at work in them and will renew them interiorly to enable them to discover how they might lead a human life in a divine manner, and how work, earthly values, and human relationships can cooperate to extend the kingdom of God, and lastly, how Christ is present in each of their fellow men. It is through such a life so transformed by charity and Godlike vision that the message of the Gospel is to be taken into and found in the world.[38]

Comparison of the Secular Institutes With Religious Communities

While these particular new institutes are considered to belong to the states of perfection, still they are not a state of perfection in the sense that, for example, the religious life is, or that of the societies in the Church which lead a common life and yet do not take vows at all — the Paulists, for example, or the Maryknoll Mission priests — or merely private vows — the Vincentians and the Daughters of Charity. Thus they are like and unlike religious congregations and orders.

They are said to be like religious orders and congregations which take vows in three respects. First, they have some kind of internal constitution and hierarchical form of government, even though this was not too specifically decided for them in the *Provida Mater*, but left rather to their own judgment confirmed, of course, by proper authority. Second, they require *complete dedication* on the part of those of their members who are considered strict members of the institute (for they do admit of those who are called nonstrict members, as orders have Third Order members); that is to say, their members must live the evangelical counsels, under some kind of promise, vow, or oath. Last, they are employed in the apostolate and the Christian ministry; that is, they are to live these counsels in the world, and this is their special mark — that they be *secular*.

They are said to be *unlike* religious orders and congregations in two ways. First, they do *not* take *public* vows as do the members of the so-called religious institutes. And, second, they do not follow the common life, that is to say, that type of canonical common life provided for in the Church's legislation for religious communities and societies of the com-

---

[38] Cf. *Secular Institutes*, J. Perrin, O.P., pp. 66–67.

mon life. Some secular institutes do have their members living together, however.

The Constitution is most explicit regarding the vows and the common life of these new institutes. So far as the vows of the institute are concerned, all three must be present. First, there must be a vow, or oath, or consecration of celibacy and perfect chastity, binding in conscience. Thus the Constitution states: "persons who desire to be ascribed in the institutes as members in the strict sense, in addition to practicing those exercises of piety and self-denial which all must practice who aspire to the perfection of the Christian Life, must effectively tend toward that same perfection also in special ways . . . by making profession before God of celibacy and perfect chastity, which shall be confirmed by vow, oath, or consecration binding in conscience, according to the Constitutions."[39]

Again there must be a vow, or promise, of obedience, so that "bound by a firm bond they dedicate themselves entirely to God and to works of charity or apostleship by a stable bond and are always and in all respects morally in the hands and under the guidance of their Superiors, according to the Constitutions."[40]

Finally there must be a "vow or promise of poverty, in virtue of which they have not the free use of temporal property, but a restricted and limited use according to the Constitutions."[41] This vow of poverty is normally worked out by each member in the form of a budget which is approved by the proper superior, and which usually depends to a great extent upon the work of the individual in question. Thus we would not expect the same budget to be kept by one who is a doctor or famous surgeon, and another who is a factory worker. If, however, special needs arise, permission must be had or at least prudently presumed, from the proper superior.[42]

The nature of these vows has been the subject of much study and discussion on the part of canonists. They are definitely not public vows as are those taken in the canonical state of perfection mentioned in Canon Law. Neither are they private vows, such as, for example, the vows taken by certain societies of the common life (the Daughters of Charity) or such as one might take in the world — the vow of perpetual chastity or dedicated chastity in the world. These vows are of such a nature that they incorporate one into a special society and state of perfection ordained and recognized by the Church.[43] So far as can be determined, in themselves,

39 Provida Mater, art. 3, § 2, AAS 39 (1947), 121; tr. Haley, op. cit., p. 134.
40 Ibid.
41 Ibid.
42 Cf. J. Perrin, O.P., op. cit., p. 68 ff.
43 Primo Feliciter, art. 5, AAS 40 (1948), 685–686; tr. Haley, op. cit., pp. 141–142.

they are private vows, but they are sometimes called *social*, because of their interest to the particular society within which they are made. However, both the terms *semipublic* and social are used by the members of the Sacred Congregation of Religious.

The secular institutes also differ from other previously recognized states of perfection, most definitely in that they do not demand canonical common life and domicile.[44] In fact, they are not encouraged to have such, because this would defeat the purpose for which they have been set up and reduce them, or raise them rather, to the level of a religious institute which they are not meant to be. But they must have one or several common houses such as the residence of superiors, central or local houses of formation, where members can live or come together for instructions and retreats, as well as houses serving for the sick and for those whom it would be unwise to leave alone. For it is *essential* to these institutes that there be a bond set up, and a *stable* bond, either perpetual or temporary but to be renewed at its expiration. Likewise it must be *mutual and complete*, so that, according to the Constitutions, the member gives himself wholly to the institute, and the institute takes care of and is responsible for the member. It can happen, however, that when many of the members work together in a given locality, they live together as with a small group of friends.[45]

Formation and Spiritual Life

The formation of the members of secular institutes is much more gradual than that of the members of a religious community or society of the common life, and this can readily be understood. For many of their members are unable to abandon their ordinary employment for a year or two, in order to make a regular novitiate. For the most part they have to receive their religious training and the training in the spirit of the institute over a period of years, sandwiching it in, so to speak, with their regular occupations. For this reason, the training and religious formation of the subjects must be continued for many years, even after they have made first profession. In many institutes, this formation covers a period of from seven to ten years. Only after this period are they allowed to make perpetual or final vows, if the institute provides for these.

The practices of prayer include assistance at daily Mass, mental prayer

---

[44] *Provida Mater*, art. II, § 1, *AAS* 39 (1470), 120: tr. Cf. Perrin, *op. cit.*, p. 110), and *Canon Law Digest*, *loc. cit.*

[45] But they cannot without abandoning their specific mission of sanctity and of apostolate in the world live the regular canonical common life. Cf. *Secular Institutes*, Canals, p. 76.

usually a half hour each day. Some institutes require of their members a longer time for this exercise, but in this case, other prayers usually are not demanded which another community would demand — for example, the vocal prayers which exist today in most of our congregations of simple vows. Devotion to the Blessed Sacrament, the rosary, and some part of the Divine Office are required by many institutes. The Opus Dei, however, despite its name, forbids its members (except those who are priests) to say the Divine Office, arguing that this is the work of priests and those religious who are bound to its recitation. On the other hand, this particular institute demands a very thorough, solid formation of its members. They must have a college education, or at least be pursuing studies which lead to a degree. In addition they take courses in philosophy and theology of university level at special Opus Dei centers. Those of them who are priests also take an ecclesiastical doctorate.[46]

*   *   *

When this new state of perfection was officially set up by the Church, it took some time for the full import and the implication of the legislation to come out. Consequently, several questions were raised regarding various points in the legislation. The following clarification was then made concerning the institutes. There are two canonical states of perfection: (1) the religious state properly so called (communities in which public solemn or simple vows are made) and (2) the state of the societies of the common life, without vows or with merely private vows. These latter, however, are not and cannot be called religious in the strict sense, but they are given equivalence with religious in many matters, and are subject to the Sacred Congregation of Religious. They, therefore, constitute a canonical state of perfection in a less absolute sense. In addition to these two canonical states of perfection, the Provida Mater inaugurated another one, not canonical but nevertheless with juridical and public status in the Church. These institutes are not in the category of religious (nor can their members be called religious) and are not made equivalent to them, even though they may approach the religious state more closely than do the societies of the common life, since their members make some profession or promise of the evangelical counsels of poverty, chastity, and obedience, and even resemble the religious orders and congregations in their spiritual life and organization. For all this, they belong to this third category of the state of perfection. The characteristic note was clearly summed up by the late Holy Father when he wrote in the Primo Feliciter:

---

[46] Cf. Spanish Catholicism Today, José Orlandos, in The Furrow, November, 1960, pp. 741–742.

In this elevation of the Societies of the Faithful to the higher form of Secular Institutes, and in working out the general as well as the particular organizations of all these Institutes, this must always be kept in mind, that in all of them their special and peculiar character as *secular* institutes, which is the whole reason for their existence, be clearly expressed. Nothing is to be subtracted from the full profession of Christian Perfection, solidly based on the evangelical counsels, and in substance truly religious; but this perfection is to be exercised and professed in the world, and therefore, in all things which are licit and which can be brought into conformity with the duties and works of that same perfection, it must be adapted to the secular life. . . . The apostolate of Secular Institutes is to be faithfully practiced not only *in the world*, but as *of the world*, and therefore with avowed aims, practices, forms and in places and circumstances corresponding to their secular condition.[47]

Requirements for the Vocation to a Secular Institute

The following points may be noted for one attempting to discern whether a person has a vocation to one or other of these secular institutes. Basically they are similar to those required for a vocation to the priesthood and to the religious life. Since we shall treat several of these requirements at length when dealing with the religious vocation, it will suffice for our present purpose merely to list them and discuss them briefly.

Attraction: There must first of all be some kind of attraction, or more correctly, usually there is some kind of attraction to one or other of these institutes. But as we shall see an attraction is merely one of the conditions which usually point to a vocation and help us to make some conjecture as to its presence. Of itself, however, it does *not* constitute the *essential* requirement, and as a matter of fact it may be, and in some cases is, entirely lacking. Thus, for example, there are some religious who have had very little attraction, either for a particular community or for the religious life in general, and yet have felt and were convinced that God wanted them there. St. Teresa mentions this lack of attraction in regard to her own vocation.[48]

---

[47] Cf. *AAS* 40 (1948), 284–285; cf. Haley, op. cit., pp. 140–141. For further information concerning the canonical and juridical aspects of these institutes, cf. especially Haley, *op. cit.* Other very excellent works from which much of the foregoing matter has been taken or from which it has been summarized can also be consulted: *Secular Institutes, a Symposium on the Modern Lay Community* (London: Blackfriars, 1952); *Secular Institutes,* S. Canals (Dublin: Scepter, 1959); *Secular Institutes,* J. Perrin (New York: P. J. Kenedy & Sons, 1960); *Les Instituts Séculiers,* J. Beyer, S.J. (Paris: Desclée, 1954). Likewise, the sources: *Provida Mater Ecclesia, AAS* 39 (1947), 114 ff.; *Primo Felicter, AAS* 40 (1948), 283 ff.; *Cum Sanctissimus,* Instruction of the Sacred Congregation of Religious, *AAS* 40 (1948), 293 ff. A rather complete list of references to this study can be found in Father Haley's work, already cited, pp. 197–210.

[48] *Life,* Chaps. 3–4, Peers, I, pp. 18–20 *passim.*

Certain intellectual qualities, at least those necessary for the particular institute in question must also be present. Thus in some institutes greater intellectual ability will be demanded than in others, just as, for example, we also see in the case of religious and priestly vocations. What is decidedly necessary for one wishing to enter the way of life set up by these institutes is a very sound judgment, even more, from one point of view, than for the religious life. The reason is more or less obvious — the member of the secular institute, by reason of his being on his own, is called upon to make many more sudden and unforeseen decisions than those called to the religious life.

There are certain moral qualities also necessary for the living of the vocation. On this score great care must be taken in the selection of candidates; for the dangers to which they are exposed are even more formidable than those which a religious in an active community has to face. And yet the obligation is one that binds in conscience. This should be pointed out by the one being asked for counsel, and some of the more difficult dangers of the life should be made known. It is above all, of course, the work of the confessor to decide whether one has the moral qualities required for such a vocation, and, on this score, it seems that he should exact a much stricter ability to live the vows, especially the vow of chastity, than he would for one entering a religious community, because in the latter, at least, there are some safeguards for the preservation of the vow, whereas in the secular institutes, there are almost none. Likewise there must be a capacity for generosity and selflessness.

There must be an interior call or vocation. The mere consciousness of the world's needs does *not* constitute a real criterion for this vocation any more than for any other, e.g., to the religious life or the priesthood. When the "I like it" becomes "I feel that I ought," in the sense of *conviction,* or persistent urge, then we have a criterion for the interior vocation, or what has often been called the divine vocation, as opposed to the exterior vocation, or the consent of the community or bishop to accept a candidate. There is a special call to this way of life, a call which although similar in nature to that of the other vocations, still is not entirely the same, any more than a vocation to the religious life and a vocation to the priesthood are the same. Pius XII, in his Constitution, mentions this vocation explicitly. "Since the older Institutes of this class have sufficiently and increasingly demonstrated . . . that even in the world, with a *special vocation* from God, and with the help of divine grace, it is certainly possible to attain a rather strict and effective consecration to God, which is not merely internal, but also external and almost religious. . . ."[49]

---

[49] *Provida Mater, AAS* 39 (1947), 118; cf. Haley, *op. cit.,* p. 131.

And even more clearly in the *Primo Feliciter* he writes:

> The Holy Spirit has called to himself by a great and special grace many beloved sons and daughters, whom we lovingly bless in the Lord. . . . [an] unfailing salt, which ever renewed by the grace of vocation, does not lose its savor. . . .
>
> To the moderators and assistants of Catholic action and of other associations of the faithful, in whose maternal bosom are being trained to full Christian living and introduced to the exercise of the apostolate so many chosen young people who are called by *divine vocation*, to a higher life, either in religious institutes and societies of common life, or in Secular Institutes, we recommend with fatherly affection that they generously promote such holy *vocations*. . . .[50]

This vocation as it matures ought to have this desire — to be fully incorporated into the Christian community, to live among the faithful. The real criterion of the vocation to the secular institutes will be this understanding, that a man will love God more deeply in this path of life, in this task, with these difficulties and responsibilities than he will in any other sort of life. One, therefore, who is called to this vocation by God, does not wish to set himself apart from a genuine interest and closeness to the whole Christian community, with its various hierarchies; rather, he wishes to keep the same life and the same subordination to the authority of the bishop and the pastor. This wish or will or firm proposal seems to be the final criterion of such a vocation. Generally speaking, however, other criteria are often found too, such as the impossibility of entering the religious life by reason of obligations toward a mother or other members of the family.

Even when these criteria seem to be present, it is always going to be difficult to discern a vocation and we can never be absolutely sure that one has the grace of a vocation (that is, an interior vocation) to such an institute, any more than we can be absolutely certain that he has a vocation to the religious life or to the priesthood or that one is in the state of grace. But if it were necessary that one should be absolutely certain that he is to follow this or that way of life, then there would be very few persons in any given way of life. What is important is that a person feel at home where he is, trusting in Providence to lead him safely through the difficulties and trials or through his compassion with Christ to the triumph of glory.[51]

---

[50] *AAS* 40 (1948), 283–286; cf. Haley, op. cit., pp. 139–142 passim.

[51] For a longer treatment of this, cf. *Secular Institutes, Their Vocation and Mission in the Church*, J. Perrin, O.P., art. in the *Symposium*, cited above.

SECTION 3.   THE RELIGIOUS LIFE

According to what we have seen above, a way of life to be a "state of perfection" requires (1) a perpetual obligation (at least intentionally) to things pertaining to perfection, and (2) a certain solemnity by which it is imposed, that is, some exterior rite that is accepted by the Church. Applying this definition to those whom we call religious, we see that they fulfill the conditions necessary to be constituted in a state of perfection. Thus St. Thomas writes concerning them:

> Both these conditions apply to religious. For religious bind themselves by vow to refrain from worldly affairs, which they might lawfully use, in order to give themselves more freely to God, in which consists the perfection of the present life. For this reason they received the name Therapeutai, i.e., servants of God, on account of their pure service and bondage. Others call them monks on account of their single-minded and indivisible life which unites them in a God-like union and a perfection beloved of God, through their envelopment in (that is, their contemplation of) indivisible things."[52]

For the religious, his state of perfection is established by the perpetuity and the public character of the contract. On the day of profession the religious renounces, for love of God, all that he might have legitimately possessed — worldly goods, the human possessions of marriage and a family, the free disposition of his activity. All this, offered to God through charity, represents an interior profession of perfect charity, and thus the religious is placed in a state of perfection.

The ecclesiastical state of perfection which is exterior, or, as we say today, canonical, signifies directly the intention of those living in the state to strive after perfection. For when they enter this state they do not profess before the world that they are perfect, that they have already reached perfection, but rather that they are tending to perfection. They are declaring their wholehearted intention to seek perfection through the observance of those things which are of perfection. In making this declaration a person would not be guilty of lying, for example, or of deceit, through his not being perfect, but only through his withdrawing his mind from the intention of reaching perfection.

From the description of the religious state as a state of canonical perfection, it is clear that the phrase status perfectionis acquirendae, "the state of striving after perfection," perhaps best describes it. This particular expression has long been used by theologians in order to indicate

---

[52] II–II, Q. 184, a. 5.

the religious state of perfection spoken of in Canon Law. This was done by these writers in order to distinguish the state of perfection of religious from the state of perfection attributed to the bishop. For this latter has received the description, or title *status perfectionis exercendae*, "the state of communicating or imparting perfection to others."[53]

It is by reason of the three public vows that the religious state is a state of perfection, for it is by means of these that one becomes obligated to those things which are of perfection. They place upon an individual what we might call a real loss of liberty, and make him enter into a permanent state of servitude, at least intentionally; and this is true even of those institutes where temporary vows are taken. For as Canon Law specifically states of religious institutes of public vows, they are taken *to be renewed after the time has elapsed*.[54] The religious by profession places himself in a condition of bondage obliging himself permanently (although with a permanency that does admit of change, even though with difficulty) to strive after a perfection that is not strictly commanded, at least under pain of grievous sin.[55]

---

[53] Canon Law, however, does not mention this particular state as a state of perfection, at least, explicitly.

[54] Canon 488, § 1.

[55] We find the meaning of "state of perfection" more clearly brought out in another work of St. Thomas where he speaks of perfection, in a more lengthy manner:

"One is said to be perfect either from the fact he has perfection or from the fact that he has the state of perfection. The first is to be sought in charity, for it is this which unites us to God. The second, that is, the state of perfection is had by those who solemnly oblige themselves to that which is of perfection, to those things which are annexed to perfection. Something is said to be annexed to perfection in one of two ways: First, as a preamble to it or preparation for it, such as poverty, chastity, and the like — those things by which a person is withdrawn from the care of and the occupation with secular things, in order that he might more freely give himself over to the things of God. Whence those things are said to be *instruments of perfection*. Whoever therefore has voluntary poverty, or chastity, etc., has something which is preparatory to perfection, but he is not said to possess the state of perfection, *unless he obliges himself solemnly by profession*.

"Secondly, these things can also be said to be annexed to perfection *as an effect* of it such as for example to undertake the care of souls; for it pertains to perfect charity that one on account of his love for God should lay aside the sweetness of the contemplative life, which he loves more, in order that he might undertake the occupations of the active life for procuring the salvation of his neighbor. Whoever, therefore, intends the salvation of his neighbor in such wise, has indeed an effect of perfection, but he does not have the state of perfection, unless we are speaking of a bishop who undertakes the care of souls by means of a solemn consecration.

"For this reason we are to distinguish between those who are said to be perfect in charity, and those who are said to be perfect in state. For those who are said to be perfect in charity are obliged by reason of an interior law, which obliges them by inclining them to what is better. These then are obliged to what is better according to the measure of that perfection which fills them. Those however, who are in the state of perfection, religious and bishops, are not obliged to what is better by

Article I.   The Theology of the Religious Life

Under this heading we shall only consider some of the more fundamental elements involved in the theology of the religious life. Most of these are contained in the following definition (not canonical as can be seen) of the religious life: a state of total dedication to God demanding the observance of the three counsels of poverty, chastity, and obedience under vow. We will attempt to consider each of the ideas contained in this definition.

A State of Total Dedication to God

We may have wondered why "religious" have received in the course of centuries the title which they bear, for certainly they are not alone in their exercise of the worship of God. All Christians, indeed all persons, have the obligation of worshiping God, and therefore of exercising the virtue of religion. In fact, we know there are persons who are not religious, in the sense that they have not entered any religious community or group of persons vowed to God, and yet who spend more time in their worship of Him than do religious, at least from an external consideration. Nevertheless, only those who have entered an institute in which public profession of vows is made are called "religious." There is a reason for this very admirably given by St. Thomas:

> That which is applicable to many things in common is ascribed antonomastically or (properly, as it were) to that to which it is applicable in some special or excellent way. Thus the name of fortitude is claimed by the virtue which preserves the firmness of the mind in regard to the most difficult things, and the name of temperance by that virtue which tempers the greatest pleasures. Now, religion, as stated above, is a virtue by which man offers something to the service and worship of God. Therefore those who give themselves up entirely to the divine service, as offering a holocaust to God are called religious antonomastically. Hence Gregory says "Some there are who keep nothing for themselves, but sacrifice to almighty God their tongue, their senses, their life, and the property they possess."[56] Now the perfection of man consists in adhering wholly to God.[57]

---

their state. They are obliged only to those things which are implied in the care they undertake or with regard to what they profess, or make profession of. Thus we might say, that these latter, bishops and religious by reason of their charity are obliged to what is better or more perfect; but by reason of their profession or consecration they are obliged only to the extent of the demands which such makes upon them" (Quodlibetal, I, Q. 7, a. 2, ad 2m).

[56] Hom. 8, in Ezech., PL 76, 1037.
[57] II–II, Q. 186, a. 1.

In treating of the virtue of religion,[58] we find that it refers not merely to the acts elicited by it, such as devotion and sacrifice, but it can also refer to other acts which are commanded by it and referred to it. The acts of all the virtues *insofar as they are referred to God's service and honor* become acts of the virtue of religion. From this it follows that since a religious is one who devotes his whole life to the divine service, his whole life belongs to the exercise of religion. It is for this reason that such a life is called the "religious" life and those who embrace it are called by this special name.

St. Gregory compares the religious life to a holocaust because the one who enters religion gives everything he has to God. He writes in one of his homilies on Ezechiel: "When one vows something of himself to God and yet retains something for himself, it is a sacrifice on his part; but when he vows to God all that he has, all that he lives, all that he relishes, then we have a holocaust, which in the Latin language is called all incense."[59] It is evident, therefore, that in the thought of St. Gregory it is in the religious life, which is a complete and total dedication of oneself to the service of God, that we have the most perfect type of sacrifice capable of being performed by an individual human being, one which involves the whole of the gift offered, and not merely a part. In the Old Testament, the holocaust was considered to be the perfect sacrifice, the most important. This, as we know, was offered each morning and evening for the chosen people. The meaning of this sacrifice was symbolic: it indicated that God was sovereign, and man owed Him complete and entire subjection. The "holocaust" meant "that which goes up," and the victim offered was considered as going up in the flames of the altar to God. It was a sign, or a symbol, or a sacrament — an outward expression of the inner worship of the soul, or of the ascent of the soul to God. It was the noblest sacrifice because of its universality, that is, the whole victim was offered and consumed, thereby indicating God's right to claim a thing entirely as His own. This is pointed out rather clearly by St. Thomas:

> There were three kinds of sacrifices. There was one in which the victim was entirely consumed by fire, and this was called a holocaust, that is, all burnt. For this kind of sacrifice was offered to God especially to show reverence to His majesty and love of His Goodness, and typified the state of perfection as regards the fulfillment of the counsels. Therefore the whole victim was burnt up, so that as the whole animal by being dissolved into

---

[58] Cf. *The Theology of Spiritual Guidance,* p. 100 ff., mimeographed notes, U. of Notre Dame Press, 1956.

[59] Quoted from the *Quodlibetals, Quod,* III, Q. 6, a. 3.

vapor soared aloft, so it might denote that the whole man and whatever belongs to him are subject to the authority of God, and should be offered to Him.[60]

Thus in the Old Testament God asked that men consecrate something of their possessions to Him through these various sacrifices, the most perfect being that of holocaust in which His universal dominion over the creature might be manifested. The New Testament, since it was the fulfillment and the perfection of the Old, would ask a more perfect sacrifice to God, to signify God's dominion over all creation and the redemption of Christ, the act of charity par excellence. And that was to be found in the religious profession. For the matter here is of much greater dignity and nobility than that of the Old Testament sacrifice, being, as it is, the most perfect of God's earthly creatures, man, made according to the image and likeness of God. Moreover, the fire by which the victim in the New Testament was to be consumed in and through this offering was not to be merely material, but rather spiritual, being a share in the very fire which moved God Himself to offer Himself up on the Cross, that is, the fire of charity.[61] Therefore, for two reasons the holocaust of the New Testament is more perfect than that of the Old: (1) by reason of the victim offered, being a human soul and body; and (2) by reason of the fire by which it is destroyed, namely, the fire of charity which is a participation in the Holy Spirit.

The perfection of the religious state, wherein one vows himself entirely to the service of God, stems from the fact that here is offered to God a sacrifice much more perfect than that of the Old Testament and one which more perfectly resembles the Sacrifice of Christ on the Cross. For the two elements essential in Christ's sacrifice, the spirit which prompted Him to offer it — divine charity, or the love He had for God and souls — and the human nature, in and through which He was enabled to offer it, are also found in the religious who dedicates and consecrates his life to God. For this reason St. Augustine says that "just as the love of oneself brought about the city of Babylon (the prevalence of sin among men) so too, is it the love of God even to the contempt of oneself, that brings about the city of God."[62]

In this consideration there is one other aspect that we must not forget. The religious life was instituted that a person might more easily reach the perfection of the virtue of charity by removing the obstacles to such a goal, namely the occasions of sin. Since it pertains to penance to cut away

---

[60] I–II, Q. 102, a. 3, ad 8m; cf. also ad 9m.
[61] III, Q. 46, a. 1, ad 1.
[62] The City of God, Bk. XIV, c. 28, PL 41, 436.

the causes of sin, it follows that the religious state or life is a most fitting place of penance. In fact, it is so penitential that one can never impose it upon another as a penance for any crime. And yet for all its being a penance, it remains a better and lighter penance than that which one would perform in the world, regardless of how severe and prolonged this might be.[63]

The Observance of the Evangelical Counsels

The religious life or state as it is understood in tradition *demands the observance of the evangelical counsels.* This is clearly indicated in the law of the Church. Religious are those who publicly profess (by vows, whether simple or solemn) the evangelical counsels. Thus Pius XII mentioned in the *Provida Mater* that the observance of the counsels under vow is necessary for one to be in the state of perfection, at least if this were to be understood in the *complete* sense, i.e., the religious state. And again in the Allocution *Annus Sacer*[64] he says that the states of perfection are those in which the evangelical counsels of poverty, chastity, and obedience are professed in some way, not necessarily by vows, but at least in the form of a promise or oath. It is in this same Allocution that he speaks of the states of perfection as states in which one *tends* to perfection (*status perfectionis acquirendae*).

A religious is not bound to keep all the counsels, but those which are essential to the point where if they were omitted, his whole life would be taken up with secular business. For there are some counsels which can be omitted without one's life being taken up with secular actions. Thus, for example, the giving of alms is of counsel, and yet the religious is not bound to give alms except this should become necessary and he has the wherewithal to do it. Again, there are certain counsels which pertain to those who *have arrived* at perfection, such as "to bless those that curse you."[65] The religious does not profess to observe these counsels. Rather he professes to observe those counsels that are instrumental in assisting him to arrive at perfection.[66]

With regard to those counsels which are consequent upon perfection a religious must intend to fulfill them and would act against this intention if he were to contemn them. In so doing he would commit a sin, not by reason of his omitting them but by reason of his contempt for them. In a similar way he is not bound to observe or perform all those things by which perfection can be reached, but only those that are definitely prescribed for him by the rule which he has professed.[67]

---

[63] II–II, Q. 186, a. 1, ad 4m.   [65] Lk. 6:27.   [67] II–II, Q. 186, a. 2.
[64] AAS 43 (1951), 26–36.   [66] II–II, Q. 182, a. 2.

Just as one who enters a school, let us say, a college or particularly a graduate school, does not profess to have knowledge, but rather declares his intention of studying to acquire this knowledge, so too one who enters the religious life does not profess to already have reached the perfection of Christian charity, but rather to strive to arrive there, to exercise himself in it, or in those things which serve as instruments to aid his quest.

Poverty

We have already seen that there is a perfection of divine love which is of counsel, and not of necessity for salvation, that is, that we should contemn those things which even though they be not opposed to the habitual presence of charity, still prevent us from the *actual* exercise of charity. It is more than clear that the human heart is attracted more intensely and completely to one object the more it is withdrawn from a multiplicity of desires. The more one is withdrawn from the consideration of or solicitude concerning temporal matters, the more perfectly will he be enabled to love God. Such a situation can be brought about by several practices. The first of these is the renunciation of external goods or the *practice of voluntary poverty*, as we have learned from our Lord Himself. His teaching has been constantly reechoed by the Fathers and theologians and the Church herself. It is the teaching of the Fathers and theologians.

The classic *scriptural* text used in order to show that voluntary poverty is the first of the means necessary in order for one to be placed in the state of perfection is found in St. Matthew: "If thou wilt be perfect, go, sell all that thou hast, and give to the poor, and thou shalt have treasure in heaven; and come follow me."[68] The young man in this gospel passage wished to have some assurance about his salvation, and for this reason he asked of Christ a sign or means by which he could be rather certain that he would be saved. As a rejoinder to the young man Christ first of all lays down or, rather, renews the obligation of the commandment of love, that of God and that of one's neighbor, which even though it is not found explicitly in the Decalogue, still is found in the Old Testament.[69] The reply of the youth was sincere. He had done all these things from his youth — the love of God, the honoring of his parents, and the love of his neighbor. This was why Christ loved the young man. Then He invited him to a perfection that exceeded that which is absolutely necessary for eternal life. If the youth would be content to have all his treasure, and so all his heart, only in heaven, then he would be fit to become a member of the inner circle of the Lord. The youth departed for the reason that he had many possessions and did not wish to give them up. On the occasion of

---

[68] Mt. 19:21. [69] Lev. 18:19; Deut. 6:5.

his departure, our Lord Himself mentioned that the possession of great wealth renders the attaining of heaven difficult, though not impossible. The Apostles were astonished at our Lord's reply, and wondered who, then, could be saved. Christ then went on to assure them that *humanly* speaking it would be exceedingly difficult for one who had great wealth to also have an efficacious desire for heaven that would offset these possessions. But He went on to explain that it is possible for grace to allow one to possess riches and wealth, and still loosen their grip on the heart.[70]

After this, following the account given by St. Matthew we are told that the reward promised by our Lord will be not only for the Apostles, but for all who having left all things and having detached themselves from them, give themselves over to the service of the Lord. In the new era, in the kingdom of heaven they occupy a special place, even though in this life their reward will be for the most part spiritual. One thing that is promised them is life everlasting.[71]

Before, in another passage,[72] He also mentioned the danger of riches in regard to the life which He had come to establish: "The cares of this world, and the deceitfulness of riches choked up the word and it became fruitless." The meaning of our Lord's words is clear. If we wish to attain to eternal life, it is more advantageous for us to renounce our possessions than to retain them.[73]

In the *early Church* we find that the earliest form of asceticism consisted especially in the practice of virginity for the sake of the Kingdom of God. Some kind of poverty was practiced, it is true, especially by way of alms to the poor, but the stark message of the Gospel did not receive a special kind of answer until the time of Antony.[74] The form of asceticism which he began was characterized primarily although not exclusively by the distribution of his goods to the poor. Soon it became the practice for all the desert spirituals to renounce all the goods and riches of this world as the first step in their peculiar spirituality. This renunciation of wealth was indispensable and allowed of no reserve. Moreover, it was characterized by a *spiritual joy* which was to find its most lyric presentation later on in the person of St. Francis of Assisi. Such spiritual joy was brought about by the *hope of heaven* or by the hope for treasures that could not be consumed, such that we can say that ultimately this

---

[70] *Catholic Commentary on Holy Scripture*, ed. B. Orchard, O.S.B. (New York: Nelson, 1953), p. 886.

[71] Cf. Mk. 10:17–31; Lk. 18:18–27.

[72] Mt. 13:22.

[73] *On the Perfection of the Spiritual Life*, Chap. 7; tr. *The Religious State*, by Fr. Proctor, O.P. (Westminster, Md.: The Newman Press, 1950), p. 21.

[74] Cf. *Vita Antonii*, PG 26, 835 ff.

formed the basis and proper motivation for the practice of poverty. To this trust in providence and hope for the reward of heaven there was joined a deep love for work which was often of an unprofitable kind.[75]

From a personal practice aimed at bringing out the perfection of hope and ultimately, of course, charity, the practice of poverty was soon transformed into a community affair especially with the spread of cenobiticism. As such it was meant to keep visible here on earth the practice of the early Church described in the Acts. This was true, certainly of St. Basil and those who followed his rule. We find that in his writings this saint enhanced the practice of poverty with a mystical note by which it became a kind of outward sign of that state of belonging to God, the true Lord and Master of the monastery. We might say that the characteristic notes of early poverty were the following: the desire for the highest perfection; the longing to establish an ideal society on earth which would be actuated by the purest form of fraternal charity, and show itself as an anticipation of our heavenly life.

This early ideal was preserved in Benedictine monasticism. For even though the rule itself very rarely mentions the words "poor" and "poverty," still the idea implied in evangelical poverty is capital to the Benedictine ideal. Upon profession the monk must once and for all strip himself of all his possessions, keeping back for himself nothing in this world. And the reason for his so doing was the same which motivated the early desert fathers and their groups: that they might truly seek God or the kingdom of heaven.[76] Common life for the most part formed the substance of the monk's practice of poverty but even in this Benedict kept to the earlier tradition: the objects possessed in common belonged to God and His worship and were considered as sacred things, so that their misuse would be considered something on the order of a sacrilege.[77]

With the arrival of the mendicant orders evangelical poverty, which had fallen into disgrace in so many monasteries of the time, was once more brought back to its full vigor. Yet the practice was much the same so far as the ideal was concerned. For it placed one in a state of continual dependence upon others and especially on the providence of God. Indeed we can say that Franciscan poverty brought out perhaps more clearly than ever before the very heart and core of all mysticism: the Allness of God and the nothingness and sinfulness of man.

With the coming of the Society of Jesus on the scene in the sixteenth century, once again the practice of poverty was aimed at the same ideal;

[75] Cf., e.g., the story of the Abbot Paul who continually made and unmade rush mats so as not to remain idle and yet not acquire remuneration! PL 73, 773.
[76] Cf. Chapter 58 of the Rule of St. Benedict.
[77] Cf. Chapter 31.

a personal and a communal asceticism ordered at bringing out the fullness of one's hope or trust and confidence in God, and ultimately the perfection of charity.[78]

The Church also has always looked upon this practice as essential for the constitution of the religious state. This is most clear from its having been included in the Code of Canon Law as one of the essential characteristics of any state of perfection which is to be classed among the canonical religious states of perfection.[79] The purpose for which it is to be practiced today as well as before has been very admirably pointed out by our late Holy Father Pope Pius XII in an address made to the General Congregation of the Society of Jesus:

> An unswerving observance of poverty should be one of the mainstays of a life devoted to the crucified Christ, since poverty was a thing so dear to the heart of your founder. And this poverty should not be one which merely excludes the independent use of temporal things, but rather one which is based on dependence and consists in the moderate use of temporal things and a lack of those conveniences which men living in the world may legitimately seek for their own. Certainly you will use for the greater glory of God those things which are helpful in your apostolic labors and which your superiors approve. But at the same time there are many things which are in no way necessary for your goal, things, rather, which are simply attractive; these you will be careful to deprive yourselves of so that the faithful may regard you as disciples of the poor Christ, and so that extra money may be saved and used in things that are useful for the salvation of souls and may not be squandered on luxuries. . . . As far as superfluities are concerned put them aside out of love for poverty and with that constant zeal for mortification in all things which is one of the marks of your Order. . . . Not in word alone, but also by example should Religious manifest a zeal for penance, without which there can be no hope of eternal salvation. . . .[80]

A similar thought was expressed by this same Pontiff in speaking to the members of the General Chapter of the Friars Minor in 1951:

> Poverty is of such a necessity and falls so much in line with the law of the gospel that a Christian would expose his eternal salvation to peril if he were not to respect it at least in his heart, and if he were not to detach his desires from the attraction of earthly pleasures. That is why it is necessary that there be in the Church those who would give a perfect example of this virtue to instruct and to form others. You are these men on condition that you do not depart from the old rule. Consequently, so that poverty may shine forth in your houses and your goods, do not touch earthly things except in fear and trembling and do not take undue pleasure in them but use them moderately according to the words of the poet: "One can live conveniently with little."[81] . . . The principal virtue which shone particu-

---

[78] Cf. Poverty, Religious Life Series (Westminster, Md.: The Newman Press, 1954), pp. 10–82.

[79] Cf. Canon 487.

[80] The Pope Speaks, 4 (1958), 451.

[81] Horace, Odes, Bk. II, xvi, 13.

larly in your founder was charity, seraphic charity. Ravished by it he walked the earth with a very light tread, and was carried away by the desire for heavenly good. Under the empire of this ardent charity he had for evangelical poverty, a remedy against all vices, such great veneration that in this great struggle he was victorious.[82]

But it remained for the reigning Pontiff, Pope John XXIII, to bring out the relationship of the counsels to Christian perfection in a most striking manner. This he did in an encyclical celebrating the centennial of the Curé of Ars:

> Even if Churchmen are not commanded to embrace these evangelical counsels by virtue of their clerical state, it still remains true that in their efforts to achieve holiness these counsels offer them and all of the faithful the surest road to the desired goal of Christian perfection. What a great consolation it is to us that at the present time many generous hearted priests are showing that they realize this; even though they belong to the diocesan clergy they have sought the help and aid of certain pious societies approved by Church authorities in order to find a quicker and easier way to move along the road to perfection. . . . The curé passed a life that was almost completely detached from the changeable, perishable goods of this world and his spirit was free and unencumbered by impediments of this kind so that it could always lie open to those who suffered from any kind of misery.[83]

Theologians likewise have attempted to show the place of voluntary poverty in relation to the perfection of charity. The general reason which most of them give is as follows, the religious state by definition is an exercise and a discipline for the attaining of perfect charity. For this, however, since charity consists in the love of God and the love of neighbor in and for God, whatever could serve as a hindrance in our reaching this goal ought to be set aside. Riches and the wealth of this world, or the possession of temporal goods, however, tends to absorb our attention, to such an extent that one does not easily give his mind and his heart over to the pursuit of divine things, or the search for God. For the attainment of the perfection of charity, then, the first foundation is that of voluntary poverty, whereby a person lives without property of his own, following the counsel given by our Lord Himself: "If thou wilt be perfect, go, sell what thou hast and give to the poor . . . and come follow me."[84]

As we can readily see, the reasoning given by theologians insists upon the negative aspect of the vow of poverty, that is, the detaching effect which it has. Too often in our asceticism of today this particular aspect of voluntary poverty has been placed in the background, so that the posi-

---

[82] May 23, 1951; cf. Qu'en pense l'église, documents pontificaux du regne de Pie XII, René Carpentier, S.J. (Paris: Bonne Presse, 1959), pp. 266–267.
[83] August 1, 1959; cf. The Pope Speaks, 6 (1959), 11–12.
[84] Mt. 19:21.

tive aspect might stand out more prominently. Such a presentation has many advantages and should be continued. But in an age in which the theology of original sin and the effects which it has left and is leaving on the soul is being pushed into the background (almost to the extent that there is a kind of a practical denial of its existence in human nature), it would also be very wise to place the negative aspect of poverty on a par with its positive aspect. There is always the danger that in reaction to perhaps an overemphasized presentation of one aspect of a matter, its other aspect will also be overemphasized. Any overemphasis, however, always brings about an impoverished vision. The truth of the matter lies somewhere in the middle. It would be unwise to insist so much upon either of the aspects of the counsel and the purpose of voluntary poverty as to neglect or play down its other aspect, because such a tendency in the practical order will always have its ramifications in the daily life of an individual.

In fact, we might say that it is only by insisting upon both aspects of the vows that a balanced asceticism can be ingrained in a person who undertakes the religious life from the very first years. The whole of our effort ought to be used in setting forth the whole purpose and the complete role of the vows in the attainment of Christian perfection.

So much could be done on this score today in our own country where the very idea of poverty and the lack of some material object is a kind of stigma. We seem to have forgotten that poverty was not meant merely to be embarrassing, as it often is, but it was meant to be crucifying. For the Lord Himself insists upon the fact that we must constantly practice self-denial, and in the Old Testament we read that "we have been chosen in the furnace of poverty."[85]

When the Angelic Doctor mentions the relation of poverty practiced by a religious to that practiced by a person in the world, he sets down its excellence in very clear language:

> The renouncement of one's own wealth is compared to almsgiving, as the universal to the particular, as the holocaust to the sacrifice. . . . For this reason St. Gregory mentions[86] that those who assist the needy with the things they possess, by their good deeds offer sacrifice, since they offer up something to God and keep something for themselves; but those who keep nothing for themselves offer a holocaust which is greater than a sacrifice.[87]

The very detachment which is practiced in and through the profession of voluntary poverty also admits of a positive action. For a sacrifice is not

---

[85] Is. 48:10.
[86] Hom. 8 in Ezech., Bk. II, PL 76, 1037.
[87] II–II, Q. 186, a. 3, ad 6.

merely a negation, but it is also, and necessarily, a consecration. So often we hear people consider this act to be unnatural, a kind of pathological self-mutilation; or we draw the conclusion that what is sacrificed must be of little value, that these persons who are called by God have received, in their grace of vocation, an understanding of the worthlessness and the very baseness of that which they give up. In fact, the notion of sacrifice, such as that is commonly understood among men, is one of negation and carries with it a kind of suggestion of compulsion, and extortion, destruction, and refusal of life. At most, they think of it merely in terms of a spiritual and mental exercise and discipline, assumed to train a strong will and bring about a self-control which tempers and fashions the natural instincts into a pliable instrument for the use of the spirit. All this is true, and we must never forget this aspect of the vows. But in the idea of holocaust there is something else that is also very important and, from many aspects, more important than the mere negative role which it plays — the offering of something good.

If we go back to the pagan concept of sacrifice, we see that it was a solemn affair characterized with a certain beauty and ceremony. For only something precious and good, something extraordinary, was offered in sacrifice — the choice, the rare, and, in general, the best. A sacrifice was for the ancients a gift, a gift that was chosen, precisely because it was *precious*. The ceremony itself was one of joy and accompanied by the singing, etc., of the persons who assisted at it. And this was true even when the sacrifice was most gruesome in our own thought, such as the sacrifice of children.

This note of sacrifice is also proper to the sacrifice of the Church, to that of the Old Testament and to that of the New Testament. The Church herself for the most part offers sacrifice with lights and song and amid the presence of incense and flowers, precisely, because sacrifice is a giving, a giving of something to God; for a sacrifice is something that should be given *only to God*. So often we have considered that what we give up through the vows is something that is evil, and that this giving up is of its very essence something painful. The inconsistency of this becomes evident only when we link up the gift given with the one to whom we give it. Since in this case it is God, the thing that we offer Him cannot be something that is evil, for that would be to insult Him. On the contrary, because a sacrifice is something that is given to God, or involves something which is offered to God, it must be of something that is good, of something that has a certain amount of value in the eyes of people. In giving this gift, the person must, of course, deprive himself of it; he must renounce it in giving it, and he finds this somewhat painful because he knows the value of it. The pain which he experiences, however, in sacrifice is something which accompanies the act, but it is not something which he considers to be the whole purpose of the action. The person sacrificing does not do so to hurt himself; he sacrifices to give, to offer, to please the receiver. The pain which accompanies the gift is, at most, the price of his precious gift, of his right to give; and he does not haggle about it or complain about the price. It would certainly be strange to think that a man should give something to God only to feel the pain involved, or that God, who is Love by Essence, should take pleasure in the gift only because it costs the giver pain. The pain connected with the giving is above all a sign; it is like the indicator on a balance, pointing to something else, to some measure or weight; and in the case of sacrifice offered to God, it indicates the love behind the gift, or the love which moved one to make the gift. Such a gift offered to God is a sign, a visible sign of something invisible, and it indicates the preciousness or importance or value of the invisible thing of which it is a sign. It has been said that "the gift, though in itself a mere 'thing,' has become wholly transparent, perfectly representative. All the love of the person, his prayer, this thanks, is put into the gift, and it is presented with one request, one repayment and one return — that God will not spurn it, that He will accept it, that it may find favor in His sight (as we see in the very prayer of the Offertory of the Mass). God does not need this sign; it is man who needs it to believe in his own love . . . (The creature tests and proves himself again and again, each time more severely, and when he triumphs achieves something for God.)"[88]

This positive approach to the religious vow of poverty or to the counsel of poverty can be more easily made when we present it from the viewpoint of the virtues. For, the act in and through which one vows poverty, or enters into the state of poverty, is an act of the virtue of liberality, that is, an act of the virtue of justice which indicates the firmness of will to use the things of this world well.[89] It is a virtue which manifests that the will of the individual is free from any undue or improper attachment to external goods. Thus the virtue serves to control the internal passions whereby one is affected by temporal goods and strongly inclined toward their possession.

The religious by professing the vow of poverty in the religious state practices the most perfect of the acts of liberality, because he gives away or renounces all possessions in effect for the love of God, as an act of

---

[88] *The Nature of Sanctity*, Ida F. Coudenhove (New York: Sheed and Ward, 1933), p. 72.
[89] *The Theology of Spiritual Guidance*, p. 129 ff.

sacrifice to Him. In the last analysis it is an act which manifests either the hope, the intensity of the person's hope, or the desire of the person to arrive at the perfection of the virtue of hope, which has as its motivating force or element the all-powerfulness of God, *Omnipotentia Dei auxilians* — "The omnipotence of God assisting one." Thus St. Peter recommended to the early Christians: "Throw back on him the burden of all your anxiety; he is concerned for you."[90] It is the omnipotence of God which becomes the security of the individual, and by having made the vow the religious begins his work of becoming assimilated to or like to God, the Father. Moreover, the corresponding gifts of the Holy Ghost — the gifts of Fear of the Lord, and of Knowledge — are allowed to develop and lead the soul to that perfection which is required for entrance into the Beatific Vision. "Suffer the little children to come unto me, for of such is the kingdom of heaven." Thus the *filial* characteristic is brought out more and more through the perfect and constant exercise of the virtue of liberality by the practice of poverty. And in the case of a religious, because it is assumed under vow, there is involved not merely an occasional act of the virtue but the *constant* and *continual* exercise of the virtue in the use of any material good or in the *denial* of such. Each act, whether of use or of denial, involves the virtue of religion, an act of devotion and of sacrifice, offered to God. In this way alone will the religious arrive at fulfilling the invitation given by God: "My Son, give me thy heart."[91] In so doing, one already, in a sense, enjoys the reward promised by our Lord: "Blessed are the poor in spirit, for theirs is the kingdom of heaven."[92] True poverty does not so much despise the goods which have been given up, but rather chooses a greater good, one that is capable of enriching it infinitely and eternally, the beatifying vision and possession of God Himself, through knowledge and love.

To view poverty (as well as the other vows) under this explanation is to give it its full import, both negative and positive: the positive, by showing that it is a gift, a precious gift, voluntarily surrendered to God as a sign of devotion and love for Him; the negative by showing that it denotes a certain painfulness. This latter element, however, pertains to poverty insofar as it exists in the present economy of redemption. As such it affords the soul an opportunity of sharing in the redemptive sacrifice of Christ. For all sacrifice in the Christian dispensation must, like the sacrifice of which it is a sign and a continuation and a participation, be redemptive. Thus the painful nature or element of the vow is something that is essential to it in the present economy of grace. To forget this is to forget one of the most disturbing of mysteries in the present economy

---

[90] 1 Pet. 5:7.   [91] Prov. 23:26.   [92] Mt. 5:3.

of salvation, the mystery of suffering, a mystery which is basically and radically one of love; for suffering involves misery, and misery is the object of mercy. Without misery God could never show us the boundlessness of his own mercy, nor could man imitate this manifestation of God's love for creatures.

Chastity

A glance at St. Thomas' treatment of the virtue of temperance will show that for him religious chastity differs from the chastity of other Christians in that it implies the *intention* of abstaining *forever* from venereal pleasure, and this *for the love of God*. In this he was merely following the early Church Fathers, who taught that voluntary chastity was not something to be praised in itself but only insofar as it was practiced out of love for God. Religious chastity adds something to what we might call common chastity, that is a greater amplitude, since it obliges one to abstain from all, even the legitimate and virtuous use of the procreative faculties. In fact, this intention of *perpetually abstaining*, is the act of *another virtue*, the virtue of virginity, which St. Thomas defines as the "purpose confirmed by vow of observing perpetual integrity."[93] The object of chastity in the case of a religious is *specifically different*, in the language of the theology of the virtues, from the object of common chastity. That is to say, it has a special excellence which common chastity lacks, an excellence by reason of which the person exercising this type of chastity is said to be living a life that is more angelic than human or, rather, more eschatological than earthly. For he lives already on earth that life of which our Lord spoke when He said they shall be like the angels in heaven. The formal and complementary element of virginity is the *firm proposal*, or the *decision confirmed by vow*, of abstaining *perpetually* from all pleasures of the flesh *for the sake of God*. It is this decision confirmed by vow which makes a special virtue of virginity.[94]

The existence of this evangelical counsel as a most excellent means to Christian perfection can easily be shown from Scripture and from the writings of the Fathers and theologians as well as from the teachings of the Church.

In general it may be said that the practice of virginity and celibacy was not the ideal during Old Testament times. It will suffice for us to mention only the example of Jepthe's daughter in the Book of Judges.[95] We are told there that she lamented her father's vow which reduced her to the state of virginity, and her reaction was to withdraw to the mountains to bewail her virginity. The reason for this abhorrence of the Israelites

---

[93] II–II, Q. 152, a. 3, ad 4.   [94] II–II, Q. 152, a. 1.   [95] 11:37–40.

for virginity seems to stem from their desire for or, rather, hope in the promised Messias. Every Jewish woman hoped to be favored with the blessing of God in the form of offspring, for it meant the possibility of her being the Mother of the promised Redeemer or Messias.

Fortunately, however, the Old Testament seems to present us with a preparation for and an anticipation of the teaching of our Lord and of St. Paul. And this we find in the person of Jeremias, the "virgin prophet" as he was called by Bossuet.[96] He is the first one to whom Scripture explicitly attributes celibacy, and indeed as a kind of state of life which he embraced. Some writers attribute this to Elias also, but the testimony of Scripture is purely negative, i.e., he is not mentioned as having a wife. In his confessions Jeremias speaks of his celibacy and explains the reasons which prompted him to embrace it. Basically, they might be indicated in a word which was later to be used by St. Paul and implied by our Lord Himself in recommending celibacy and virginity: *propter instantem necessitatem* — "because of, or in view of, the impending distress."[97] It might be said that celibacy was imposed progressively upon the prophet by circumstances — his isolation and the persecution that made him an outcast. Because of the Hebrew tendency to disregard secondary causes he attributed this vocation to celibacy as coming from God.[98]

There are two passages in the New Testament in which the excellence and superiority of virginity and celibacy over the institution of marriage are clearly indicated. One occurs in the Gospel of St. Matthew[99] and the other in Paul's First Epistle to the Corinthians.[100]

The passage in Matthew where our Lord speaks of the excellence of virginity and celibacy over matrimony occurs in one of the famous "divorce without the right to remarry" passages. It is His answer to the disciple's conclusion that if the institution of marriage is so strict that one is not permitted to remarry without committing adultery, it would seem that it is better not to marry at all — for fear that if your marriage does not work out, you must endure the union for life. The answer is rather categorical: "That conclusion (it is better for man not to marry at all) cannot be taken in by everyone, but only by those who have the gift. There are some eunuchs who were born so from the mother's womb, some were made so by men, and some have made themselves so for the love of the kingdom of God. Take this in you whose hearts are large enough for it."[101]

---

[96] Cf. *Méditations sur l'évangile*, 109th day.

[97] 1 Cor. 7:26; cf. Jer. 16:1-4.

[98] Cf. *The Prophetical Meaning of Celibacy*, L. Legrand, Scripture, 12 (1960), 97-101.   [100] Cf. 1 Cor. 7:1, 5-8, 25-38, *passim*.

[99] Cf. Mt. 19:10 ff.   [101] Mt. 19:11-12.

The text seems to be so clear as to need no prolonged commentary. After having indicated the nature and, in a sense, the greatness of the state of marriage he proceeds to indicate that there is a way even higher to procure, or to better assure oneself of, entrance into the kingdom of heaven, and that is through voluntary celibacy or virginity. But only those whose hearts are large enough to make this sacrifice, only those who are called to make it have the right to do so.[102] Our Lord not only permits men and women to follow the way of voluntary celibacy and virginity, but He clearly indicates that it is a better way for one who wishes to better assure himself of his salvation. In fact, it would seem that the only real reason for observing voluntary celibacy and virginity is for the sake of the kingdom of heaven. These last words indicate that there is question here of a spiritual chastity, that is, a chastity that is practiced at the dictate of the Spirit, because of a special gift from God. The reason for which one ought to embrace it is not purely philosophical; it is not to give oneself over to study or to the pursuit of any natural goal. The reason rather is spiritual — for the sake of the kingdom of God.[103]

Proceeding to the investigation of the passage on celibacy occurring in the First Epistle of Paul to the Corinthians, the same ideal is presented with further development of the motives moving one to practice this way of life. The Epistle was written in answer to various questions that had been addressed to the Apostle by the Church of Corinth. And among these questions was one concerning virgins or unmarried girls among the members of the Church of Corinth. While eventually dealing with the subject Paul took this occasion to treat the entire question of celibacy or virginity and marriage, showing the relation of one to the other in the Christian dispensation. The pertinent passages are as follows:

> As to the matters of which you wrote me it is an excellent thing for a man to remain unmarried. [Then the Apostle goes on to show that this might be difficult for some and these should marry rather than give themselves over to immorality.] To all who are unmarried and to widows I would say this: It is an excellent thing if they can remain single as I am. But if they cannot control themselves, let them marry. For it is better to marry than to be on fire with passion. . . . About unmarried women I have no command of the Lord to give you, but I will give you my opinion as that of one who by the Lord's mercy is trustworthy. I think that in view of the impending distress it is well for a person to remain as he is. Are you bound to a wife? Do not seek to be free. Are you free from a wife? Do not seek

102 L'Évangile selon saint Matthieu, trans. and notes by P. Benoit, O.P. (Paris: éd. du Cerf, 1950), p. 114.

103 Cf. "Évangile selon Matthieu," in La Sainte Bible, D. Buzy, S.C.J., Pirot-Clamer, IX, 1935, 251–252 note on this passage.

marriage. But if you marry you do not sin, and if a girl marries she does not sin. Yet those who marry will have *worldly troubles* and *I would spare you that.* I mean brethren, the appointed time has grown very short; from now on let those who have wives live as though they had none, and those who mourn as though they were not mourning, and those who rejoice as though they were not rejoicing and those who buy as though they had no goods, and those who deal with the world as though they had no dealings with it. *For the form of this world is passing away.*

I want you to be free from anxieties. The unmarried man is anxious about the affairs of the Lord, how to please the Lord, but the married man is anxious about worldly affairs how to please his wife, and *his interests are divided.* And the unmarried woman or girl is anxious *about the affairs of the Lord,* how to be holy in body and spirit; but the married woman is anxious about worldly affairs, how to please her husband. I say this for your own benefit, *not to lay any restraint upon you,* but to promote good order and to secure *your undivided attention to the Lord.* And if anyone considers that he is behaving unsuitably towards a girl who is in his charge, on the ground that she is now past her prime, and there is no way of avoiding it, why let him please himself. There is nothing sinful in it; let her marry. Whereas if a man remains fixed in his resolution and makes up his mind to keep the girl unwed, although there is no necessity for it, and he is free to choose for himself, such a man is *well advised.* Thus a man is *well advised to give* his ward *in marriage* and still *better advised not to give* her in marriage. As for a wife she is yoked to her husband as long as he lives; if her husband is dead she is free to marry anyone she will so long as she marries in the Lord. But *more blessed is she if she remains as she is* in my judgment; and I too claim to have the Spirit of God.[104]

There is very little doubt that Paul here follows exactly the teaching of our Lord in Matthew's Gospel, that is, that virginity or celibacy is a more excellent way of life than marriage, and that it is to be practiced for the Lord, with a view to giving oneself more undividedly to the things of the Lord or, as Christ said, to the things of the kingdom of heaven. But Paul adds another thought which is not found in the passage relating our Lord's discourse on this same subject, or perhaps three thoughts or reasons for the practice of chastity. To some these might appear to be different reasons. However, upon closer analysis they would be found to be basically the same as the one just given, but looked at from another aspect, and that is, eschatological, not in the final and terminative sense of that word, but in the actual working out of that covenant which leads directly to eternal life.

Catholic commentators see three reasons for the practice of detachment from the things of this world which is in a sense symbolized perfectly by abstension from marriage or by the practice of celibacy and virginity: (1) There is, first of all, the growing *hostility of the pagan world* which was

---

[104] 1 Cor. 7, *passim.*

being centered on the Christians at this precise time. Before this only the Jews had shown themselves opposed to this new sect. But at the time at which Paul wrote this opposition was coming from pagan sources as well. Since an unmarried person was better able to meet these persecutions and trials than one who was married, Paul pointed out the excellence of celibacy over marriage. (2) Another reason, perhaps even more prominent in the mind of the Apostle, was the *possibility of an early second coming of Christ.* While we do not have to suppose — in fact, it seems as though it would be rash for us to do so — that Paul was convinced of a very near second coming, still the possibility of such at any moment was always vividly before his mind. Nor do we have to suppose that the second coming was that of the universal judgment; the second coming that Paul may have had in mind was the particular judgment which comes to each Christian at the moment of his death. Since life is short, the stakes are high, why not put all our effort into attaining as perfect a disposition for this moment as we possibly can?[105] (3) The last reason given by the Apostle bears out the idea of the second coming being the particular judgment of each individual which for all of us is very near. He does not advise us to neglect earthly concerns. He advises us to *concentrate* on those which are eternal, and to keep those which are temporal in their proper place, *as of secondary although real interest.*

In the next few verses the Apostle goes on to apply these general ideas regarding detachment in the life of the Christian to the institution of marriage in particular. But he is careful to insist that this choice should be a *free* choice, and not one that is forced on anyone, that no one observe this practice out of fear: "I do not wish to lay any restraint on you" ("I would not hold you to a leash," as Msgr. Knox translates it). But he does strongly suggest it *so that our service of the Lord might not be divided.* We are to understand by this, of course, that these persons will most probably be or are most likely to be divided, or perhaps, that the institution of marriage *by its very nature* demands a division of our attention, at least, as it exists in the present economy after the Fall. However, the advice of the Apostle is not to be construed as a precept, but rather as a *counsel,* a counsel that is addressed to all who are in a position to accept it, that is, especially those who are not married — widows or virgins.

When we examine Paul's vocabulary we find that this *eschatological* interpretation is not something that is being read into the text. It is something that is really present. The words used, although they could be understood in a sense that is not eschatological, still by reason of their convergence and context make it quite clear that the Apostle is establishing

---
[105] Cf. vv. 29–31.

virginity in an eschatological background. And perhaps we might say that he like Jeremias is thinking of virginity *as a testimony that the last times have come*.[106]

In all this we are to consider not the question of the *time* of the Parousia, but rather of its *significance*, that is, an attitude of a mind that is truly Christian, that has truly adopted the mind of Christ. This is clearly brought out by John in his Apocalypse where he pictures to us the soul, or the whole Church — the Bride of Christ — as a bride waiting and expecting, looking forward to her meeting with her husband or to her marriage with the Lamb. Thus the soul or, in fact, the entire Church is according to the mind of John a virgin, one that is not yet married, but that is preparing for marriage, or at least for the final stage of a marriage that has already been begun during her earthly sojourn.[107] This interpretation seems to be borne out by recalling that for Paul also the incorporation of the Christian into Christ through Baptism already in a sense gave him *a share, a part* of eternal life. It was not just a ticket as it were to eternal life; it was already eternal life begun here below.[108]

It seems that we are correct, then, in concluding that for Paul as well as for the Christian Faith of which he is a witness appointed by God, virginity and celibacy are a *visible* sign or symbol or "sacrament" of an *internal* attitude that *ought* to characterize *every Christian*, since our incorporation into Christ demands that we no longer live as pertaining to this world, but with Christ who dwells in the glory of the Father. The virgin and the celibate in this sense are visible signs or symbols to the world that marriage with God is not only possible, but that it is obligatory since in heaven there will be no marriage or giving in marriage, since the Holy City, the New Jerusalem belongs to the Lamb, to Christ as His bride.[109]

This conclusion is not at all contradicted by Paul's eulogy or hymn concerning the beauty and grandeur of marriage.[110] Rather, it is brought out all the more strongly if we stop to consider this passage. Paul encourages those who are married in Christ, that is those who are members of the Church of Ephesus, to consider their marriage as reflecting, as being a "sacrament" or sign or symbol of the union existing between Christ and the Church. Lest they lose sight of the *Christian purpose and meaning of* marriage and fall to the level of mere carnal considerations, he shows them that an earthly marriage between man and woman is not just earthly. It is partially at least heavenly, since the husband is to look upon his wife

---

106 Cf. *The Prophetical Meaning of Celibacy*, L. Legrand, Scripture, 12 (1960), 102.
107 Cf. Apoc. 22:17 ff.; 19:7 ff.
108 Cf. Jn. 6:55 ff.; Ephes. 1:13; 4:30; 2 Cor. 1:21.
109 Apoc. 21:9.
110 Cf. Ephes. 5:25 ff.

not just as a woman, but as Christ looks upon the Church. And the woman is to look upon her husband not just as a man but, rather, as Christ. What married persons are to do through intermediaries, the celibate and the virgin do *directly* without the use of any intermediary and in that way they show that they are attempting the heroic, to live on earth as though they were already in vision, as though they were already celebrating that marriage which is not temporal or passing, but which is instantaneous and eternal.

Virginity and celibacy might be considered to be a special charisma that characterizes the New Covenant, that indicates and points constantly in a tangible and visible way to the superiority of the doctrine of Christ over that of the Old Law. For the law of Christ is written not on tablets of stone but rather on the hearts of those who believe. It is the law of the Spirit, breathing where He wills; it is the law of generosity, a generosity that imitates and reflects that of Him who gave birth to the Church, the virginal Eve who was to be His immaculate Bride until the consummation of the world. The observance of virginity or celibacy is *not* the result of an attitude of fear or panic at the approach of an imminent disaster. It is much more than this. It is an act of faith, of hope, and especially of love. It is an act of *faith* in the significance of the Paschal Mystery, which is the beginning of the end. It is an act of *hope*, because it can be undertaken only at the invitation of the Lord, upon whose strength and assistance those whose hearts have been made large enough depend. But it is above all an act of *love*, for it indicates a preference of love for the Person or Persons who alone can fulfill the hidden depths of the human heart's desire to love.

When we approach the *writings of the early Fathers* of the Church regarding virginity we find ourselves presented with the richest and perhaps fullest development of expression ever reached in regard to this institution.[111] Briefly we might say that any study of both the Latin and Greek Fathers regarding marriage and virginity would disclose that their teaching on these two states does not at all serve to oppose them to each other. Rather they overlap. Virginity goes all the way along a road on which marriage stops at the halfway mark. Consequently, virginity is situated along the same line of life as marriage though further on. As such it far transcends the earthly state of the *Magnum Sacramentum* spoken of by St. Paul. It attains *directly* what several Fathers predicated of Christ and the Church

---

[111] I will treat this subject at rather great length elsewhere. Cf. Ch. 5: "The Excellency of Consecrated and Dedicated Chastity Over Marriage," in *The Sacrament of Matrimony: A Dogmatic Study*. Also in this work in Ch. 5.

— the actual substance of eternal marriage. It is merely a formulation of the eschatological theology of the betrothal of the soul with the Word. Thus true marriage for the Fathers is the marriage of virgins with Christ, and our earthly marriage is merely a counterpart of this in the temporal and material order. To indicate by way of summary the thought of the Fathers regarding the excellence of virginity the following points might be set down.

The excellence of virginity lies in its very nature and not, as is true of marriage, in some good that lies beyond the union of the two persons. The state of virginity consecrated to God is a state of supreme perfection for it is a marriage that is eternally indissoluble since it is a marriage with God, or with Christ, the Son of God. An earthly marriage is one that is dissolved with death.[112]

Virginity is a state of perfect integrity since it puts a soul in possession of God. The circle of a human family is rather narrow and the joys of human love are ephemeral. The most perfect created spouse is still very limited in his perfection. But the divine Spouse Christ, true God and true Man, possesses every perfection, human, angelic, and divine.[113]

The essential work of virginity is the contemplation of God, a contemplation which is loving and solicitous for His welfare and His honor and glory. This work which might also be called communion with the Word of God or undivided service in His cause is that work which has been chosen for virgins by God Himself. And it is ordered toward the good of the soul and toward the good of the body, toward the contemplation of God rather than toward the propagation of the human race. The fruit of virginity is the possession of the Word of God who is the Word of Infinite Love.[114]

Virginal fruitfulness is the most perfect since it is, as it were, divine and eternal. The work and the happiness of virginity is to see God and to beget in one's soul the Word of God. Such, however, is also the divine fruitfulness of God the Father, which He communicates in some mysterious way to those whom He calls to the state of virginity. In this way the virgin is like Holy Mother the Church who engenders spiritually through the power of the Spirit of the Son of God, Christ, in the souls whom she

---

[112] Augustine, De S. Virginitate, 8, 11, 12, PL 40, 400 ff.; Ambrose, De Virginibus, I, 5, PL 16, 195; Gregory of Nyssa, De Virginitate, 3, PG 46, 334 C; Gregory of Nazienzen, Exhortatio ad Virgines, 1–6, PG 37, 632–634; In laudem virginitatis, PG 37, 537–538.

[113] Cf. Ambrose, De Virginibus, I, 5 ff., PL 16, 199–203.

[114] Cf. Augustine, De S. Virginitate, 27–29, PL 40, 410–412; De Bono Conjugali, 7, 8, PL 40, 379; Gregory of Nyssa, De Virginitate, 2, PG 46, 323, A, 414 D; Gregory of Nazienzen, In laudem virginitatis, PG 37, 521, 537–539.

begets unto eternal life. This is also the work of those called to this state. For by their prayers, their example, their devotion or devotedness, and their charity they beget the Son of God, Christ, in souls.[115] Thus those who embrace this way of life are said to have divine fruitfulness *in regard to the fruit produced* (the Son of God in souls);[116] *in regard to its principle* (the Father);[117] and *in regard to its vital moving force* (the Holy Ghost, or the Person of Love).[118]

In comparison with other states of men *virginity is to be placed at the summit* since it is the definitive perfection of man, or the perfection of man at the very term of his progress. It represents the highest possible union of man with God, that which the soul is meant to enjoy for all eternity where there will be neither marrying nor giving in marriage. In this sense *it is eschatological,* or an anticipation of the life of eternity here on earth.[119]

Virginity is an angelic virtue or an angelic way of life, since it is a property of incorruptible natures. Marriage has been given to man because he will die and therefore in order to insure the continuation of the race God has provided for this through marriage. The angel, and the virgin likewise, is delivered from this work since both in a sense pertain already to eternal life, to a life in which they are incorruptible.[120]

Virginity is the most striking example of Christ, the Mother of God and Holy Mother Church in this sense that virgins, those who have consecrated their lives to God are called into being in the Church in order to continue as it were the *exemplarity* and symbolism of Christ, Mary and the Church in a *concrete* and *tangible* sort of way.[121]

Virginity is a gift from God. Thus neither flesh and blood nor the will of man produces it. It is something which is so peculiarly divine that it must come from God Himself. Since it is integrity and holiness, it is something that is the property of God since He alone is perfect and holy by nature. Moreover, it is a gift which elevates man to a state of most

---

[115] Cf. esp. Augustine, *De S. Virginitate*, 3, 5, 6, 7, *PL* 40, 397 ff.; Gregory of Nyssa, *De Virgin.*, 2, *PG* 46, 323 A; 13, 379; Ambrose, *De Virginibus*, I, 6, *PL* 16, 197.

[116] Cf. Augustine, *De S. Virginitate*, 2, 3, 5, 6, 7, *PL* 397–400.

[117] Cf. Gregory of Nazienzen, *In laudem virginitatis*, *PG* 37, 538–552.

[118] Cf. Augustine, *De S. Virginitate*, 4, *PL* 40, 398, 401; Ambrose, *De Virginibus*, I, 3, 5, *PL* 16, 191 ff., 194 ff.; Gregory of Nazienzen, *In laudem virginitatis*, *PG* 37, 536 ff.

[119] Cf. Ambrose, *De Virginibus*, I, 3, *PL* 16, 191; Augustine, *De Bono Conjugali*, 2, *PL* 40, 373–378; *De S. Virginitate*, 13, *PL* 40, 401 ff.; Gregory of Nazienzen, *In laudem virginitatis*, *PG* 37, 523–525.

[120] Cf. Ambrose, *op. cit.*, I, 3, *PL* 16, 191 ff.; Gregory of Nyssa, *De Virginitate*, 13, *PG* 46, 379; Gregory of Nazienzen, *In laudem virginitatis*, *PG* 37, 533 ff.

[121] Cf. no. 115, immediately above.

intimate society or life or companionship with God. It is evident that the virgin enjoys very intimate relationships with the three divine Persons, Father, Son, and Holy Ghost, as we have seen above. [122]

All of the Fathers are unanimous in teaching that virginity is not a precept of the Lord. It is merely a counsel. Consequently, no one is obliged to embrace it (prescinding for the moment from the question of whether or not one who is called by God interiorly is obliged to follow this vocation). Marriage, although inferior to virginity, is not at all condemned, for such would be to go against the teaching of Scripture itself. Those to whom God has given the gift of chastity should prefer their blessing to marriage in such a way, however, that they may not consider marriage an evil. They are to "surmount it (marriage) as a hill of inferior blessing that they come to rest on the mountain of the greater blessing of continence."[123]

From all this it is clear that it is the unanimous teaching of the Fathers of the Church that virginity consecrated to God is superior to the state of marriage even though this latter be a sacrament of the Church. While we must admit that the sacramentality of Christian marriage was not understood in the precise sacramental language which we have today, still this would not at all interfere with our conclusion. The Fathers were acquainted with Christian marriage as such, and nonetheless considered chastity dedicated to God as a state far superior to that of this institution. It would perhaps, in our own day, be most wise for teachers and preachers to point this out occasionally to the faithful indicating to them the reasons just given as those which have been advanced by persons who are considered to be faithful witnesses not to a personal opinion, but rather to the teaching of our Lord and His Church.

Moreover, this teaching on the excellence of virginity over marriage has also been extended to the state of widowhood. Suffice it to quote the clear thought of Augustine on this matter: "For while either one is in error (to make nuptials equal to virginity, or to condemn marriage as an evil) these two errors in their overeagerness to avoid each other attack from opposite extremes since they have refused to cling to the middle position of truth in which both from reason and from the authority of the Holy Scriptures, we find that marriage is not sinful, yet we do not

---

[122] Cf. Gregory of Nyssa, De Virginitate, PG 46, 319–323; Augustine, De S. Virginitate, PL 40, 420; Gregory of Nazienzen, Prima Virgo est Sancta Trinitas, PG 37, 523 ff.; St. Ambrose, op. cit., I, 3, 5, PL 16, 191 ff., 194 ff.

[123] Augustine, De S. Virginitate, 14–18, PL 40, 402 ff.; Jerome, Letter 22, 18; Letter 50, 5; Letter 48, 2, PL 22, 405, 516, 494–495.

make it equal to the blessing either of virginal or even widowed continence."[124]

When we come to another of the sources — the proximate norm of our faith and belief — we find that the Church herself has not issued a large number of documents in regard to this question.

Perhaps one of the first documents indicating more than just the teaching of heads of the various and individual local Churches on our problem is that issued by the Council of Elvira (Granada) in Spain, in 300 or 303. Some of the legislation dealt with the conduct of unfaithful virgins. Canons 13 and 14 divided them into two categories: (1) consecrated virgins or those who have dedicated themselves to God and (2) others who had no special commitment to God. The former were considered to have incurred excommunication if they violated their promises. They could, of course, repent and if they remained faithful they could be reconciled before their death. If they did not, then they were to be considered as excluded forever. In the case of the other category, offenses against the moral law made them liable to five years of penance.

From this document it seems that we can clearly assert that in this area of the Church, a Council, at which many bishops assisted, declared officially that virginal consecration involved entrance into a category of persons. Moreover, the Canons indicate that the Church herself had some kind of responsibility over a group of consecrated virgins and that their state was superior to that of matrimony and subject to disciplinary sanctions which were juridically laid down.

Later on, in the fifth century, there existed rituals for the consecration of virgins, rituals of a more or less fixed nature, proper for the occasion. While some formula of consecration or other was used earlier (as, for example, we know from Ambrose's report on the consecration of his sister Marcellina by Pope Liberius in 353) still it does not seem that any definitive form was had at this time. The forms which we have knowledge of have come from about the time of Pope Leo the Great (fifth century). In them the consecration of virgins borrows all its emphasis from the nuptial rite. A restrained prayer for the grace of fidelity is followed by the formula of blessing which is a marvelous act of homage to the Word Incarnate, Friend and Model of pure souls, and Bridegroom of virgins.

It should not come as too much of a shock, then, that the Council of Trent in treating of the Sacrament of Matrimony specifically touched upon its relationship with chastity. This it did in connection with Holy

---

[124] De Sancta Virginitate, 19, PL 40, 405.

Orders and religious profession. The teaching of the Fathers can be found stated in the following two canons:

> Can. 9: If anyone says that clerics in sacred Orders or regular clergy who have made solemn profession of chastity can contract marriage and that the contract is valid despite the law of the Church and their vow; and that the opposite opinion is nothing but a condemnation of marriage; or if anyone says that all those who feel that they do not have the gift of chastity even if they vowed it can contract marriage; let him be anathema. For God does not deny that gift to those who petition it in a correct manner nor does he permit us to be tempted beyond our strength.[125]

> Can. 10: If anyone says that the marriage state is to be preferred to the state of virginity or of celibacy and that it is not better and holier to remain in virginity or celibacy than to be joined in marriage:[126] let him be anathema.[127]

It is clear, then, that it is a *dogma of our faith* that celibacy or virginity vowed and consecrated to God is a better way of life and a holier way of life (objectively speaking, of course) than matrimony. Moreover, the Fathers clearly indicate that solemn profession of chastity is a diriment impediment to marriage, but they also indicate that in so stating they *do not at all wish to declare that this is to be considered as a condemnation of marriage.*

It seems that this subject of the superiority of virginity and celibacy over marriage was not challenged to the extent that it drew any great number of statements and declarations from the magisterium — until rather recently. With the reign of Pius XII, however, this topic was the subject of several pronouncements and was included in many others. Since I will treat of this at greater length elsewhere,[127a] it will be sufficient for me to give merely the conclusions of these addresses:

1. Virginity or celibacy is more excellent than marriage. This is a *dogma of faith.*
2. The reasons for which it is embraced are *to think of the Lord, to be more entirely devoted to His service or to the good of our neighbor, to realize more numerous advantages for advancement in the spiritual life.* The underlying motive for all this is a *preference of love.* For it is out of love for Christ that one undertakes this way of life.
3. *Perfect chastity effects a spiritual marriage between the soul and Christ.*
4. *Perfect chastity deserves the name of the angelic virtue* since it is an eschatological state or way of life anticipating here on earth the life that all of us will be obliged (and privileged) to live in eternity. Thus those who have vowed their chastity to God are *signs or images of the* perfect integrity of the union between Christ and the Church.

---

[125] Denz. 979.
[126] Cf. Mt. 19:11 ff.; 1 Cor. 7:25 ff., 38, 40.

[127] Denz. 980.
[127a] Cf. note 111.

5. While the state of perfect chastity is not a sacrament and does not confer grace *ex opere operato*, still it does afford those who embrace it something spiritual which far exceeds the mutual helps which married persons confer upon each other. The personality of those who take this way of life upon themselves does not at all suffer harm; rather it gains immensely. For God shares with these persons His own divine life in a more abundant manner.

6. The *fruits* of virginity and celibacy are many, especially with regard to the *sanctification of souls*. Thus, far from abdicating any fatherhood or motherhood, those who embrace this way of life increase it immensely, since they beget not for an earthly and transitory sort of life but for the heavenly and eternal one. A deeper faith and holiness and the wonderful example which they afford to the whole Church are likewise to be enumerated among the fruits arising from this practice.

7. *Priests are to encourage vocations* to these walks of life, and *parents are also to willingly offer* to the service of God those of their sons and daughters who feel called to it. They are *not to interfere* with a vocation in any way but consider it a great honor to see their son elevated to the priesthood or their daughter consecrate her life to God.

8. Although *marriage is inferior* to dedicated chastity, we are *not to conclude that marriage is an evil*. Nor is virginity or chastity necessary for Christian perfection. Holiness of life can be attained even without chastity that is consecrated to God. Marriage, therefore, is a good, but a lesser good than the life of chastity consecrated to God.

9. Virginity is something that is *not of precept but rather of counsel*. Hence it demands *free choice* and *supernatural help* and assistance from God.[128]

The reasoning often employed by theologians is again taken from the negative aspect of the vows. The religious state requires the removal of whatever prevents man from devoting himself entirely to God's service. The use of the procreative faculties, however, prevents the mind from giving itself entirely to the service of God and this for two reasons. First, the strong pleasure connected with its use, and frequent repetition increases concupiscence. Thus it draws the mind from the consideration of divine things. Second, it involves man in solicitude for the care of his family and temporalities which serve for their upkeep, in accordance with the words of St. Paul in the epistle which we quoted previously. Therefore, perpetual continence, as well as voluntary poverty, is requisite for reli-

---

[128] Cf. the following pertinent documents: *Women of Catholic Action*, October 21, 1945, in *The Teachings of Pope Pius XII*, ed. by M. Chinigo, pp. 62–63; Apostolic Constitution, *Sponsa Christi*, AAS 43 (1951), 5 ff.; (for tr., cf. *Canon Law Digest*, III, p. 221 ff.); *Sacra Virginitas*, AAS 46 (1954), 161 ff.; *Sacra Virginitas*, AAS 46 (1954), 161 ff. (cf. NCWC ed., Washington, D. C.; *Address on Marriage and Parenthood*, May 19, 1956 (*The Pope Speaks*, 3 [1956], 196); *Address to Nursing Sisters*, April 25, 1957 (*The Pope Speaks*, 4 [1957], 136–137); *The Young Woman's Calling*, July 13, 1958 (*The Pope Speaks*, 4 [1958], 97).

gious perfection. "Just as Vigilantius was condemned for equating riches to poverty, so was Jovinian condemned for equating marriage to virginity," St. Thomas remarks.

While marriage is not to be considered evil in any sense of the term, still it is not so excellent as perpetual chastity undertaken for the sake of the service of God, of dedicating oneself completely to the works of the Lord. There is a difficulty involved in its practice, as is very clear from Scripture itself. Thus we read that it is a *gift* of God. "I knew that I could not be continent unless God gave it to me."[129] Moreover, both St. Paul and our Lord mentioned this in the texts cited above — that each one has received his proper gift from the Lord, and that only those whose hearts were large enough could take this counsel in. Any gift, as we know, is something that comes to us from the Father of all gifts, God Himself. Since the firm purpose of perpetual continence is a special gift that is given to us or suggested to us efficaciously by God, it manifests a special concern or love on His part for us. For no one is said to be better than another unless he shall have received a greater good than the other has received.[130]

Voluntary chastity would not have been asked of man by the Lord if man had not fallen into original sin. This St. Thomas teaches very clearly.[131] But because of original sin and the disorder which is set up in our tendencies, it safeguards and fosters the movement of the mind to God. Throughout all his parallel works on this subject St. Thomas comes back to this aspect of the practice of chastity. In order to preserve it, he writes in his "On the Perfection of the Spiritual Life," we must avoid all that might prove an obstacle to it. There are three principal difficulties to continence. The first arises from the body, the second from the mind, and the third from external circumstances, whether they be persons or things.

The *body* is an obstacle to continence, for concupiscence is the law of the flesh. The more the flesh is pampered by superabundance of food and by effeminacy of life, the more will its concupiscence increase. He who desires to undertake a life of continence must chastise his flesh, by abstension from pleasure, and by fasts, vigils, and such exercises. Another obstacle to continence arises also from the *mind*, if we dwell on unchaste thoughts. The first and chief remedy is to keep the mind busied in prayer and in the consideration of divine things. The second remedy is to study Scripture. For as St. Jerome mentions: "love the study of Holy Writ and thou shalt not love the vices of the flesh." The third preservative is to occupy the mind with good thoughts. Thus St. John Chrysostom remarked

---

[129] Wisd. 8:21.   [130] Cf. I, Q. 20, aa. 3–4.   [131] Cf. Q. 98, a. 2, ad 3m.

that physical mutilation is not so great a curb to temptation and such a source of peace of mind as is the habit of bridling the thoughts. The fourth help to chastity is to shun idleness and to engage in bodily toil. A fifth remedy lies in a certain kind of mental disquietude. St. Jerome relates that in a certain congregation of cenobites, a young man dwelt who could not by means of fasting, or any laborious work free himself from temptations of the flesh. The superior of the monastery, seeing that the youth was on the point of giving up, adopted the following means. He commanded one of the most discreet of the Fathers to constantly upbraid the young man, to load him with insults and reproach, and after treating him thus to lodge complaints against him with the superior. Witnesses were called in to take the part of the elder Father. This was continued for a year. Then the superior questioned the youth. "Father," he said, "I am scarcely permitted to live, how could I be inclined to sin."

The third danger, seen above, arises from extrinsic circumstances, persons, etc. For this reason there must be the avoidance of unnecessary, useless contact with others of the opposite sex. This Pius XII also insisted on in his *Menti Nostrae* written for priests.

There is, however, another side to the presentation of religious chastity, the positive side. The reason for which one undertakes this is to devote oneself more completely to the things of God. It is a consecration or a setting aside of something good and precious to offer as a pleasing gift to one whom we love. What was mentioned previously concerning the true meaning of sacrifice can also (one might say, especially) be brought into the presentation of the beauty of religious chastity. It is an act of offering, of immolation of one of the best things that we have, and it is only this that makes it acceptable to God. For if it were not a good, one of the most precious goods that we have, it would not be worth offering to God. The *positive* aims of religious chastity ought to be explained whenever treating of the various states of life. These have already been given elsewhere,[132] so here it will suffice merely to recall them briefly.

Chastity effects:

Freedom of spirit: for it establishes the whole person in a quest for God.

The closest possible union with God: for the union of the soul with God is something like that of man and wife. It is through this separation, which is first of all a dedication and consecration to God, that one gives to Him complete determination and disposal of one's body for the good of the Church. For a man who dedicates himself to the service of God through his vow of chastity there is signified a second baptism, death to

---

[132] Cf. *The Theology of Spiritual Guidance,* p. 167 ff.

self and sin and resurrection in and unto Christ. For a woman, through the assumption of this vow, there is signified a spiritual marriage with the Son of God, a life of the closest possible union with Christ, a life with God. In her the signification is much more positive and clear than in the case of the man.

A *holocaustal offering:* just as we saw with regard to the counsel of poverty, the sacrifice involved in chastity is also holocaustal, that is, it is a complete sacrifice in which not merely a part of a gift is offered to God, and set aside and consecrated, but the whole gift is surrendered to Him. In the sacrifices of the Old Testament, one thing very noticeable is that God always demanded that only that which was pure and undefiled be offered and set aside for sacrifice — the first fruits of the field, an unblemished animal, a turtledove — something known, for its innocence and purity. The whole of the tradition of the Church has shown us God's preference for innocence and purity as having something that is more than pleasing to Him. We find this personalized in the Mother of God, St. John the Baptist, St. Joseph, and St. John. Thus St. Ambrose wrote concerning chastity: "You have heard parents, that a virgin is a gift of God, the oblation of parents, the priesthood of chastity. The virgin is a mother's victim by whose daily sacrifice the divine anger is appeased."[133] St. Paul mentioned something similar concerning the offering of Christ on the Cross.[134] Consecrated chastity continues to show in a most visible manner the innocence involved in the sacrifice of Christ. In order that this aspect of His sacrifice might be visibly continued and kept present before the eyes of men reminding them that there is another world and other realities, divine and eternal, the institution of virginity was inaugurated by Christ in the New Law. It is not merely something that pertains to the realm of the individual, although it is this — the individual's consecration

---

[133] *De Virginibus,* Bk. I, Chap. 7, n. 32, *PL* 16, 198.

[134] Cf. "The blood of bulls and goats, the ashes of a heifer sprinkled over men defiled, has the power to hallow them for every purpose of outward purification; and shall not the blood of Christ who offered himself through the Holy Spirit as a victim unblemished in God's sight purify our consciences, and set them free from lifeless observances to serve the living God? Thus through his intervention a new covenant has been bequeathed to us, a death must follow to atone for all our transgressions under the old covenant, and then the destined heirs were to obtain forever, their promised inheritance. Where a bequest is concerned it is necessary that there be the death of the testator; for a will has no force while the testator is alive. Thus the Old Testament needed blood for its inauguration . . . and the law enjoins that blood shall be used in almost every act of purification; unless blood is shed, there can be no remission of sins. And if such purification was needed for what was but a representation of the heavenly world, the heavenly world itself will need sacrifices more availing still." Hebr. 9:13 ff.

to God — but it is also, at the same time, social, the holocaust of the people, the collectivity, before God.[135]

The perfection of love: this stems from the very purpose for which the vow or the counsel is embraced. For the end of chastity is the pursuit of charity, or of divine love, which is the love of God and the love of neighbor. Religious chastity although by its very nature it aims at reaching the perfection of charity and is undertaken as a personal act of asceticism, still has its repercussions in the social order of the Church. The person who embraces chastity learns to love the world of souls with a selfless and impersonal love one which bears the mark of the personal love of Christ and Mary. Thus one's love is not annihilated by following the counsel of chastity; rather it is brought to its highest development, and becomes universal and all-embracing.

Someone has said that coldness of heart is no more the way to God than cowardliness. In fact, we might say that if we examine the lives of the saints we shall discover that the capacity for love is the only indispensible natural sign or foundation for holiness. A saint need not be wise or learned or even highly gifted to become holy, but he must be one who can love God and man. He must possess the power and the impetus to be able to forget himself for another's sake. Since a vocation to the religious life or to the priesthood is the invitation of God to seek the perfection of charity and love, then we might safely say that within the framework of this vocation, there is also given the power to love which is so important for the growth of the Church.

Obedience

Obedience likewise belongs to the perfection of the religious state. It is a virtue by which one is inclined to submit to the authority of another, precisely insofar as this authority is had by the other from God. The superiority of one will over another comes not from the fact that this person has more talent than another, but from divine determination, by reason of some delegation on the part of God. We might define obedience as a permanent disposition or quality or habit, by which one is rendered capable of submitting to a higher authority, in regard to those things in which this will has authority over us, an authority which shares in the authority of God and which has at heart the interests of the common good. By obedience a person either by some circumstance or voluntarily makes over to another person's will the service of his own.

---

[135] Cf. *The Cloister and the World,* Ida F. Coudenhove (New York: Sheed and Ward, 1936), p. 39 ff.

The relation of this practice or observance to religious perfection can be shown to be the teaching of Scripture, the Fathers, of theologians and the magisterium of the Church.

Our Lord Himself manifested the excellence of obedience on several occasions. Thus, for example, when speaking to the rich young man who wished to live the perfect life, He mentioned that he should go sell all that he had, and then come back and follow Him.[136] This injunction, or rather, counsel, on the part of our Lord, clearly indicates that the selling of what we might have does not constitute us in the state of perfection, unless there be joined to it the following of Christ, the will to go where Christ might wish to send us. The following of Christ demands the imitation of Christ. But among the things which are most remarkable and most mysterious in Christ is the perfect obedience which He displayed toward His Father. For it is this which is commended most of all in Him: "He became obedient even to the death of the cross."[137]

Again in this same Gospel we see Him counseling those who wished to follow Him to take up their cross, deny themselves, and follow Him.[138] Here we have the counsel of Christ to follow Him, wherever that may take us, and in whatever He might command or ask us to do.

In these particular texts the excellence of obedience is insinuated. There are many other texts, however, in which the obedience of Christ is commended and held up as a model of conduct for ourselves. Thus in the Epistle to the Romans Paul commends obedience to the lawful rulers of the state.[139] Likewise in the Epistle to the Ephesians He commends this same virtue and practice.[140] It is in the Epistle to the Hebrews, however, where the inspired author signifies the sublimity of obedience on the part of Christ.[141] In this passage we find him describing the announcement of Christ that He had come to abolish the sacrifices of every sort which prevailed under the Old Dispensation, and that He was replacing them by another, that of His own sacrificial obedience even unto death. Thus he speaks of Christ coming into the world with the words of the psalm on His lips: "See then I said, I am coming to fulfill what is written of me, where the book lies unrolled; to do thy will, O my God."[142]

When we come to the *historical* appraisal of the place obedience occupied in the thought of the early Christians we find that it has always been regarded as an essential to reaching Christian perfection. In the eyes of the Fathers of the desert, for example, obedience was one piece in the multitude of things which the ascetic had to bring with him in leaving

---

[136] Cf. Mt. 19:21.   [139] Cf. Rom. 13:1 ff.   [142] Ps. 39:7–9.
[137] Phil. 2:8.   [140] Cf. Ephes. 6:1 ff.
[138] Cf. Mt. 16:24.   [141] Cf. Hebr. 10:5 ff.

the world to test his courage and strength against the temptations of the desert. The heart of man was so contaminated by concupiscences of various kinds that he would be rash if in attempting to reach perfection he did not seek and rely on direction in a spirit of humility. Thus, obedience for these men was the corollary of a frank soul testifying to his confidence in his spiritual father or master from whom he sought advice.[143] In these small groups following the teaching of a master, obedience was not regulated by any positive institution or organic legislation as it is today. It was an element of interior perfection and could almost have been reduced to the practice of humility. Death of self-will was part of the overall ascetical program which anyone embraced who entered upon this life.

At this time obedience began to take on an ever greater preeminence in striving after perfection, with the result that the cenobitical life became more esteemed than the eremitical.[144] Certainly since the time of the rule of St. Pachomius, the very essence of the religious life, as it were, has been obedience. But we must note that these early cenobites always saw obedience in its proper perspective, as a means to the perfection of charity and, therefore, inferior to it.

When we come to examine the *motive* underlying the practice of obedience, we find that it was the same for all the early cenobites and for the monks that followed them. The example of the Redeemer and of His sacrifice is considered to be the essential motive of the monk's obedience. This practice, however, was always referred or related to humility, this latter being, as it were, the touchstone of the former.

From the juridical and moral viewpoint it is difficult to say whether the first cenobites were regarded as having vowed obedience to a spiritual father or not. From all the documentary evidence at our disposal it seems as though the practice of vowing obedience came to the fore only with the arrival of St. Benedict on the monastic scene. Nonetheless, for the early cenobites no less than for the later monks of the West, the practice of obedience always remained fundamental and basic in any common and safe pursuit or quest after Christian perfection. It was always regarded as the supreme instrument in the attaining of charity. Consequently, we must conclude that the basic elements which ought to mark even the contemporary practice of obedience, the love of Christ, the following of His obedience, and the practice of faith and humility form, as it were, the very heart and core of this same practice as we find it presented to us in the writings of the early Fathers and Church legislators. The one difference, and it is in some respects rather extensive, between the practice of obedi-

---

[143] Cf. *Conferences of Cassian*, Col. II, 11; *Dict. de Spiritualité*, art. "Asceticism," p. 245.   [144] Cf. Cassian, 19th Conference, Rule of St. Basil, PG 31, 933.

ence in these early times and that prevalent today is the functional character of the latter and all that this implies. But to undertake an exposition of this would go far beyond the scope of the present considerations.[145]

That obedience pertains to the religious life has been constantly maintained throughout the history of the Church and in her *legislation and pronouncements* concerning the religious life. We find the Code of Canon Law stating explicitly that this counsel must be taken under vow if one is to be considered a member of the canonical religious state of perfection.[146] Its relationship to Christian perfection has not been questioned and so has not been extensively treated in papal documents. This was left to treatises on the spiritual life. Recently, however, this relationship has been taken up due to objections that have been raised against the so-called traditional practice of religious obedience. Only recently Pius XII in several addresses felt the necessity of indicating the Church's position in this regard:

> If the number of candidates wishing to enter the enclosed garden of the religious life is diminishing especially among young women, the reason very frequently is that they find it too difficult to divest themselves of their own judgment and surrender their freedom of action as the very nature of the vow demands. Indeed some praise as the real peak of moral perfection, not the surrender of liberty for the love of Christ, but the curbing of such surrender. The norm, therefore, to be preferred in the formation of a just and holy person would seem to be this; restrict liberty only where necessary, otherwise give liberty free rein as far as possible.
>
> We by-pass the question whether this new foundation on which some are trying to erect the edifice of sanctity will be as solid and effective in supporting and augmenting the apostolic work of the Church as was the one which through fifteen hundred years has been provided by that ancient rule of obedience undertaken for the love of Christ. What is now of supreme importance is to examine this proposal thoroughly to disclose what lies concealed beneath the surface. This opinion if carefully considered not only fails to appreciate the nature of the evangelical counsel, but it somehow twists it to a meaning in accord with its theory. No one is obliged to choose for himself the counsel of perfect obedience which essentially is a rule of life which surrenders the control of his own will, no one, we repeat, be it an individual or a group. They can if they wish conform their will to this new rule. But words must be understood and accepted according to their obvious meaning and if this norm is compared with the vow of obedience it surely does not possess the same supreme value nor is it an adequate expression of the wonderful example recorded in Holy Scripture.[147] "He humbled Himself becoming obedient even unto death."[148]

---

145 Cf. *The Religious Vocation*, J. Leclercq, p. 128 ff.; *Obedience*, Religious Life Series, III (Westminster, Md.: The Newman Press, 1953), p. 50 ff.

146 Cf. Canon 487.

147 Phil. 2:8.

148 *Annus Sacer*, December 8, 1950, AAS 43 (1951), 31. Eng. tr. *The States of Perfection*, ed. Gaston Courtois (Dublin: Gill & Son, Ltd., 1961), pp. 178–179.

In a similar manner seven years later this same Pontiff spoke against those who maintain that the religious state, especially by reason of the practice of obedience which it demands, acts as an obstacle to the harmonious development of the human personality and gives rise to a certain infantilism. He wrote at that time:

> The Church has always regarded obedience as a means to lead man to God. Because the motive which inspires it is that of union with God and because it is ordered ultimately to the increase of charity, the superior can never be regarded as an obstacle placed between the inferior and God and turning to his own advantage homage or reverence addressed to God alone. The superior cannot command except in the name of the Lord and in virtue of those powers of his charge. And the subject ought not obey except out of love for Christ and not for motives of utility and convenience let alone by pure constraint. Only in this way will he conserve in the most complete submission the joyful indifference of one who ratifies by the concrete acceptance of each day the total gift of oneself to our only Master.[149]

Here again we are presented with the traditional teaching of our Lord: obedience is one of the basic and fundamental means which lie at our disposal in our quest for the perfection of charity, since it imitates the wholehearted obedience of Christ who became obedient even to the death of the Cross.

Theologians, generally speaking, still advance among many reasons, the basic one given by St. Thomas in reference to the same problem: the relationship of the practice of obedience to Christian perfection. The religious state is an exercise or a school or a discipline for tending to perfection. For persons tending to perfection, or those who are being instructed or exercised in order to attain an end, it is only right that they follow the direction of someone under whose control they are instructed or exercised so as to attain that end as disciples under a master. For this reason, religious need to be placed under the instruction and command of someone as regards things pertaining to the religious life. Thus it has been said that the monastic life denotes subjection and discipleship. And this, of course, comes about by one's being subject to another's command and instruction through obedience.[150]

It is interesting to note that regarding the counsel of obedience, St. Thomas does not take a negative approach, that is, that it is a denial of the most precious thing that one has, but rather a kind of a positive approach. This he does by viewing the religious life as a school of perfection. One entering the religious life does so in order to reach perfection. For this reason he places himself under a master, who can lead him or instruct

---

[149] *AAS* 50 (1958), 41. Eng. tr. *The States of Perfection*, p. 313.
[150] Cf. II–II, Q. 186, a. 5.

him in his pursuit. In other places, however, he does approach obedience from the negative side, that is, as an act of self-denial, and of abnegation, by which one yields the most precious thing that he has to another, his own will.

Today more than ever before, a strict theological approach to the practice of religious obedience is most important. It is only on condition that a religious understand and learn to discipline himself in the practice of this counsel and virtue such as he has it in the religious life, that he will reap from this life the merit and the peace of spirit which he seeks in entering a religious community. Unless both aspects involved in religious obedience are presented to those in formation, and some, at least general, idea to those who are desirous of entering a religious community, sometimes difficulties can come up later on in life. Unless true convictions are generated in the early formation, and unless the habit of obedience is exercised continually, a young religious could very easily go through years of the religious life, "following the crowd," without any conviction, and without any real merit accruing to him from the practice.

Since these theological aspects of religious obedience have already been treated at length in another work[151] it will be sufficient here merely to recall some of the main points:

It adds greater amplitude to the virtue of obedience, for one becomes obliged to follow the will of another in more things than he would be obliged if he had not taken the vow. Thus St. Thomas writes in the present article: "The vow of obedience taken by religious, extends to the disposition of a man's whole life, and in this way it has a certain universality, although it does not extend to all individual acts. For some of these do not belong to religion, through not being of those things that concern the love of God and of our neighbor, such as rubbing one's beard, lifting a stick from the ground, and so forth, which do not come under religious obedience. Some acts are also contrary to religion."[152]

The end to which superiors of a religious community are to lead their subjects is different from that to which a natural society intends to lead its subjects. For in the case of the former, the end is intimate union with God through the perfection of charity. Moreover, a religious is more certain of doing God's will under obedience than in any other way. For the certitude of faith teaches us that obedience to a lawfully constituted representative of God in the society which we call the Church puts us into more immediate contact with the will of God in our regard than any other kind of obedience. There can be nothing truer than to think of religious

---

151 Cf. The Theology of Spiritual Guidance, p. 123 ff.
152 II–II, Q. 186, a. 5, ad 4.

superiors in the same light as we would the Eucharistic species. For although materially and visibly superiors seem so human and fallible (and are so oftentimes) still *as far as we are concerned*, they represent God and His will for us immediately. Considering the negative aspect of obedience, which is to divest oneself of all self-will, we can say that the concrete person and the will of this or that person is the thing to which one submits oneself. And we can say that if one is to draw the *full fruit* of obedience *in the way of renunciation*, then it is to a concrete will that he must subject himself.[153] It is for this reason that religious superiors would not be wise in giving up a traditional practice in regard to obedience, that is, of not always giving a reason for asking something of a subject. When reasons are always given, obedience can and usually will ultimately be performed out of mere natural motives. While we ought to remember that obedience flourishes most perfectly in a family atmosphere, still this does not mean that a reason must be given or even ought to be given for sending one about this or that task or duty.

For this reason we ought to note that the modern craze for efficiency is an ever present danger to the spiritual life of religious. Their activities are increasingly governed by other people who do not share their life or ideals — educational authorities, government officials, the parents of children, doctors and patients in hospitals, and so on. Because we wish to see our works efficient and acceptable to secular interests which largely control funds, and in the face of almost cutthroat competition even among Catholics in hospital work or in teaching, we often adopt a short-term and shortsighted policy which gets work done but merely through appealing to human motives. The rule to follow on this is "Let no one in the monastery be troubled for this is the house of God and the family of God. There are times when the preservation of this peace will require a file to take off the rough edges and not merely a sponge. But always be careful that in scraping off the rust, you do not break the vessel and cut through it."

Religious obedience in comparison with common obedience is like the offering of a *holocaust* compared with a sacrifice. This we have already seen in regard to the other counsels taken under vow in a religious community. It is the sacrifice of the *whole* and not merely of a *part*. Through the vow of obedience one offers to God the complete good of the soul, for by the vow he offers to God his own will by which he makes use of all the faculties and habits of the soul. It is precisely because this vow touches the will of man that it is the *perfect instrument of charity*, for it puts us into immediate contact with the will of God. It is the most perfect means

---

[153] Cf. M. Nicolas, O.P., *Religious Sisters*, Religious Life Series, I, p. 70.

of putting one's will in direct contact with that of God, and of conforming one's will with that of God. And we know that to love God is not merely to give up something of one's own will for Him, but above all to adhere positively and firmly to His will. This one can be absolutely certain of doing in and through the exercise of religious obedience. The more constant and actual is the union of wills the more actual and constant is one's love of God. The role of obedience is to enable the religious to lead a life of *constant union of will* with the will of God through the exercise of obedience performed out of charity or pure love. It should, then, be the normal way in which the will of the one loving is transformed into the will of the one loved. Thus obedience should be both a *means* to charity and a *sign* of charity. Obedience can, and in a sense should, go beyond mere justice. It should become an occasion for our pure love for God, an act by which we adhere to the will of one we love.[154]

Religious obedience brings about the perfect practice of docility to the Holy Spirit, and particularly an increase in one's *faith* and the gifts which accompany it, those of *understanding* and *knowledge*. The virtue of humility is increased and thus one of the greatest obstacles to obedience is offset, the vice of or tendency to pride, the independence of one's own will.

Finally the union of the individual *with the redemptive act of Christ* must also never be removed from the meaning of obedience. Christ saved the entire human race through His Passion, through what was an apparent failure. The growth of the Church takes place through the perfect fidelity of a religious to obedience even when this means the annihilation of a talent or all five or ten of them. Souls are saved not in accordance with our own will or what we think we should be doing, but rather in accordance with the will of God. They are saved through that Passion and through our union with that Passion, and as such all obedience and all other acts in the life of a religious can and should become, to some extent, coredemptive.

Of the three religious vows, the vow of obedience is the most important. Indeed it includes the other two vows in its makeup, for one remains poor and chaste under obedience. The reason for its excellence is that of all the goods which a person could possibly offer to God, the highest which he has is his own will. This he does through obedience.[155]

---

[154] Cf. Reginald Buckler, O.P., *The Perfection of Man by Charity* (St. Louis: B. Herder, 1954), p. 188.

[155] In addition to the work cited above several others that might be read with reflection and profit are *The Religious Vocation*, Jacques Leclercq (New York: P. J. Kenedy and Sons, 1955), pp. 128–145; and *To Live is Christ*, R. Gleason, S.J. (New York: Sheed and Ward, 1961), pp. 137–160.

Under Vow

For the state of perfection which is called the "religious" state, these counsels should come under vow. On this point the teaching of the Church is most explicit. We read in Canon Law that the religious state is a permanent mode of life by which the faithful undertake to observe not only the precepts common to all, but also the evangelical counsels by the vows of obedience, chastity, and poverty.[156] The profession of these counsels must be under vow, that is, it must be external, and not merely secret; it must be public, that is, not private, accepted by the Church. Moreover, these must be at least virtually perpetual, i.e., at least accompanied by the intention of renewing them as soon as the term for which they have been taken has expired.[157]

This was once again reasserted by Pius XII in the Provida Mater Ecclesia in placing the secular institutes in their relationship to the religious state and the societies of the common life. He writes in part: "In it[158] the Church decided to give full measure of equality with the canonical state of perfection to those societies which had deserved well of her and frequently of civil society also. These associations, though lacking certain juridical forms, public vows for example, required for full constitution in the canonical state of perfection[159] are nevertheless closely allied to religious orders properly speaking by close resemblance and by a certain necessity, because they possess the other features that are regarded as belonging to the substance of the life of perfection." "Art II: Since Secular Institutes neither take the three public vows of religion[160] nor impose community life or domicile in common on all their members, according to Canon Law,[161] by law ordinarily they cannot strictly speaking be called religious orders or societies of the common life."[162]

Theologians generally try to explain this juridical fact in the following manner. The religious state is a state of perfection, and, as we have seen, the state of perfection requires an obligation to whatever belongs to perfection and this obligation consists in binding oneself to these things by vow. For they firmly establish themselves in the proposal to strive after the heights of Christian perfection when they make a promise to God stabilizing themselves in this purpose or resolve. As we have seen, how-

---

156 Cf. Canon 487.
157 Cf. The Sacred Canons, Abbo-Hannan, I (St. Louis: B. Herder, 1952), pp. 480–482.
158 Cf. Title XVII, Bk II, of the Code of Canon Law.
159 Cf. Canons 488, §§ 1, 7; 487.
160 Cf. Canons 1308, §1; 488, 1°.
161 Cf. Canons 487 ff. and 673 ff.
162 AAS 39 (1947), 117; trans. in Perrin, Secular Institutes, pp. 109–110.

ever, poverty, chastity, and obedience belong to the perfection of the
religious life, freeing us from those things which could prevent us from
giving ourselves up completely to the worship and life of service for the
glory of God in perfect sacrifice. For as Gregory says: "When a man vows
to Almighty God all his possessions, all his life, all his knowledge, it is a
holocaust" which is the most perfect sacrifice of praise which we can offer
to the Lord. For this reason, the religious state requires that one be
bound to these practices or observances by vow. This reasoning is merely
one of fittingness, since there are other states of perfection which constitute one in a stable manner in the pursuit after perfection, in which
public vows are not made. In some of the societies of the common life
and in the secular institutes these promises or oaths or vows are private,
social, or semipublic. But if such a society is to be considered among the
religious institutes, according to the present discipline of the Church, then
the evangelical counsels must be followed under public vow.

It is only fitting that these three counsels should be observed under vow,
because of the excellence of the state which is one of permanent holocaust
to God. It is only in such a state that a person can truly be said to give
to God His whole life in such a way that he no longer possesses the right
over what he has given to God. Because a man's actions are successively
performed in time, it would be impossible for him to give to God his
whole life, once and for all, except in and through a solemn promise which
he makes to God. Only in this way can a person fulfill the injunction of
our Lord, to follow Him and not to turn back, for "no man putting his
hand to the plow and then turning back is fit for the kingdom of God."[163]
This unwavering following of Christ is made fast by a vow, by which one
offers to God not only the act of a faculty, but the faculty itself, thereby
once and for all giving over to the service of God the very faculty of action
which He has received from Him. In and through the religious vows a
person does not give God merely an isolated act of poverty or of liberality,
of obedience, of chastity, but he gives Him the very faculties from which
such acts proceed. Once and for all he establishes himself in liberality
and chastity and obedience, giving God not merely the fruit of the tree
but the very tree itself, so these things, external goods, the body, and the
will belong exclusively to God.

St. Thomas in speaking of the excellence of a work done under vow
points this out rather clearly:

> It is better and more meritorious to perform some work with a vow than
> without a vow for three reasons: first, because "to vow" is an act of latria,
> or of religion, which is most excellent among the moral virtues. Now the

[163] Lk. 8:62.

more excellent the virtue the better and the more meritorious the deed. Wherefore the act of an inferior virtue is the better and the more meritorious for being commanded by a superior virtue, whose act it becomes through being commanded by it, just as the act of faith or hope is better if it be commanded by charity. Hence the works of the other moral virtues (for instance fasting and chastity) are better and more meritorious, if they be done in fulfillment of a vow, since thus they belong to divine worship, being like sacrifices to God. Wherefore St. Augustine says, that "not even virginity is honourable as such, but only when it is consecrated to God, and cherished by godly continence."[164]

Secondly, because he that vows to do something, subjects himself to God more than he that only does it; for he subjects himself to God not only with respect to the act, but also with respect to the power, since in the future he cannot do something else. In a like manner he gives more who gives the tree with its fruit than he who gives only the fruit, as St. Anselm observes.[165]

Thirdly, because a vow fixes the will on the good immovably and to do anything from a will that is fixed on the good belongs to the perfection of virtue, according to Aristotle, just as to sin with an obstinate mind aggravates sin and is called a sin against the Holy Ghost.[166]

Thus, the doing of a virtuous and meritorious work becomes even better and more meritorious when we do it under vow. For a vow is an act of the virtue of religion and stabilizes the will for the future in some good exercise. We have mentioned previously that the exercise of an act of one virtue can become in some manner the act of another virtue when it is commanded by this virtue. This same truth is applicable here. For every act of virtue belongs to religion or latria, by way of command insofar as it is directed to the reverence of God, which is the proper end of latria. The direction of actions to their end belongs to the commanding virtue, such that the direction of the acts of any virtue to the service of God is the proper act of latria or the virtue of religion. A vow, however, by its very definition is a promise made to God or a directing of the thing promised to the Person to whom the promise is made. To vow something to God is merely to direct the thing vowed to the worship or service of God. While it might very well be that the matter of a vow is sometimes the act of another virtue, the promising of that thing to God belongs to religion. Thus there are some things which of their very nature are acts of the virtue of religion, such as sacrifice and devotion and adoration, while there are other actions which belong to religion by reason of their being ordered thereto by vow.[167]

---

[164] On Virginity, Chap. 8, PL 40, 400.
[165] Actually it was not Anselm but Eadmer, On Likeness, Chap. 84, PL 159, 655.
[166] II, II, Q. 88, a. 6.
[167] Cf. ibid., a. 5.

While it is true that one becomes obligated to the performance of an act that he has promised to God, still it is what St. Augustine calls a happy necessity: "Repent not," he says, "of thy vow, but rejoice rather that thou canst no longer do lawfully, but to thy own harm. Happy the necessity that compels to better things."[168]

*   *   *

From the foregoing considerations — that the three evangelical counsels pertain to the state of perfection and that they must be undertaken by vow for the religious state — we can conclude that religious perfection, or the perfection of the religious state, consists in the profession of these three vows. St. Thomas brings this out rather admirably:

> the religious state may be considered in one of three ways:
>
> 1. As being a practice of charity or of tending to the perfection of charity; and under this consideration it is constituted by the three vows seen above. For in order to practice perfection or tend to it, a man is required to remove all those things from himself which could prevent his affections from tending wholly to God. These, however, are of three kinds: external goods, and this obstacle is removed forever, through the vow of poverty; secondly, the concupiscences of sensible pleasures and these are removed by the vow of chastity; thirdly, the want of order in the human will, and this is removed by the vow of obedience.
> 2. As quieting the human mind from outward solicitude. Likewise we see that this worldly solicitude is aroused in man in reference especially to three things. First with respect to the dispensing of external things; this solicitude is removed through his taking the vow of poverty. Secondly with respect to the control or government of a family which is cut away by the vow of chastity. And thirdly, with respect to the disposal of one's own actions, and this disquiet is removed by the vow of obedience whereby a person commits himself to the disposal of another.
> 3. As a holocaust whereby a person offers himself and his possessions wholly to God. Under this consideration of the religious state we can see that it demands these three vows also. For man has a threefold good: first, the good of external things, which he wholly offers to God by the vow of voluntary poverty; secondly, the good of his own body, and this good he offers to God especially by the vow of chastity, whereby he renounces the greatest of bodily pleasures; and thirdly, the good of the soul, which man wholly offers to God by the vow of obedience, whereby he offers God his own will, by which he makes use of all the powers and the habits of the soul.[169]

All the religious observances which we find in communities are somehow or other contained under these three vows, such that they cover all the external actions of an individual, directing them to God. For if there

---

[168] Letter to Paulina and Armentarius, 126, PL 33, 487.
[169] II–II, Q. 186, a. 7.

are any external actions ordered toward the procuring of a livelihood, such as labor, begging, teaching, nursing, or preaching, they are to be referred to poverty, for the safeguarding of which religious seek a livelihood by these means. Other observances whereby the body is chastised, such as watching, fasting, and the like, are directly ordered to the observance of the vow of chastity. Those religious observances which regard human actions whereby a person is directed to the end of religion, namely the love of God and his neighbor, such as reading, prayer, visiting the sick, and the like, are grouped under the vow of obedience which applies to the will, directing its actions to the end in accordance with the ordering of another person.

Article II.   Works Compatible With the Religious State

In this article we shall discuss rather briefly some of the various works which are in keeping with the religious state. While in general it can be said that almost any spiritual or corporal work of mercy can be the objective of a religious order or congregation, still it seems as though certain types of work have been most frequently undertaken. A few ideas would perhaps be a stimulus for further investigations on the part of the reader.

Teaching and Preaching

The work of teaching and preaching seems to be very much in keeping with the profession of the religious state. This is more than clear from the Church's having approved so many orders and congregations which have this as their peculiar end. For this reason alone we can be most certain that such work is work through which the Church of God is built up in love. But in addition to the fact of approbation there are several arguments which can be pointed out showing the reasonableness of this action of the Church.

In the overall picture of the Incarnate Redeemer, we find three aspects which are united in the One Person of the God-Man: Priest, Teacher, and King. And if we were to search the Gospels in an attempt to discover which of these three roles our Lord exercised most often we would very quickly have to conclude that it was that of teacher and preacher, one who was sent to make creation once more act as a sign or symbol leading man back to God. In this work He was to associate others so that these latter would carry on the mission which had been entrusted to Him by His Father. And it is right here where we find the excellence of the apostolate of teaching and preaching. It is a share in the work of the Word Himself, to express the riches of the Godhead to man. In this work we find the loftiest use of human speech. Such a mission is not at all forbidden to religious. In fact, we can say that they are especially fit for such an office in the Church. This was very forcefully indicated by St. Thomas by reason of an historical difficulty encountered in his own day with those who felt that religious priests should not be allowed to preach or teach since they belonged in the monastery. He writes in part:

> It is foolish to say that a man is rendered less fit for spiritual duties through advancing himself in holiness. Consequently, the opinion of those who declare that the religious state is an obstacle to the fulfillment of such duties is foolish. For unless they have vowed not to perform these duties there is nothing in their profession which would make such a work contrary to it. In fact, they are more apt for performing these things than others who have not the religious life because they have taken upon themselves the practice and the occupation of holiness and perfection under vow. The more perfect a person is, the more effective is he in the works of the spiritual life.[170]

While it is true that St. Thomas had in mind the teaching of theology and philosophy, still a similar conclusion could also be drawn in regard to other subjects and fields of intellectual endeavor. Moreover, it should be drawn since in many cases the intellectual apostolate is being more and more looked down upon, especially by those entering the ranks of the priesthood. The need for religious and priests to dedicate themselves to this work stems from the need we have of seeing the whole of knowledge viewed in its proper perspective. Not that all knowledge is religion or religious in the strict sense of the word. No, each subject has its own contribution to make to the overall product which is the Christian in search of God. We human beings are like polygons. We have many sides, all of which must be developed with a view to some ultimate end, with a view to harmonious development and unification. But this unified view can come only from one who has the proper vision of all things: Christ's vision. For we are called upon to impress upon a student God's gaze on all things. Of all persons, however, those whose lives are most perfectly ordered to the attaining of this vision are those who are dedicated to God. Because their life is a constant pursuit or quest after God, after holiness and perfection, after purity of heart, it is only logical to conclude that such a life in itself is much more conducive to the acquisition of the overall image which must be impressed upon the minds and hearts of men. The very vows themselves enable one to free himself from those preoccupations which could so easily impede one from giving himself almost entirely to his work. They enable his vision to be clear, unobscured by the cares and difficulties which we find among people of the world. The

---

[170] Ibid., Q. 187, a. 2.

constant endeavor of going out of the world, of withdrawing from it, enables him to see it more advantageously, not in piecemeal fashion like the person dwelling in the valley, but rather in one grand view like the person dwelling on a mountaintop. His perspective should be better, more perfect, more calm, more detached, and more universal.

Today perhaps more than ever before there is need to stress the apostolate of teaching, both on the higher levels and on the lower levels. For it is only in and through these various activities impregnated with the spirit of Christ, that we can hope to restore all things in Christ. Even though the subjects taught may seem to be almost entirely secular, nevertheless the presence of religious and priests in those fields serves to keep the science or discipline in its right perspective, in its right position and order in the overall plan of divine Wisdom such as that has been parceled out to men. All truth converges upon the First Truth of which it is merely a share, and therefore we can say that all learning should and can bring us closer to God. But it is only in proportion as the individual religious sent into these fields learns to strive after the sight of, or the perfections of, God found in them that such an ideal will be attained. While we admit the difficulty of such work for religious or priests, still it is only from their presence in these fields that we can hope to make the reign of Christ permeate the whole range of knowledge and wisdom which reaches from end to end.

The dignity of the religious and priest teacher on *all* levels of education should be placed before the minds of those entering a religious community or desirous of contributing something to the apostolate. For there are some who are attracted not to teaching on the higher levels of learning, and yet are very much interested in doing a similar work on the lower levels in which the moral influence and guidance of the priest can play an important role. We are told of St. Anselm that his interest in youth was so great that it drew the attention of others, who marveled that such a profound and brilliant mind could be so attracted to them. His answer was that

> the age of youth is like that of soft wax. It is most fit to take the impress of a seal. If the wax be ever so little too hard or too soft it can in nowise take the seal. But if it be firm enough, and yet also soft, and the seal be discreetly impressed thereon, then it will receive the form in all its entirety. Thus it is with the state of men. Take one who from his infancy unto old age has been occupied with the passing vanities of this world. He has no taste for aught but earthly things. Treat with such a one of spiritual matters, speak to him of the marvels of divine grace, seek to teach him the secrets of eternity, and you will find him incapable of perceiving what you would teach him. Nor is this to be marveled at for the wax has hardened.

On the other hand consider a child tender in years and knowledge as yet unable to distinguish between good and evil and thus incapable of following you as you discourse. The wax is oversoft, ready to pour forth in a liquid stream, and in nowise capable of retaining the impress of the seal.

Midway between these two, stands the boy who by reason of his yielding yet firm disposition is most fitly tempered. When you instruct such a one you shall be able to teach him whatsoever it pleases you. This have I noticed and with greater solicitude have I watched over these young souls having a great care to root out from them all vice so that through the fit exercise of all holy virtues, they may form within themselves the likeness of the spiritual man, the likeness of Christ.

Even though the dignity and nobility of such work is more than evident, nevertheless because of the weakness of man and the inordinate tendencies of our nature, which could so easily lead us to make a god out of study and the pursuit of truth, we would do well to keep before our minds the words of St. Augustine:

And what did it profit me that I read and understood for myself all the books of what are called the Liberal Arts, that I was able to get hold of, since I remained the vile slave of evil desires. I enjoyed the books while not knowing Him from Whom came whatever was true and certain in them. For I had my back to the light and my face to the things upon which the light falls, so that my face, by which I looked upon the things in the light was not itself in the light. . . . Of what use to me then was my intelligence, swift to run clear through those sciences; of what use were all those knotty books I unravelled without the aid of any human teacher, when in the doctrine of love of You, I erred so far and so foully and so sacrilegiously?[171]

The only secret to avoiding the evil of which St. Augustine speaks, and of realizing the ideal of which we have spoken above, is to constantly purify the intention in which and because of which one engages in the study or the teaching of those sciences not immediately pertaining to divine things. This constant purification of intention or direction of one's intention will serve to put the intellect at the service of Christ, and by reason of the perhaps deeper faith needed to engage in such works God Himself will grant a more ample reward. Fidelity to one's religious duties, and these always first of all, will safeguard one in the pursuit of such knowledge.

The Medical Apostolate

Another apostolate in which we see many religious engaged is that of the medical apostolate, which can be called a true and sacred ministry. For when it is undertaken with a supernatural motive it becomes as it were a

---

[171] *Confessions*, Bk. IV, Chap. 16, PL 32, 706.

continuation of the work and ministry of our Lord Himself toward the sick. So often throughout the Gospels we are presented with scenes telling of the loving meetings or encounters of the Son of God with our suffering humanity and of the infinite pity which He manifested in its regard. This ministry of mercy He left to the Church to be carried on through her members. It is these persons who are to recognize Christ in every sick person and who are to act as Christ would act with him. This end of the medical apostolate has been very beautifully pointed out by Pius XII in an address made to nursing Sisters in 1957:

> But let no one imagine that the Church can or will abandon her maternal duty of comforting the sick who have not only bodies but also souls which are often more in need of help than their bodies. We believe that the first to be convinced of this are the good doctors themselves who are well able to evaluate the benefits conferred by the presence and care of Catholic Sisters. Hence our will does not waver from the way we have chosen which has as its end the preparation of an ever-growing multitude of chosen souls ready to meet the duties that await them at the bedside of the sick and the infirm. For this reason, beloved daughters, you have left your families those you had and those you might have had. . . . It is certain that every sick man is the image of Christ. "Lord when did we see thee sick and come to thee? As long as you did it to one of these the least of my brethren you did it to me." If you had this living faith, if behind the human faces you were able to see the Face of Jesus in every ward, in every bed, expressionless in the mysterious solemnity of the operating room, you would never notice that you had passed from the chapel to the hospital corridors; you would not entertain the slightest fear that religious observance would be a hindrance to your care for the sick or that this care for the sick would do any harm to your religious observance. You would continue to love Him as much, however, and wherever he chose to conceal Himself. You would permit no interruption in your converse with Him, no distraction, no forgetfulness of what He is and what He wills.[172]

Such an ideal with regard to the medical apostolate should be most perfectly realized by one who has vowed or consecrated her life to the service of God in and through His sick. The obligations of the religious life enable one to broaden his or her vision in regard to the sick, and above all these obligations make it necessary to continually reimpress on the mind the sight and gaze of Christ Himself on those who are afflicted with suffering. Thus the freedom which the vows give, the lack of preoccupation with other cares proper to those who do not have the vows and yet are engaged in work with the sick, the obligation of meditation and reading and prayer, all these contribute to forming and deepening the image of Christ the healer on those whom He has called to this apostolate.

---

[172] *The Pope Speaks,* 4 (1957), 138–140.

Suffering like everything else in life pertains to the unfolding story of God's love for man. For this is not merely made up of events that are pleasant and agreeable to mankind, but also, in the present economy, of events that are painful and disagreeable to nature. Yet it is oftentimes by these that the redemption of both the individual and society is most efficaciously brought about.

In a sense, we can say that if ever the saying "Be ye holy and spotless you who have the vessels of the Lord in your charge" is true, it is true of the vocation of those who have been called to this apostolate. For in the sick and suffering and the dying the vessels of God's election are entrusted to their care. It is their mission in the Church to draw out of souls the most efficacious healing power that lies in the human race. We can truthfully say that the most precious instruments of sanctification are entrusted to their hands and it is their mission to draw from these instruments the song of praise and glory to the mercy of God. In a very real way, then, does this apostolate allow one to carry on the mission of Christ and of His Church: to be love, to be mercy, to give life, and to be the cause of the joy of the human race.

Care for the Poor and Abandoned

Still another apostolate that is exercised by many religious communities is that of the care of the poor and the abandoned. The purpose of this work is to incarnate throughout the whole of human history God's concern, Christ's concern, and the Church's concern for these members of the human family. Like the other works mentioned above, this too is a work of mercy, of pity, and consequently ought to be seen within the framework of the redemptive Incarnation which is an act of mercy or pity par excellence. In the Old Testament the excellence of such a work has been very well pointed out for the members of this covenant: "Spend thyself giving food to the hungry, relieving the afflicted. Then shall light spring up for thee in the darkness and thy dusk shall be noonday . . . ease the insupportable burden, set free the over-driven, share thy bread with the hungry, give the poor and the vagrant a welcome to thy house; meet the naked, clothe him; from thy own flesh and blood turn not away . . . the Lord will give thee rest continually, fill thy soul with comfort, thy body with ease. Not more secure, the well-watered garden, the spring whose waters never fail."[173]

These ministries allow the Church to carry on the mission entrusted to her by Christ. This also has been pointed out by Pius XII: "With the assistance of your maternal hands, beloved daughters, the Church is able

---

[173] Is. 58:7 ff.

to support the aged in their declining years; with your heart-beats the Church is able to warm the hearts of tiny orphans; with the fervor of your self-dedication the Church is able to minister to the sick."[174] It is easy to see why persons who desire to consecrate themselves to God's service embrace the state of virginity as a liberation in order to be more entirely at God's disposition and devoted to the good of their neighbor. How otherwise could they accomplish the gigantic tasks they do if they had to look after the corporal and spiritual needs of a wife or husband and children. It is for this reason that we see works of charity being entrusted for the most part to consecrated persons, both because they are freed from the obligations and cares of others and because they are better able (objectively, of course) by reason of their way of life to bring to this work the calmness and universality of vision which is so proper to God as He looks upon the needs and miseries of mankind.

Manual Labor

In the course of formation, particularly for those communities in which some of the religious are going to be engaged in domestic or manual work, the dignity and the role which it occupies in the life of the community ought to be pointed out. This should be done frequently even if merely by way of example in the discussion of other points of community life, or virtue and spirituality. It would serve much to raise the occupation in the minds of the religious. Just in passing we might mention that domestic work of its very nature does not so absorb the mind that this cannot be given over to thought and reflection on divine things, on the mysteries of salvation. Thus it is a work compatible with the contemplative life. A religious, even though a member of an active community, could rather easily live a life that was more contemplative than active if he or she were engaged in such employment within the community. The work is regular and steady, and usually allows time for prayer and reflection, which appeal to certain types of temperament. Second, the role of such employment in the community should also be made clear. It is an economic asset to the community, and above all contributes to the general well-being of the community, "for even the army of Christ marches on its stomach." The work of those employed in domestic work in a community helps greatly in preserving the spirit of cloister, which is being broken down more and more with very serious consequences to the religious spirit. When it becomes necessary to employ lay people in religious houses, the result is that sometimes the closest secrets of the community life are soon

---

[174] Nursing Sister, loc. cit.

known in the surrounding areas. This revelation of the intimate secrets of community life, with the faults and failings and shortcomings of those who live in it, is one of the keenest sufferings in the life of a religious. For this reason the employment of religious in such houses serves to preserve the spirit of cloister. While it is true there is very little recognition given to those who do such work, and they lead lives which are for the most part hidden and almost completely neglected by the other members engaged in more prominent and public work, still the *spirit of faith* animating their work and life is usually profound, something like that of Mary and Joseph at Nazareth. As St. Teresa remarks, "God walks among the pots and pans just as much as He does in the choir."

Article III. The Different Kinds of Religious Communities

The present investigation is important both for one entering the religious life as well as for one engaged in directing others to the religious life. Upon the decision for or against a community or a diocese rests oftentimes the happiness and the degree of perfection which a person will reach, and, consequently, the value of this person to the Church and her mission. Each community presents a certain spirit in the Church, and attracts those persons whom God has willed from all eternity to possess or become, so to speak, the incarnation of that spirit. Wrong direction in the choice of a community is occasionally the reason for which the person withdraws from the religious life or from a seminary and becomes a kind of misfit for the rest of his or her life. Concerning this problem of the different religious communities in the Church the following observations might be of some help.

Religious orders do not differ from one another in regard to the obligation which they impose upon their members of devoting themselves wholly to the service of God. In no religious order is one allowed to retain something for his own use and free disposal. This *complete* dedication to the service of God is of the *very essence* of the religious life and must be found in all religious orders. They do differ, however, in this that they have or afford different works whereby one aims at the perfection of charity, or if not different works then at least different exercises whereby one strives after the perfection of the Christian life. If the exercises are almost exactly the same (as is true in most modern congregations), then the manner in which these exercises are practiced differs slightly, so that we can say there is a spirit in this community which is not found in another. Sometimes, as we must admit, the difference seems scarcely discernible; yet if one were to take the time and the trouble to discover the spirit of a given community, it seems, at least to the present writer, that it would appear clearly enough. Perhaps too many of our modern communities have failed to make their spirit apparent and for this reason have lacked the unifying principle that would give vitality to the community and perfect it in its work for the growth of the Church. For when a community fails to communicate its own spirit as well as it possibly can, we have a family that is without life or at least the intensity of vitality which would give it its true position in the Church.

Religious orders may be differentiated in one of two ways: First, according to the different things or works to which they are directed. Thus, for example, one may be directed to the taking care of the sick, or of poor and abandoned children; another may be directed to the apostolate of teaching; another to the foreign mission apostolate, etc. Second, they may be differentiated from one another according to the diversity of practices which they have. Thus, for example, the body is chastised in one order by abstinence from food; in others it is chastised by the practice of manual labor, or teaching, or preaching, or nursing, etc. Of these two ways, however, as is evident, the various religious orders differ from one another more by reason of the first diversity than by reason of the second, that is, in accordance with the various works or ends rather than in accordance with the various practices which they employ.

From this we can readily see that while the three essential vows of religion pertain to the practice of the religious life as principles to which all other practices may be reduced, there are, nonetheless, many ways of disposing oneself to the observance of each of them. One order disposes its members to the observance of continence by solitude of place; another, by abstinence; and yet another, by community life. If there were absolutely no differences in two religious orders, then it seems that such a state would lead to confusion rather than to the good of the Church. For confusion is opposed to distinction and order. Thus a multitude of religious orders and communities would lead to confusion if they were directed to the same end and in the same way, without necessity or utility. To prevent this from happening the Holy See has commanded that orders shall not be instituted without its being consulted. With these principles for diversifying and distinguishing religious communties St. Thomas makes the following observations in regard to our problem.

1. A religious community can be fittingly directed to the active life. The reason for allowing this from a theological viewpoint stems from the fact that charity, which is the end of the religious life and state, admits of a

twofold direction, that is, toward God and toward our neighbor. As we have seen, the contemplative life seeks to devote itself to God alone and therefore directly belongs to the love of God; the active life, on the other hand, which ministers to the needs of our neighbor, belongs directly to the love of one's neighbor. Just as by charity we love our neighbor for the sake of God so the services which we render him redound to God according to the teaching of our Lord: "Whatsoever you do to these the least of my brethren you do unto me."[175] Those services which we render our neighbor insofar as they are referred to God are described as sacrifices, which are acts proper to the virtue of religion.

Even though one engages in the active life, total and complete service of and subjection to God are not at all precluded, because the religious engages in these for the sake of God. Because this service is undertaken for the sake of the Lord, it follows that the action of active religious results from contemplation of divine things. For although they may be in the world, still this particular phrase admits of two different meanings; for one may be in the world merely according to bodily presence, or one can be in the world according to the bent of his mind and heart. Religious engaged in the active life are in the world according to bodily presence, but they are not supposed to be in the world with regard to the bent of their mind, for their very profession indicates that they have withdrawn from the world in this regard, and that whatever could be considered to be worldly, or the delights and pleasures of worldlings, are excluded from their lives by their profession. They occupy themselves with exterior works and things not as though they were seeking anything from the world but merely for the sake of serving God, for they are like those of whom St. Paul said: "Who use this world as though not using it."[176] For this reason St. James has spoken of such religious when he wrote that religion pure and undefiled is to visit the fatherless and widows in their tribulations and to keep oneself unspotted and unstained from this world.[177]

Cajetan notes in his commentary on this article of St. Thomas:

The works of the active life have a twofold relationship with divine contemplation. First they can be regarded as an effect of contemplation. And thus to preach is said to be a work of the active life emanating from contemplation or flowing from it. Secondly, they can be said to be an effect of God Himself Who is contemplated as an end. And thus all works of mercy whether they be spiritual or corporal are derived from contemplation. It is for this reason that the Angelic Doctor says in the article that as long as religious with their eyes on God give themselves over to the works of the active life, they are not deprived of the fruit of contemplation.

[175] Mt. 25:40.   [176] 1 Cor. 7:31.   [177] Cf. Js. 1:17.

For unless they have fixed the peak of their mind on God as the end, their will would never move them to the works of the active life to be exercised for God.[178]

2. A religious order could be, as was true in the past, directed toward soldiering or toward the performance of some military service. We have just seen that an order could be founded not only for the contemplative life, but also for some work of the active life that is for the service of one's neighbor, redounding, of course, to the service of God. The occupation of soldiering can be directed to the assistance of the Church and of our neighbor. For this reason, then, a religious order could be established for soldiering, not for any worldly purpose but for the defense of divine worship and public safety or also for the defense of the poor and the oppressed.[179]

3. A religious order can also be founded for preaching and the hearing of confessions, retreat work, etc. The reason given is almost the same as that given above: that a religious order can be established for the works of the active life, or for the service of one's neighbor, or it can be directed to the service of God and the upkeep of divine worship. The good of one's neighbor is advanced even more by spiritual works of mercy than by means of corporal works of mercy to which religious can dedicate themselves. In excellence the spiritual works of mercy surpass the corporal for three reasons: first, because the *offering* is more excellent since it is a spiritual gift; second, because the *object helped* is more excellent, namely the soul; third, because *spiritual* acts are more excellent than corporal acts.[180]

---

[178] Commentary on art. 2, in the Leonine edition of the works of St. Thomas.

[179] The fact that a military order can be founded in which religious vows could be professed is not something merely of theory, for the history of the Church has seen the existence of such orders. The Crusades afforded an opportunity for their foundation, and thus they were introduced into the organism of the Church around the twelfth and thirteenth centuries. Their chief aim as we know was the defense of the Church and the Christian State. Among these orders were the following: the Order of St. John, founded at the beginning of the twelfth century, the members of which were later called Rhodian Knights (1291), and, even later, the Knights of Malta (1530). Certainly one of the most famous was the Knights Templar (1118–1312) which received its Rule from St. Bernard; another order was that of the Teutonic Knights founded in 1199; and finally we have the Order of the Knights of St. Lazarus (1250–1490).

[180] Thus, for example, we have the following line-up of the most important of the spiritual and corporal works of mercy:

Spiritual
{
Prayer, by which one prays for another
Instructing the ignorant as regards their speculative intellect
Counseling them as regards their practical intellect (moral life)
Comforting them in time of sorrow
Forgiveness of injuries.
Bearing with the weaknesses of others
}

4. A religious order may also be established for the purpose of study. The reasoning given by St. Thomas in his treatment of this question is most clear and to the point. We could do no better than recall his own thoughts on this subject:

A religious order may be directed to the active or to the contemplative life. Among the works of the former type of life, the active, the chief are those which are ordered to the salvation of souls, such as preaching and other similar works. Given this division of the religious orders, it follows that the study of letters is a fitting occupation for religious from three different viewpoints:

First with regard to the *contemplative life*. For study assists this life in a twofold manner:

(1) by helping directly to contemplate insofar as study enlightens the intellect. For the contemplative life is directed chiefly to the consideration of God and divine things to which man is directed by study. Thus, even in the psalms we read that "Blessed is the man that shall meditate day and night on the Law of the Lord."[181] "The wise man will seek out the wisdom of all the ancients and will be occupied with the prophets."[182]

(2) by helping indirectly, removing the obstacles to contemplation, namely, the errors which in the contemplation of divine things frequently beset those who are ignorant of the Scriptures. Thus St. Gregory writes that "some through seeking contemplation more than they are able to grasp, fall away into perverse doctrines and by failing to be humble disciples of truth become the masters of error."[183]

Secondly, with regard to the *active life of preaching and other like works*. For by studying and embracing the faithful word which is according to Doctrine or teaching they may be able to exhort in sound doctrine and convince others.

Thirdly, the study of letters is becoming to religious as regards that which

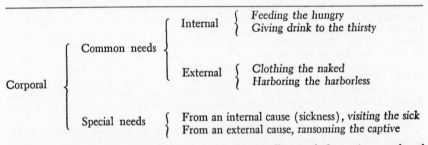

This is, of course, an analysis of the *objective* excellence of the various works of mercy for which a religious order could be founded. For it could very well happen that one of these works, even though less noble *in se*, in itself, would nevertheless be more important and more noble in a given circumstance.

181 Ps. 1:2.
182 Ecclus. 39:1.
183 *Morals*, Bk. VI, Chap. 37, PL 75, 761.

is common to all religious orders. For it helps us to *avoid the lusts of the flesh*. Wherefore St. Jerome says: "Love the science of Scripture and thou shalt have no love for carnal vice." For it turns the mind away from lustful thoughts and tames the flesh on account of the toil that study entails. . . . It also helps to *remove the desire of riches*, wherefore, it is written: "I esteemed riches nothing in comparison with her"[184] and "We needed none of these things namely assistance from without, having for our comfort the holy books that are in our hands."[185] It also helps *to teach us obedience*, wherefore Augustine says[186] "What sort of perverseness is this to wish to read, but not obey what one reads?"[186a]

Religious are encouraged to engage in study whether they be enrolled in the active life or in the contemplative life. They should, however, devote themselves chiefly to the study of letters in reference to the doctrine which is according to Godliness.[187] "For it becomes not religious," St. Thomas mentions, "whose whole life is devoted to the service of God, to seek for other learning save insofar as it is referred to Sacred Doctrine. Thus St. Augustine writes concerning this question: 'While we think that we should not overlook those whom heretics delude by the deceitful assurance of reason and knowledge, we are slow to advance in the consideration of their methods. Yet we should not be praised for doing this, were it not that many holy sons of their most loving mother the Catholic Church had done the same under the necessity of confounding heretics.'"[187a] In general, then, because this employment in the teaching of subjects other than religion seems to create difficulties for so many religious they should be advised that the work they are assigned under obedience should be done and well since it has some contribution to make in reference to that doctrine and life which is according to godliness. Yet in order to accomplish this work they must never disregard the demands of their rules in respect to the spiritual reading so necessary to offset the absorbing effect of other studies, that is to say, if they wish to advance in perfection.[188]

---

[184] Wisd. 7:8.
[185] 1 Mach. 12:9.
[186] De Oper. Monarch., 17, PL 40, 565.
[186a] II–II, Q. 188, a. 5.
[187] Cf. Tit. 1:1.
[187a] Loc. cit.

[188] Whether all would agree with the thought of Fr. Leen I do not know; but it is worth setting down for reflective consideration:

"What is bad or of a dangerous tendency must be wholly shunned by all who aspire even to ordinary Christian living. It is unfortunate that parents and teachers do not understand how utterly un-Christian can be the mentality created by works to which they so readily give their approval, if they find nothing in them contrary to faith or morals. For those who aim at intimacy with God, the selection of recreative reading must be much more careful; everything taken into their hands with a view of affording mental relaxation should tend at the same time to elevate and ennoble the mind. Nothing should be provided which would *only* stimulate and excite the imagination. Books turning upon the interplay of human passions, and without any supernatural

5. As we saw at the outset of this article, the difference and excellence among religious orders depends chiefly upon the end to which they are ordered, and only secondarily on the exercises which they employ to reach this end. We might formulate the general rule as follows: That religious order is more excellent or more perfect which is ordained to a higher end, either because it is a greater good, or because it is directed to more good. If the end of two communities is the same, then their excellence is to be measured in respect to the proportion of the exercises to the end in view.

We have already seen that the direct work of the contemplative life is the love or the contemplation of God, and as such is more perfect

---

background to the dramatic representation of the loves and hates of mankind, vitiate the taste and take away all relish for books that deal with the spiritual experiences of those who have given themselves to the life of intercourse with God.

Books that derive all their charm from the vividness with which they portray the deep emotions of earthly and natural affection are dangerous for souls which have consecrated the love of their hearts to God. The heart of the priest and the nun must be virginal, and should be carefully shielded from everything that would excite in it an interest in the play of human passions. The imagination of those who, turning their back on secular life and renouncing by vow the joys of domestic life, have bound themselves to tend towards perfection, should as far as depends upon their efforts, be kept free from all images of profane love. . . .

Consecrated souls must keep in close touch with God for the sake of others as well as in their own interest. They must be always prepared in mind and will to be a guide to the supernatural world, for those who are broken by the trials of earth; for it is to that supernatural world and the God Who reigns in it, that the human heart when crushed under the burden of existence, will immediately turn for healing and hope, if once it has known the goodness of that God. If they, whose function it is to play the part of intermediary with God, allow their minds to be formed to the same pattern as the minds of those who live in habitual neglect of divine things; if they waste their time, dissipate their energies and enervate their imaginations with the same type of literature as fashions the taste and charms the leisure of the worldling, then they cannot fulfil satisfactorily what is expected of them. It is true that sometimes those who are devoting themselves seriously to the cultivation of an interior life, are obliged in the discharge of their duties to make an acquaintance with the books that are in vogue. But while doing this they should hold themselves well on their guard against the seduction of that reading, and keep their literary taste pure and uncontaminated. Interior souls should beware of making the perusal of romantic literature a recreation: they should give themselves to it as to a task and regret the time that may have to be spent in it. Where possible an interior soul should renounce all indulgence in light or romantic literature. If one who desires to give himself to spirituality has not a taste for spiritual books, then that taste should be cultivated, for it can be acquired. . . . When our minds are by constant reading steeped in the thoughts of God and divine things, it will be easy for us to think of Him, and it will come natural and easy for us to speak to Him and to speak of Him out of our full hearts and well-stored minds.

After one is grounded deeply in spirituality it becomes possible to touch these works of fiction without being defiled; they will have lost their appeal; they will be read only through necessity; they will be read not for amusement but in order that one may be a service to and guidance to others." *Progress Through Mental Prayer*, by Edward Leen, C.S.Sp., published by Sheed and Ward, Inc., New York, pp. 225–227.

than the work of the active life which is the service of one's neighbor. However, we have to recall a distinction made previously. The work of the active life is twofold. First, there is that which proceeds from the fullness of contemplation, such as teaching and preaching. This work is more perfect than simple contemplation; for even as it is better or more excellent to enlighten than merely to shine, so too, is it better to give to others the fruits of one's contemplation than merely to contemplate. Second, the other work of the active life consists entirely in outward occupation, for instance almsgiving, receiving guests, and in general some of the other corporal works of mercy. This is, of course, less excellent than the works of contemplation, except in cases of necessity.

From these principles we can draw the following order of excellence with regard to religious communities. The highest place belongs to those directed to teaching and to preaching sacred doctrine. These are also nearest to episcopal perfection, since their work is the chief work of the bishop.[189] The second place among religious orders belongs to those which are directed to contemplation. Third place belongs to those which are occupied with external actions.[190]

In each of these three grades one religious order may surpass another in objective excellence through its being directed to a higher action in the same genus. Among the contemplative orders, for instance, it is better to pray than to study; among the active orders it is better to ransom captives than to receive guests. Likewise one is said to be better than

---

[189] Concerning this St. Thomas mentions in one place that it is simply better or more excellent to teach sacred doctrine, and also more meritorious, if it be done with the right intention, than to busy oneself with particular care for the salvation of this or that individual. Whence the Apostle said that the Lord did not send him to baptize but rather to evangelize (cf. 1 Cor. 1:17). Thus he likens this work to that of an architect regarding a building who is said to be simply better or to occupy a more excellent position than one of the manual laborers who carries out the plan conceived by him. Whence he receives more money for the building than those who put it together in accordance with his plan, even though he himself does nothing as far as the manual work goes. In the spiritual edifice, they are said to be manual laborers who in a particular manner are concerned with the care of souls, namely by administering the sacraments or doing something of this sort. The principal artisans, however, are the bishops who command and dispose in what manner this work shall be done; for this reason they are called the overseers. In a like manner doctors or teachers of theology are, as it were, principal artisans who seek out and teach how others ought to procure the salvation of souls.

"However, in some case of imminent necessity, both Bishops and teachers of theology have to lay aside their proper office, and care for souls, in a particular manner.

"We must be careful then, not to accuse those who teach theology, or dispose themselves for this through study, of wasting time." Quodlibetals, Quod. I, Q. 7, a. q. c. and ad 1m.

[190] Cf. II–II, Q. 188, a. 6, c. and ad 3m.

another in regard to the means which it uses to arrive at the end it has in view. Contrary to what is often thought among the faithful and even among religious, the austerity of observance is not the chief object of commendation in a religious order. A religious order is not more excellent merely because it has a more austere observance, but rather because its observances are directed by greater discretion to the end of the religious institute.

Consequently it would be no obstacle to a community's rating in excellence were it to have sufficient external goods, whether movables or immovables, for a livelihood, if we consider poverty in relation to the *common* end of religious orders which is to devote themselves to the service of God. If, however, we consider poverty in relation to the *special* end of a given community, then a greater or lesser degree of poverty will be more perfect in relation to the special end for which the order has been established. An order will be most perfect in its observance of poverty in relation as it professes and observes a poverty that better allows it to reach or attain its end.[191]

6. The religious life of those called to live in community is less perfect than that of those called to live in solitude. Solitude, like the vows, is a means to arrive at the perfection of charity, and, as a means, its value lies in the measure in which it brings about the end in view. Since solitude is ordered to contemplation rather than to action, solitude is not suitable to those religious orders that have as their end the works of the active life whether these be spiritual or corporal works of mercy, except perhaps for a time. On the other hand, solitude is most suitable to those religious orders that are devoted to contemplation. But even here we must be cautious in understanding this correctly. Solitude belongs to one who has arrived at perfection, for the solitary is one who is self-sufficing. Consequently, for those who have not attained this state either by practice or by means of a special gift of God, it is not right to seek the solitary life. For in order to arrive at this state by practice they need the assistance of others by way of instruction, example, and reproof. For tending

---

[191] From this principle St. Thomas draws the following conclusions regarding the practice of poverty:

a) A religious order that is established for the active apostolate, that is, certain external works as taking care of the sick, the homeless, and the abandoned, etc., should have an abundance of riches in common, not for the religious but for carrying on their work.

b) A religious order that is established for contemplation only should have more moderate wealth.

c) Those who aim at giving to others the fruits of their contemplation should have a life that is most exempt from external cares, and this is accomplished by their laying up the necessaries of life procured at a fitting time. II–II, Q. 188, a. 7.

to perfection, a social life is necessary, whereas for the living of perfection already attained, it is not. The solitary life is more perfect for such a life. Just as that which is already perfect surpasses that which is being schooled in perfection, so the life of solitaries, if properly practiced surpasses life lived in common. It should not be undertaken, however, without preparation unless the grace of God should supply for this.[192]

The Choice of a Religious Order

In concluding this treatment of the difference between religious orders we should note that all of them have something in common as well as something by which they differ from one another. The common note which they all have is the intention to seek the perfection of charity — the general end of the religious life. The individuating note is found in the means adopted by a community to realize this end.

We have seen that the Church is surrounded about with variety, and this in accordance with the designs of God Himself. For He has dispersed His perfections among creatures so that they represent Him according to the different excellences which He has. For a similar reason there are different religious orders in the Church. Each of them contributes to her perfection, the perfect reflection of the beauty and nobility of the virtues of Christ. Thus we have in the Church the Bene-

---

[192] Cf. II–II, Q. 188, a. 8. We might mention here that these principles are not as abstract as they might seem. Solitude has a twofold relation with perfection. It acts as a *disposition* for it and aid to reach it; for this reason all communities insist upon a certain amount of solitude for their members. And as we have seen it pertains to the *terminal point* of perfection. As a result a young priest or religious should not be missioned to a parish or house wherein for all practical purposes he or she is going to be asked to live a life of solitude, either because the person is alone or because the age differences of the members of this house is such that it makes it very difficult for social contact. Pius XII recently pointed this out rather emphatically in an exhortation addressed to priests: "Here we cannot refrain from strongly urging you venerable brethren to take particular care of the young priests. The passage from the sheltered and tranquil life of the seminary to the active ministry may be dangerous for the priest who enters upon the field of the apostolate if he has not been prudently prepared for the new life. You should realize that the many hopes placed in young priests may fail if they are not gradually introduced to the work, wisely watched and paternally guided in the first steps of their ministry.

"We approve therefore, the gathering of young priests when possible for some years in special institutions where under the guidance of experienced superiors they can develop their piety and perfect themselves in sacred studies, and be put on the path toward that form of the ministry more closely corresponding to their temperaments and aptitudes. For this reason we would like to see institutions of this nature established in every diocese or for a number of dioceses together." (*Menti Nostrae,* AAS 42 (1950), 691–692; NCWC ed., pp. 36–37). This was made legislation for clerical religious institutes by the *Sedes Sapientiae*, and it would be most wise for all religious communities of men and women to follow a similar practice for their young members. Many vocational problems and crises could be met more easily.

dictines, whose life is dedicated to the solemn and perfect execution of liturgical prayer; not that these monks have monopoly over such a piety, but it is their work, their spirituality, par excellence, their special movement toward God. The Franciscans, for their part, find the ideal in the exercise of the virtue of liberality, so closely connected with the state of the spirit of poverty. In the Society of Jesus the virtue and the exercise of obedience receives the principal stress and emphasis.

We might say that where we find differences that are pronounced, in a combination of accidental differences which come together to form an organic whole, we have what is called a school of spirituality. This does not mean, however, that where these pronounced differences are lacking we are to conclude that there is no particular or peculiar spirituality to be discovered. No, each group, just as each saint, individuates the grace of Christ which pours into creatures and is received in them according to various limitations and various dispositions of mind and of heart, and even of sex. Thus, the axiom, "*Quidquid recipitur ad modum recipientis recipitur*," also applies to religious communities and their distinctive spirits and spiritualities. For a spirituality is merely the abstract notion of the spirit of a religious community; it arises out of the community, and very often is something which is not set forth in one neat packagelike whole by the founder of the community. It may be dispersed and scattered throughout his or her writings, and yet it is something which he or she certainly is instrumental in giving birth to. It is important to discover what this particular spirit is in every community, because it serves to unite its members to the vital influence of the founder, and to preserve them in the close-knit unity so essential for a strong and vigorous apostolate in the Church. We can notice throughout the history of the Church that those orders and communities which have a definite central theme and ideal or spirit stand out in the Church, and where they have remained loyal to it, they have given invaluable and singular service to the Church.[193]

---

[193] Cf. Joseph de Guibert, S.J., "En quoi different réellement les diverses écoles catholiques de spiritualité," in *Gregorianum*, 19 (1938), 263–279. Cf., likewise, John of St. Thomas, *Isagoge*, Introduction to the *Summa* of St. Thomas, in II–II, QQ. 188–189; H. Brémond, *Histoire de sentiment religieux en France*, VII, p. 682; Père Langlais, O.P., *Le Maître des novices et le Maître Spirituel, dans Les États de perfection* (Rome: 1951), pp. 11–12. This latter writes: "The perfection of the monk or the cloistered nun is one thing, and the sanctity of this or that Institute is different, following the thought of God, who inspires it, and the will of the Church who approves it, with its proper ideal, its particular Constitutions, and its duties or offices of state which it gives it. From this there arises a definite spirit, which the community is to communicate to each of its individual religious, giving them a special form of perfection and a personal, if I may use the word, or individual physiognomy."

Fr. Valentine Breton, O.F.M., similarly notes: "A specific type of spirituality is an organized system of principles and convictions as well as certain pious practices which

The tinkering with the *essentials* of any religious spirit is always a dangerous thing. To do so would be to introduce into the religious community a profound modification which would not be proper to it nor in accordance with the intentions of those who have entered it. It would be to interfere in the long run with the grace of vocation which God has given. This does not mean that accidental modifications cannot be made in the course of years. In fact, we know that a religious order can conserve its spirit and fulfill its mission throughout the centuries only by adapting itself, its external forms, to the changes and demands of the different epochs. Thus when St. Teresa of Avila reestablished the primitive observance of the Carmelites, she once more reinstated the silence of the desert so necessary for the purpose for which she was founding this group of religious, and yet at the same time she used the clothing which was being sold in her day, although it was very definitely penitential in its weave.

The cult or the worship of what is ancient, an overexaggerated fidelity to tradition which would remain indifferently attached to all the primitive forms of the spirit of the order, would risk in the long run putting it to death; it would hinder it in its existence, and certainly in its apostolate in the Church. However, we must remember that to distinguish between external forms to be kept and those that must disappear at any given epoch belongs neither to inexperienced fervor, nor to any new desire of modernization. "It is not a right of authority or of the superior who is charged with conserving rather than modifying; it is the exclusive right

---

convert these convictions into action and into habits promoting the dutiful service of God. . . . We can speak of Benedictine spirituality, or Dominican, or Carmelite. We can point out the Jesuit system of spirituality and show how the Salesian and Liguorian spiritualities have developed from it. We have Franciscan spirituality from which descended also the spiritual systems of the Oratory, that of St. Sulpice, and the Eudists. The differences of these various systems stem mostly from doctrinal and theological and especially from philosophical systems of these families, their conceptions of God and of Christ, of grace, nature, and sin. They can be classed as Theocentric, Christocentric, and Anthropocentric.

"Theocentric spirituality is centered upon God; it is wrapt in the contemplation of the absolute Transcendence of God, be it by the Liturgical life of Benedictine Piety, or by the intellectual contemplation of Dominican Piety. Christocentric spirituality lives on the facts and mysteries of the Son of God made man. Thus, St. Bernard, St. Francis, and his posterity, Cardinal de Berulle and his disciples — all follow simply Him who called Himself the Way. Finally Anthropocentric spirituality studies and cultivates the duties and obligations of man towards his Creator. It promotes the correspondence of the will or psychological approach according to various conceptions of the relationship of nature and grace. The great exponent of this school is St. Ignatius though he falls back on the traditional sources of the Gospels and Christian practice. Similar more modern spiritualities follow in his path." *Franciscan Spirituality,* tr. by Flavian Frey, O.F.M. (Chicago, Ill.: Franciscan Herald Press, 1957), pp. 7–10, *passim.*

of sanctity which is alone capable of moulding into a living and authentic form the spirit of which it possesses the fullness."[194]

It is God's grace of vocation which puts into a given soul a certain motion toward a certain religious community. Therefore, the grace of vocation and the grace of a particular institute correspond with each other, and that is why it is so essential that an individual be directed to the spirit which corresponds most perfectly with his or her grace of vocation. To misdirect a soul along the lines of a supernatural vocation would be to interfere with God's handiwork, and might entail the loss of that vocation and the loss of much vitality in the Church; for the more perfectly one fulfills in his or her life the will of God for himself or herself, the more perfectly does that one contribute to the vitality and growth of the Church and family of God. Usually, it is only in a given family that the life-giving grace of vocation will find the nourishment necessary for it to grow and to flower. For a plant cannot live for long outside its own environment.[195]

Along more practical lines the following points of investigation have been laid down by Lessius for helping one choose a community:

1) Are the essential vows observed in the order, so that there be no private property, and no superfluity; that there be no exemptions and no freedom to live as one pleases.

2) Is the religious discipline observed? This can be determined by the religious bearing of the members of the community, by the reverence they show for the divine service, by their modesty in company, by their guarded speech, their moderation at table, by their silence in the house, the quiet in the rooms — in fine, by the exact observance of the rule as it applies to external conduct. For there is nothing more beautiful and edifying than exact observance of the rule.

3) Is there harmony and brotherly unity there? This is evidenced by the presence of respect for one another, the mutual assistance which they give to one another, each speaking well of the other.

4) Is there ambition present among the members? For the religious life is a school of humility and mortification.

5) Does the order have an apostolic spirit? For according to the mind of the Angelic Doctor, this is the most perfect type of life, i.e., where the contemplative life is combined with the active, in imitation of

---

[194] I Want to See God, Fr. Marie-Eugène de L'enfant Jesu (Chicago: Fides Publishers, 1953), p. 94, footnote 33.

[195] It is for this reason I believe, that Sedes Sapientiae placed the following statement in the "Statuta": "In order to be admitted to the Novitiate or comparable period of probation they must give signs already of a true religious, sacerdotal and apostolic vocation and indeed a specific one, that is, to a "definite institute." Title VI, art. 31, § 2. 1°.

Christ and the Apostles. Therefore other things being equal, this mode of life is to be preferred.[196]

St. Alphonsus advises the candidate to investigate the following points:
1. The duties and occupations that he may be required to perform.
2. The acts of penances and mortification which one is expected to be capable of in this order.
3. The talents that the order requires.
4. The health he must have.
5. His own natural inclinations and qualities in comparison with the various demands which the order requires.

On the part of the counselor it would be wise to put these queries before the one seeking advice, and then perhaps suggest some literature available on the various institutes which appeal to him. After this has been done, then the counselor can examine the attraction of the individual to see whether it is in keeping with his qualifications.

For the most part, however, the difficulty of discerning the proper order is not as great as it may seem from the foregoing discussion. God usually works through natural or, let us say, better, created causes, or instruments which are responsible for the attraction to one or another order or community. Thus, for example, we have priests in parishes who have attracted vocations to the diocesan priesthood, or priests of a religious order teaching school, or Brothers or Sisters engaged in nursing or teaching or the care of the poor and the abandoned who have also attracted vocations. Coming into contact with one or other of these is usually the starting point of the vocation, or rather the milieu in which God has determined to make the vocation come to the fore.

SECTION 4. THE THEOLOGY OF THE RELIGIOUS VOCATION CONSIDERED AS THE DIVINE CALL

So far we have been concerned with the theology of vocation considered in the external sense, i.e., of the various walks of life to which one can be called by God. In this particular section which is to some extent, the most important from the viewpoint of the individual called by God, we intend to lay down the theological notions concerning the interior call, or the divine vocation, or the grace of vocation. The notions given here are the same basically for all the vocations which we have considered

---

[196] *On the Choice of a State of Life*, quoted in Vermeersch, S.J., *The Religious and Ecclesiastical Vocation* (St. Louis: B. Herder, 1930), pp. 60–62.

and which we will consider. Consequently, we will not go over them again when we come to treat of the other vocations in this work.

Article I.   Theories Concerning Religious Vocation

While to some the theology behind religious vocation may seem to have been practically settled by the appearance of the *Sedes Sapientiae* in 1956, there are still remnants of other theories proposed in the course of the centuries which continue to influence modern and contemporary thought on the problem. It is the aim of the present article to present and evaluate them. For the most part they may be classified under two headings each of which admits of further subdivisions. These are the "general vocation theories" and the "special vocation theories." Since some of these have not enjoyed any widespread popularity, relatively little space will be devoted to them. Others, however, have enjoyed or still enjoy a rather large following. To these greater consideration will be given.

The General Vocation Theories

The first of these is usually called the *general external vocation theory.* This is defined by the authors that mention it in their writings as "the invitation addressed by Christ to all souls to follow Him in the perfect life, that is, in the practice of the evangelical counsels." Such a vocation is addressed to all the faithful by our Lord and is usually brought to their attention through the reading of Scripture, through classes in doctrine, through retreats, and the like. This general vocation does *not* give the grace to embrace the counsel(s), but this grace can be obtained by prayer.

The criticism theologians usually advance against this particular theory is that it is correct — as far as it goes. But it seems to beg the question of the divine vocation. While it is true, as the proponents of this theory say, that it is the teaching of Sacred Scripture and of the Church Fathers that the invitation to the religious life was given by our Lord to all, still it does not answer the question why some are said to be called and others are said not to be called. Hence there must be some other element in the religious vocation which this theory does not explain. For this reason neither the Church nor the better theologians of the past nor any today will sanction a vocation which is *merely* external, that is, one which does not admit of some divine call or interior movement of God's grace. There must be, according to these authorities, an internal element present in the complete concept of religious vocation. Thus St. Thomas maintained that the general external vocation is merely an *objective* invitation addressed to all, a vocation in a kind of a dispositive sense, rather than in the strict sense or usual sense such as that has always been understood by the Church.[197]

One thing to be noted, however, is that the Fathers seem to maintain that if one should ask for the grace of a religious vocation with a constant and persevering prayer, and *if this should be for the salvation of the individual*, God will not fail to grant the grace, the internal grace which is needed to embrace this way of life.

The second of the general vocation theories is called the *general internal vocation theory*. It maintains that a special grace is given to one who is called to embrace the religious life, but not in the form of any special illumination making the person absolutely certain that God is calling him to the religious state. These authors do admit that some of the canonized saints and others have received special illuminating graces from God with regard to vocation.[198] Still this is not something that is given to the majority. In fact, it is something very rarely given.

This theory was proposed by Father Arthur Vermeersch, S.J.[199] For Father Vermeersch a vocation is said to be either *ordinary* or *extraordinary*. It is said to be *ordinary* if it is the "result of deliberation under the influence of grace whereby the individual perceives under the light of the Gospel and from other considerations that the way of the counsels is to be preferred by him." It is said to be *extraordinary* if there is an illumination of the mind and incitement of the will, such that before any reflection is made or has taken place, one is strongly attracted or drawn or inclined toward the religious state.[200]

In listing the signs of a vocation Father Vermeersch says: "they are two: (a) the absence of impediments, and (b) the firm resolution with the help of God to serve Him in the religious life. Perhaps you will demand also a certain inclination of the will. But we maintain that this inclination unless it be identified with the right intention is something that cannot be clearly defined and can only give rise to useless doubts and mistakes. For your hearer will probably understand this inclination to mean that natural relish or desire which is only too often wanting in the best of vocations."[201]

---

[197] Cf. St. Thomas, *Contra Retrahentes*, Chaps. 9–10, *Opuscula Theolo.*, II, Marietti ed., 1954, p. 172 ff.

[198] E.g., St. Ignatius Loyola, St. Peter Nolasco, etc.

[199] Cf. *Religious and Ecclesiastical Vocation*, 2 ed., tr. by Joseph Kumpf (St. Louis: B. Herder, 1930), p. 48 ff.

[200] Cf. op. cit., p. 47.

[201] *Op. cit.*, p. 50. And in another place he defines the religious vocation in the following manner: "a special gift of those in the Church of God who follow the

In discussing this theory, theologians, especially strict Thomists, mention that it seems to imply that the final efficacy in regard to the firm intention comes not from grace but rather from the free will of the individual. Vocation does not seem to be so much a special favor on God's part as an heroic act on the part of the individual, so to speak, who *determines* the general internal grace which he has received to make it bend or incline him to the religious life rather than to some other form of life. This seems to be contrary to the mind of St. Thomas when he writes that "no one is said to be loved more than another, unless God shall have given to that person a special grace or good which He has not given to another." This theory is an application of the theory of grace known as congruism to the problem of vocation. Thus, here as well as in the grace of sanctification the authors who follow this opinion wish to preserve the free will and activity of man and therefore deny the existence of any divine decree antecedent to man's use of free will. This they deem necessary, because otherwise the counsels would be reduced to the status of a command and man would not be responsible for his own destiny. According to many Thomists, however, no divine decree depends upon the will or the activity of man. For God would then be one who would have to depend upon man and this would deny the truth that God is Pure Act and dependent upon no creature. For in God there is only one divine decree, and one that is in nowise modified by the action of man. He is not dependent upon the freedom of man because it is He who inclines man's will this way or that since He alone has the power of inclining the will of man, even of changing the inclination which He finds there. In this there is a mystery, but it is one in which the power and majesty and mercy of God stand out in all their splendor.[202]

While the authors who hold this position maintain that the religious vocation is a special gift, nevertheless, the role of grace in it does not seem to be entirely clear. Rather than say that they have erred, perhaps it would be better to say that the solution proposed does not seem to solve the

---

evangelical counsels with the proper intentions. The elements are the interior and exterior helps, the efficacious graces which have led to the taking of the resolution and all the graces which produce meritorious perseverance. Unlike the gratuitous gift, the *gratia gratis data*, this gift can be obtained by humble prayer. In this it resembles the grace of perseverance and requires our cooperation." *Op. cit.*, pp. 46–47. In this theory he follows St. Robert Bellarmine, S.J., cf. *Controversiae*, II, Contro. 2, Bk. II Chap. 31.

[202] Concerning this theory of Father Vermeersch and others, one author has recently said: "If the necessity of grace be admitted, must we exclude an interior divine vocation at all costs by imagining that grace is something, a sort of general spiritual force which we direct whither we will — canalized as it were, to do the work of our independent choosing?" Ed. Wuenshel, C.Ss.R., "The Traditional Notion of Vocation," in *Missionary Union of the Clergy Bulletin*, March, 1945, p. 28 ff.

problem entirely or to explain it fully. What seems difficult to admit in this theory is the assertion "that there is no evidence of a divine plan whereby God assigns to each man antecedently to the use of his free will a particular state so that he who embraces another state will find himself in a state not his own."[203]

It seems that God does assign to each of us a certain position in the world of creation and gives to each the necessary graces to reach or to fulfill the mission for which he is destined. Nevertheless the creature can reject the graces offered, and since the rejection of these graces is not always a serious sin, for they are graces of counsel, the outcome of his action is not necessarily eternally harmful. But we shall see more of this later on when treating of the obligation to follow a vocation.

The Special Vocation Theories

In this category as far as could be determined, there are three different opinions regarding religious (and priestly) vocation. They are usually referred to as the special external vocation theory, the "attraction" theory, and the special internal vocation theory.

Special External Vocation Theory

This theory, proposed by Canon Joseph Lahitton at the turn of the present century, caused quite a disturbance in many circles. In fact, it was deemed wise to have a special commission of cardinals pass judgment on his work. They finally vindicated it, at least, with regard to faith and morals. The work was written in order to offset what Lahitton considered an overemphasis on the interior element of vocation. It seemed to him that the authors of his day were requiring a miraculous grace almost pushing one into the seminary, or a grace of special illumination revealing to one God's decision in his regard. As a result of this tendency, he thought, France was losing vocations and the seminaries themselves were not receiving the subjects necessary to carry on the sacerdotal ministry.

In answer to this the Canon proposed a theory of vocation in which there were two elements, one material and one formal. The *material element* was the *interior* one. It included the mental and physical qualifications required on the part of the candidate as well as the right intention. The *formal element*, on the other hand, was the call of the bishop or of a religious superior in the case of a vocation to religion. From this he concluded that God calls to the religious life or to the priesthood *only those who are called by the bishop or admitted to profession by a religious*

---

[203] Vermeersch, *op. cit.*, p. 12.

superior; or, more correctly, God calls *formally* to these vocations only those who are admitted to them by legitimate authority. The material element does *not* constitute a divine right to the priesthood, for this right or vocation does not exist purely and simply except by the hierarchical act of the bishop or the authoritative act of the proper authority.[204]

Concerning the material element or at least a part of it — the intention of the candidate — he admits that this can come from one of three causes: (1) from a divine formal revelation, whether this be through an interior word or an external word; (2) from a divine inspiration, an inclination which precedes deliberation; or (3) from a supernatural election which is the fruit of a free and personal election of one's own initiative, having concomitant with it the action and excitation of grace. This election, however, is not provoked either by revelation or by the direct touch of or contact with the Holy Ghost who works in the soul mysteriously through His Gifts, the soul itself being more or less passive to this action.[205]

In regard to these different manners in which the material element, or that part of it which we call the right intention, is produced he says that a vocation in the first two cases is something sent from on high, whereas in the third case, it is the person, the soul which presents to itself the priesthood as a goal freely attainable with the help of God.[206] But because these conditions of fitness — physical, moral, mental, and the right intention — constitute only the material element of vocation, "they can be considered as constituting a vocation only by using the word improperly, or let us say by abusing the word and committing a useless equivocation which is to say the least, confusing."[207]

Because of the very forceful way in which this opinion was put forward at that time, it became the subject of many debates and finally, as has been said, was examined by a committee of cardinals. After having examined the book, the committee made the following decision: The author is not to be condemned, but rather approved especially when he writes:

(1) That no one ever has any right to ordination antecedently to the free choice of the bishop.

(2) The requisite on the part of the one to be ordained which we call the priestly vocation, does not by any means consist, at least ordinarily and necessarily, in a certain interior attraction of the subject or an invitation of the Holy Ghost to enter the priesthood.

(3) On the contrary, in order that one may rightly be called by the bishop,

---

204 Cf. *La Vocation Sacerdotale*, 2 ed. (Paris: 1914), p. 20.
205 *Op. cit.*, pp. 46–47.   207 *Op cit.*, p. 115.
206 Cf. *ibid.*

nothing further is required beyond the right intention, together with that suitability which is based on such gifts of nature and grace, which is proved by such goodness of life and sufficiency of knowledge as will give well-founded hope that he will be able to discharge the duties of the priestly state properly and fulfill the obligations of that state in a holy manner.

These findings announced by Cardinal Merry del Val, were approved in an audience with Pius X on June 26, 1912.[208] As a result of the approbation of the book, this theory was supported by several later writers on the subject of priestly vocation.[209]

The "Attraction" Theory

Still another theory which seems to fall under this category of special vocation is that called the "attraction" theory. It was this which was the occasion for the book of Canon Lahitton. Very briefly, it asserts that certain signs must be present to prove that God has whispered His call to the soul of a young man seeking ordination.[210] It is a divine call that is addressed immediately to a man's soul urging him instinctively or perhaps even sensibly, as it were, by a secret voice, to enter the clerical or the religious state. Thus it implies three things. First, it implies a peculiar supernatural attraction, a strong and permanent inclination or a sweet impulse which is felt in the depths of the soul and leaves little or no doubt that the person has been called by God. Second, unless a person has this, he may not even consider the possibility of his becoming a candidate for the religious or clerical state. Third, by the very fact that he feels this attraction present in him, he has a right to demand that the doors of the cloister or the sanctuary be opened to him.[211]

Father Blowick, in trying to trace the history of this particular vocation theory, mentions "that the earliest references we can find to it are in the Letters and Conferences of St. Vincent de Paul and the theory is mentioned with a view to the lectures to be given at the first exercises of 1628. The Saint writes 'the lecturer will treat of vocation to the ecclesiastical state and he will impress upon the ordinands the necessity of having been called by God before they present themselves for orders. . . . He will explain to them in what this vocation consists, what are the marks and what are the means by which they may corre-

---

[208] Cf. AAS 4 (1912), 485.

[209] Cf., for example, *Priestly Vocation*, J. Blowick (Dublin: M. H. Gill and Son, Ltd., 1932); in fact this writer maintains that the theory of attraction which we are now going to discuss was condemned by Pius X. Cf., op. cit., pp. 114–116.

[210] Cf. Blowick, op. cit., p. 21.   [211] Cf. J. Lahitton, op. cit., p. 6.

spond with it.' "[212] This statement, Father Blowick then goes on to say, refers to the exercises or retreat held in 1628. "From this year we may date the origin of the theory of vocation which came to be universally held and received by ascetical and moral theologians until it was challenged and disproved in 1900 by Lahitton."[213]

If we were to accept this "attraction" theory just as it is presented to us by Canon Lahitton and others, we would perhaps have to agree with their condemnation of it. But an examination of the authors to whom it is attributed would indicate that they did not at all understand it in this way. They were not speaking of a kind of a charismatic gift or gratia gratis data, a special overpowering illumination or revelation made by God to the soul. They were speaking merely of the necessity of there being present a special internal grace of vocation, which God gives only to those whom He calls to the religious state or the priestly vocation. As such their theory is basically the same as that which shall be given next: the special internal vocation theory. However, the manner in which they presented their position in some passages of their works could easily be misunderstood. Thus, Hallier, a theologian whom St. Alphonsus follows, writes: "God gives this call by means of a secret voice whereby He speaks to the soul of the aspirant and invites him to embrace the clerical state. No one should be admitted to sacred orders whom God has not invited to the ministry at least by a secret voice."[214]

Subsequently this same writer points out that one can know of the presence of this voice by three signs: purity of life, purity of intention, and the absence of unworthy means and deceitful wiles in the seeking of ordination. It is the position of the bishop either personally or through those who act on his authority to investigate the signs of vocation and to pronounce on their genuineness. The bishop's verdict given after a thorough and searching investigation is an authoritative declaratory sentence that the candidate has or has not the recognized signs of a vocation and therefore that the vocation or secret voice itself exists, or does not exist. This same thought, with the necessary changes being made, is applicable to the religious vocation.

Canon Lahitton interpreted this position of Father Hallier (later adopted by St. Alphonsus) in the following manner: This attraction consists in this that the subject "feels himself from day to day in the depths of his soul drawn more strongly to the ecclesiastical state or profession; he feels himself quite suddenly set free from the uneasiness

---

212 J. Blowick, op. cit., p. 21.   213 Ibid., p. 22.
214 De Sacris Electionibus et ordinationibus, in Migne's Cursus Theologicus, XXIV, col. 375.

and irresolution by which he had been previously tormented and that not by any idea of his own worthiness but by a sweet acquiescence in the will of God and by the efficacy of His interior voice."[215] In other words Canon Lahitton as well as all those who follow his lead on this score consider this attraction theory in this light — that one must receive a very special extraordinary grace from God in order to advance to the reception of Holy Orders, and, therefore, that vocation consists in receiving this call.

Such an interpretation is not at all warranted, if we investigate the author's overall thought on the matter. In fact none of those who held this theory — Hallier, St. Alphonsus, St. Vincent de Paul, Concina — speak of one who has a vocation as being necessarily struck from on high as was St. Paul or some of the other saints, as we have mentioned above. They merely exact the so-called signs or marks of a vocation with regard to its interior aspect. They do not deny that one validly ordained priest or validly professed in some religious institute has a vocation or that he is not a priest or not a religious. They merely maintain that one should not advance to either of these ways of life without an internal vocation, without something, some signs that indicate by way of moral certitude this is a person's place in life. For without these, without this divine vocation, it is most difficult — if not impossible — to fulfill the obligations of the state and obtain salvation. These theologians appeal to the Council of Trent in support of their theory. Regarding the ministers of the altar the Council states: "The holy Synod teaches furthermore that in the ordination of bishops, priests, and of other orders, the consent or call or authority of the people, or of any secular power or magistrate is not required for the validity of the ordination; but rather it decrees that those who are called and instituted only by the people or by the civil power or magistrate and proceed to exercise these offices and that those who by their own temerity take these offices upon themselves are not ministers of the Church, but are to be regarded as 'thieves and robbers who have not entered by the door.' "[216] The Council in these words certainly demands some internal vocation or call from God before one dares to assume the responsibilities of the priesthood. This is also the mind of the Popes down through the centuries, as we shall see when treating of the next theory.[217] It was the opinion of these authors that it was gravely unlawful for one to receive orders or to enter

---

[215] Op. cit., p. 6.

[216] Council of Trent, sess. 23, On the Sacrament of Orders, Chap. 4, Denz. 960.

[217] Cf. Great Means of Perfection and Salvation, Complete Works of St. Alphonsus, III, tr. by Father Grimm, C.Ss.R. (Brooklyn: Selva, 1927), Chap. 10, p. 488 ff.

a religious community, unless he shall have been called to this by God, and this call which they likened to some inner or secret voice was something that could be known through conjecture, through signs, and not through some special illumination, as was thought by Canon Lahitton and his followers.[218]

What is most important to remember is that when these authors speak of this secret voice they do not mean to imply that one must have received a special internal revelation of the fact or the presence of vocation; this is more than evident from the fact that they give certain *visible* signs, the very same signs which all authors give, from which one can conjecture with moral certitude that a vocation is present. The use of the words or phrase "secret voice" may not have been the most fortunate, but what we must look for is not so much the expression as the reality or the thought which these authors were trying to convey. On this score they remain faithful to the entire tradition of the Church.

The Special Internal Vocation Theory

This is the last of the vocational theories that have been proposed. In the last analysis it is the same as the one attributed to St. Alphonsus and the other theologians mentioned, when their position is correctly understood. It is the theory which is commonly held today and is almost certain by reason of the many papal documents which may be cited in its favor. We might attempt to explain it as follows.

At the very beginning of this section we divided vocation into divine and ecclesiastical. The first of these, the divine vocation, can be further divided into a general external divine vocation and a special internal divine vocation. The general external divine vocation is merely the call addressed by Christ to all the faithful to follow the way of the evangelical counsels. The special internal divine vocation, on the other hand, is the call which God addresses to the heart, as it were, a *special grace* which moves or inclines one to embrace this life. St. Thomas has attempted to indicate this difference between the two in his *Contra Retrahentes:*

> It has already been shown that the message by which the Lord speaks to us in Scripture has the same weight of authority as if the words were

---

[218] Cf., e.g., Haine (*Theologiae Moralis Elementa*, II, 255; Aertneys-Damen, C.Ss.R., *Theologia Moralis*, I, 427 ff.; A. Lehmkuhl, S.J., *Theologia Moralis*, I, 305 ff.; C. Marc. C.Ss.R., *Institutiones Morales Alphonsianae*, II, 607 ff.; J. Gury, S.J., *Compendium Theologiae Moralis*, II, 61. None of these authors maintains that one has a right to demand that the doors of the cloister or the seminary be opened to him. They merely assert that one who feels that he should be a priest or a religious should respond to this call and do what lies in his power to be accepted for the service of God in either the priesthood or the religious life.

pronounced by our Lord Himself. There is, however, another manner in which God speaks to man interiorly which is to be placed before every kind of exterior message. . . . If therefore one must obey immediately the voice of the Creator speaking in an external way as they say, then even more so ought one not resist the interior voice by which the Holy Ghost changes the mind. Rather he ought to obey it without hesitation.[219]

The so-called ecclesiastical vocation, or the ecclesiastical element involved in a vocation to the religious life (or to the priesthood), the call of the bishop or the acceptance on the part of the proper religious superior, can be viewed either theologically or juridically. *Theologically*, the ecclesiastical call or vocation is the confirmation used by Divine Providence to perfect and strengthen the internal vocation on the part of the candidate.[220] *Juridically*, it is the Church's stamp of approval or the conferring of the privilege on the candidate to enter into or make religious profession or to advance to orders.

---

[219] *Opuscula Theologica*, II, Chap. 9 (Rome: Marietti, 1954), pp. 173–174. In a very excellent work Father Edward Farrell (*The Theology of Religious Vocation* [St. Louis: Herder, 1952], pp. 79–80) has interpreted this passage in the following light: "In thomistic language God wills all Christians by His antecedent will to establish themselves in the state of perfection. By His consequent will He wills that certain ones and not others actually do become religious. By analogy with the division of grace into efficacious and sufficient, the external vocation can be denominated a sufficient call; the internal, an efficacious call which infallibly moves a man to choose freely the religious state."

While the author seems to be on the right track in bringing into the problem the question of sufficient and efficacious grace, still I feel that this distinction has not been properly placed. Rather than place it in relation to the external and the internal calls, it would seem to be more in keeping with the general Thomistic viewpoint on grace to place it within the concept or confines of the internal call itself. This internal call is accepted by the one to whom it is addressed and then it would have been efficacious. It can also be rejected by the individual, and then the grace, though offered, would have been sufficient. From this viewpoint the analogy given by the above-mentioned author might prove to be a little confusing. It is possible for a reader to conclude that if one did not answer the external call he would be *resisting* a vocation. What is more properly the case (and this I think would be the thought of Father Farrell also) one would be said to resist the internal call if he chose not to follow the inspiration of God's grace. If he chose not to follow the *external* call, it might be because he felt that God was not calling him. Thus, if a person were to examine the counsels and his own capacities and temperament under the light and activity of God's grace and were to decide that the religious life was not his vocation we could not say that he resisted the call of God to the religious life. Rather, we would say that God has not given him the grace of vocation, whatever mysterious reality would be meant by that phrase. One *could* commit a fault, I believe, at least against prudence, by *willfully* not giving any consideration to the words of our Lord. But this is a very delicate problem demanding many refined distinctions which cannot be gone into here.

[220] Cf. E. Farrell, O.P., *op. cit.*, p. 81. Fr. Colin remarks similarly: "The call of authority is merely the official verification and as it were the authentic confirmation of the former, the call of grace." *The Practice of the Vows* (Chicago: Regnery, 1955), p. 21.

Both the internal and the ecclesiastical vocations are so necessary for there to exist a vocation in the complete sense of the word, that the following conclusions regarding vocation can be established: (1) without the interior vocation, the exterior vocation would be valid but illicit; (2) without the ecclesiastical vocation, the divine vocation is neither authentic nor operating; (3) the total vocation is interior and exterior (vocatus intus et extra).[221]

Such a concept of vocation while not demanding a special illumination or revelation (or what Lahitton called the "attraction" theory) does still demand a special internal grace moving a person to seek admission into a religious order, or into a seminary. This is what we mean by vocatur intus. God, of course, could grant some special grace or grace of illumination or revelation, but this is not the normal thing.

This theory admits that God invites all through the words of Sacred Scripture to follow the way of the counsels, at least, the spirit of these norms of perfection. It also claims that the internal call is made through the channel of a special grace, through which one's thoughts and aspirations are inclined to the religious life. But it denies that this action of God depends upon the free choice of the individual and that the grace involved in a religious vocation or a priestly vocation is the same grace as that given to all men, rendered efficacious in the last analysis. by the consent of man. Most of these ideas can be readily substantiated from a quick look at the sources as well as from theological principles. And this we shall now do.

Examining the Sacred Writings, there seems to be no doubt that texts could be pointed out indicating favorable leanings both to the general internal vocation theory, and to the special internal vocation theory. Thus, for example, in some of the texts referring to the observance of the counsels, the passages would seem to indicate that man himself makes the decision as to whether or not he shall observe them: "If thou hast a mind to be perfect, go, sell what thou hast and give to the poor and so thou shalt have treasure in heaven; then come back and follow me."[222] Again we are told: "If any man has a mind to come my way let him renounce self, and take up his cross and follow me."[223] Finally, in regard to the observance of chastity, both the texts referring to this would seem to warrant a similar interpretation. For we read in Matthew: "There are eunuchs who have made themselves so for the sake of the Kingdom of heaven."[224] And Paul says: "I am thinking of your own interest when I

---

[221] Cf. Fr. Sempé, in "Vocation," Dictionnaire de Théologie Catholique, XV, 2ième part, col. 3174.

[222] Mt. 19:21.   [223] Mt. 16:24.   [224] Mt. 19:11–12.

say this. It is not that I would hold you on a leash. I am thinking of what is suitable for you and how you may best attend the Lord without distraction. . . . Thus a man is well advised to give his ward in marriage and still better advised not to give her in marriage . . . if her husband is dead, she is free to marry anyone she will . . . but more blessed is she if she remains as she is."[225]

All of these texts would seem to indicate that it is the individual person who chooses whether or not he or she will observe the counsels. The idea of there being a special grace required for making the choice is not indicated in them. However, this idea does seem to be implied in several of the contexts wherein these passages occur. Regarding the observance of chastity, for example, both in Matthew and in 1 Corinthians we find at least insinuations that such an observance is possible only because some special gift has been given to an individual. In the passage in Matthew we read: "If this be the case between man and wife, it is better not to marry at all. That conclusion, he said, cannot be taken in by everybody, *but only by those who have the gift.*"[226] And in 1 Corinthians we read: "For I would that all men were even as myself (unmarried). But every one has *his endowment from God,* one after this manner, and another after that."[227] These texts would seem to indicate that such a way of life, while indeed the result of an individual's free choice, is nonetheless also due to some gift of God, which is different from some other gift. Paul clearly indicates that both chastity and marriage are gifts, although the first is objectively speaking a more excellent gift than the latter.

From these texts of Sacred Scripture it would seem that we can rightfully conclude there is such a thing as a divine vocation or an internal "grace" or gift, as it is designated in Scripture, which God gives to those who observe chastity for the sake of the kingdom of God. This gift is different from that given to another, for example, who would enter into the state of marriage, even though such a state would be due to a gift also and in some sense, perhaps, a divine vocation. While all are invited externally, still only some are invited internally, in a special way, since they alone have received a gift from God to undertake this way of life. The texts do not indicate the exact nature of this gift, but it does not appear to be a kind of special illumination or revelation, even though this certainty has been given in the case of some vocations.[228]

If the testimony of Scripture does not seem sufficient to some, the writings of the *Fathers and theologians* do present a proof that is beyond question. For present purposes we might limit ourselves to some of

---

[225] 1 Cor. 7:25 ff.   [226] Mt. 19:10–11.   [227] 1 Cor. 7:7.
[228] E.g., Isaias, Jeremias, Paul, the Mother of God.

the more important periods of the history of this question, attempting to see the problem as it was presented by the Church Fathers, by some of the Scholastics, and by several authors writing after the Council of Trent.

The Early Church Fathers

The early Church Fathers furnish ample testimony to the position which we have said is commonly held and is almost certain today. In one of his letters, St. Antony[229] points out the presence of a divine or interior call or inspiration to the monastic life, without which one should not attempt it. The exact nature of this call is not described, and the Saint furthermore admits that God also furnishes certain external stimuli or helps to enable one to hear this call, such as the hearing of the Gospel, the reading of Scripture, and the divine punishments.[230] Nonetheless, the idea of an internal call is clearly insisted upon. On this point he is closely followed by Cassian[231] who clearly distinguishes between what we have called the ecclesiastical and divine vocation: "God moves one interiorly to embrace the monastic life which, however, must be approved by the monastic authorities," in order to be authenticated.[232]

St. Gregory the Great, in speaking of priests who have not been really called to the ministry, indicates that ordination alone is not sufficient to constitute a complete vocation: "They are really priests who have been ordained, but this ordination is merely permissive or one that is tolerated by God. By themselves they rule and not by the will of the Supreme Rector, those who do not have virtue and who are in no wise divinely called."[233] The sense of his thought seems to be that even though one may have been validly ordained, he has nonetheless received the order illicitly since he has in no way received from God the interior vocation which the external rite of ordination presupposes in the ordinand. An idea very similar to this can be found in St. Bede's Commentary on St. Mark. There he mentions that "the Lord in calling exteriorly by means of the human word, enkindles the desire to follow Him promptly by means of a divine inspiration interiorly put into one's heart."[234]

The Scholastic Period

Moving to the Scholastic period, we might cite merely three of the greater authors of this time. St. Bernard, in one of his letters touching on the question of impeding a vocation, teaches that this would be to inter-

229 (356).
230 Cf. Letter 1, PG 40, 999 ff.
231 Cf. 435.

232 Cf. Coll. 14, Chap. 5, PL 49, 959.
233 Regula Pastoralis, PL 77, 13.
234 Commen. In Marcum, PL 92, 150.

fere with something that comes from God: "The angel of Great Council calls. Why do you offer any counsel that would be foreign to this? It is God who works in the hearts of men in order to incline their wills wherever He wishes."[235] A century or so later, St. Bonaventure, in an exposition of the Rule of the Order of Friars Minor, mentions that to enter the order one must have received some inspiration, and such inspiration cannot be had unless it shall have been given from above.

But it is perhaps St. Thomas who has given us the most lengthy treatment of our problem. Almost the whole of Chapters 8 and 9 of the *Contra Retrahentes Homines* — "Against Those Who would Prevent Men from Entering Religion" — deals with this subject of the interior and exterior vocation or call. He writes in part:

> There is another manner in which God speaks to man interiorly, which is to be preferred to all exterior calls. If therefore, we must obey the voice of the Creator calling us exteriorly, and this by an immediate response, then even more so no one is to resist the interior call or invitation, by which the Holy Ghost changes the mind. . . . He does not act by the power of the Holy Ghost who resists it or who proceeds to accomplish it only after hesitation. . . . Since therefore a person is moved to enter religion by the inspiration of the Holy Spirit, he is not to be put off in order that he might seek human counsel; rather he ought to follow this inspiration immediately. Whence it is not praiseworthy but rather worthy of censure that one after having received an interior or exterior vocation given either by word or writing, should put it off or seek counsel. Either one is ignorant of or tries to resist the power of the Holy Ghost who attempts to delay the movement of the Spirit by seeking counsel.[236]

What Thomas is arguing against is the tendency to delay answering God's call when a person is certain of its presence, under the pretext of seeking counsel. Thus if one were not certain that the inspiration was there and truly present, he would not be forbidden to seek counsel; in fact, in this case he would have to seek it in order to come to a correct evaluation of the inspiration. How often such a situation would occur is very difficult to say. What is noteworthy for us is that Thomas does speak of there being a special internal inspiration in the case of one truly called by God.[237]

---

[235] Letter, 382, PL 182, 585.

[236] *Contra Retrahentes, Opuscula Theologica,* II (Rome: Marietti, 1954), p. 173 ff.

[237] Cf. also II–II, Q. 189, a. 10: "The saying try the spirits to see if they be of God applies to matters admitting of doubt as to whether the spirit really be of God. Thus those who are already in religion may doubt whether he who offers himself to religion be led by the Spirit of God or whether he is moved by hypocrisy. Consequently, they must try the postulant to see whether he be moved by the divine Spirit. But for him who seeks to enter religion there can be no doubt that the purpose of entering religion to which his heart has given birth is from the Spirit of God. For it is His Spirit that leads man into the land of uprightness." *Loc. cit.*, ad. 1.

After the Council of Trent

This same position of the early Church writers and the Scholastic theologians was continued after the Council of Trent also, and perhaps even more strongly, as the reaction of the early part of the 17th century would seem to indicate. Two of the outstanding writers of this period, St. Francis de Sales and St. Alphonsus Liguori, might be brought forward as witnesses to this continued tradition. The former in speaking of the vocation to the religious life writes:

A good vocation is simply a firm and constant will which the called person has to serve God in the way and in the places that Almightly God has called him to: that is the best mark that one can have to know when a vocation is good. Not that it is necessary that such a soul should do from the beginning all that it must do in its vocation with so great a firmness and constancy as to be exempt from all repugnance, difficulty, or disgust in the matter of its vocation; still less that this firmness and constancy must be such as to make it exempt from committing faults, nor has it to be so firm as never to come to waver or vary in its undertaking to practice the means which may lead it to perfection; since all men are subject to such passions, to change, to vicissitude, and are not to be judged by these different movements and accidents so long as the will remains firm as to the point of not quitting the good which it has embraced, though it may feel some disrelish and coldness. . . . To know whether God wills one to be a religious man or woman, one is not to wait for Him sensibly to speak to us or to send us an angel from heaven to signify to us His will, nor is there any need to have revelations on the subject. Neither is there need of an examination by ten or twelve doctors of the Sorbonne to try whether the inspiration is good or bad, to be followed or not, but one must properly cultivate and correspond with the first movement and then not be troubled if disrelish or coldness supervene.

For if one try to keep the will always firmly fixed upon seeking out the good which God shows us he will not fail to make all turn to His glory. From whatever side the motive of the vocation may come it is enough to have felt the inclination or movement in the heart to seek after the good to which one is called and to remain free and constant in its pursuit although this may be with repugnance and coldly.[238]

As the quotation clearly indicates, St. Francis does not demand the presence of an extraordinary grace in order to determine the presence or absence of any vocation. All that he demands is the presence of a firm and constant will to serve God, which he calls an *inclination* or *the movement of the heart* to seek after the good to which one is called. He advises one to follow the *first movement*, and then not be troubled by any supervening difficulties.

---

[238] *Letters to Persons in Religion* (Westminster, Md.: Newman, 1943), pp. 385–386.

The position of the other writer, St. Alphonsus, is rather well known as we have indicated. It can be found expressed in several places in his works. The following passages, however, will suffice since they seem best to represent his thought on the matter. "To enter any state of life," the Saint writes, "a divine vocation is necessary; for without this it is, if not impossible, at least most difficult to fulfill the obligations of our state, and obtain salvation. But if for all states a vocation is necessary it is especially true of the ecclesiastical state. That is why the Church has called any one who assumes or takes to himself this state without having a divine vocation a thief and a robber." After having laid down this principle, the Saint goes on to indicate the signs of this vocation which are practically the same as those given in Canon Law. The presence of these signs indicates the presence or the absence of the secret voice or the call of God. Consequently, it would seem that for St. Alphonsus as well as for others this secret voice refers not to some extraordinary revelation or illumination which one receives from God but rather to a special internal grace or gift which those whom God calls receive from Him.[239]

> God destines (he continues) according to the order of His providence a state of life for each individual and according to the state to which he calls him prepares abundant graces and helps. In the distribution of graces, says St. Cyprian, the Holy Spirit takes into account His own plan and not our caprices. . . . Ask the Lord of the harvest to send laborers into His harvest. It is our duty not so much to ask men but rather to ask God to send worthy men into His harvest. For it is God who chooses men for this work: You have not chosen me, but I have chosen you. It is perfectly right and fitting that one should make persons aware of the religious state and of its advantages. But we must be careful that we do not use means that are merely human and without the divine backing for a vocation.[240]

Ecclesiastical writers from the very earliest days have insisted upon the necessity of some interior call before one should advance to assume the duties of either the religious life or the priesthood. This need not be something that is in the realm of the miraculous, but merely a conviction that one is called by God to embrace this or that state of life or a firm will to serve God in one or other of these ways of life. This interior call is not something emotional but rather something of the will or of the volitional faculty of man. What tradition has never demanded is the necessity for any extraordinary grace or special revelation made by God to one called to the religious life or to the priesthood.

---

[239] Cf. *Great Means of Perfection* (*Complete Works of St. Alphonsus*, III), tr. by Fr. Grimm (Brooklyn: 1927), pp. 488–490.
[240] *Ibid.*, p. 503.

The Documents of the Church

If there has ever been any doubt (and there has been, as the theories which we have enumerated indicate), it is safe to say that today there is none whatsoever as to the necessity of this interior divine vocation. This clarification of affairs has been brought about by many rather recent documents issuing from the magisterium of the Church. It will be sufficient for our purpose to indicate the thought of Pius XI and Pius XII in this regard.

Pope Pius XI

In his encyclical on the Catholic priesthood Pope Pius XI points out three things in regard to our present considerations. First of all, he indicates that an extraordinary grace is not required for one to enter upon the sacred ministry of the priesthood. Second, he does require that a man be called interiorly, or by a special call or grace from God before he embark on this way of life. Otherwise he exposes himself to the risk of becoming a stumbling block to himself and to others, with peril of eternal ruin. Third, this interior call can be known only with moral certitude by reason of the presence of certain positive signs of fitness, those which are listed in Canon Law. The following excerpts from this encyclical will substantiate these claims:

> His [the rector of the seminary] watchful and experienced eye will perceive without difficulty whether one or other has or has not a true priestly vocation. This as you well know Venerable Brethren is not established so much by some inner feeling or devout attraction, which may sometimes be absent or hardly perceptible; but rather by a right intention in the aspirant, together with a combination of physical, intellectual and moral qualities which make him fitted for such a state of life. He must look to the priesthood solely from the noble motive of consecrating himself to the service of God and the salvation of souls. . . .[241]

> Such false mercy [allowing a man to continue who does not have the signs of a vocation] would be a real cruelty not only towards the Church, to whom would be given an unfitted minister, but also toward the youth himself; for thus embarked upon a false course, he would find himself exposed to the risk of becoming a stumbling block to himself and to others, with peril of eternal ruin.[242]
> . . . the chief responsibility rests with the bishop who according to the severe law of the Church should not confer holy orders on anyone unless from positive signs he is morally certain of canonical fitness. Otherwise he

---

[241] *Ad Catholici Sacerdoti, AAS* 28 (1936), 40; *The Popes and the Priesthood* (St. Meinrad, Ind.: St. Meinrad Press, 1944), pp. 65–66.
[242] *Ibid.,* pp. 39–40; 65.

not only sins grievously, but also places himself in danger of sharing in the sins of others. This canon is a clear echo of the warning of the Apostle to Timothy: "Impose not hands lightly on any man, neither be a partaker of others sins." To impose hands lightly our Predecessor Leo the Great expounds is to confer the sacerdotal dignity on persons not sufficiently approved: before maturity of age, before merit of obedience, before a time of testing, before trial of knowledge; and to be a partaker of other men's sins is for the ordainer to become as unworthy as the unworthy man whom he ordained. Hence do not fear to seem harsh if in virtue of your rights and fulfilling your duty you require such positive proofs of worthiness before ordination.[243]

[It is] God Himself who liberally sows in the generous hearts of many young men this precious seed of vocation; but human means of cultivating this seed must not be neglected.[244] . . . Yet it must be confessed with sadness that only too often parents seem to be unable to resign themselves to the priestly or religious vocations of their children. Such parents have no scruple in opposing the divine call with objections of all kinds; they even have recourse to means which imperil not only the vocation to a more perfect state, but also the very conscience and eternal salvation of those souls they ought to hold so dear.[245]

The presence of this inner call, if you will, had already been singled out by this same Pontiff in other places, two of which are rather striking in their wording. In *Rerum Ecclesiae* he writes: "There is no room in seminaries for those who show no inclination of will toward the priesthood. We all know that no fewer youths are called today than heretofore, yet many fewer obey the movement of divine inspiration. . . . No one should, however, be refused the priesthood if he is inspired and called by God."[246] And again he points out: "They will not infrequently hear in their hearts [in the course of a retreat] the mysterious voice of God calling them to the sacred functions and to the salvation of souls and impelling them to undertake the fullness of the apostolate."[247]

Pope Pius XII

This same teaching has been frequently restated by our late Holy Father Pope Pius XII on many occasions. For example in the encyclical letter *Mediator Dei*, in distinguishing between the character of Baptism and that of Holy Orders he wrote:

In the same way that Baptism is the distinctive mark of all Christians and serves to differentiate them from those who have not been cleansed in this purifying stream and consequently are not members of Christ, the sacrament of Orders sets the priest apart from the rest of the faithful who

---

[243] *Ibid.*, pp. 42; 66–67.
[244] *Ibid.*, pp. 45, 70.
[245] *Ibid.*, pp. 48, 71–72.

[246] AAS 18 (1926), 76.
[247] *Mens Nostra*, AAS 21 (1929), 701.

have not received this consecration. For they alone *in answer to an inward supernatural call* have entered the august ministry, where they are assigned to service in the sanctuary and become as it were the instruments God uses to communicate supernatural life from on high to the Mystical Body of Jesus Christ.[248]

A similar note is struck in the two documents dealing with the secular institutes, the *Provida Mater* and the *Primo Feliciter*. In the former he states: "While remaining in the world, they are able *through a special vocation from God* to devise new and unrivalled forms of confederation which particularly answer the needs of the times and in which many can lead a life wholly conducive to the attainment of Christian Perfection."[249] And in the latter he points out the special activity of the Holy Spirit in these vocations: "The Holy Spirit who unceasingly re-creates and renews the face of the earth which in these days has been made desolate . . . *by a great and special grace has called to Himself* many dear sons and daughters."[250]

In his apostolic exhortation to the clergy of the world this same Pontiff, having spoken of the priest as having been admitted to the sublime ministry of the altar by a call from heaven, later on takes up the question of vocational recruiting. In this particular part of the document he writes: "But it is also necessary that the souls of those called by God be *prepared for the impulse and the invisible action of the Holy Ghost.* To succeed more efficaciously in this (the recruiting of vocations) every priest must make an effort to be and to show himself an example of the priestly life which for the young men whom he approaches and among whom he looks for the *signs of the divine call* can constitute an ideal for imitation."[251]

Perhaps the most important document, however, that takes up our present problem in a most clear and forthright fashion is the *Sedes Sapientiae*, dated May 31, 1956. Since it is so vital to the understanding of the mind of the Church on our question, it is worth quoting at length:

First of all we want all to be aware that the foundation of the entire religious, priestly, and apostolic life, namely, the *divine vocation*, consists of *two essential elements, the one divine, the other ecclesiastical*. As to the first element, God's call to embrace the religious or priestly life, this must be considered *so necessary* that in its absence the foundation upon which the whole structure is to rest is absent. *A man whom God has not called is not moved or aided by His grace.* Inasmuch as God is the principal author of every state of life and of every natural and supernatural gift and disposition, a real vocation to any state, must, in a sense, be called divine. If this be so, how much more must one call the religious and priestly

[248] *AAS* 39 (1947), 538.
[249] *AAS* 39 (1947), 117.
[250] *AAS* 40 (1948), 283.
[251] *AAS* 42 (1950), 683–684.

vocation divine, since it is invested with a sublime dignity and adorned with so many natural and supernatural gifts that could be bestowed only by the Father of Lights, from whom comes every good and perfect gift.

But now let us pass on to the second element of the religious and priestly vocation. The Roman Catechism teaches that they are said to be called by God who are called by the lawful ministers of the Church. Far from contradicting what we have said concerning God's call, this position is actually in close agreement with it. For by a divine vocation to the clerical and religious state, a person undertakes publicly to lead a life of holiness in the Church, a visible and hierarchical society and to exercise this hierarchical ministry. Such a person ought to be authoritatively tested, approved, and directed by the hierarchical rulers to whom God has entrusted the administration of the Church.

This point must be kept in mind by all those whose duty it is to bring together and test such vocations. They must then, never compel a person in any way to embrace the priestly or religious state. They must not invite or admit one who gives no sure signs of the divine call. They should not advance to the clerical ministry one who shows that he has been called by God only to the religious life, or force or divert into the secular priesthood one who has received this twofold vocation. Finally they are not to turn away from the priesthood anyone whose vocation is manifest.

Furthermore, it is evident that when the seed of a divine vocation and the endowments this requires are present, it needs education and formation if it is to develop and mature. For a thing is not instantly perfect at birth, but only acquires perfection by a process of gradual growth. And if the desired goal is to be attained successfully, external circumstances must be considered in the guidance of this development; the persons whom God has called, the times, and the place.[252]

From these documents, the following observations seem in order concerning the mind of the Church with respect to the interior vocation and the exterior vocation:

a) No special impulse is needed for one to feel called by God to the priesthood, i.e., it is not necessary that one should be aware of God speaking within the soul, or that he should feel himself forced by God through some special illumination or force, to embrace one or other of these vocations.

b) A divine vocation or the divine element of a divine vocation is one which is known by others only through the presence of certain visible signs.

c) The role of the bishop or that of the religious superior is to judge whether these signs or marks of a divine vocation are present. If they are not present, their lack is to bar one's path either to the religious life or to the priesthood, or to both. If they are present, however, then the subject or the person is to be admitted to profession or ordination. This last point, i.e., that they must be admitted to profession or to

---

[252] *AAS* 48 (1956), 357–359; tr. *The Pope Speaks*, III (1956–1957), 290–292; *Canon Law Digest*, IV, p. 169.

ordination, is clear from the statements of Pope Pius XII in the *Sedes Sapientiae*, just given. Thus, the Code of Canon Law states that after the end of the novitiate and if the candidate is judged suitable or fit, he is to be admitted to profession. A response of the Sacred Congregation of Bishops and Regulars, when asked whether this implies a necessity, was in the affirmative.[253]

Theological Explanation

It would seem that the fundamental theological explanation, or, as theologians say, reasoning, that lies behind this accepted position is as follows. We have seen at the very beginning of this work that for God to love one thing more than another is for Him to will for the one a greater good than He wills for another. In the case of a vocation to the religious life, we are presented with such an occurrence. Those whom God is said to have called to this life by a special interior grace have always been referred to in the tradition of the Church as the chosen portion of the flock of Christ. The gift that they have received from God, through His loving action in their regard, is objectively speaking a more excellent gift than that which is given to those who are called, let us say, to the state of matrimony. Consequently, in a sense, religious can be said to be loved by God more than those who are called to an inferior state (again, we must insist, *objectively*).[254]

Whatever good there is in a creature has not been placed there, at least in any ultimate analysis, by the creature itself or by any other creature. Rather, it has been placed there by God since he is said to be the cause of all goodness in things and nothing good can be said to exist which does not have Him as its cause. Since the religious and priestly vocations are recognized by all as ways of life that are superior to others, it would seem that we must conclude that those who are called to these walks of life have received a greater gift or grace from God than others. They have in some way been the object of God's mysterious and special activity. And to this extent they can be said to be loved by God more than others are said to be loved by Him. While the choice or election that we make of something is caused by some good which already exists in the thing we choose, the *divine election* is not caused by any good present in the thing chosen, but

---

[253] Cf. *Fontes*, V, 2649. Father Ladislaus a Maria Immaculata, C.P., mentions that this holds true for the perpetual profession also; that is, that the community must admit the professed to final vows, or the novice has a right to final vows (cf. *De Vocatione Religiosa* [Rome: 1950], p. 152). Passerini is of the same mind: "And therefore where it is ascertained by means of a diligent and sufficient investigation, that one is called by the Holy Ghost the religious institute must cooperate with the Holy Ghost, because otherwise it would extinguish the spirit and resist it" (*De Statibus hominum, et officiis inspectiones morales* [Lucae: 1732], III, q. 189, a. 1, n. 19).

[254] Cf. I, Q. 20, a. 3.

on the contrary causes or places some good in it. It is God's election or choice of something that demands the presence of some good in one that is not to be found in another. St. Thomas indicates this quite clearly in the case of something analogous to what we are considering, namely, justification.

> In the case of the rational creature, certain ones are chosen for glory, certain ones are among the reprobates. The Lord knows His own for in a great house there are not only gold or silver vessels, but those of wood and clay. That is to say, there are certain vessels which are used for noble purposes and others which are used for less noble purposes. Thus there appears a diverse order among men. While in some the mercy of God shines forth and is resplendent in those whom He prepares for grace without any preceding merits, still in others, the justice of God appears, as for example when He consigns them to punishment for their faults, even though this may be far less than what they deserve.[255]

> Why He should especially draw this individual rather than this other one, no one reason can be given other than the divine good pleasure. Similarly the reason for which He makes some Apostles, some Confessors, some Martyrs, etc., is for the beauty and the perfection of His Church. But why He made Peter an apostle, Stephen a martyr, and Nicholas a confessor, there is no other reason that can be assigned except that such is His will.[256]

From these considerations it seems that we are justified in saying that the internal vocation, or the special grace which God gives to those whom He chooses for the religious life or for the priesthood and which manifests itself by way of the so-called right intention, is the effect in Thomistic language of God's grace-helps. This right intention presupposes the internal movement or communication on the part of God moving one to make this particular decision — to enter the service of God in one or other of these walks of life. This has been well indicated by Father Edward Farrell: "An internal vocation," he writes, "in man finds its expression chiefly in the act of intention, or the *propositum religionis* the purpose of entering religion, in which man tends to a definite goal under the inspiration of grace or a movement of grace."[257] This firm purpose of entering religion (or following the priesthood) is not always sudden. In fact, it is very rarely sudden. It is usually gradual in its formation, as we shall see immediately in treating of the genesis and nature of the interior vocation.

The Nature and Genesis of This Interior Vocation

When we stop for a moment to consider the nature of this special grace

---

[255] *Super Joannem*, Chap. 15, lect. 3 (Rome: Marietti ed., 1952), p. 381.
[256] Chap. 6, lect. 5, p. 176.
[257] *The Theology of Religious Vocation*, p. 48.

which God plants in the souls of some individuals we ought not forget the adjective which denotes it — "religious." We have already said, when treating of the theology of the religious life, that one is said to be a religious antonomastically, or properly, as it were. It belongs to the virtue of religion to render service or worship to Almighty God, and because one binds himself to divine service exclusively through his profession, he is said to be a religious. Thus the word "religious," while applicable to all persons performing acts of the virtue of religion, has been and is today appropriated (with an appropriation that has passed into propriety) to those who make public profession of the evangelical counsels.[258] We would expect that in the case of the spiritual physiognomy or the spiritual or supernatural organism of one called to the religious life, the virtue of religion would be in some way affected by the grace which he receives from God. Not that we mean to imply that this state, and this state alone, implies a modification of the virtue of religion. This would be to oversimplify and distort the truth. All vocations imply some way to God and therefore include the notion of service of God. All vocations are more or less rivulets into which the Christian life is channeled in its leading men to fulfill the very reason of their existence — to know, love, and serve God. But in the case of the religious vocation we are dealing with a manner or mode of life in which an individual is completely mancipated to God. Consequently, it would seem as though the virtue of religion would be in some way or other especially affected. This we might attempt to analyze.

The Nature of the Religious Vocation

As we have mentioned, the religious vocation, at least in facto esse, demands the presence in the soul of the recta intentio, the right intention, which consists in the firm proposal on the part of an individual to dedicate himself to the service of God in the religious life. Such an action would seem to be an externalization, as it were, or the ultimate effect of the activity of the virtue of religion. This stems from the fact that the whole of vocation seems to center around the service and reverence to which a creature dedicates himself in making this firm proposal. Because it pertains to the virtue of religion to elicit or command those acts through which one serves God or reverences and subjects himself to Him, vocation would seem to pertain, or to be an act that pertains, to this particular one of the infused habitual inclinations of the soul. In every vocation that is entered into out of service and subjection to God we find this virtue (and

---

258 For a parallel, cf. I, Q. 36, a. 1, ad 1m.

the others also but only in relation to religion) modified or "bent" in some way to elicit the firm proposal that is required for the vocation in question. This modification comes about, of course, as a result of the divine activity working in the soul.[259]

Moreover, it would seem that we can pinpoint, so to say, the activity of God involved in vocation even more minutely. In the theology of St. Thomas, we find that every virtue has at least one action that is proper to it — the virtue of faith, the act of confession; the virtue of charity, the act of dilection; the virtue of fortitude, the act of martyrdom; etc. The virtue of religion is no exception to this rule. It too has several actions which it elicits, such as the internal acts of devotion and prayer, and the external acts of sacrifice and adoration. Any analysis attempting to discover which of these would be involved in the firm proposal mentioned in the preceding paragraph would point to the *act of devotion* which is defined by St. Thomas as the "will to give oneself readily to things concerning the service of God."[260] Consequently, it would seem that any and every Christian vocation would in some way be related to this particular act of the virtue of religion. In fact, it would seem that we could readily conclude that the difference of vocations would be due to God's moving the will through His grace, or, as St. Paul called it, His gift, to make an act of devotion, one that would differ in some way according to the vocation in question. Thus, the firm proposal to serve God in this or that walk of life would be an elicited act of devotion differing in intensity and extension according as the vocation demands a more or less complete service of God, according as it might be conceived as a holocaustal act or a sacrificial act, as it were, demanding total or partial offering of the object given, that is, oneself, in service.

We have mentioned that the difference of vocations lies in the difference of (1) the *extent* to which a person gives himself in service and (2) the *intensity* required on the part of the act of devotion to meet the demands of the offering involved. This warrants an explanation. When we speak about the extension of a virtue, we are referring to the number of objects which fall within its scope. St. Thomas brings this out rather clearly in treating of the virtue of charity:

> A habitus may receive increase through extending to objects to which it did not extend previously. Thus the science of geometry increases in one who acquires knowledge of geometrical matters which he did not know hitherto. This cannot be said of charity because even the slightest degree of charity extends to all that we must love by it.[261]

---

[259] Cf. II–II, Q. 81, a. 3, *ad* 2m.   [260] II–II, Q. 82, a. 1.   [261] II–II, Q. 24, a. 5.

There is question, here, of the *material* object of the habitus of geometry, that is, the various things which fall under its scope. While the *formal* object *quo*, as they say, or the peculiar power or ability or motivating force under which the habitus of geometry operates, remains the same, the material object can increase *by way of extension*. Similarly in regard to the virtue of religion and its act of devotion, we find that the material object admits of a greater or lesser extension according to the excellence of the vocation in question. In the case of one who makes the complete and total or holocaustal offering and surrender of self to the service of God in the firm proposal to enter religion, we find an increase in the material object to which this virtue extends. For the grace of the religious vocation moves him to dedicate his *whole life* to divine worship and service by withdrawing himself from human affairs and by laying aside those things which could prevent him from giving himself entirely to God. In his case there is present the firm proposal or desire to give everything that he has or is to the service of God and this directly, or more directly than he could through any other vocation, to the point where he becomes the property of God much as a slave is said to be the exclusive property of his master. As St. Thomas mentioned in his treatise on the vow, he gives not only the acts of his faculties, but the faculties themselves to God; or to put it figuratively, he gives not only the fruits of the tree, but the tree itself to Almighty God. Thus, even though another might give God all the fruit of the tree, but still retain possession of the tree itself, the action of devotion required would still not be as holocaustal and extensive as if he gave the tree also. His action would still have the value of a sacrifice in relation to a holocaust. In the one case there is the giving of everything, whereas in the other there is a giving of only a part, even though a very great part. This idea is brought out by John of St. Thomas. He notes that the virtue of religion has a twofold object divided in the following manner:

Formal
{ quod: the cult to be rendered to God
  quo: the imperfect equality between God and the creature. This is why it is a potential part of the virtue of justice. No one can render adequate or perfect cult to God outside, of course, of Christ.

Material
{ body
  soul
  intellect and will which are offered to God or subject to Him
  other natural goods

In the case of the religious, there is the firm proposal to offer to God the body, the soul, the intellect and the will and one's possessions in cult or out of reverence and subjection to Him, in acknowledgment of His supreme rights and dominion over us. This offering is radical, including not only the acts that are involved in regard to these things, but the thing itself insofar as it can be given over.[262]

An example might serve to illustrate this point. Both in marriage and in consecrated virginity the body of an individual is given over to Christ, yet in different ways. In marriage one's body is given to Christ not directly, but *indirectly* in the person of the one who acts as the representative of Christ. Marriage sanctifies, as it were, all that is bodily in such a way that man even to his very depths is plunged into Christ and his most instinctive bodily reactions can become sanctified. In Christian virginity, however, one gives his or her body *directly* to Christ, bypassing all representatives. It is for this reason that Christian tradition has always regarded the virgin as the spouse of Christ. While marriage is the total donation of heart and soul and body *in* Christ, virginity is the total donation of these same things *to* Christ Himself, such that He alone possesses exclusive rights over these things. In an address to nursing Sisters Pius XII brought this out most strikingly:

> virginity is a higher state than married life because the virgin soul binds itself by the ties of complete and indissoluble love directly to God, or more exactly to the God-man Christ. Actually all that she has received from the divine goodness in order to be a wife and mother is offered up by her as a whole burnt offering upon the altar of entire and perpetual renunciation. The virgin soul in order to be united to the heart of God, to love Him only, and to be loved by Him in return does not advance toward Him by means of other hearts, nor does she linger to converse with other creatures like herself. . . . Even though marriage is a true sacrament, one of the seven sources of grace instituted by Christ Himself, and even though it involves a mutual offering of one spouse to another and cements a real union of lives and destinies, still there remains something that is held back, something that is not actually offered or given, or at least not given wholly. Only virgin souls can make that offering of self that for other loving souls is *an unattainable goal.*

Again the act of devotion that seems to be needed for making the firm proposal to enter religion is objectively speaking *more intense* than that which is required to enter an inferior state of life. In the former case, it seems as though God in giving one the grace of a religious vocation somehow or other works on the virtue of religion enabling it to elicit a most intense act of devotion. Father Farrell remarks quite accurately in this regard:

> a religious vocation is distinct from others because of its greater intensity, indeed the greatest intensity possible to the virtue of religion. For it fulfills

[262] Cf. *Cursus Theologicus*, VII, Disp. 19, a. 2, nos. 6 and 10.

religion's power of dedicating a man totally to the divine service perfectly. It is precisely this that constitutes the religious vocation: a most intense act of devotion intending religion's greatest object, that is, the religious state. We may thus define the religious vocation as an intense act of devotion in which an individual intends to dedicate himself to a wholehearted pursuit of perfection by fulfilling the evangelical counsels of perfection.[263]

From this it follows that vocations can be measured for their excellence according to the objective degree of intensity and extension which the walk of life places upon the virtue of religion and its act of devotion. The more excellent the walk of life, the more excellent also, normally speaking, is the act of devotion made by the person embracing it. Consequently, devotion can be said to play its most dramatic role in the pronouncing of the religious vows. In a sense we can say that it actually outstrips itself by prompting a man to go beyond the demands of nature, of justice, even of the divine precept of love, in order to bind oneself irrevocably to the service of God.[264]

This explanation, one in which both the intensity and the extension of the virtue of religion come into consideration, seems to the author to be more adequate than others. The idea of extension seems to imply more the notion of establishing one in a given state, or office, or function, or way of life. Intensity, however, seems to imply the idea of interior holiness or perfection of life, or perfection of charity, ultimately, since the virtues are proportionately intense. Yet we must make a distinction between the two ideas. It is possible for a person who possesses the firm proposal to enter religion not to have as intense a virtue of religion as someone in the

---

[263] Op. cit., p. 103.

[264] Cf. Farrell, op. cit., p. 55. Here we might also note an analogy. It comes from an analysis of the grace of Christ. We know that St. Thomas teaches that Christ is said to have had grace according to the greatest perfection in which it could possibly be had, according to the ordinary power of God or according to the decree of His divine wisdom in relation to the present economy of salvation. It was perfect with regard to its intensity both because His soul was the closest to the very source of grace that any soul could possibly be because His soul was hypostatically united to the Word of God, and also because He was to be the font from whom all grace would flow to men. It was perfect by way of extension since He possessed it in reference to all its possible operations and effects in the present economy. III, Q. 7, a. 9.

While it is true that both those who are married and those who profess the evangelical counsels could and should arrive at sanctity, still the fullness of grace required for sanctity in one case and in the other would be different since one state objectively speaking demands a more intense act of devotion (and proportionately of all the other virtues) than does the other. Each may be said to possess a fullness of grace but this fullness would be relative to the particular way of life in question. Both the Mother of God and St. Stephen were said to be full of grace, and yet the fullness of grace possessed by the former far surpassed that of the latter. The example used by one of the Sisters of St. Therese of Lisieux seems most apropos here — the two glasses both full but of different capacities. III, Q. 7, a. 10.

married state. In this case the acts of the virtue of religion of the latter could be much more intense than those of the former. Thus, objectively speaking, there is required a more intense act of the virtue of religion called devotion to enter the religious state than that of matrimony. Yet subjectively it could happen, and perhaps relatively often does happen, that a person in the state of matrimony makes a more intense act of devotion (and not merely emotionally intense) than one entering upon, or in, the religious life. Normally speaking, however, the act of devotion implied in giving to God one's entire life, body, will, and possessions is more intense than the act or devotion implied in entering the state of matrimony: and the reason — more is given to God, or at least, more is given *more directly* to God in the religious vocation than in the vocation to matrimony. This is good for us to recall because the loss of intensity in the act of devotion and its virtue, religion, could very easily mean the loss of vocation, since one would find it impossible or most difficult to fulfill the demands which the increase of extension implies. This latter never changes; it is constant. The former is susceptible to change for better or for worse since a person can starve or beat his vocation to death, or leave it unguarded. In fact, the younger the vocation, the more susceptible it usually is to harmful influences which could easily snuff out the light and life and love which have been infused by God.[265]

From this investigation I would like to propose the following definition of a religious vocation: "An intense act of the virtue of religion which we call devotion, implying an extension of the material object of this virtue, in and through which one firmly proposes to dedicate himself to the whole-hearted pursuit of Christian perfection by fulfilling the evangelical counsels of perfection, thereby intending to make a holocaustal offering of himself to the service of God."[266] This is what I think St. Thomas implied when he wrote: "Religious antonomastically (or properly by way of appropriation) are said to be those who dedicate themselves entirely to the service of God, offering to Him as it were, a holocaust. The religious vocation is nothing else than the firm proposal to do this, to be *totum incensum ante Deum*, all incense burning before the Lord."[267]

---

[265] Normally speaking the intensity of the virtue should be increased in proportion as the extension of the virtue increases. "For God so prepares and disposes those whom He chooses for some mission that they might be found capable of that for which they are chosen. Thus the Blessed Virgin was chosen to be the Mother of God and therefore we cannot doubt that she received the grace necessary for her to fulfill this role. The angel said to her, 'thou hast found grace before the Lord.'" III, Q. 27, a. 4.

[266] II–II, Q. 186, a. 1.

[267] Cf. On this score, regarding the nature of the religious vocation, we should note that another author, Father Bonduelle, O.P., considers the firm proposal to enter upon

Genesis of the Religious Vocation

To arrive at the proposal spoken of in the foregoing section, or the right intention, a whole previous formation of mind and heart and soul is necessary, somewhat in the manner in which a disposition is needed for the reception of habitual grace. This is brought about by God although He may use any of various kinds of instruments in so doing. While it is true that this call can take place like a thunderbolt, still most often it becomes only gradually perceptible. It is God, as it were, gradually revealing Himself in all things. Things that are human begin to lose their meaning so that one gradually begins to make plans always with reference to God. It is not at all strange that at the outset most people have only a confused consciousness of what is taking place and the moment in life when confusion is greatest is that of adolescence, which is also the usual age for vocations. It could easily happen that one who has been seized by the call is unable to analyze what is taking place within. That is why sometimes when a young person approaches a superior or recruiter of a religious community, and the recruiter asks why the individual wishes to consecrate himself or herself to God, the candidate cannot find the definite response that would assure the one approached that there is truly a vocation present within himself. This inability to formulate the proper response does not at all indicate that there is no vocation present, since the most deeply felt impressions are often the most difficult to put into precise words or formulas.[268] The principal fact at the source of every religious vocation, however, is that God is manifesting Himself to the individual as a person, as a living Being, and a dialogue has begun, the first word of which comes from God speaking in the depths of the soul; for the religious life will always be a life with God and in God. As the actual graces

---

religion or to be a religious, to be an act of the virtue of prudence. ". . . we see that the act by which a person turns to the religious life is a decision involving an extremely important choice, as it determines a permanent state of life, and therefore bears on all the moral and spiritual acts of a lifetime. For the whole life is marked from this time on with a special stamp coming from the virtue of religion and imposed more particularly in virtue of charity. However prominent the part played by religion and charity as the motives of this important decision the choice depends upon supernatural prudence because it involves planning for the future and arranging the whole of life. The person is trying to discover the will of God for himself. The situation is complicated, the individual has to take his bearings, try to see things clearly, classify the various factors that influence him from without as well as from within. He must discover what may be called from different viewpoints the virtuous solution, or the reasonable one, the Christian solution, of simply duty, or to speak in simple and more traditional terms, the will of God." Vocation, Religions Life Series, II (London: Blackfriars, 1952), p. 30.

[268] Cf. The Religious Vocation, J. Leclercq (New York: P. J. Kenedy and Sons, 1955), pp. 14–15.

or stimuli coming from God increase and multiply, the soul becomes aware of an active presence, of a divine reality, a reality of love in which it perceives the living God within it asking it for itself in a union of love that can only be compared with the union of bride and bridegroom in marriage. For the bride the bridegroom is the one being in the world who is most actively present to her. But as we said this comes about only gradually and usually leads to the intense act of devotion spoken of above.

If we were to inquire as to the causes of this awareness of God and of the intense act of devotion we should find that they are several, perhaps innumerable. Certainly the first cause is God, the extrinsic cause of devotion, as St. Ambrose has so clearly pointed out: "God calls whom He wills, and whom He wills, He also makes religious."[269] Second, there are other causes, one which St. Thomas calls the intrinsic cause of devotion, that is, meditation or the consideration of the goodness of God and of our own shortcomings.

> But [says St. Thomas] the intrinsic cause of devotion on our part must be meditation or contemplation. For it was stated above that devotion is an act of the will to the effect that man surrenders himself readily to the service of God. Now, every act of the will proceeds from some consideration since the object of the will is a good that is understood. Consequently, meditation must be the cause of devotion in so far as through meditation a person conceives the thought of surrendering himself to God's service. Indeed a twofold consideration leads him thereto: God's goodness and loving kindness toward him and his own shortcomings.[270]

Perhaps, the proper secondary cause of this act of devotion, or rather of its intensity, is the activity, the growing activity, under God's graduated stimuli or actual grace-helps, of the virtue of *magnanimity*, not so much, it seems to me, considered as a special virtue, as rather a condition or influencing factor responsible for the intensification of the act of every virtue — in this case, of religion and its act, devotion. Without the activity of this virtue an intense act of devotion, or of any other virtue for that matter, could not be made. For the virtues grow proportionately. The works which the magnanimous man undertakes are great and not merely by reason of the weakness of the man undertaking them. To dedicate oneself to God's service in the religious vocation is an act which objectively demands intensity on the part of an individual. Something similar can be seen in the so-called volunteer missions which occur during time of war or volunteer assignments even within religious communities. All these, like the religious vocation itself, demand the influence and activity of magnanimity which is a potential part of the cardinal virtue of fortitude,

[269] *Commen. on Luke*, VII, c. 9, v. 53, *PL* 15, 1793.
[270] II–II, Q. 82, a. 3.

This is brought out clearly by St. Thomas in his treatment of this virtue: "Every virtue has a certain propriety or adornment by reason of its own species. This is proper to every virtue. But there is superadded to it another adornment by reason of the very greatness of the virtuous work undertaken, through magnanimity which makes all of the virtues greater."[271]

From this we can see that the object of every virtue can become the object of the force of magnanimity so that this latter attains the status of a general condition or virtue which surrounds the acts of all the virtues or at least some of them, that is, those which are considered to be worthy of great honor and are recognized as being heroic ordered as they are toward a great and difficult good. Because the very nature of the religious life demands the presence of greatness and difficulty in the acts which it implies, the virtue of magnanimity as a general condition influencing the activity of the virtue of religion and its act devotion, must be found wherever we find a vigorous and growing religious life. Greatness and difficulty are stamped on the religious life. That is why it is called a state of perfection. Thus, precisely by reason of the holocaustal nature of this state and of the acts which one in it is required to perform throughout his or her entire life (greater liberality, greater chastity, and greater obedience), the presence of this virtue is most essential. In this sense we can say that the virtue of magnanimity enters into the act of the virtue of religion which we call devotion, being responsible for the firm proposal or the right intention required on the part of the candidate seeking the religious life. This adorning action, as St. Thomas calls it, of magnanimity with reference to the virtue of religion is brought about usually gradually and by the communication on the part of God of successive actual graces leading up to the firm proposal.[272]

However the case may be with regard to the influence of the virtue of magnanimity on the virtue of religion in regard to the religious vocation, we are not to consider this as an exclusive property which it enjoys. The act of devotion is not only the result of the special activity of the virtue of magnanimity. It is the result of the activity of all of the virtues, certainly of charity, of prudence, of intense liberality, intense obedience, and intense chastity or virginity. Practically all of the virtues have their special roles to play in enabling the virtue of religion through the act of devotion to elicit this firm proposal. But in the activity of all these virtues, there will always be the influencing factor of magnanimity. For the acts of intense liberality, of intense obedience, and of intense chastity imply something of greatness and difficulty about them. Consequently, each of these

---

[271] II–II, Q. 129, a. 4, ad 3m.
[272] Cf. Farrell, op. cit., p. 65, who differs slightly from the above presentation.

virtues in their activity needs to be strengthened by the adorning presence of magnanimity. It would seem that we must conclude that in the case of the grace of religious vocation, God gradually increases the strength of the *entire* supernatural organism and not only of the virtue of religion. When we say that the grace of religious vocation is an intense act of the virtue of religion and its act, devotion, we do not intend to exclude the presence and the activity of the other virtues. We merely intend to point out the *specific* eliciting virtue of the act required to mancipate oneself to the divine service.

In trying to explain the genesis of vocation, we could not have recourse to a better analogy than the work of God on the soul in justification. While it is true that this sometimes takes place very suddenly, as in the case of the conversion of St. Paul, still it is usually the end result of many previous actual graces or stimuli by which God has prepared the soul for this permanent gift. Oftentimes we tend to think of these actual graces as merely transient, passing, leaving no impression or modification on the soul, like flight of a bird through the air or the passage of a ship through the sea. This is not a true picture. There is no *accepted* actual grace which is so transient that it does not leave some trace of its passage on the soul, some remnant of its passage, or some disposition which becomes more and more pronounced as these stimuli multiply and increase. It is in this way that God disposes a subject gradually for the reception of that final grace which we call justification uniting the soul immediately with the three Divine Persons in loving companionship.[273] This is brought out by St. Thomas in treating of the vocation to the Christian life:

> Vocation is twofold; the first is *external* such as that which is had when a preacher extends an invitation to it. This is not justification but rather disposes to it. The other is *internal* and at times does not attain its end because of some obstacle or defect in the one receiving it. This interior vocation is nothing else than a kind of instinct or motion toward good sent to a person by God. This vocation is not the same as justification, but rather a way to it — an actual grace leading to it. Sometimes however, this interior vocation does attain its goal when one listens to the one calling and comes to Christ. Substantially this vocation is the same as justification and differs from it only *logically*. For it is called vocation in so far as a man is withdrawn from sin through the infusion of grace and through help which is given to him. It is called justification in so far as we consider the *terminus ad quem* or the terminal point which is a state of righteousness before God.[274]

These notions can be applied by analogy to the problem of vocation.

---

[273] Cf. I–II, Q. 109, a. 6, ad 1m, ad 4m, ad 4m; I–II, Q. 112, a. 2, ad 1m, ad 3m.
[274] IV *Sent.*, Q. 1, a. 1, qcl. 2.

There are internal actual graces which ought to lead to a religious vocation and fail to do so because of some defect in the subject. And there are others which do attain their effect when the subject listens to the one calling and comes to Christ. Substantially the religious vocation is the same as the firm proposal of religion or the firm desire or purpose of being a religious. The two differ from each other only logically. It is called "religious" vocation insofar as one is withdrawn from life in the world, through the infusion of grace and through the helps which are given him. And it is called "the firm proposal of religion" insofar as we consider the *terminus ad quem* or the term to which this call leads, namely, the firm desire to dedicate oneself to the divine service through the religious life.

The graces which are given are essentially supernatural, in nature and in character, because the object around which they center is supernatural. In fact, in a sense, we can say that these actual graces leading to a religious vocation or the firm proposal are *virtually* the religious vocation itself since the motion or movement ought to be judged in accordance with the terminal point to which it should lead.

*   *   *

From what has been seen regarding the nature and genesis of religious vocation it might well be considered as a special mark of God's love for a given individual by which He calls him out of the ordinary tasks of life, dispensing him, so to speak, from these tasks in order to entrust others to him. For the religious is called to be not so much the mold according to which all Christians are to be formed, as a *sign* of man's goal — intimate and complete union with God. The religious receives this grace, which makes of him the virtue of religion incarnate, precisely to hold and to keep before men the ultimate goal of all human life. Unless this sign is visibly present to men in some vocation or in some walk of life, they too easily forget the end for which they have been created. The overall picture of the religious life, with the habit, the discipline, the houses in which it is lived, has, as at least as one of its purposes, to keep before the eyes of men their own eternal or eschatological goal — consecration to and complete service of God. Because this service requires a spiritual union of the soul with Christ, the religious life in its very makeup *represents* this spiritual union by demanding of its members complete severance from union with the things of the earth. For the religious vocation is a call to imitate the perfection of the union which exists between Christ and His Church in the purely spiritual realm, that is, with regard to its integrity and purity and immaculateness. That is why religion, according to St. Thomas, is considered to be really the same as sanctity, which is defined as the inclination by which and through which the mind of man applies itself and its acts to God. It implies two things: cleanness of heart, without which the mind could not be given over to God; and stability, in this application. This is exactly what the goal of the religious life is; and it affords the most excellent means for one to arrive at these two conditions requisite for sanctity: *firmitas et munditia*. Thus St. Thomas mentions that sanctity is attributed to those who are applied to the divine service or worship, and that is, as we have seen, the whole purpose for the being of the religious vocation and life.[275]

Article II.   The Obligation of Following a Religious Vocation

Another of the speculative difficulties that has been much discussed concerns the obligation an individual has of following a vocation. The issue is most involved and complicated, to be sure. Nevertheless, we will attempt a presentation of the basic two positions *pro* and *con* together with an appraisal of each. We must remember that here we are dealing with something that lies in the realm of opinion. Consequently, the position that will be adopted by the author is not necessarily the correct or only one.

The *first opinion* maintains that because a religious (or a priestly) vocation is not of precept, but merely of counsel, it cannot oblige under pain of sin. That is to say, that if one felt that he were really called by God or that he possessed a religious (or priestly) vocation and nonetheless neglected to follow it, he would be guilty of at most a positive imperfection. One of the authors holding this position, Father Vermeersch, writes as follows:

> But is he who chooses the less perfect state not guilty of contempt? We cannot put on a par mortal sins and venial sins or imperfections; in a similar manner the refusal of the grace inviting us to better things which are not absolutely necessary must be distinguished from the refusal of the grace by which we perform necessary things that are commanded. In the latter case we are guilty of contempt and insult; in the former we merely prefer a lesser to a major grace. We have already indicated that when a certain state is preferred by some individual, it is not a question of electing a state of life which is not his own, but of following a secondary call to any good state.
>
> In the stricter opinion there is implied the false premise that God has designated a particular state for each human being, so the selecting of another state can scarcely be pleasing to Him. Habert goes so far as to say that any state but the one thus predetermined for each man is positively displeasing to God. These are his words: "He who enters though not called, commits a grievous wrong against the supreme authority of God. . . . Without a vocation, the office of the priesthood though good in itself is adminis-

---

[275] Cf. II–II, Q. 81, a. 8.

tered in opposition to God, contrary to His will. It is far more dangerous to make a mistake concerning vocation than concerning any single command of the law."[276] We have here [Father Vermeersch says] an extraordinary example of confusing interior and exterior vocation, or the will of one who invites and of one who commands or forbids.

We do not admit this principle or premise that God has designated a particular state for each individual human being. On the contrary, any honest state can be called a gift of God even if it is chosen by those who have been invited to a state of higher perfection.[277] . . . One who neglects to follow a special vocation [result of an extraordinary illumination of mind and incitement of will] becomes guilty of a positive imperfection.[278]

Note that it is not quite proper to say that the ordinary state, if chosen by one who seems to be called to a more perfect state, is chosen as a "less good." This would indicate something faulty or bad, whereas that state must be considered as something *really good*. We have the same thing constantly in the choice of good works, of which some are better than others, but all are good.[279]

How could that be called a counsel which imposes a virtual command?[280]

After giving this opinion, Father Vermeersch notes that *by way of exception* there are some who are in duty bound to embrace the religious life while for others that state is morally impossible or not to be advised. The moral necessity of entering religion may arise from a vow or exist in consequence of a divine law either natural or positive. For God can command some particular person to do a thing which is ordinarily only advised. If His will to this effect is revealed, then that person is bound by a positive command. This right belongs to Him by reason of the fact that He is the Supreme Being and Lord of the human race. Moreover, if a person is really convinced that he cannot save his soul except by entering a religious community, he is bound by the duty of self-love to choose the safer way. "This we grant," he says, "but it rarely happens." Others cannot enter by reason of impediments divine or human and these are given in the Constitutions of every religious community. Usually they merely repeat the dictates of Canon Law in this regard.[281]

---

276 Theologia Dogmatica et Moralis (De. Sacra. Ordinis, Pars III), Chap. I, #2.

277 Religious and Ecclesiastical Vocation, tr. by J. Kempf, 2 ed. (St. Louis: B. Herder, 1930), pp. 42–43.

278 Ibid., p. 47–48.

279 Ibid., p. 44.

280 Ibid.

281 In support of this opinion which Father Vermeersch calls the "original teaching of theologians and one based on Sacred Scripture, and the Fathers of the Church, and more simple than the other opinions advanced," we find several theologians: Father Berthier, M.S., in his Opusculum on the States of Life of the Christian and Vocation, According to the Doctors of the Church and Theologians (Paris: 1897); Father Bouvier, S.M., "Vocation According to the Masters of Theology," in Le Recruitment

In support of this opinion Father Garrigou Lagrange can also be cited. According to his terminology, *Minus bonum non est malum* — "Something which is less good is not evil, or bad, and therefore, is not sinful." For him such a refusal, at least as far as the ordinary vocation would be concerned, would not be sinful, but would involve merely a positive imperfection. He gives the following reasons for his position:

a) Acts are specified by their objects; if the object and the motive for which it is willed are good, then the act is good, although it may be less good than another which could be done at that time. A less good act is still a good act. It is not bad or sinful.

b) A counsel, by its very nature, does not oblige, but only invites us to what is better. Nor can it be said, as is sometimes said, that a counsel becomes obligatory if and when it appears opportune to a person here and now. "We might just as well say that in the concrete a counsel loses its nature, its very essence, and becomes a command; should any counsel here and now oblige anyone it would do so not of itself but in a wholly accidental fashion, because not to follow the counsel would involve sloth or contempt. Sin (however) has elsewhere been defined as any word, deed or desire against the eternal law, whatever is contrary to precept, *sub gravi* or *sub levi*, whether this bind seriously or lightly."

c) God Himself does not always choose that which is best in itself, for He can create beings more perfect than those to whom He has given existence.[282]

Father Edward Farrell also holds this opinion. He admits that it might provide some difficulty, however:

Some difficulty may occur in grasping the fact that no fault at all may be involved in the loss of a vocation (and a fortiori for the initial grace of vocation). But the difficulty is subjective and by no means objective. Since the withdrawal of actual graces by God takes place here some semblance of a real difficulty might be based on the observation of St. Thomas that whatever is granted by the grace of God is never recalled without guilt.[283] That this principle has a limited application, however, is obvious from the transient nature of the charismatic gifts, and exception must be made also for the religious vocation. St. Thomas is insistent upon the fact that a person's withdrawal from religion does not indicate the lack of religious vocation; it simply means that, although the grace was given by God to enter the religious life, the grace of perseverance was not.[284]

Sacerdotale, June 15, 1901; St. Robert Bellarmine, S.J., *Contro.*, T. 2, Contro. 2, Bk. 2, Chap. 31, and Chap. 12; Suarez, *De Religione*, Tract. VII, Bk. V, Chaps. 4, 8, and 9; Father Sempé, art. "Vocation," *DTC*, XV, col. 3155: Aidan Carr, O.F.M.Conv., *Vocation to the Priesthood, Its Canonical Concept* (Washington, D. C.: C. U. Press, 1950), p. 14.

[282] *The Love of God and the Cross of Jesus* (St. Louis: B. Herder, 1947), pp. 322–325.

[283] III, Q. 50, a. 2, c. *Id quod per gratiam Dei conceditur, numquam absque culpa revocatur.*

[284] *Op. cit.*, p. 217.

The *second opinion*, as we would imagine, holds that one has an obligation to follow a vocation, whether religious or priestly. This is held by several theologians, all of the highest repute in theological circles.

Cajetan writes: "It is evident that if the religious institute finds nothing that would exclude the novice from making profession, if they were to refuse to admit him to profession they would be reprehended by any wise and prudent person. Nor would they be said to be in good faith with that novice. *It is equally true* that the novice would be in bad faith if merely from his own free will he withdraws from the institute, although in the eyes of the Church nothing can be said against him." [285] Then he adds: "If one does this who has vowed to enter religion, then he would sin mortally; if he has not vowed to enter religion, then he would sin venially."

St. Alphonsus Liguori is of a similar opinion:

The Divine call to a more perfect life is undoubtedly a special grace and a very great one which God does not give to all: hence he has much reason to be indignant against those who despise it. How greatly would not a prince think himself offended, if he should call one of his vassals to serve him near his person, and this vassal should refuse to obey the call. And should God not resent such conduct?

Whenever God calls to a more perfect life or state, he who does not wish to expose his eternal salvation to great danger must then obey and obey promptly. Otherwise he will hear from Jesus Christ the reproach he made to that young man who when invited to follow him said I will follow thee Lord, but let me first take my leave of them that are at home. And Jesus replied to him that he was not fit for the kingdom of God. The lights which God gives are transient, not permanent gifts. Whence St. Thomas says that the vocation of God to a more perfect life ought to be followed as promptly as possible. He proposes in his *Summa* the question whether one ought to enter religion without having asked counsel of many and without long deliberation. He answers in the affirmative saying that counsel and deliberation are necessary in doubtful things, but not in that matter which is certainly good. St. Thomas says that if the vocation to religion should even come from the devil, we should nevertheless follow it, as a good counsel even though coming from an enemy.[286]

This particular position of St. Alphonsus comes from the fact that he as well as some of the theologians mentioned above, Habert, e.g., held that our eternal salvation depends principally upon the choice of our state of life. This is evident from the following statement:

Father Granada [he relates] calls this choice the chief wheel of our whole life. Hence as when in a clock the chief wheel is deranged the whole clock

---

285 Commentary on Q. 189, a. 4, n. 6.

286 *Great Means of Salvation and of Perfection*, tr. by Eugene Grimm, C.Ss.R. (New York: Benziger Bros., 1886), pp. 383, 386–387.

is also deranged, so in the order of our salvation. If we make a mistake as to the state to which we are called, our whole life will be an error. If we wish to secure our eternal salvation in the choice of a state of life, we must embrace that to which God calls us in which only God prepares for us the efficacious means necessary for our salvation. For St. Cyprian says that the "grace of the Holy Spirit is given according to the order of God and not according to our own will."[287]

Another author, one very famous for his work on the states of life, *Father Passerini*, O.P., also upheld this theory. He writes: "A counsel in general does not oblige, but one in particular does, that is, one that is given here and now concerning this world. This carries an obligation because the divine inspiration is a certain counsel addressed to an individual, through which God calls someone to do something."[288]

"If under the impetus and the help of God, a man in particular is illuminated so that he knows what is better right here and now and that he can do it, or prudently thinks that he can, then he is held to elect that which is better and if he does not do this, then he sins in some way."[289]

The reasons which he gives are about what one would expect: (1) it is a certain kind of ingratitude not to accept a gift from God once one knows that it comes from Him; (2) a certain irreverence is committed in refusing to recognize God as our leader and teacher, wishing to do that which is opposed to what He teaches we ought to do; (3) it would be not to do that which is better, [290] for that which God inspires in us is always better, all things being considered. The choice in this case is not for a right end, and consequently is not morally good, but rather evil. [291] He chooses evil, by the fact that he chooses a less good.[292]

Together with Cajetan he also holds that "where there is a diligent and sufficient investigation, and one knows that he is called by the Holy Ghost, the religious institute ought to cooperate with the Holy Ghost; otherwise they are extinguishing His work and are resisting Him."[293]

---

[287] *Ibid.*, p. 381.

[288] *De Statibus Hominum et officiis inspectiones morales* (Lucae: 1732), T. I, Q. 184, a. 3, n. 39.

[289] *Ibid.*, n. 52; cf. also nn. 43, 49, 54.

[290] Cf. n. 46.

[291] Cf. n. 51.

[292] Cf. n. 54.

[293] *Op. cit.*, T. III, Q. 189, a. 1, n. 19. Others among more recent authors have also held this opinion, although according to Father Vermeersch, while they have "otherwise done well in theology, they do not treat this matter with the necessary precision, and often contradict themselves" (*op. cit.*, p. 34). Thus Father Gautrelet, S.J., mentions that a person who does not choose the state in life to which he is guided by Divine Providence, remains in a state not his own all through life (*Treatise on the Religious State*, I, pp. 216–217 ff., 1885 ed.). Likewise Father I. Coppin, C.Ss.R., holds this same theory following St. Alphonsus and Habert (*La Vocation au marriage*,

In recent years this second opinion has been sustained by an ever grow-ing list of writers. Perhaps the reasons which are leading more and more theologians to sustain this view are (1) a deeper understanding of the law of Christ which is a law of love, or the interior law of charity, and (2) the significance of religious profession.[294] Father J. Leclercq seems to indicate this in his work on the religious vocation:

> The normal age when the call makes itself heard is in adolescence, the season of life when the mind opens out and becomes aware of beauty. But men change and this change may be in the way of corruption. To keep a vocation healthy that purity of heart must be maintained which allows the divine voice to be heard freely in the soul. Thence come those forms of self-denial which are codified in the religious life. . . . Faithfulness to the vocation thus becomes a detachment which enables the call to be heard. . . . He who hears the call sees that his life will be devoid of meaning unless he gives himself, and the word "gift" here is used in the fullest sense. . . .

au célibat, a la vie réligieuse, 4 ed. [Paris: 1914], Part I, Chap. 4). Aertneys, C.Ss.R., also hold this opinion (Theol. Moralis, I, Bk. V, Chap. 2, #3).

Concerning these authors, Father Vermeersch notes: "If we accept the opinions of these theologians, the divine call scarcely differs from a command. For while admitting that no obligation arises from the Evangelical Counsels, in the final analysis the choice is relegated to a purely speculative consideration of the matter. Indeed, in practice those who do not follow the call commit per se a venial sin. This assertion made with some hesitation by St. Alphonsus (Theol. Moralis, V, # 78) is boldly maintained by others, e.g., Passerini, as we have seen, and C. D'Annibale (Summul, III, 215)." Thus there is actually no choice left to anyone since it is impossible to enter the religious state if one is not called to it, or to refuse to enter if he is called, without committing sin. This conclusion is distinctly set forth by Scavini who says: "those who are not called cannot enter the religious state; those who are called must enter, or what would be the use of the call?" (Theol. Moralis, 14 ed. I, # 473, op. cit., pp. 36–37).

[294] Some of the authors that may be cited in favor of this position are the following: Jacques Leclercq, Essai de morale catholique, I, Le Retour a Jésus (Paris: 1946), p. 112, and again, in The Religious Vocation (New York: P. J. Kenedy & Sons, 1955), p. 17; G. Corallo, "Libertà e dovere nel problema della vocazione," in Salesianum, 11 (1949), 231–278; E. Zafolli, "L'Obligo di corrispondere alla Vocazione," in Vita Cristiana, 18 (1949), 361–401, and again, "Libertà e dovere nella problema della vocazione," in Vita Cristiana, 18 (1949), 402–409. Another article appeared the following year. "A Quanti Negano L'Obligo di corrispondere alla vocazione," in Vita Cristiana, 19 (1950), 169–183. Other authors are J. Osbourn, O.P., The Morality of Imperfections (Westminster, Md.: Carroll Press, 1950), pp. 73–74, 132, 205; Walter Farrell, O.P., "Virtues of the Household," in The Thomist, 9 (1946), 337 ff.; A. Plé, O.P., "Unconscious Attraction to the Religious Life," in Vocation, Religious Life Series, II, pp. 109–110; and apparently two other authors in this same volume, A. Motte, O.P., pp. 27–28, 36; A Bonduelle, O.P., p. 40. Other authors are not quite so categorical. Father Ladislaus a Maria Immaculata writes: "Quae tamen vocatio temporanea non facile est admittenda," De Vocatione Religiosa (Rome: Passionist House of Studies, 1950), p. 168. Father Brouillard, S.J., remarks: "Si elles existent, elle ne peuvent être que fort rares, marquées de signes assez clair pour permettre a l'autorité réligieuse de les reconnaître" "La Vocation Réligieuse," in R.C.R., 4 (128), 136. It has well been remarked "In the opinion of Fr. Veermersch we find a kind

Thence comes the vow. The vow is in a certain sense the essence of the religious life, for one is giving no true gift unless one has pledged oneself. The natural tendency of love is to say "forever." Love which gives of itself for as long as it pleases and reserves the right to resume possession of itself is only passion or fantasy. . . . The gift is only complete if one gives it for life with the determination to remain given whatever may be the difficulties and troubles.[295]

Evaluation of the Opinions

Perhaps the best approach to this consideration would be to state a preference for one of these two positions, the reasons for which this preference has been made, and then answer the objections which the opposite position makes against it.

The *second* opinion given above seems to be preferable and more according to the mind of the Church, and theology.

Church Documents

We have seen above that the Council of Trent spoke of one assuming the duties and the office of the priesthood without a vocation as a thief and a robber. Thus the fact that one receives the sacred order of the priesthood does not exonerate him of any guilt. If he has not had an interior vocation, he has no right to assume this office, and is to be considered as a thief and a robber.

Moreover, the Popes have constantly spoken of the necessity of one having the right intention of receiving orders, that they were not to receive orders if they did not have this right intention. This we have defined as the *propositum sacerdotii*, or the proposal to receive orders. Again there is question here of an interior vocation required as the foundation for the exterior call of the religious superior or bishop. While it is true that this fact does not imply that one who does not follow this vocation commits some kind of sin, still it does indicate that an interior vocation must be possessed before one can enter upon this way of life. Pius XI,

of echo of the position of Fr. Lahitton. Even if one seeks the priesthood with an intention that is not entirely pure, God with His consequent will wishes him to be a priest after orders and will give the necessary grace or assistance to live this life if he prays. . . . Consequently, it might be said that those who are entrusted with the direction of men or aspirants are not so much to look for men with vocations as they are rather for men for vocations. But I do not believe that Fr. Vermeersch would go along entirely with this analysis of his position. Both Lahitton and Vermeersch, it would seem, base their understanding and analysis of vocation on the Bellarmine and Suarezian doctrines of grace, predestination, and free will, the doctrine which has been called Congruism, whereas the Thomists base their understanding of vocation on the Banezian or Thomist doctrine in regard to these same entities." Cf. *Diocesan Priest Saints*, Father Hutchinson (St. Louis: B. Herder, 1958), pp. 82–88.
[295] *Op. cit.*, pp. 15 and 17.

himself, sanctioned to a certain extent one of the reasons given by St. Alphonsus, that otherwise "thus embarked upon a false course, he would find himself exposed to the risk of becoming a stumbling block to himself and to others, with peril of eternal ruin."[296] Certainly, if this means anything at all, it means that one must not advance to the priesthood (and we can apply this to the religious state) without having the proper, that is an internal, vocation.[297]

From these documents may we not draw the following conclusion, at least with some probability: If one should *not* embrace a vocation *at least* to the priesthood or the religious life without having a vocation to it, then it *seems* that he *is* to embrace that vocation to which he is called by God.

Theology

Perhaps the basic theological reason that could be advanced in favor of this position is the following. Whatever is granted by God's grace is never recalled without some guilt on the part of the individual involved. The grace of a religious vocation is a grace granted by God to certain individuals and this not merely by way of an exterior counsel but by way of an interior inspiration. Therefore, to consciously resist this special grace would be, as St. Thomas states, to resist the inspiration of the Holy Ghost, and to commit sin.[298]

Certainly from a thorough reading of the various works of the Angelic Doctor, we would have to conclude that this seems to be his mind. In the *Contra Retrahentes*, in speaking of this interior inspiration of the Holy Ghost to enter religion, he is speaking of merely the interior grace of vocation, and not of some special or gratuitous miraculous grace of illumination. In this place, however,[299] he specifically states:

> If we must obey the voice of the creator calling us exteriorly and this immediately as they say [that is if Christ were to come and appear to give us an order, or God were to do this, as Father Vermeersch also agrees]; then even more so *no one must resist the interior message* by which the Holy Ghost changes the mind. He does *not* act by the impetus of the Holy Ghost *who resists* it or who *tardily proceeds to accomplish* it. It is *not praiseworthy but rather worthy of censure (vituperabile)* that one after having received an interior or exterior vocation, given either by word or by writing, should put it off as it were and seek counsel. Either one is

---

[296] *The Popes and the Priesthood, Ad Catholici Sacerdotii*, p. 65.

[297] Cf. also *Sedes Sapientiae:* "For God by His grace neither moves nor assists anyone He does not call. This fact must be kept in mind by all those seeking to find and examine vocations of this kind. Let them never force anyone (to any state for which he does not show the proper signs) . . ." *AAS* 48 (1956), 357–358.

[298] Cf. III, Q. 50, a. 2.   [299] Cf. Chap. 9.

ignorant of, or tries to resist the power of the Holy Ghost, who attempts to delay the movement of the Holy Ghost by seeking counsel.[300]

In a parallel place the same idea seems to be expressed: "The example which is given in proof of the newly baptized not being commanded to fast until Pentecost, shows that no difficult things are to be laid on them as an *obligation before the Holy Ghost* inspires them inwardly to take upon themselves the difficult things of their own choice."[301] While there are certain things which are not of obligation before they are suggested by the Holy Ghost even to those who are of the Faith, still these would seem to become obligatory when the Holy Ghost inwardly inspires us or moves us to them.[302]

Again he writes: "When we say that the perfect are held to that which is better, this is true, if we understand this of those who are said to be perfect by reason of the perfection of charity. These are obliged by reason of an interior law which obliges them by inclining them [to these actions]."[303]

The reasoning of St. Alphonsus and many other reputable theologians together with St. Thomas Aquinas makes the second opinion at least a strong probability. To refuse a gift of God and to do this knowingly and willingly seems to indicate some slight offense against Him, at least so far as gratitude and prudence go on the part of the subject. While a vocation remains of counsel, when considered exteriorly, still if the interior grace of vocation is present (this we can usually determine with moral certitude only), then there always is a slight obligation to embrace the state, and, at times, as even the authors of the other opinion admit, a serious one if one were to understand that he could not possibly otherwise secure his eternal salvation. *The slight obligation would be one imposed by the virtues of prudence and/or gratitude.*

Answers to the Objections Advanced by the Authors of the Other Opinion

It would not be entirely fair merely to give the two opinions, take a stand for one, and fail to give the reasons for not holding the other

---

[300] Chap. 9, op. cit., p. 174.

[301] II–II, Q. 189, a. 1, ad 4m.

[302] In speaking of divine inspirations St. Francis de Sales writes: "Although the inspiration should continue during the whole life, yet we could not render ourselves pleasing to God if we took no pleasure in it. On the contrary, His Divine Majesty would be offended with us. . . . If after receiving an inspiration and taking pleasure in it we refuse our consent we should show ourselves extremely ungrateful and we highly offend His Majesty by our contempt for His favors." *Introduction to a Devout Life*, P. II, c .18.

[303] *Quodlibetal*, I, art. 14, ad 2.

opinion. At least the reasons advanced in favor of the other should be investigated and weighed.

The reason advanced by Father Farrell, that the statement of St. Thomas cited in the basic theological reason given above, although applicable in some considerations of theology does not apply here, is not proved. He merely makes this assertion without giving any solid reason in support of his position. The difficulty, therefore, remains. Why should this premise be true in regard to sanctifying grace and yet not true with regard to the grace of a religious vocation, or with regard to other inspirations of counsel? Do these not also pertain to the order of sanctifying grace, at least, virtually?

Nor do the reasons advanced by Father Garrigou Lagrange seem entirely cogent. First of all, we must remember that the sin or fault involved in refusing to embrace a walk of life or follow a counsel lies *not in the choosing of the lesser good*, or tending to this lesser good objectively considered, but *in refusing to follow a movement of God*. In other words, there are two objects to be considered, the object from which one withdraws and the motive leading one to withdraw from it, and likewise the object to which one tends and the motive moving one toward it. In the present case the objects are both good, but the motives moving one to the one and away from the other also have to be taken into consideration. If the motives are selfish, (with a disordered selfishness), then there seems to be some fault on the part of the one acting. The selfishness involved in one's withdrawing from a *known* interior grace would lie along the lines of imprudence and/or ingratitude. Thus by reason of some disordered desire, the person would commit a slight sin of imprudence and/or ingratitude in not following what he knows to be the will of God for him. The sin, therefore, lies not in the choice of the lesser good, but rather *in the turning away from another good to which we are inclined by God*. Unless this internal grace is present, one cannot be said to be refusing the grace of vocation.[304]

---

[304] The reasoning of Passerini and the other theologians which seems to agree perfectly with that of St. Thomas is preferable. Suarez has called this a negative ingratitude as opposed to a positive ingratitude. Whereas the latter is sinful, the former would not be. Thus, he writes: "I think that in things of this sort a kind of negative rather than positive ingratitude comes into the picture *per se* speaking; this because of the fact that one does not follow or correspond to the divine gifts as much as he can and as he ought, in order to conduct himself in the better manner. But, I say that it is not privative because in the demands of justice it does not deprive one of honor, nor is it a fault. As long as we cannot prove that the inspiration of the Holy Ghost has an obligatory force, there can be no question of an obligation to follow out a call from God."

"We agree with Suarez that there is no question of an obligation from the consideration of the virtue of justice. But what of the obligation from some other virtue,

When sin is defined as Father Garrigou Lagrange defines it, this must be interpreted in the light of the teaching of St. Thomas concerning sin. He understood this as the definition of *serious* sin, however, as is clear from the following passage:

> The division of sin into venial and mortal is not a division of a genus into its species, which have an equal share of the generic notion. It is a division of an analogous term into the parts of which it is predicated, of the one first, and of the other afterwards. Consequently, the perfect notion of sin which Augustine gives applies to mortal sin. On the other hand, venial sin is called a sin in reference to an imperfect notion of sin and in relation to mortal sin, even as an accident is called "being" in relation to substance, in reference to the imperfect notion of "being." For it [venial sin] is not against the law, since he who sins venially neither does what the law forbids nor omits what the law prescribes to be done. But he acts beside the law, through not observing the mode of reason which the law intends.[305]

To the third reason advanced by Father Garrigou Lagrange, we would answer that it is true that God has not made the best possible world, or the best possible creatures in it, considering these in merely a kind of abstract way. But in accordance with the whole plan of God it must be admitted that it is the best which He could have made, that is, in order that His wisdom and justice and mercy might be manifest according to the manner in which He judged it best to be manifested.[306]

Father Vermeersch using the argument "a counsel can never become a command" writes: "nowhere does he [St. Thomas] threaten with eternal ruin or the deprivation of sufficient grace one who though he be fit for it neglects the more desirable state. He would not write otherwise for he is the theologian who says that command differs from counsel in this 'that a command implies obligation, whereas a counsel is left to the option of the one to whom it is given' and adds that it is in accord with the evangelical law of liberty that besides and above the commands there should be counsels, the following of which is not necessary for salvation."[307]

First of all there seems to be a confusion in his intepretation of the

---

as prudence and/or one of the minor virtues connected with justice, gratitude? Can we say that there is no slight obligation from either of these considerations? This seems to be hard to accept" (cf. A. Motte, *art. et loc. cit.*, p. 28). Also J. Osborn (*op. cit.*, pp. 230–231): "The material of the better good though indeterminate and not formally obligatory while in the order of abstraction can and does become formally obligatory whenever it is determined to the concrete better good for the individual by God, either directly through the channels of divine inspirations or indirectly through human reason's ability and diligence in exploring the marginal implications of the principle of finality."

[305] I–II, Q. 88, a. 1, *ad* 1.   [307] *Op. cit.*, p. 27; he cites I–II, Q. 108, a. 4.
[306] Cf. I, Q. 25, a. 6, *ad* 3.

remark made by St. Thomas. For it is more than evident that St. Thomas is considering the counsels insofar as they are held up for us, so to speak, from the outside, proposed to us externally, in general, and not in special, that is, not through some special internal inspiration on the part of the Holy Ghost. Then, of course, there is no doubt. If the counsels are proposed to us in this light, they do not oblige under pain of sin or even of moral imperfection. But when these counsels are suggested to us, through some special internal or inward grace, the grace of religious vocation, this no longer holds, because there is an obligation for one to follow out the call of God, and that obligation we have already said consists in one of prudence and/or gratitude.

*   *   *

In conjunction with this question of the obligation of following a vocation we might note the following points:

First, per se the evangelical counsels do not oblige anyone, that is, insofar as we consider them as addressed to all persons, as it were from the outside. But when there is question of an interior inspiration to follow them (religious vocation in fieri) and even more of the firm proposal to embrace them (religious vocation in facto esse) then it seems more probable, that to refuse this inclination given to us by God would be to commit a sin, a venial fault involving a lack of fervor in the service of God, and of fervor that ought to have been given. The venial sin is, as we mentioned, one against the virtue of prudence and/or gratitude.[308]

This sin could be grievous if the decision deliberately exposes the person to danger of damnation, or proceeds from a thorough contempt for the teaching of God. The guilt is venial if the decision does not proceed from contempt, but merely from a lack of fervor and does not seriously endanger salvation. There is no guilt at all if the moral dispositions of

---

[308] Father Motte, in treating of this same problem writes: "Because it is Christ Who speaks through the counsels, this attention will be characterized by a special note of religious gravity. Once again the unrivalled excellence of Christ's counsels does not change them into commands (although as we have seen, a command may be superimposed upon them), but it does lead us to rate exceptionally high the advice they give. To take no notice of them would be a want of respect for Christ; it would also involve the loss of guidance invaluable for making a good decision. This would be gravely imprudent when by reason of its cardinal importance, the decisions require a maximum of application on our part.

"Imprudence is thus likely to be the gate through which culpability first enters the soul of one refusing to follow his vocation.

"The decision not to enter religion without prejudice to the culpability one may incur by reason of bad dispositions in the will, may offend against prudence by precipitation, or excessive slowness, thoughtlessness, timidity of judgment, inconstancy, or negligence," Vocation, Religious Life Series, II, "The Obligation to Follow a Vocation," A. Motte, O.P., pp. 32–35. Cf. also The Theology of Spiritual Guidance, p. 94 ff.

the subject are good and the decision not to enter religion has been taken without there having been any offense against the virtue of prudence and/or gratitude. In this last case no grace of vocation would have been given.

In practice, in judging the conscience of someone turning from a religious vocation or seeking advice before doing so, the first thing to do is to check the moral dispositions — humility, detachment, straightforwardness, charity, and then the workings of the practical reason when faced with the hypothesis of the religious life. The efforts made to note and to decipher all of the various factors in the divine call, and the degree of fidelity all along the line to those personal acts by virtue of which the vocation itself is nourished, will become increasingly firm and evident. As Fr. Motte notes: "if the inclination towards the perfect life becomes clearer they should be urged to follow it. Then if they refuse, it will be difficult to clear them of at least a venial sin of imprudence. This culpability the Christian instinct and its authorized interpreters have always detected more or less behind refusal to follow Christ's call to the perfect life, even though that call does not come as one of the common precepts of the divine law."[309]

Second, a general vocation must be contradistinguished from a "*special vocation*" which itself is divided into *extraordinary* (that is, one that is given by means of some special illumination or revelation) and *ordinary*, that is, an *internal* grace which moves one in the direction or actual making of the firm proposal to enter the religious life or the priesthood. If one were to commit a sin against the virtue of prudence in making his decision or choice regarding a state of life too hastily (with precipitation), or in putting off making a decision on it, or in making a decision thoughtlessly, or in being inconstant in his resolve (by reason of the defect of the will in commanding the one to proceed to action), or through negligence, then a *fortiori*, he would commit a fault against this virtue *in refusing a known grace* of vocation. The sin is one of turning away from an object which is supposed to be his by divine ordinance or dispensation. Such an action seems to be a manner of acting that is not *entirely* virtuous, because it is to choose a good, which is less, *leaving aside or neglecting* that which is *here and now better*.

Some authors, e.g., Father Ladislaus a Maria Immaculata, C.P.,[310] object that this would be true only in certain instances. Sometimes it happens that although a religious vocation is in itself better than a vocation to a lesser state, still *de facto* under certain circumstances for a given individual

[309] *Art. et loc. cit.*, pp. 35–36.
[310] Cf. *De Vocatione Religiosa* (Rome: 1950), p. 153 ff.

it would not be the better state, but rather the less good state. This objection, however, is to beg the question. For we are considering the problem of the better state as opposed to the less good state, not merely in the abstract, but *in the concrete*, here and now, with all the circumstances involved in the action taken into consideration. Moreover, we might add that God certainly would not give the *internal* grace of vocation, or the movement of the Holy Ghost, where He Himself knew that *this* grace would lead one to damnation. While it may be that in the designs of God the religious life may be the occasion or the environment in which one does work for his own condemnation, still this will *not be because of the grace of vocation* but by reason of the person's failure to cooperate with it, or because he has never received it.

Father Ladislaus' argument, of course, is based upon the reasoning of Suarez "that often the Holy Ghost gives one a desire for something whose execution he does not wish. For the Holy Ghost sometimes sends such a desire for the good and the merit of the individual although the outcome or the realization of this will be not had."[311]

This is true but *what* will is he speaking of? Again we come back to the distinction of efficacious and sufficient grace, God's permissive will and His efficacious will. The responsibility of one's not cooperating with the grace of vocation is not God's, but rather the individual's. It is the same with respect to the loss of sanctifying grace or the refusal of the person to embrace the faith and a life of Christian virtue. We cannot say that God wills this, but rather that He permits this. What He wills is the order of justice, to punish the individual's guilt, for which not He but the individual himself is responsible.

Third, by reason of the importance of making the right decision in regard to one's vocation, and by reason of the role which the virtue of prudence contributes to the making of this right choice, it should be pointed out to those who have not yet made a final decision and who are in the process of arriving at it that they should avoid the following:

1. *Precipitation:* An individual should be warned about making a hasty decision concerning his entire future life. It should be pointed out that he ought to think the thing through and seek help from those who are in a position to give it.

Pointing out to youth that the religious vocation is a counsel (of the Lord) and that such a counsel ought not to be considered lightly, but at length, is one way of helping them avoid this difficulty. To take no notice of the evangelical counsels would be to show a lack of respect for Christ and for God Himself. This defect of prudence is opposed to the first act

[311] *De Virt. et Statu Religionis*, Vol. III, Bk. V, Chap. 8, n. 4.

involved in the overall makeup of this virtue — the taking of counsel. It should be pointed out that often one's decision is made by reason of the influence of the lower appetites and tendencies.

2. *Indecision:* This is a defect likewise opposed to the taking of counsel. It implies that one puts off making the decision and so does not come to a judgment concerning the matter at hand.

3. *Thoughtlessness:* The defect involved in this is that one although sufficiently examining the possibility of vocation, has not attributed sufficient importance to one or other element involved in it, for example, the consequence of one's refusal to enter, or the consequences of one's leaving a religious community or a novitiate of such. Perhaps they have minimized a positive sign of a vocation. This defect of the virtue of prudence is opposed to its second act which is *judgment*.

4. *Inconstancy:* This defect with respect to the virtue of prudence denotes a withdrawal from a definite good proposed or purposed. The origin of this is the appetite. A person does not withdraw from a previous firm proposal unless something has come in meanwhile, to change this decision. If this something is not according to right reason, then it is the result of the movement of an inordinate appetite. Pressure then from the opposite direction or from difficulties that loom up on the horizon usually causes this. This defect of the virtue of prudence arises with respect to the third act which it involves, namely, the act of *command*. For a person is said to be inconstant because his reason fails in commanding what has been counseled and judged ought to be done.[312]

---

[312] Because of the danger of inconstancy St. Thomas points out that a vocation to the religious life or to the priesthood is not always to be made known immediately to one's family or relatives: "Even as the flesh lusts against the spirit so too carnal friends often thwart our spiritual progress, according to Michaeas (7:6): 'A man's enemies are those of his own household.' Therefore Cyril expounding the text of St. Luke (9:61): 'Let me first take leave' of them that were at his house, shows he was somewhat of two minds. For to communicate with his neighbors and consult with those who are unwilling to relish righteousness is an indication of weakness and turning back. Hence he hears our Lord say 'No man putting his hand to the plough and looking back is fit for the kingdom of God,' because he looks back who seeks to delay in order to go home and confer with his kinsfolk." II–II, Q. 189, a. 10, ad 2m.

St. Alphonsus is even more to the point concerning one's own parents: The vocation must be kept secret from one's family and relatives. Thus practically speaking oftentimes when the person knows or suspects strongly that his vocation will be opposed in the family, he ought to keep it secret, until the latest possible moment. The reason for this opposition is, of course, more or less evident. They know so very little about the life into which one is going, and therefore fear it, and form prejudices about it. In such a state or disposition of mind, they are not to be considered the best of counselors. A person, for example, who is desirous of becoming a doctor does not consult a machinist on the advisability of his embarking upon this profession. On the application of this principle we must be very cautious. The advice of a good confessor and director should be followed. There are ways of preparing people for such a shock.

5. *Negligence:* Negligence is opposed to the solicitude which is demanded in the exercise of the virtue of prudence. It is a defect centering around the third act of prudence, namely, command. A negligent man fails through lack of a prompt will to carry out the proposal, and thus indicates that his will is remiss or slack and flabby in its movement.

The means to overcome these possible defects against prudence which could hinder us from making a right decision are prayer, the reception of the sacraments, and a training along the lines of personal thought and responsibility. Perhaps one of the best means of making one make this decision in the presence of God is to teach and exhort him to a knowledge of self and a knowledge of God.

A further practice that should be urged upon youth is that of mercy toward and help of one another. For the Beatitude which corresponds to the virtue of prudence is that of the merciful. It is mercy which enters into each vocation in a most fundamental manner. For a vocation is merely a call to the service of God, to imitate God in some walk of life, by communicating goodness to others. Every vocation falling under the general Christian vocation will have this as one of its characteristic marks, and the more perfect the vocation, the more perfectly does it show mercy. From this fact springs the hierarchy of vocation — the priesthood, the religious life, and finally Christian marriage. All vocations have as their very basic meaning the communicating of goodness. Thus a person will be led to place before himself a vocation in the following question: "How can I best communicate God's goodness to others, and how does He wish me to communicate this goodness to others?" These two notions come to the same thing. For the best way that an individual can communicate God's goodness to others is the way that God has chosen for him.[313]

Vocation should be placed before youth as a call to render service and love to God, and the objective measure of this service and love for God will always be found in accordance with the objective amount of good that we give to others. This is an action of mercy, for all others stand in need of our help just as we stand in need of theirs. This presentation will serve to give the choice of vocation a supreme importance in the minds

---

[313] Father Gardeil brings this out quite clearly in a work on the gifts of the Holy Ghost and their work in the spiritual life. "The gift of counsel brings to perfection in a kind of divine manner, the work of Prudence. Now what does prudence counsel us? Without any doubt, to take the best means of saving ourselves. The gift of counsel must lay quite open in an altogether divine fashion this best means, which is precisely mercy. There is no precept more inculcated in the gospel than that 'In what measure you measure out to others, it shall be measured out to you.' We are thus warned that the only way of attaining mercy is by exercising mercy." *The Holy Spirit in the Christian Life* (St. Louis: B. Herder, 1954), p. 85.

of youth, one which shows them that the desire so deeply rooted in all of us to communicate goodness to others can be found in the most perfect manner in the religious and supernatural sphere, in the religious life or in the priesthood.

The attitude of Samuel in regard to vocation ought to be adopted by all, "Speak Lord, for thy servant heareth."[314] St. Augustine sets forth this same thought in his *Confessions:* "O Lord You reply to all who ask of Thee, and at the one time You answer all even though they consult You on diverse matters. All may ask advice of Thee on whatever he wills though they do not always hear the answer they desire. He is Thy best servant who looks not so much to hear from Thee what he himself desires, as to will what he hears from Thee."[315]

Fourth, it seems to be the mind of the Angelic Doctor that once a vocation, or the grace of vocation, is given by God, it is not lost except through some fault on the part of the individual. Whatever grace is given by God, if nourished and properly cared for should develop and grow and become stronger, until the perfect day. The Book of Isaias mentions that "although youth may weaken and the warrior grow tired and faint, those who trust in the Lord will renew their strength like eagles new-fledged; hasten, and never grow weary of hastening, march on, and never weaken on the march."[316]

Father Walter Farrell has written very solidly and beautifully on this subject of the continuance of the grace of vocation:

> There is a lifetime obligation, incumbent on every religious, of protection and nourishment of his vocation, or prompt and aggressive attention to the threats of vocation and of quick recognition of the symptoms of its corruption. Surely it is clear that the entrance into a religious Order does not encase a vocation in a protective covering that assures its unchanged endurance; for the years of a lifetime, that vocation can be threatened; it can be starved, it can be corrupted. . . . [This also] has direct relevance to our own vocations for no one of us is ever finished with the work of nourishing, protecting, fostering, and perfecting our own vocation.
>
> Two essential conditions are necessary for the preparation of and preservation of vocation, cleanness and stability, and this both of mind and of heart, of intellectual and moral cleanness; this gives the basic meaning of our separation from the world; it is not that we at any time attempt to desert men, but that we shake ourselves loose from those things that so fill the mind as to impede its soaring to God. If there is a change in one's stability, the change is in us, and that change is a change for the worse, a moral decay that has deadened our hearts and weighted down our feet. A "tempo-

314 1 Kings 3:9, 10.
315 *Confessions*, Bk. 10, Chap. 26, PL 32, 795. Cf. *Guidance for Religious*, Gerald Kelly, S.J. (Westminster, Md.: Newman, 1956), p. 226.
316 Is. 40:30–31.

rary vocation" is a modern euphemism for a vocation that has been un-
protected, undernourished, exposed to threats, and finally beaten to a bitter
death. There should be a constant change in religious life, but the kind of
change induced by our perpetual discovery of new heights, and depths in
the infinite perfection of the Divine Master. Such discoveries are not a
threat to the stability that is inseparable from the virtue of religion.[317]

It can be readily seen that for this author there is no such thing as
a temporary vocation. A vocation once had from God is lost only through
infidelity. Like the life of sanctifying grace it must be nourished if it is to
remain and to reach to new heights and depths of love and service for God.
Only when this development is interfered with is a vocation once realized
lost, and here we are speaking of an *interior* vocation, that is, the firm
purpose to serve God in the life of complete dedication. As we have seen,
this is also the thought of Father Motte and others supporting the second
opinion. Either a vocation is lost or it was never had, in the case of a
so-called "temporary vocation." And the latter is true only where we can
definitely find the lack of the firm purpose to serve God in the religious
state. If this purpose were ever present (and not simply a *velietas*, or
wishful thinking, or emotional burst of enthusiasm, but a true and strict
firm desire and purpose of serving God in the religious state), then if
this no longer appears in the life of an individual whether before entering
a community or after entering it, we have a "lost" vocation. This can only
be due to the fact that some other love or preference has entered into
the life of the individual to lead him away from his first love.[318]

---

[317] Quoted from a mimeographed talk.

[318] Here I believe it is worth mentioning several statements made by Father Elio
Gambari, S.M.M., a member of the Sacred Congregation of Religious. They are
certainly not official pronouncements but they do perhaps indicate the mind of at
least some of the members of that congregation. The following questions were put to
him:

1. Is there such a thing as a temporary vocation to the religious life? A Sister
thinks she has a vocation and her superiors accept her. The Sister makes her vows
and after a year finds the religious life is not for her. Did such a Sister have a temporary
vocation?

"Is there a temporary vocation to the religious life? No, because the religious state
is the state of perfection. State — every state — requires stability. Where there is no
stability there is no state. Juridically, you know, Canon 574 foresees vows for a period
of time, one year, three years, five years, and renewal at the expiration. But intentionally
as a background, the Sister intends to give herself to God forever; but this intention to
remain forever, although it must be real, does not inhere in the substance of the vow.
Juridically vows bind for one year, two years, three years with the intention of
renewing them at expiration. But if at the expiration something new happens, or the
religious knows herself better, or the superior knows the religious better (and that is
more frequent) then the religious leaves or the superior tells her to leave. Coming
back to the question — Juridically the vows are temporary, but in the intention it must
be to renew them at the moment of their expiration." *Proceedings of the 1957 Sisters*

While it is true that this fault is not always of a serious nature, still if the individual has starved or not protected and safeguarded a vocation which he truly had, then he certainly seems to be somewhat responsible for its loss. Other factors may be present such as the lack of sufficient training, or counsel, or guidance, or the failure of the community to pre-

---

Institute of Spirituality (Notre Dame, Ind.: U. of Notre Dame Press, 1958), pp. 155-156.

2. Is it the mind of the Church that when one has taken final vows in a particular community one has *ipso facto* a vocation to that community; that is, it is not possible to have made a mistake? Does every dispensation indicate therefore a lack of correspondence with grace coupled with defection?

"The vocation we would say and the different steps in a community rest upon the Divine Providence which helps, inspires things, so that, unless we have a manifest, quite evident proof to the contrary we have to say that the person who has entered that community and has pronounced final vows has the vocation for that community. This is the ordinary way to judge and the judgment that we have to formulate in every case, unless there is quite evident proof to the contrary that a mistake has been made.

"Is it possible to have made a mistake? Unfortunately it is possible. Unfortunately, it happens that sometimes the person shows herself after final vows not fit for the religious life. So we cannot say that she has made a mistake, *but she has not corresponded with her religious vocation.* If a religious lives so badly that superiors are compelled to dismiss her, we must say that she has not been faithful to her vocation. If a religious does not feel right in a community, does not feel apt and does not want to bear the burden of the religious life and asks for a dispensation, commonly we say that she has not corresponded with divine grace. Because when the Sister has been loyal, has been sincerely trying to do what superiors tell her to do, through the postulate, novitiate and temporary vows, it is very difficult for a mistake to go through all these days without it being noticed that she is not fit.

"No, I would say to Sisters who ask about dispensation of vows: really to ask for dispensation from vows means to take back what we have given to God, to refuse to God what we have given to Him, telling Him 'give it back, give me a divorce' — it is a kind of divorce. Juridically they are allowed to ask for a dispensation. But this does not mean that *morally their conscience may be in peace.* That is another question. Probably the institute after their leaving has more peace than before. That may happen but not their soul. There might be some person who thinks 'Yes, there is always a way to put an end to vows — dispensation.' We should remark a dispensation is something that the Church has been obligated to introduce to avoid worse evil. So the poor Sister who asks for a dispensation should realize that before God and her conscience." *Ibid.,* pp. 146-148.

The following year in answer to a similar question, he said: "I would suggest to the mistress of novices that when she explains the possibility of dispensation from vows she makes it very clear. She should show that this dispensation is not a natural way by which the vow expires. It is only something that the Church tolerates as was true of divorce in the Old Testament. It is a toleration in order to avoid something worse for the community. And the dispensation from vows is rather for the good of the community than for the advantage of the individual Sister, because generally when they leave the community they are not happy. But the community is happier than before." *Proceedings of the Sisters Institute of Spirituality,* 1958 (Notre Dame, Ind.: U. of Notre Dame Press, 1959), p. 241.

Moreover, several official documents from the Sacred Congregation seem to substantiate this view. In a letter of the S. C. of the Sacraments given in 1931, we find the following: "In case it clearly appears that a subdeacon who is about to be raised

serve the safeguards normally required and contained in the Constitutions.[319] But in the last analysis the person himself is responsible for his own lost vocation. Consequently, both communities and individual religious must constantly protect their vocations, avoiding anything that could weaken and destroy them. All engaged in working with religious or in vocations must be constantly on their guard lest they become too much attuned to the mind of the outsider. The religious and even one who is thinking of entering the service of God must constantly look upward at the things that are above because a centering of one's interests and concerns unduly in creatures makes one faint in his quest and search for God whom he is to love with an everlasting love. As a person immerses his heart in things beneath him, putting his heart to the service of sin, he becomes a slave to it and gives to sin the service that he ought to be giving to God. The cramming of one's head with inferior things is always a serious threat to the consideration of God.

Sometimes in opposition to the above opinion (and it is still in that realm, I admit), the following thought from the Angelic Doctor is brought out: "A man who has entered religion gives neither scandal nor bad example by leaving especially if he do so for a reasonable motive; and if others are scandalized it will be passive scandal on their part and not active scandal on the part of the person leaving, since in so doing, he

to the diaconate either never had a vocation, or has lost it through habitual sins, then further investigations should be made in accordance with what follows regarding the advancing of a subdeacon to the deaconship and the reception of the priesthood." AAS 23 (1931), 120 ff.; cf. Canon Law Digest, I, p. 470. And again, in a document issued by the S. C. Rel., in February, 1961, regarding religious priests who ask for reduction to the lay state, the following ideas are expressed: "In general the aforesaid religious claim that they entered on this way of life without a genuine divine vocation or that they lost their vocation during the period of their formation or in the early years of their active life. The causes they assert: undue influence of their family, undue influence of superiors and directors, who threatened them with the danger of eternal loss if they left the clerical state, and insufficient knowledge of religious and clerical obligations, esp. celibacy, uncertain will or resolve in entering and mere following of the crowd. There can be no denying that frequently the charges of these priests in their petitions have only a semblance of truth. It is a fact that these reasons are often alleged only by the petitioners who are the interested parties, and are not substantiated either by witnesses or by documents brought forth in the hearing. They not infrequently take their present state of mind and psychic crisis which has gradually evolved over a period of years and unconsciously transfer it to the time of their profession and ordination, being unaware of the inner change which has taken place within themselves."

[319] "When a religious leaves his order, the Superior of the same order, if he has diligently examined his conscience before God, will very frequently be well aware that he himself is not without fault and has failed in his duty. This neglect of duty is often verified either in the admission of candidates or in training them to the religious life or, after they have made vows, in keeping watch over them." Enchiridion de Statibus Perfectionis, n. 286, p. 341.

has done what was lawful and expedient on account of some reasonable motive, such as sickness, weakness and the like."[320]

Certainly, when speaking of a reasonable motive, he indicates something that would point to the lack of one of the signs of vocation — the physical, moral, mental or spiritual or psychological qualities necessary for a vocation. This would very definitely be a sign that now, at this time, the person is not called. Whether at one time or another he was and why he is not at the present time is a matter that must always remain between the individual and his God. Here we must be careful, of course. Rather than frighten anyone who wishes to leave a novitiate or a religious community or seminary, we would do well to place the various opinions of authors before them (perhaps not always, but most of the time) and allow them to make the decision as to whether or not they have a sufficient reason for withdrawing. If a reasonable motive is present, they may certainly leave with a clear conscience. But it would seem in this case that what was thought to be a vocation perhaps never was one. Consequently, the basic principle used in the theological reasoning given above — God never withdraws a grace except because of some fault on the part of the one to whom it has been granted — can be invoked in the case of the religious (or priestly) vocation as well as in that of justification. If a vocation arrives at maturity and grows and becomes stronger, it is God's work primarily, for we are "fields of God's tilling and structures of his designs."[321] If, however, the grace of vocation does not arrive at maturity, does not grow, but remains stunted or even becomes corrupt, the fault is due not to God and His sufficient grace, but rather to man's failure to cooperate and to use the grace which he has received.[322]

Regardless of which of the opinions the reader may choose to follow, it can safely be said that today we should take a stronger stand on the

---

[320] II–II, Q. 189, a. 4, ad 2. On this point Father Fanfani remarks: "A novice may freely leave the institute, that is, by leaving she does no injury to the institute, nor has the institute any right to constrain her to remain. This does not apply to a person who feels she has a vocation. No one may flee from this obligation since prudence demands that we do all that is possible to follow the vocation to which we have been called." *Canon Law for Religious Women* (Dubuque, Iowa: Priory Press, 1961), p. 181.

[321] 1 Cor. 3:5.

[322] Cf. R. Butler, O.P., *Religious Vocation: An Unnecessary Mystery* (Chicago: Regnery, 1961), p. 129. He does make some reservations, however: "those who may incure some prohibitive impediment such as poor health or family needs, which makes their departure from religion necessary and proper. Religious in perpetual vows would not be required to leave under these or any other circumstances." I am wondering whether we are to understand by this that those in temporary vows would be *required* to leave because of poor health contracted after profession, or because of family needs that arose after profession.

sacredness and meaning of the religious vows and the intention of making them. We can do this best, I believe, not by referring to the *possible* sin committed in rejecting a vocation, or to the scandal that might be involved, or to the lack of generosity that might be present, but rather by pointing out again and again the sacredness, the sanctity, and the beauty of consecration to Christ. Like the Church, we should use means that are suitable for our times to meet the attacks aimed to destroy an edifice which in itself is sublime, which pertains more to the order of glory than to the order of time. If the vocation is eschatological, then it is a call from God to pertain already here on earth in some mysterious manner to participated eternity, to be assimilated into the *nunc stans* of the Godhead, while still in some manner immersed in the *nunc fluens* of time. Perhaps an overemphasis on the juridical elements involved in vocation has obscured our vision of its meaning.

This eschatological aspect of the religious profession and vocation stands out very clearly in one of the vows that is essential to it, the vow of virginity. Of itself virginity is intrinsically indissoluble because it is a marriage with God. If it is soluble, this is only accidental to it; it comes from its earthly condition. It comes not from the bond itself, but rather from the defect of the subject who can fall from the perfection of his engagement with Christ just as he can from the perfection of charity. The vow of virginity is soluble by the Church not *per se*, it would seem, or by reason of the weakness of the bond or by reason of some condition that is better than virginity *in se*, or in itself. It is soluble, *per accidens*, as theologians say, by reason of some defect on the part of the subject, *ob duritiam cordis*, because of the hardness of our hearts. Just as God permitted or indirectly allowed the Jews of the Old Testament to practice divorce, *ob duritiam cordis*, until the time of Christ, so too, does He allow a dissolution of the vow of virginity, *ob duritiam cordis*, until the law of the New Testament opens up into the law of eternity. The solubility of the bond, then, comes from the weakness of man in the face of the perfection of heaven.[323]

---

[323] Cf. *La Virginité Chrétienne*, F. Bourassa, S.J. (Montreal: 1952), pp. 124–129. Is this not the thought of Pius XII writing in the *Sacra Virginitas*: "since they have eagerly embraced the state of virginity or celibacy, they will certainly receive from God that gift of grace through whose help they will be able to carry out their promise. Wherefore if there are any who do not feel they have the gift of chastity even though they have vowed it, let them not declare they cannot fulfill their obligations in the matter. For says the Council of Trent quoting St. Augustine, God does not command the impossible, but in commanding serves notice that one do what he can and pray for what he cannot, and He helps us to accomplish it. This truth so full of encouragement We recall to those also whose will has been weakened by upset nerves and whom some doctors, sometimes even Catholic doctors are too quick to persuade

Article III.   The Signs of a Religious Vocation

As we have pointed out, a divine vocation to the religious life (and to the priesthood) is essentially something that transcends the order of the senses so that its existence is incapable of *immediate* scrutiny or direct proof. This does not mean that we have no proof whatsoever of its existence. For if the approbation of some exterior norm is required to certify its existence (at least with moral certitude), then this exterior norm must be presented with certain signs or indications by which it can judge the presence or absence of such vocation. The good of the faithful demands that the selection of priests and religious should be sufficiently accurate as to preclude serious danger of error in their choice. It is for this reason that the Code of Canon Law admits the existence and recognizability of certain criteria or signs for determining whether one has a probable vocation to the priesthood or to the religious life. We cannot have mathematical certitude to be sure. But we can have moral certitude and this is sufficient. These criteria can be divided into two categories (1) positive criteria, and (2) negative criteria, each of which we will now consider rather briefly and schematically.

Positive Criteria

St. *Alphonsus Liguori* gives the following signs of a religious vocation: (1) that there be a good end in view which includes the removal of self from the dangers of the world, or the better assurance of salvation, or a more positive union with God. Very often all three of these reasons are found together. (2) That there be no positive impediments as regards health, talents, or parents in need. (3) That the person in question be admitted by the superiors of the institute.

St. *Francis de Sales* lists almost the same signs. He is, however, somewhat more clear with respect to the right intention than St. Alphonsus is. He insists that for the right intention there is no need that there be any sensible attraction; but it is sufficient that the will be firm and remain firm and constant and that there be *some affection* for the call, that is, the desire, or the *will* (that is the *habitual* presence of this firm will) to submit to God's will or to do God's will rather than our own. He adds, moreover, that we should not care whether this call comes from this quarter

---

that they should be freed from such an obligation, advancing the specious reason that they cannot preserve their mental balance. How much more useful and opportune it is to help the infirm of this type, to strengthen their will and to advise them that not even to them is chastity impossible according to the word of the Apostle 'God is faithful who will not suffer you to be tempted above that which you are able; but will make also with temptation issue, that you may be able to bear it.'" NCWC. ed., p. 17.

or that, for wherever it comes from, *if it is firm and constant*, it must receive its efficaciousness from God.

Father Edward Farrell mentions two groups of signs, primary and secondary:

The *primary signs* are three: (1) the absence of impediments both natural and legal; (2) the firm resolution to serve God as a religious with His help; (3) a generous and magnanimous spirit which recognizes the difficulties of the religious life and is willing to try to meet them.

The *secondary signs* admit of two classes. (A) Those which proceed from the activity of the *virtue of religion and its act of devotion:* (1) *spiritual joy and satisfaction in the choice* of life one has made; (2) *peace of mind*, which follows upon the decision; (3) *facility and promptitude in performing the various acts of religion and of the other virtues.* (B) Those which proceed from the activity of the *virtue of magnanimity:* (1) *a generous disposition to give oneself without expecting anything in return;* (2) *a love for virtue;* (3) *frankness and honesty in all dealings with others;* (4) *a balanced appreciation of the things of the world, avoidance of pre-cipitation, and involvement in many affairs.* This latter is a sign insofar as one who intends a great thing usually withdraws his consideration from many small matters and concentrates it on the one thing that he intends.[324]

Father Walter Farrell, O.P., in treating of the signs of vocation writes:

A search for the signs of vocation will consist in our looking for the activity of the virtue of religion in this particular youngster, particularly noticing the fundamental notes of this virtue which are reverence and subjection. Irreverence and stubborn pride, uncleanness and fickleness will be fairly dependable signs of the absence of a vocation. We can be reasonably sure only when we see evidence of devotion in an eminent degree: an eager and prompt will to serve God. There is special evidence of this devotion perfected by the Gifts in the presence of humility, poverty of spirit and to a lesser degree, a tender conscience in matters of modesty, continency, and chastity. To protect a vocation will demand the preservation of the two essential requisites of cleanness and stability. Concretely, that means fighting against the things that enslave the heart of a man, against the service of sin, particularly against the service of carnal sins. It means caution against immersion in the activities of the world, which though not sinful, so fill the mind of a man and accustom it to looking down that it becomes increasingly difficult for him to consider the things of God. There must be the insistence on the development of moral habits, the virtues that release a man from the changing whims and passions and fix his heart firmly on the supremely desirable and absolutely unchanging goodness of God.[325]

In a rather excellent article written in the work on "Religious Sisters,"[326]

---

[324] Cf. *The Theology of Religious Vocation*, pp. 160–164.
[325] Mimeograph talk cited above.
[326] Religious Life Series, I (London: Blackfriars, 1952), pp. 209–225.

Father Loret, C.Ss.R., has given the following categories of signs that a guide or counsel or ought to keep before him:

1. The motives which have brought forth the desire for the religious life or for the priesthood;
2. The lack of impediments to admission to this way of life;
3. The aptitudes of the one seeking admission;
4. The intention of the one seeking admission.

Very briefly we shall consider each of these categories and their division.

1. The motives which have been the cause of the vocation include all those factors which have had some bearing on making one think of the vocation, desire it, and ask about entering some way of life. They can be reduced to three: attraction, inspiration, and circumstances:

a) *Attraction:* This is to be considered both on the part of the walk of life itself and on the part of the corresponding movement of the individual toward this way of life, that is, the *inclination* felt by the individual with respect to entering some religious community or diocesan seminary. With regard to this one ought to consider the following factors:

(1) OBJECT OF THE ATTRACTION: What is the object? Is it the religious life in general, or the priesthood in general, or is it some very definite form of life in this or that institute? Is the attraction to some mere detail of the religious life, such as silence, the peace of the cloister, or the desire to devote oneself to the care of the sick or the teaching of youth? Or is it an attraction for the very essentials of the religious life, that is, the desire to dedicate oneself wholly and completely to the service of God? Is it the desire to escape from the world or to live a life of penance? In these latter two instances the attraction seems well founded, and the future seems at least promising, and usually is, if these desires and motives are furthered and developed.

If the attraction centers around certain secondary things or elements of the religious life which might be accidental to it, certain personal advantages, etc., then it is the duty of the guide or the counselor to discern whether underneath these accidental things there are the substantial attractions mentioned above. It is then his duty to point out to the individual the difference between the two and to try to develop the attraction with respect to the things that are essential to the religious life or the priesthood.

(2) CONSTANCY OF THE ATTRACTION: Does it persist and stand firm despite opposition, or long waiting, or temptations, or other obstacles? Does the person remain steady and calm under all of it; or is it rather something of a shadow without substance, a passing, will-o'-the-wisp sort of thing?

(3) PSYCHOLOGICAL BASIS OF THE ATTRACTION: Is it merely sensitive or instinctive, based more on the emotions than on reason? Is it something that has been thought out and derived from reason or from faith? For when it is this latter, then the attraction is really the firm purpose or right intention spoken of in the Canon Law.

(4) SUBJECTIVE VALUE OF ATTRACTION: Does one tend to dwell frequently on the attraction, and to consider it as an indubitable proof of vocation to this or that way of life? Does one tend to give it an origin that is directly from God? Or build it up in any way? If this is the case, then we ought to be cautious of the importance of the attraction. It should be noted, however, that Divine Providence uses many things in order to bring a person to the religious life or to the priesthood. For example, personalities of priests and religious are often factors that contribute much to one's being drawn to the service of God. However, this attraction to an individual should be ordinarily *ultimately* and basically the *religious* character and decorum of the individual in question, or, better, the *religious* qualities rather than the sensible qualities which the individual religious might possess.

In older persons the attraction usually manifests itself in a volitional sort of way; whereas in younger persons, it often manifests itself in an emotional sort of way. And yet, beneath this emotional attraction one can detect the signs of faith and devotion.

b) *Inspirations* or suggestions that come from without, in the shape of visions or intuitions, or words which propose the idea of vocation and the urge to follow it. These we have already seen with respect to the charismata, and the value which should be attached to them. The best thing for the guide to do is to consider not the source of the inspiration but rather the effects which it leaves. By their fruits you shall know them.

c) *Other Circumstances or Motives*: retreats, sermons or readings, meetings with religious of a given community, the example of a priest in the parish, etc. These should be given their proper considerations, but the vocation must be judged on its own merits.

2. The lack of impediments or those obstacles to admission laid down by the Church in her Canon Law, as well as special ones which the community being considered may also have in its own Constitutions is another positive sign. These can usually be found in the Constitutions of a given community. The impediments of Canon Law are of two kinds: those pertaining to *valid* admission to a novitiate and those pertaining to *licit* admission to a novitiate.

a) *Valid Admission:* The following cannot be validly admitted to the novitiate:

(1) Those who have been enrolled in a non-Catholic sect, that is, Catholics who have apostatized and openly passed over to a schismatic, heretical, or atheistic sect.

(2) Those who have not reached the age required for the novitiate (15 years complete).

(3) Those who enter religion out of force, acute fear, or fraud; and those accepted because the superior is under the same influence when he admits them. Violence is not very common today. Fear, however, is something that cannot be overlooked, for in some cases pressure is brought on an individual to enter either the convent or a seminary. Usually, however, the opposite is true, at least, in our own country: pressure is brought upon an individual to stay out of the convent and seminary. Fraud may take many forms: sickness or other defects — physical or mental — or even the pretense of having qualities and degrees (academic) which would facilitate one's being accepted. Usually, however, these things are discovered very quickly in the course of the novitiate.

(4) Married persons as long as the bond remains.

(5) Those who are or who have been bound by previous religious profession, unless proper steps have been taken.

(6) Those liable to punishment for a grave misdemeanor of which they may be accused. This can be either ecclesiastical or civil.

(7) Bishops, whether residential or titular; even those who have only been designated by the Sovereign Pontiff and have not yet been consecrated.

(8) Clerics who by ordinance of the Holy See are bound under oath to devote themselves to the service of their dioceses or of the missions for as long as the obligation created by the oath lasts. This impediment affects only those who have undertaken to serve in their dioceses or missions for a given length of time. For as long as this time endures, they cannot validly enter a religious community. This impediment, however, does not affect those diocesan priests who are ordained under the title of diocese or mission.

b) *Licit Admission:* The following cannot be licitly admitted to the novitiate:

(1) Clerics in Holy Orders, if they fail to consult their Ordinary or if the Ordinary opposes the step on the ground that their departure would be gravely detrimental to the good of souls, and that this harm could not be avoided unless they stayed. The Canon does not go so far as to require the Ordinary's consent but merely obliges the cleric to ask his opinion. The Ordinary, however, can veto the proposal if the departure of the cleric would result in serious harm to souls, and the harm could not be

otherwise remedied. Serious harm and the impossibility of finding another solution are the two conditions which must be found *together*, if an Ordinary is justified in objecting when one of his clerics wants to enter a religious order. Usually a slight delay is sufficient to enable the bishop to meet the needs of his diocese. This impediment for licit entrance touches only those in major orders, not those in minor orders.

(2) Those burdened with debts they cannot pay.

(3) Those with some special responsibility, or other temporal business to attend to, by reason of which the institute might become involved in lawsuits or troubles.

(4) Children bound to help parents (father, mother, grandfathers, and grandmothers) in really straitened circumstances, and parents whose services are needed for the maintenance and education of their children. While there is no positive law regarding, for example, brothers or sisters, still their need is to be interpreted in the light of the need of the parents. One, therefore, may be obliged to forego entrance into religion by reason of the obligation to take care of the brothers and sisters of his or her family.

In connection with this, canonists and moralists ask the question whether grave need affecting the parents *after* the child has gone into religion would create an obligation for the child to give up the religious life. Speaking very broadly, the reply must be in the *negative*. Help can be given by the superiors, or the religious may be exclaustrated for a given period. This is very much in keeping with the teaching of St. Thomas who mentions that once a person has entered religion he is said to have died to the world and therefore has no need of returning to it in order to help his parents or relatives. Our Lord, Himself, seemed to have sanctioned this when he said that no man putting his hand to the plow and turning back is fit for the kingdom of heaven. Let the dead bury the dead.

(5) Those who in religion would be destined for the priesthood but are debarred from it by irregularity or some other canonical impediment.

(6) Catholics of the Eastern rites may not be received into the novitiate of an institute of the Latin Church without written permission or leave from the Sacred Congregation for the Eastern Church.[327]

3. *Aptitudes:* This word can be understood in the negative sense and in the positive sense, that is to say, that there is nothing in the person that seems opposed to his having a vocation; or there are very definitely positive aptitudes or requisite qualities that would seem to indicate the pres-

---

[327] Cf. *Vocation, Religious Life Series*, II, *Canonical Impediments*, E. Bergh, S.J., p. 85 ff.

ence of vocation. When these latter are present we ought to note, however, that such a person *is qualified for any walk of life*. They are, briefly, family, health, moral character, mental capacity, piety, and sociability.

a) *Family*: The family background of every candidate ought to be thoroughly checked, in order to ascertain the environment in which the vocation was engendered. Two factors are to be especially noted: *broken homes* and *opposition on the part of the family*. When these things are found, it usually is better to have the young aspirants carry on their education in some Catholic high school, under, of course, the guidance of those teaching in the school. If the authorities of the school are notified of the situation, they will be able to assist the child in realizing the vocation. This practice has been found to be effective, although each case will have to be judged on its own merits.

b) *Health*: Sufficient health is required to enable the person to perform the duties of the religious life. The common life should be kept uppermost in mind, for too many exemptions would tend to destroy the regular discipline of the community.[328]

c) *Morality*: The superiors of a religious community or the directors of a diocesan seminary have the right to investigate the moral qualities of the youth seeking admission. Those asked for information on this score must also be most frank as the ordination ceremony itself mentions: "let them speak out now for the good of the Church." Very often today it happens that a person receives a recommendation for an aspirant from a pastor or Sister which is not a genuine picture of the applicant and does not give precise information concerning the moral character of the individual in question. Generally speaking, the authorities of a school in which the person is enrolled can be counted on to give a good evaluation of these qualities, particularly when the recruiter visits the school personally in search of this information. The following are the moral qualities that will have to be determined:

(1) Purity, either preserved or firmly recovered if lost, so that public scandal may be avoided. This does not exclude the possibility of a fault or faults against this virtue, but it does demand that the *virtue* or the *habit* of chastity should have been *firmly* recovered, that the individual is solid in his desire and ability to preserve chastity.

(2) Honesty and Frankness

(3) Generosity: This is, as we have seen, very essential; for the whole religious and priestly vocation springs from it, and its presence will greatly

---

[328] For more detailed ideas on this score, cf. *Medical Guide to Vocation*, Drs. Biot and Galimard, tr. by Dr. Robt. Odenwald (Westminster, Md.: Newman Press, 1955).

determine the preseverance or lack of it in any given individual.[329]

d) *Mental Capacity:* The amount of mental ability will depend much upon the vocation in question. Greater ability will have to be demanded of those wishing to study for the priesthood than for those wishing to be working Brothers in some community. What is most important along these lines is the presence of sound judgment.

e) *Piety:* Since the very essence of the religious life is reverence and worship, the exercise of the virtue of religion, the aspirant must have a solid piety and a real desire for the service of God, a real desire to dedicate himself to the quest for God. Emotional devotion must be looked upon as something that is not at all a guarantee for the permanence of a vocation.

f) *Sociability:* This is very necessary in the case of those who seek admission to a community or diocesan seminary where the ability to get along with people is so essential and will determine the individual's capacity to move freely in his own vocation. Cheerfulness and pleasantness

---

[329] On the question of moral aptitudes, St. Thomas speaks of the case of whether one who is not practiced in the keeping of the Commandments ought to be admitted into a religious community. He answers the proposed question in the affirmative: that one ought to be admitted, for the religious state is a state of tending to perfection; therefore, we cannot demand proved virtue of one entering. Thus he says that they will the more easily avoid sin and attain to perfection in the practices of the religious life. Several years ago, among a group of those engaged in formation from various religious communities, this same question was brought up. The verdict was not unanimous. For there were two very definite divisions: those for admitting (and these included especially those from the monastic orders) and those against admitting (these were, for the most part, from active communities).

I believe that the solution to the question might be that a person who is not practiced in the observance of the Commandments could be admitted to a monastic community or order, precisely because here he would have the means to deepen himself in the practices of the Commandments more readily and under more favorable conditions. Thus a man could very easily be admitted to a monastery with this in mind: to make this his conversion to God. The seclusion and the lack of the many dangers which he found in the world would certainly be most conducive to his conversion.

When there is question of such a person entering an active community, however, then it seems that this advice is not to be followed. For the dangers which he met with in the world will be very much his even in a religious community that is engaged in the many and varied apostolates of our day. He would not be freed from these dangers, but rather place himself in their presence again after a few years. It seems that in regard to active communities, particularly here in our own country, it would be wiser to demand of candidates practice in the observance of the Commandments. This does not mean there will be complete absence of falls, but it does mean that there are no vicious tendencies that are not as yet brought under control. Experience teaches that those who have had these tendencies for many years of their life do not easily within a few years break themselves, so as to insure their observance of the vows under the same difficulties in which they found themselves weak while in the world. This is especially true of older candidates seeking admission to the priesthood.

of character and disposition indicate the presence of this quality. To say that it is necessary in communities where the common life is observed definitely refers also to contemplative communities. Indeed, it is most necessary there, for the lack of it contributes much to the many disorders which could possibly occur in these orders. St. Teresa's advice should never be forgotten: "Better to make no foundation at all than to put melancholic people in them."[330]

4. *Right Intention:* This is the most crucial of the signs; the others are merely conditions for it. We have already seen what this is in the case of a religious vocation: the desire or the firm purpose of dedicating oneself to the service of God in and through the religious life; or it is an intense act of devotion necessitated to meet the demands of the object which one has in mind — the complete holocaustal offering of oneself to God. This firmness need not prevent one from feeling the sacrifice involved in the act, to the point even of a kind of natural repugnance, as has been pointed out. In order for this right intention to exist, objectively, the person must have *knowledge* of the religious life or of the priesthood and of what it demands (this, of course, in accordance with the aspirant's capacity) and *full freedom of choice.* One must know the sacrifices involved also, especially that included in the vow of chastity. Otherwise, one could enter and merely "drift" along for much, if not all, of the religious life. A right intention, we must always remember, is an act of the will, or the volition of the *end,* insofar as it is the reason of willing those things which are for the end. It is an *efficacious* volition of the end, not a mere *velietas,* or an imperfect willing or volition which is simply a kind of complacency of the will in the good apprehended by the intellect. This right intention consists in the wish, the firm wish of the individual, to obtain the end of religion — Christian perfection through the observance of the vows.[331]

The right intention is not to be considered present in the person who desires to enter, but merely for a time. For the very nature of the religious *state* demands that the one entering have the intention of remaining there. Canon Law demands that for even temporary religious profession, the will to persevere in religion must be present. Not that this can never change, but the intention here and now of the one making profession should be that of persevering in the vocation which he is embracing. It is not necessary that this will be manifested explicitly, but it should appear from certain circumstances of the candidate's life, in his exterior conduct and

---

[330] *Letters,* 315, Peers, II, 702.
[331] Cf. "La Vocation Réligieuse," E. M. Lacome, in *Récruitement sacerdotale,* 28 (1928), 238.

activity. Thus it should, in short, dominate his manner of conduct in the religious life.[332]

Negative Criteria

The following are the negative criteria or signs which indicate that one is not fit for the life of the cloister or the seminary:

1. *Difficulty in Remaining Continent:* Those who find it difficult to keep continence to the point where they do *not* give proof of their ability to keep it perpetually. Thus, the mere fact that one finds it somewhat difficult but nevertheless with the help of God's grace does keep continence, would not *ipso facto* indicate that he was not fitted for the religious life or the priesthood. As long as the will is strong enough to control the lower nature, then grace is doing its work, and we should expect that it will continue to do its work.[333]

---

[332] *Ibid.*; cf. also *La Vocation au Sacerdoce*, J. Hurtaud, 2 ed. (Paris: 1911), p. 252. Another program for the discernment of vocations is the following: One can consider in the individual who seeks advice, regarding vocation (1) the gifts of grace which he has received; (2) the gifts of nature with which God has endowed him: (3) acquired training, that which he may have received in the course of his education, etc.

1. *The Gifts of Grace:* refer to those things which he has received from God, that is, through the supernatural workings of grace in the soul. When we find the presence of magnanimity and of the virtue of religion, stability and cleanness of heart and mind, we have a sign of a religious vocation. For this reason, then, one must be most careful to insist upon the presence of these tendencies or habitual inclinations, for they indicate very strongly the activity of God in the soul and the intensity of the act of devotion.

2. *The Gifts of Nature:* refer to these gifts or aptitudes which one may have received from God, the temperament that an individual has been endowed with by God in the natural order of things. This would include, of course, physical, mental, or intellectual talents, and certain moral aptitudes or natural inclinations, such as kindness or humility or chastity. The habitual dispositions of soul and body, then, are gifts which individuals receive from God and greatly facilitate the exercise of the supernatural infused virtues. For these latter would find it very difficult to proceed to exercise unless they found no obstacle hindering their activity. God, then, in His providence, determining the individual to a given work in His Church, endows an individual with those qualities that will be necessary or useful for it.

3. *Acquired Training:* refers to the habits of knowledge, whether practical or speculative, which one may have developed in the course of the years. Moreover, the moral training that one has been subjected to and has realized in the passage of years would be included among the things of this category. These acquired talents or habitual inclinations, whether they be moral or intellectual, and sometimes physical, often give some indication as to what way of life one ought to choose — whether he ought to teach or do manual labor, and whether he ought to enter a monastic community or one that is devoted to the works of the active life: teaching, taking care of the sick, etc.

[333] Father Gerald Kelly, S.J., remarks: "To assume extraordinarily difficult obligations without special reasons may be the equivalent of exposing oneself unnecessarily to occasions of sin and even giving scandal to others. It is not wise to assume or to encourage others to assume the duty of observing perfect chastity when one's past

2. *An Ill-Regulated Temper:* Persons afflicted with this failing would be described as *habitually* irritable, touchy, impatient, and inclined to take things amiss. They do not get along with others very easily and lack the social virtues necessary for making a go of community life or of the duties involved in the pastoral ministry. Experience teaches that such persons do not continue in the vocation, even though they may be admitted to profession. If such a defect comes to the fore after profession, then, of course, the community has to be somewhat forebearing and try to remedy some of the causes for this — overwork, obedience that does not fit the temperament of the individual, etc. If this defect is discovered in the postulate or novitiate, then, if it seems that it is not being corrected with the proper guidance and assistance the person should not be encouraged to continue.

3. *Lack of Docility:* The reason for which one of this nature is not to be admitted or encouraged to continue is rather obvious. It indicates an improper spirit of independence and will give rise to difficulties along the lines of obedience. It was for this reason that Pius XII in his exhortation, *Menti Nostrae*, mentioned concerning the obedience of the priest: "Nothing can be lamented more in the conduct of the future priest, than that it is not in conformity with the Will of God." On this score we must be careful in distinguishing a rebellious subject from one who is not properly instructed or lacks home training. Sometimes these defects, with time and grace and the proper education, can be remedied, and the person can become quite capable of meeting the requirements of the religious life or the priesthood.

4. *An Overly Domineering Disposition:* This must be carefully watched because, if not checked early in life, it will usually cause trouble later on. Hence, it is essential that persons of this disposition show definite signs of improvement either outside a seminary or novitiate or postulate or, at least, in such a place, if it has been discovered there. If a person is incapable of taking second place, it is a good and strong sign that no vocation exists; for in the religious life especially they would be *cantans extra chorum*, "singing outside the choir," or out of tune with it.

5. *Jealousy:* If this defect is deeply rooted and pronounced, then it constitutes a serious impediment to entrance into religion or the seminary.

---

record or one's temperament indicates that the fulfillment of this duty is problematical. Difficulty even great difficulty is not in itself an obstacle. But difficulty with manifest weakness or with inability to confide in a director or with lack of appreciation for the safeguards of chastity is certainly a sufficient reason to make one hesitate or encourage the assumption of this obligation. To tell one that this will clear up in the novitiate is the height of ignorance. It may clear up in the novitiate only to return with even greater force later on." *Op. cit.*, p. 233.

For usually it indicates also a strong tendency to pride of one sort or another; and if it so exists in an older person, it is something which can be removed probably only with great difficulty. The assertion, that "you cannot teach an old dog new tricks" is very applicable in the present case. It is most difficult to acquire habits and dispositions after one has reached maturity. If, of course, there is proof or strong indication that one can overcome this fault with the natural and supernatural means at his disposal, then it would not be considered an insurmountable obstacle.

6. *Lack of Judgment:* This defect is more or less serious depending upon the community in question. For in some communities, by reason of the apostolate or some other circumstance, a greater need for sound judgment is required than would be demanded in others. There is a minimum, however, below which no community can go and this minimum is tending to become more and more the same for all communities.

7. *Lack of Balance:* This includes habits of mind resulting from family, social, and racial backgrounds, together with a religious training that may have produced in the individual erroneous ideas about religion. Sometimes they are spoken of as *idées fixes,* "fixed notions or ideas." Instability also is included under this phrase. Sometimes these things are not present at the time a person enters a community or seminary but develop in the course of the years through factors that have been introduced into the individual's life as a seminarian, religious, or priest. The influence of others have often been responsible for the presence of these notions; sometimes even the community may have been in some way responsible for them.[334]

Appendix to "Criteria"

Often enough, despite all these seemingly rather definite norms set up for determining the presence or the absence of vocation, the counselor, or those who have candidates in their charge may meet cases about which they are doubtful. The following general norms might be laid down as approved and capable of being safely followed:

1. If the doubt turns *in* favor of the candidate, such a person can be accepted for the seminary or for the novitiate of a religious community.

---

[334] In a much less detailed analysis of these defects of character which act as negative criteria, Father Vermeersch notes that they can be summed up as follows:
1. Those who find it difficult to observe continence.
2. Those who are so attached to their own will that they will hardly be found to be docile.
3. Those who have a disposition different from the rest or who are prone to be envious or suspicious of others, or singular in their behavior, and, consequently, apt to prove unsociable and disagreeable in community life.
4. Those who are so dependent upon human consolation that they will most probably fall victims to sadness and dejection in the cloister. *Op cit.,* p. 43.

For these have been instituted partially for the purpose of seeing whether a person has the qualifications required by the Church and the community for the ministry or religious life. However, this attitude of doubt should be settled on the part of the candidate; that is to say, he should have made up his mind to give it a try because he feels that he would like to be a religious. Here again, we come face to face with the firm purpose or the right intention which is required of a candidate desirous of pursuing one or other of the lives in question — the religious life, or the life under the counsels, or the priesthood. If this is not present, then we simply have to conclude that the person lacks the most essential of the requisite qualifications. Hence, doubtful candidates should not be encouraged to make profession, not even temporary, or take orders, if a *real* doubt exists, and not just an imaginary one, which would be more or less on the lines of groundless anxieties or fears. For these, experience shows, often arise in the lives of religious and seminarians, especially on the eve of profession or ordination. Thus a doubt which is practically all shadow and no substance should not be considered an obstacle to either of these steps.[335]

2. A doubt which *turns against* the person in question. In this case one might defer a definite decision until the situation becomes a little clearer. If this does not happen, or if there is no opportunity for delay, then the person ought to be discouraged. Where the doubt is of this nature, particularly with respect to those who are still in high school, the person ought to be encouraged to finish high school in some Catholic institution where he can be guided and watched by those in charge.

3. If the doubt is such as to render the motives for admitting or rejecting *just about equal*, then, perhaps, some kind of trial might be attempted, with the *definite understanding* with the candidate that if there is no improvement or resolution of the doubt he cannot be admitted to profession or the novitiate, or to continuance in the seminary. Sometimes a retreat in the environment in which one is thinking of leading the seminary or religious life, or a few days there as a kind of guest seeing at firsthand the routine, and yet not being committed to it, often helps in resolving the doubt. At the same time it gives the community or the seminary authorities an opportunity to observe the individual in question. Thus at the end of the third year of high school, for example, for those who are thinking of vocation to the religious life or seminary, some sort of workshop could be instituted. Something of the life of the seminarian or religious, let us say, the postulant and the novice could be observed at firsthand, without the observers being in any way committed to the institute or to the seminary.

---

[335] Cf. *Contra Retrahentes*, Chap. 10, *ed. cit.*, p. 176.

4. With regard to one who is *continually wavering* between the desire for the religious or priestly life and the married life, the counselor should try to clarify the issues and strengthen the will, suggesting retreats or consultation with some member of the order or community which the person is thinking of entering. If, despite all efforts, the hesitation persists, the person should be advised *not* to enter the religious state or the priesthood, but rather to choose the opposite state if the opportunity offers; for experience proves that such hesitation will be probably a perpetual thing in either state. The person should be told plainly that there is *no definite sign* of a vocation to the religious life or the priesthood and, consequently, that he has no obligation whatsoever of trying either. In fact, we might say there is a definite lack of the essential sign — the firm proposal already spoken of.[336] The director should advise the person that the recurrence of the desire should cause no scruples or regrets in later life. For he can practice the counsels *according to his state of life.*

Article IV.   The Means of Nourishing a Vocation

As we have seen, there is a lifetime obligation of nourishing and protecting a vocation already realized. Likewise, there is a way in which a vocation can be fostered, not given, of course, since it can be given only by God. If this is to be done efficaciously, we have to understand something of the ways in which the virtue of religion and its act of devotion are nourished and fostered and made to grow. St. Alphonsus Liguori has summed them up as follows:

1. *Prayer and Meditation:* In his treatment of this he mentions that one ought to devote a half hour in the morning and again in the evening, if possible, to meditation! He suggests the following topics: how the soul's salvation is secured by one entering the religious state; the happy death of a religious; the immense glory of a religious in heaven; the account that each one will have to render at the time of judgment; the interior peace which religious enjoy; the debt that we all have to God for all that He has given us; and how this debt can best be repaid through the religious life.[337]

St. Thomas certainly understood meditation to be the means *par excellence* of developing and protecting a vocation to the religious life or to the priesthood. For he mentions in his treatment of the act of devotion that it is the intrinsic cause of devotion:

> For while it is true that the *extrinsic* cause of devotion is God, still the intrinsic cause on our part is meditation or contemplation. For devotion is

---

[336] Cf. A. Vermeersch, *op. cit.*, p. 56.
[337] Cf. *Great Means of Salvation*, p. 418 ff.

a kind of act of the will. Every act of the will proceeds from some kind of consideration, insofar as it is an understood good that is the object of the will. For this reason it is necessary that meditation be the cause of devotion insofar as a person comes to the conclusion that he should give himself over to God's service through meditation.

This should center on two things: the greatness of God, and the benefits which He has given to us and the defects of the creature, from which one is led to see his complete dependence upon God. "I lifted up my eyes to the mountains whence help shall come to me." The first arouses love or dilection which is the cause of devotion, and the second excludes presumption through which one would posit some impediment to his being helped by God, for it makes us rest on God Himself. This meditation should center around the humanity of Christ in His relations with us.[338]

We can truthfully say that where there is no meditation there is no vocation. And experience teaches that in the case of abandoned meditation, we soon arrive at an abandoned vocation. In the course of teaching the states of life in high school it would be well to suggest this practice — just a few minutes a day of reflective thought on the meaning of life; on the end for which God has created us — to know Him, to love Him, and to serve Him; the meaning of the word "service" and its relationship to vocation; the ways in which we can serve God, and among these the grades of excellence, and the like. To get youth accustomed to reflect even for a few minutes each day on some truth such as this is already to train the person in religion and in devotion. Whether this will lead to a religious or priestly vocation depends, of course, upon God, but at least it is a good preparation or environment for it, or for any other truly Christian way of life to which the person may be called. To foster and nourish a vocation, means that we have to fill it with the things of God, and that can only be done by thoughtful reflection or meditation on the things of God, particularly on the mysteries of Christ's humanity.

2. *Recollection, or the Withdrawing From Worldly Interests:* While to some minds this might seem to be merely of the ancient past, still it is according to the saints one of the most efficacious ways of fostering and nourishing and protecting a vocation. And perhaps because this has not been followed in treating of the ways of the Christian life, we have failed to take into account one of the essential steps to the fostering of vocations. It is, we must admit, a negative means to the end; nevertheless it is an essential one. For we must constantly direct our efforts against the immersion of the mind and the heart in the things that are inferior, that serve only to clutter up the mind and enmesh it in trifles. Thus, we must caution young minds against becoming immersed in the activities of the world which, even though not sinful, still fill the mind of man and so

---

[338] II–II, Q. 82, a. 3, c. and ad 1m.

accustom it to look down that it finds increasing difficulty in looking up. Only if we insist upon the exclusion of undue contact with inferior things will we prevent loss of the spiritual cleanness of mind and heart and of stability which belong to religion and to its act of devotion. St. Alphonsus speaks of advising one to keep apart from worldly conversations and amusements. And Father Walter Farrell writes concerning this matter: "It is true at this moment and it will be of every moment of our lives that we protect that vocation in proportion as we keep away from the things that distract us from God, that immerse us in the things that are beneath us and hold us back from giving ourselves completely to the divine things above us."[339]

3. *Insistence on the Virtues of Generosity or Magnanimity, Chastity, Liberality, and Obedience* according to the state of the individual in question. If these virtues are to grow, we must warn the person of the dangers involved in frequenting things that could be harmful to his vocation. Overfamiliarity with those of the opposite sex, for example, should be discouraged for one who seems to show signs of a vocation to the priesthood or the religious life. And whereas this may seem rather Jansenistic to the modern mind, still it is the advice of *all the saints* who have written concerning the ways and means of fostering religious and priestly vocations. Any other opinion seems to be more or less influenced by the naturalistic trends of the day.

4. *Development of the Spirit of Sacrifice:* St. Alphonsus calls this the spirit of detachment. One who goes to serve God in His house ought to consider that he is going there not to be well treated, but rather to suffer for Him. This also includes detachment from relatives, from self-esteem, and from our own will.

5. *Secrecy:* That is, the vocation or the desire should not be "proclaimed" openly in circles where great opposition can be expected. A gradual revelation is usually the better procedure.[340]

From this analysis of the means of fostering a vocation, and of the very nature of vocation as pertaining to the overall picture of *gratia gratum faciens*, we can easily deduce the important conclusion that a vocation, once realized, is not by that very fact exempt from the possibility or even

---

[339] Talk cited above.

[340] These in general seem to be the means that are to be suggested in order to foster and protect a vocation to the priesthood or the religious life. Father Edward Farrell mentions a similar program: "charity, meditation, knowledge of the religious life, the exclusion of undue contact with inferior things, the insistence on the development of the virtue of magnanimity, the practice of liberality, chastity, and obedience from the earliest years." *Op. cit.*, pp. 174–179; cf. *Great Means of Salvation*, p. 391 ff.

the likelihood of corruption. Like all life, in order to mature and develop and grow strong even to the perfect day, it must be protected and nourished until the final breath.

The vigor of a vocation can always be measured or determined by certain signs: deep reverence, easy and eager humility, poverty of spirit with the manifestation of liberality and magnanimity, of generosity, which this implies, complete subjection. Moreover, the reverence for God's perfections as found in man is also something that is regarded as highly sacred in character. The image of God, man and woman, will always be considered with deep modesty, continency, and chastity. To preserve and to deepen the meaning of vocation, constant, frequent, and wise use of the sacraments, of prayer, and of meditation must be encouraged. What must be done in order to preserve or help along the vocation of a child must also be done by the one that has been in religion for fifty years, because to no one has the gift of perseverance been promised. This is something that must be constantly and humbly asked for throughout the entire course of a religious or priestly life. And God gives it — to one who is meek and humble of heart, to one who understands and realizes his own weaknesses and takes the proper measures to offset them and their influence on the spiritual life. Vocation, then, is not an act of virtue performed once and for all when the profession is made or solemn obligations are contracted. No. It needs constant attention, like a small plant, for it never finishes growing any more than does the life of grace itself. This is constantly in motion until we reach the terminal point — which was the point of our departure also — the mystery of the Trinity.

There is no excuse for the comfort of obscurity or vagueness in the matter of vocation. There should be nothing of cloudiness contained in our statement that a certain individual has a vocation. By this we should mean that we have seen in this person an act of devotion in a high degree, an eager, prompt will to give himself to God, confirmed by humility, reverence, subjection, cleanness, and strong, firm habits of virtue. Father Walter Farrell remarks: "If you don't mean this, you don't mean much of anything; you are committing the life of another on no more evidence than your 'feeling' in the matter. There is much indeed that is mysterious in vocation, but not in the field in which you are called to help; the divine love flowing into this youngster, the divine fruit of love in the individual's soul, the divine invitation that has started a conflagration within the heart. What must be seen by you is something that can be seen, taken apart, nourished, encouraged, protected — or betrayed."[341]

---

[341] Loc. cit.

Article V.   When Discernment of Vocation Is Called For

Sometimes we feel that the only occasion when a vocation comes up for discernment is at the outset, and that, once settled, it requires no further examination. This is not entirely correct, at least, from the viewpoint of experience. For while a vocation is of its *nature* something stable, and admits of only progress and advancement, nevertheless in a given individual it may also admit of regression, decay, and even death, as we have seen. Hence it may be wise to point out some of the more general cases where a guide will have to go through the process of discernment.

1. *Upon Seeing the Signs of a Religious or Priestly Vocation*, one who is engaged in vocational work can and should place this way of life before another, particularly when this has not been previously done or has been done inadequately. "Have you ever thought about the priesthood or the religious life?" is an introduction to such a move on the part of the guide or counselor. Opportune situations ought to be taken advantage of.

2. *Upon Seeing Signs of Hesitancy* in asking about vocation or counsel concerning it, one should offer to give any help possible. For often a youth is just a little hesitant about asking for information or guidance in regard to this problem.

3. *When There Is Uncertainty About the Precise Order or Congregation, or Type of Priesthood*, diocesan or religious, counsel is again called for. Here, however, the help of the confessor is of prime importance, for he sees the deep interior inclinations and tendencies of the individual in question, and can give counsel that is, perhaps, just a little more individual and personal and, therefore, more certain. It is, however, perfectly possible that one who is not the confessor, in fact, not even a priest — a Brother or a Sister — might be closer to the individual in question than even the confessor and could be of immense help in assisting the person to arrive at this decision. What is most important is that we must remember that we are not to tinker with a vocation and try to channel it along lines of our own choosing rather than of God's. Because this method of procedure has not always been followed, serious and harmful mistakes have been made and lives ruined, either consciously or unconsciously, by those asked for advice. Both individuals and institutes have had to suffer much from this, and something sacred (for the grace of vocation is sacred) has been profaned. There may be occasions when little or no fault has been involved, but if we look over the integral parts of prudence, it is often hard not to see that when misdirection is given, there has often been some slight departure from the virtue of prudence in the form of precipitation, neglect, or thoughtlessness.

In helping one choose a particular order or congregation or diocesan seminary, the entire "natural plant" of the individual ought to be considered — i.e., mental and physical — as well as the "supernatural plant." The use of a good psychologist, psychological test, or psychiatrist, is not to be underestimated — nor overestimated either. For some of the things that are revealed by such an examination can be of immense help to superiors for the channeling of talents and aptitudes, for the correction of possible defects of character, which, as we know, will ultimately be overcome only through the right use and therapeutical effects of nature and grace. They will serve to indicate along what lines a candidate may develop the natural virtues so indispensable for the easy and strong exercise of the supernatural virtues. On the other hand, it must be understood that *no psychological or psychiatrical process* can enable us to tell whether a person has a vocation or not *insofar as its supernatural side is concerned.* Thus Pius XI wrote: "We condemn those who say that we are able to test by ordinary purely secular examination or experiment, the supernatural factors that may enter into a child's education, such as the divine vocation to the priesthood or to the religious life and in general the mysterious effects caused in the human soul by grace, which though it elevates the powers of nature, yet infinitely transcends them and can in no way be subject to physical laws since the Spirit breathes where it will."[342]

---

[342] *AAS* 22 (1930), 70. Pius XII reaffirms this same teaching in the recent Constitution *Sedes Sapientiae:* "As for educational methods, it is evident that none of those supplied by nature or the human research of our day ought to be rejected, provided they are good. Such methods ought to be rather highly esteemed and wisely employed. There is *no greater error,* however, in the formation of such select students than excessive or exclusive reliance on these natural methods and their preference to the means provided by the supernatural order or the neglect of these latter means in any way. For supernatural means, such as the sacraments, prayer, mortification and the like are not only necessary to the attainment of a religious and clerical perfection crowned with apostolic success; they are altogether basic and of its essence.

"With this hierarchy of methods and activities preserved, nothing should be slighted which will contribute in any way to the perfection of body and mind and the cultivation of the natural virtues and the formation of an integral human personality. Thus the supernatural training whether for the religious life or for the priesthood will be based on the solid formation of natural integrity and refined personality. Although the humane and natural education of the religious clergy is to be highly esteemed, still first place in the program of formation must be given to the supernatural sanctification of the soul. If the words of the Apostle, 'For this is the will of God, your sanctification' apply to all Christians, they bind all the more one who has not only received the priesthood, but has made a public profession of his resolve to pursue evangelical perfection." *AAS* 48 (1956), 359–360. Cf. *Canon Law Digest,* IV, 175 f.

In its commentary on this Constitution, the Congregation of Religious writes in the General Statutes: "In order that the work of fostering, safeguarding and aiding

At the same time the grace of vocation is not afraid of the human soil or nature in which it takes root. And not to take into consideration the defects of this human nature would not be a sign of prudence. The knowledge that can be gained from these tests will enable one to make decisions later on that will be of great advantage both to the Church and the institute and will, in the long run, work for the well-being of the subject also. Many mistakes can be avoided in the way of assigning religious their obediences and the like, merely from an understanding of their temperaments and aptitudes.

What is important is that we remember that when these means are used in regard to candidates, they have a limited effect and result and that they can never bring about the ultimate cure for which we hope. And the reason for this is that every defect is in some way or other due to original sin and that, in the last analysis, only grace can bring any person to the level required for the religious life or the priesthood, a level which is essentially of the supernatural order. By reason of the theology of original sin and the principles of sacramental grace, we must not underestimate the effect which grace can have on the unconscious life and the psychic part of man, for it can be a therapeutic often much more potent than any that medical science could bring forward. The exact determination is again something that can be measured only by experience, by the experience of older persons who have been engaged in similar work and cases. And we must remember that we can never hope to avoid all mistakes.

4. *At the Time of Entrance Into the Novitiate and to Religious Profession:* On this score, from the viewpoint of the institute this inquiry is most important, for some communities have it as a written rule that "no one is to be admitted to the taking of the religious habit unless there is moral certitude that the individual will be received for profession. This is the momentous time when prayer should be resorted to and every effort made in order to know the will of God, and thus avoid a grave injury to the community and to the individual. When this has been done religiously and after mature deliberation, but little responsibility will rest on the final examination for perpetual vows. How much wiser it is to prolong the trial until the conviction can be reached." Certainly this rule is in perfect keeping with the theology of vocation such as it has been given above.

5. *Finally, in Regard to a Vocation Once Realized, then Called Into*

---

vocations to the states of perfection have abundant fruits, supernatural means must first of all be used, such as fervent prayer, the shining example of religious sanctity, ardent and perpetual exercise of apostolic zeal." Art. 32, § 1.

Question: When this occurs, prudence demands that the case be studied in order to determine whether the original decision was wrong, whether the solidity of the motives either for the first step or for the future step can be established. For it is a fact that some persons have embraced the priesthood or the religious life without having had the divine or interior call. And it is likewise a fact that in the mysterious design of Providence, a soul can be lead from one institute to another, as, for example, from an active one to a contemplative one.[343]

Article VI.   The Role of the Advisor or Counselor in Regard to Vocation

To give just a few basic ideas on the role of one who is asked for advice about entering one or other walk of life, the following might be suggested: first, he can be considered as exercising this role in a *general* capacity; and, second, in a *special* capacity:

1. *In general:* One is said to act as a counselor in a general way when, for example, he presents the notion of vocation to others in and through sermons or talks to various organizations or clubs, instructing those who have made a choice, as well as those who have yet to make this choice. Thus, for example, one acts in this capacity when he gives a vocation talk to a Serra Club or to a high school or grade school. In such a general presentation of the idea of vocation, the method used by Christ and the

---

[343] St. Thomas speaks of the possibility and advisability of passing from one institute to another in the following manner: "It is not commendable to pass from one religious order to another apart from the case of great usefulness or necessity: both because this frequently gives scandal to those who remain; and because other things being equal, it is easier to make progress in a religious order to which one is accustomed than in one in which one is not habituated. Hence in the Conferences of the Fathers, Abbot Nesteros says 'It is best for each one that he should according to the resolve he has made hasten with the greatest zeal and care to reach the perfection of the work he has undertaken and in no way forsake the profession he has chosen.' And further on he adds by way of reason: 'It is impossible that one and the same man should excel in all the virtues at once, since if he endeavors to practice them equally, he will of necessity, while trying to attain them all end in acquiring none of them perfectly,' because the various religious orders excel in respect of various works of virtue."

"Nevertheless one may commendably pass from one religious order to another for three reasons. First through zeal for a more perfect life which excellence depends as stated above, not merely on severity, but chiefly on the end to which a religious order is directed, and secondarily on the discretion whereby the observances are proportionate to the due end. Secondly, on account of a religious order falling away from the perfection it ought to have; for instance, if in a more severe religious order, the religious begin to live less strictly, it is commendable for one to pass even to a less strict or severe order if the observance is better. Thirdly, on account of sickness or weakness, the result of which sometimes is that one is unable to keep the ordinances of a more severe religious order, though able to observe those of a less severe one." II–II, Q. 189, a. 9.

Apostles and the Fathers and the Scholastics should be used; that is, they should present the religious life and the priesthood as special vocations willed by God for certain members of the Church, more perfect ways of life according to which one might render more complete service to God in an easier and more secure manner.

It is his office to place before these groups the *motives* which lead a person to embrace one of these states of life, that is, devotion or promptness and the desire to dedicate oneself to God and to the salvation of souls in a special way. Moreover, he should place before them the *rewards* which Christ Himself has promised to those who leave all to follow Him.

From this, he can pass on to the *superior excellence* of the life and how it fulfills in the highest possible manner the aspirations of a human being — of giving oneself to others for the sake of Christ, of entering into the eternal salvation of individual souls.

Likewise it is the duty of such a counselor or recruiter (for that is what his office amounts to) to show very clearly that a vocation does not imply special illumination and does not usually manifest itself in any extraordinary manner. As a rule a boy will simply mention to his mother or dad that he wants to be a priest or Brother, or in the case of a girl, a nun. It is then the *duty* of the parents not to discourage this wish, but to encourage it, without using any force either to persuade one to follow this call or to dissuade one from it. Thus parents are to encourage such a desire, but with proper moderation. They should realize, however, that it is a good thing to take precautions in certain respects, such as have been mentioned, with regard to the nourishing and fostering of vocations.

2. *In Special:* One who exercises the role of special counselor is usually either a director of souls or a confessor. It is his office to point out to penitents seeking a way of life that there are various ways open to a person, showing them their excellence and their requirements. He should emphasize that a vocation is something of God and from God and that it is a way of serving Him. If he sees that a person has the qualifications for the priesthood or the religious life, he might ask the question which was recommended previously: "Have you ever thought of the religious life or the priesthood?"

What he must insist upon is that the person act from his own knowledge and choice. One usually knows what he wants and he knows his own reasons for wanting it. Therefore, just as he makes a decision to do or not to do other things from his knowledge, so too must he act in regard to vocation — on the knowledge he himself has.

It is most important, however, that the director and the confessor recognize that it is not their obligation to test the spirit or to prove it, in the case of one well disposed. This pertains rather to the superiors of the institute. Thus, when one has the firm resolution to enter a particular community or seminary, then the director's or confessors' role is finished, unless, of course, he be the director of a person in the seminary or in the community. For this reason St. Thomas mentions that probation is not required of the individual to determine his right intention. This is the province of the religious community. Thus, in short, the spiritual director is not to act, or consider that he must act, as the novice master would.[344]

The confessor or counselor should also realize that it is perfectly possible that while human motives may have entered into one's choice of a state of life, this fact does not at all indicate that a genuine vocation is lacking. What he must do is to ascertain whether or not at the basis of the desire, there exists one or several of the true supernatural motives mentioned above — the desire to insure one's own salvation, or the desire to save souls, etc. If the motive is *purely* human or predominantly human, then it is the duty of the counselor to point this out, or to seek to purify it; if this prove impossible then he should discourage the "vocation." He should keep in mind, Father Edward Farrell writes, "the period of probation and the canonical novitiate which all candidates must undergo or the years of seminary training are designed to test and to discover the shaky foundations or improper motivation; it is there that they will be bolstered or collapse entirely." The novitiate partially serves as a proving grounds, as we have seen, from the standpoint of the individual (who enters with the right intention, that is, the firm resolution to make this his way toward God unless, during the course of that time, God shall point out otherwise), and from the standpoint of the community. Likewise, it will serve to train and to form the candidate for the religious life in something of the way that the seminary trains and forms young students for the priesthood.

Moreover, the counselor should know the individual quite well before giving any decision; that is, he must know his religious spirit, his generosity, his dispositions or aptitudes, the kind of companions with whom he associates, his spirit of prayer, and his frequentation of the sacraments.[345]

*   *   *

As a conclusion to this section on the religious life and vocation to it, probably no better paragraph than that given by St. Thomas in closing his treatise on the states of life could be cited:

The building of the tower signifies the perfection of the Christian Life, and the renunciation of one's possessions is the wherewithal to build this

[344] Cf. *Contra Retrahentes*, Chap. 10, ed. cit., p. 176.
[345] Cf. Felix Duffy, C.S.C., *Testing the Spirit* (St. Louis: B. Herder, 1947), p. 26.

tower. Now no one doubts or deliberates about wishing to have the where-withal or whether he is able to build the tower if he have the wherewithal, but what does come under deliberation is whether one has the wherewithal. Again it is not necessarily a matter of deliberation whether one ought to renounce all that one has, or whether by so doing one may be able to attain perfection, while it is a matter of deliberation whether that which he is doing amounts to the renunciation of all he has, since unless he does so he cannot, as the text states, be Christ's disciple, and this is to build a tower.

The misgiving of those who hesitate as to whether they may be able to attain to perfection by entering religion is shown by examples to be un-reasonable. Hence Augustine says: "On that side whither I had set my face, and whither I trembled to go, there appeared to me the chaste dignity of continency, honestly alluring me to come and doubt not, and stretching forth to receive and embrace me, her holy hands full of multitudes of good examples. There were so many young men and maidens here, a multitude of youth and every age, grave widows and aged virgins. And she smiled at me with a persuasive mockery as though to say: 'Canst not thou do what these youths and these maidens can? Or can they either in themselves and not rather in the Lord their God? Why standest thou in thyself, and so standest not? Cast thyself upon Him; fear not, He will not withdraw Himself that thou shouldst fall. Cast thyself fearlessly upon Him; He will receive and heal thee.' "[346]

. . . Religion is the sweet yoke of Christ, for as Gregory says[347] "What burden does He lay on the shoulders of the mind Who commands us to shun all troublesome desires, Who warns us to turn aside from the rough paths of the world?"

To those who indeed take this sweet yoke upon themselves He promises the refreshment of the divine enjoyment and the eternal rest of their souls, to which He Who made this promise bring us, Jesus Christ our Lord, Who is over all things God blessed for ever Amen.[348]

The whole of the religious vocation has as its ultimate purpose to bring about the perfect disposition required for intimate union with God or for the ultimate of Christian perfection. And this particular spirit or dis-position, which is often called poverty of spirit, has been wonderfully summed up by one of the mystics in the following words:

My soul was enlightened, and I saw how all things are in God. After which I saw a very pure and abundant spring welling up out of the side of a mountain and flowing thence down upon the earth, where it divided itself up into a multitude of streamlets, more or less limpid or muddy according to the ground through which they coursed. Crowds of people ran to seek these streamlets, but very few went to draw water from the source itself. And our Lord said to me, "see how men, instead of seeking the pure and uncreated source and principle of all things, run to those streamlets which are either muddy or insufficient to quench their thirst. All things are in Me

---

[346] *Confessions*, Bk. 8, Chap. 27, PL 32, 761.
[347] *Morals*, Bk. IV, Chap. 33, PL 75, 673.
[348] II–II, Q. 189, a. 10, ad 3m.

as in their principle. Wherefore those who seek Me leaving all things, shall find them all in Me."

That is the religious life. For as St. Thomas says: "*Humanum cor tanto intensius in aliquid unum fertur quanto magis a multis revocatur. Sic igitur tanto perfectius animus hominis ad Deum diligendum fertur quanto magis ab affectu temporalium revocatur*" — "The human heart, the more it is recalled from many things, is so much the more intensely carried to one thing. Thus the more the soul of man is recalled from affection for temporal things, the more perfectly is it carried to the love of God."[349]

· APPENDIX

Another state of perfection recognized by the Code is that which embraces the so-called Societies of the Common Life, such as the Vincentians, the Paulists, the Maryknoll Fathers, the White Fathers, and the Daughters of Charity of St. Vincent de Paul. The members of these societies practice the evangelical counsels, it is true, but by means other than public vows. This they do either by private vows, or a promise, or an oath of stability, or something else. Such an engagement, when recognized by the Church either in a diocesan institute or one of pontifical status, establishes them in a state of perfection, objectively speaking, according to a canonical and juridical consideration at least, inferior in rank to a religious order or congregation. This engagement is not to be considered merely as a kind of manifestation of one's personal piety. It encompasses certain very definite juridical norms laid down by the Holy See. For the most part, they are for all practical purposes the same as those laid down for religious communities. That is why they are under the control and direction of the Sacred Congregation of Religious.

Yet for all this they are *not religious* in the *strict* sense of the word since they lack the element essential to religious and to constituting a religious institute, namely, vows received *in the name of the Church*. That is why they are called "societies without vows," not because no vows are ever taken in them, for the opposite is true in many cases, e.g., the Vincentians and the Daughters of Charity; but because they are not considered to be *public vows*. These societies are characterized by four special notes: (1) the living of the common life; (2) submission to a legitimate superior; (3) approved constitutions; and (4) a way of life that imitates that of religious in reference to acquiring perfection. Thus they approach the condition of the religious state especially by reason of their living the common life and it is by this same token that they are distinguished from certain

---

[349] *De Perfectione Vitae Spiritualis, in Opuscula Theologica, II, 1954 ed. p. 118.*

pious associations of the faithful. Consequently, it can be said that the essential element of these states of perfection is the living of common life. That is why they are called by this name.[350]

Generally speaking, however, the practice of the common life and of poverty in these societies is not as strict as it is in religious institutes. While it is true that whatever the members of these societies acquire in consideration of the society, belongs to it, still, they may retain, acquire, and administer other personal goods somewhat more freely than religious. This matter is usually determined by the Constitutions of each society and varies from one to another. It is precisely because of this juridical difference that we may conclude that the consecration of oneself to God in such a society is not as perfect objectively speaking as that realized through the public religious profession. Consequently, it would seem that we are correct in saying that the act of devotion involved in such a consecration would not have to be (again objectively speaking) as extensive or intensive as is required for the profession of public vows. In this sense it can be said that the juridical difference implies in the mind of the Church certain theological implications precisely in reference to the external and personal consecration made by one entering upon one or other of the two states of perfection, i.e., the religious life or societies of the common life. This difference in regard to the external consecration which is more complete in the case of religious strictly so called than it is in the case of the members of these societies, would imply that a lesser intensity of the activity of religion is required in the latter case than in the former, again objectively speaking. This would not at all prevent the possibility of there actually being a more intense act of devotion present in the case of one entering a society of the common life than would be true of one entering a religious institute.

Concerning this last point it would be well for us to keep in mind a passage from a note sent by the Sacred Congregation of Extraordinary Affairs to the Bishop of Namur in Belgium on July 13, 1952.

> It is not the personal perfection of the individual that is under discussion. This perfection is measured by the degree of love, of "theological charity" that has been realized within him. The criterion for the intensity and the purity of love is according to the Master's words, the fulfillment of the will of God. The individual is thus in the eyes of God the more personally perfect in the measure that he fulfills the divine will the more perfectly. In determining this, the state in which he lives matters very little, whether it be the lay or the ecclesiastical state, and for the priest whether it be the secular or the regular priesthood.
> It follows that it would not be correct to say that the secular priest with

---

[350] Cf. T. Schaefer, O.F.M.Cap., *De Religiosis* (Rome: 1947), p. 998.

respect to his personal holiness has a lesser call to perfection than the regular priest; or that a young man's decision to follow the vocation of the secular priesthood involves the choice of a lesser personal perfection than if he had chosen the religious state. It may happen that this is the case; it may happen just as well that the choice of a state other than the state of perfection will come from a greater love of God and from a nobler spirit of sacrifice than the choice of another to enter the religious state.[351]

SECTION 5. THE EPISCOPATE

In the earlier part of this work in listing the various states of perfection, we pointed out that the episcopate was also placed among the various states of perfection, at least, by most authors. This might at first seem to be rather strange. For no bishop is obliged to take the vows of religion, or to enroll in a society which is recognized as a state of perfection by the Church. Yet notwithstanding that it is the teaching of many theologians that every bishop is said to be in a state of perfection and, indeed, in one that is superior to the states of perfection that we have examined thus far. To understand this more fully we might consider the episcopate as a state of perfection and as a state of perfection more excellent than or superior to all others.

A State of Perfection

When treating of the state of perfection we mentioned that two elements were required: first, a perpetual obligation of some sort in relation to those things which were of perfection, e.g., the evangelical counsels; and second, that this perpetual obligation be assumed with some type of solemnity. Religious, we saw, are said to be in a state of perfection by reason of their having assumed the counsels of perfection in an institute approved by the Church. With a bishop something similar occurs. He is said to assume by episcopal consecration a perpetual obligation of caring for the flock of Christ entrusted to his care. The relationship of these two elements to both the religious state and the episcopate are rather clearly pointed out by St. Thomas:

> As has been said, for a state of perfection there is required a perpetual obligation with a certain solemnity to things which pertain to perfection. But both of these apply to religious and bishops. For religious bind themselves by vow to this, namely, that they abstain from secular things which they could licitly use in order that they might the more easily and freely have time for God; and in this consists the perfection of the present life.

---

[351] *Parish Priest*, E. Masure, tr. by Angeline Bouchard (Chicago: Fides, 1955), pp. 254–255. Also *The States of Perfection*, ed. G. Courtois (Dublin: Gill & Son, 1961), p. 211.

In like manner bishops bind themselves to things pertaining to perfection when they take up the pastoral care, to which it pertains that a shepherd lay down his life for his sheep, according to John 10:15. Therefore the apostle says[352] "Thou hast confessed a great claim before so many witnesses," that is to say, when he was ordained. Again a certain solemnity of consecration is employed together with this profession according to the words of Timothy[353] "Stir up the grace of God which is within thee by the imposition of my hands," which the gloss ascribes to the episcopate. And Dionysius says "that when the high priest, that is the bishop, is ordained, he receives on his head the most holy imposition of the sacred oracles, whereby it is signified that he is a participator in the whole and entire hierarchical power and that not only is he the enlightener of all (which pertains to his discourses and actions) but that he also confers this on others."[354]

The consecration of a bishop is very much like that of religious profession. It lays upon the one receiving it the perpetual obligation of that which pertains to perfection, not the living of the three vows, but, rather, the laying down of one's life for the flock should that ever become necessary. The entire symbolism of the ceremony points to this perpetual obligation. Through it the bishop becomes wedded, as it were, to a diocese, residential or titular, receiving a ring in token of the bond which is established. Consequently, the spiritual care of his subjects is not a matter of choice for a bishop. He may not legitimately abandon his diocese unless he is explicitly relieved of its care by the supreme authority of the Church. And even then he is transferred to another residential or titular see, indicating that the indissoluble marriage bond between him and some portion of the flock of Christ still exists, even though at times he may be legitimately prevented from exercising this duty because of prevailing circumstances. It is in this sense that the bishop is said to be in a state of perfection: at the moment of his episcopal consecration he encounters a duty that is perpetual, an obligation that implies all the stability and permanence that is required to establish one in a state of perfection.[355]

According to some authors, the Angelic Doctor seems to indicate that the bishop takes a vow at the time of his consecration. For he points out that the bishop does not have the right to forsake the episcopal charge in order to enter religion and there work for his own salvation. He cites Pope Innocent III in this regard and then goes on to say that the Pope alone can dispense from the perpetual vow by which a person binds himself to the care of his subjects when he takes on himself the episcopal office. It pertains to the state of perfection proper to the bishop that he occupy

---

[352] 1 Tim. 6:12.
[353] 2 Tim. 1:7.
[354] De Ecc. Hierarchia, 5, 3, sect. 7, PG 3, 313; II–II, Q. 184, a. 5.
[355] Cf. art. "Evêque," in Dictionnaire Théologie Catholique, V, col. 907.

himself perpetually in working for the salvation of others, and he would be going back on this promise if he were to pass to the religious state to busy himself only with his own salvation, since he has bound himself not only to work for his own salvation but also for that of others.[356] It is only when this obligation is impeded in some way that he can be allowed to pass to a religious institute (at least, in St. Thomas' day).

In his commentary on this question, Cardinal Cajetan points out, however, that even though St. Thomas might seem to indicate that a vow is implied in episcopal consecration, still we must be very cautious as to how we understand this word "vow." When a bishop is said to vow, or to make a vow, concerning those things which are of perfection, we are to understand that he takes upon himself something of the *effect* of a vow, but not its essence, that is to say, the obligation which he assumes is almost the same as if he had made a vow. But it does not seem that he has really taken a vow, such that if he in some way were to transgress this obligation he would be guilty of a sin against the virtue of religion.[357] His reason for saying this is that there is nothing in the law which gives any indication of this, such as there is, for example, in regard to the vow of celibacy which a subdeacon in the Latin rite assumes at the moment of his reception of this order. This position of Catejan seems to be held by the majority of modern writers. Nothing besides the episcopal consecration is needed to supply or to account for the permanent obligation necessary for a state of perfection.[358]

Superior to the Religious State

The second element contained in the episcopal state of perfection is that it is more *excellent* than that of religious. Several reasons for this are given by theologians. The fundamental one is that given by St. Thomas:

> The agent is always more perfect than the patient. Now, in the genus of perfection the bishops are in the position of perfectors, while religious are in the state of being perfected. The former pertains to action and the latter to passion. From this it is evident that the state of perfection of the bishop is more excellent than that of religious.[359]

The fundamental difference between the state of perfection proper to bishops and that proper to religious lies precisely here: the one involves

---

[356] Cf. II–II, 185, a. 4; Q. 184, a. 6.

[357] Commentary on Q. 185, a. 4, in the Leonine edition.

[358] Cf. E. J. Mahoney, "Our Priestly Obligation of Perfection," in *American Ecclesiastical Review*, 72 (1925), 570; Dom O. Lottin, O.S.B., "Doctrine de St. Thomas sur l'état religieux," in *La Vie Spirituelle*, 7 (1923), 391; M. J. Nicolas, O.P., "Sacerdoce diocesain et vie réligieuse," in *Revue Thomiste*, 46 (1946), 180; G. Thils, *La Nature et Spiritualité du clergé diocesain* (Bruges: 1946), p. 393.

[359] II–II, Q. 184, a. 5.

a solemn obligation of perfecting others, whereas the other involves the obligation to seek perfection for oneself. This difference is well expressed by the Latin phrases chosen to describe the two states: for the state of perfection proper to the bishop — *status perfectionis communicandae seu exercendae* — "the state of communicating or exercising perfection"; and for that of religious — *status perfectionis acquirendae* — "the state of acquiring perfection or seeking perfection."[360]

Several other reasons might be advanced to show that the state of perfection proper to the bishop is superior to that of religious. In the first place, the episcopal state presupposes personal perfection as we are given to understand from our Lord's asking Peter if he loved Him more than the others before committing to him the pastoral care of the Church. This is most reasonable. For one who is a perfector of others ought to be perfect himself in order to bring others to perfection, or at least, this is most fitting.[361] For the only general law that can be given for the selection of a bishop is that he be one who is capable of governing the Church, one who is capable of instructing, defending, governing, and administering the Church peacefully. If there are several who are equally capable, then according to St. Thomas we are to look for the one among them who is preeminent in the love of God.[362]

It is for this reason — that bishops, other things being equal, would be preeminent in the love of God — that many theologians speak of their state of perfection as being a state of acquired perfection (*status perfectionis acquisitae*). In fact, one of them mentions that this term is the one that is so correctly applied to the episcopal state that it ought to be referred to as "the state of acquired perfection to be exercised or communicated":

> There actually is a "*status perfectionis acquisitae et exercendae,*" in the Church Militant. In order to prove this conclusion it is sufficient to demonstrate two things: First, that the character of a real state is to be found in the episcopate; secondly, that this state requires that a bishop has already acquired perfection. But both these points are certain. The first is shown from his having a moral obligation of remaining permanently in office. . . . And he is deputed to the office of perfecting others in such a way that he himself ought to be the light of the world; and that he ought to exhort to perfection not by his words, but that he should shine as a light in the Church by the actual exercise of perfection. Therefore, exercising perfection

---

[360] It seems as though Pope Pius XII in the *Annus Sacer* was alluding to this distinction. *AAS* 43 (1951), 29–30; for tr. of this Allocution cf. *Canon Law Digest,* III, p. 119–ff.

[361] Cf. II–II, Q. 185, a. 1, ad 2m.

[362] Cf. Q. 185, a. 3, c. and ad 1m.

is incumbent upon bishops by reason of their state. But that which is not possessed cannot be exercised. Therefore, this state presupposes and *per se* demands a perfection already acquired.[363]

The more common way of referring to the state of perfection proper to the bishop is, however, "the state of perfection to be exercised or communicated," since by his very office he is one who communicates those things which are of perfection to his flock and this by way of a permanent obligation accepted with episcopal consecration.

In the second place, the superior excellence of the bishop's state of perfection comes from the element of choice involved in the assumption of these two states. A religious freely chooses the state of perfection, whereas a bishop is chosen for it even though he freely consents to the election once it has been made. This difference stems from the very basic difference which we pointed out above: the one, the state of perfection proper to the religious, is one wherein he sets out to seek perfection, whereas the other, the state of perfection of the bishop, is one wherein he is called upon to communicate perfection. The agent is always, or should always be, more perfect than the patient, the teacher than the student.

This superiority is also indicated, I believe, in two very practical norms which modern Church law establishes for the episcopacy and the religious life. Under the present discipline of Canon Law, a bishop, or a bishop-designate, cannot validly enter a religious community. Such a move, according to St. Thomas, would be a regression, a going back from a higher state to a lower state. So long as he can procure the spiritual welfare of the subjects entrusted to his care, the bishop has no right to neglect this, either for the sake of contemplation, or for the sake of avoiding hardships, or for the sake of acquiring any gain. Moreover, a religious who is elevated to the episcopacy, although he retains his vows is nonetheless dispensed from some of the usual implications of their observance where this would interfere with his office. St. Thomas has given a rather masterful analysis of this problem:

> The religious state pertains to perfection as a way of tending to perfection, while the episcopal state pertains to perfection as a kind of a teacher of perfection. Hence the religious state is compared to the episcopal state as the state of the disciple to that of the master, and as a disposition is com-

---

[363] D. Bouix, *Tractatus de jure regularium* (Paris: 1857), 1, 16. St. Robert Bellarmine and F. Suarez are often cited in favor of this same position. But I think that a thorough reading of their works would indicate their teaching to be practically the same as that given by St. Thomas. It is fitting that the man appointed to the episcopal office should be perfect, or have acquired perfection, but the exact degree is not laid down. *Controversiae, De Membris Ecclesiae*, Bk. II, Chap. 2, n. 7, *Omnia Opera*, II (Paris: 1870), p. 507; for the reference in Suarez, cf. *De Religione*, tr. 7, Bk. I, Chap. 15, n. 7, *Opera Omnia*, XV, p. 73.

pared to a perfection itself. Now, the disposition is not voided at the advent of perfection, except as perhaps what is incompatible with perfection, while as to that in which it is in accord with perfection it is confirmed the more. Thus when the disciple has become master, it is no longer fitting for him to be a listener, but it is fitting for him to read and meditate even more than before.

Accordingly we must assert that if there be among religious observances any that instead of being an obstacle to the episcopal office are a safeguard of perfection, such as continence, poverty, and so forth, a religious even after he has been made a bishop remains bound to observe these, and consequently, to wear the habit of his order, which is a sign of this obligation. (In modern communities, a bishop does not wear the habit of his order, but only retains the initials of his community). On the other hand, a person is not bound to keep such religious observance as may be incompatible with the episcopal office, for instance, solitude, silence, and certain severe abstinences or vigils and such as would render him unable to exercise the episcopal office.

For the rest he may dispense himself from them according to the needs of his person or office and the manner of life of those among whom he dwells, in the same way as a religious superior dispenses himself in such matters.[364]

While it is true that a religious priest elevated to the episcopacy is to some extent freed from his vows and to such an extent the perfection of the former over the latter is indicated, still he remains bound by his vows wherever their obligation helps him rather than hinders him in the performance of his office. While he is not bound to obey his religious superiors, this is by reason of his now coming directly under the authority of the Head of the Church, as it were, and those who exercise His authority. And yet it seems as though he would have to comply with any command which these latter addressed to him, and this by reason of his vow.

---

[364] II–II, Q. 185, a. 8.

CHAPTER FIVE

Other Forms of the Life of Christian Perfection

IN THE introductory chapter we saw that the "secular" states were three: the priesthood, the life of consecrated virginity lived in the world, and the married state. In this chapter we shall attempt to consider each of these states according to the limited scope of the present work.[1]

SECTION 1. THE PRIESTHOOD

In the introductory part of the present work, we divided the categories of vocations into those which pertained to the states of perfection and those which pertained to the "secular" order. At that time, we mentioned that while there was a dispute as to whether the priesthood ought to be placed with the states of perfection or whether it ought to be placed with the "secular" states, still we would include it among the "secular" states for the reasons that will be pointed out in the course of our discussion.

It seems to the present writer that much of the difficulty in deciding the placement of the priesthood can be traced to the obscurity still to be found in the relationship between the simple priest and the bishop. This, as yet, has not been solved satisfactorily for all; for the opinions that were advanced prior to the *Sacramentum Ordinis* are still being proposed by theologians of both camps, each maintaining that its position is upheld by the constitution. Consequently, it seems wise to give a brief treatment of the distinction between the orders, according to Scripture, the writings

---

[1] For a fuller treatment, the reader is referred to the many dogmatic, moral, and canonical works in which one or other of these states is considered. It is hoped a work entitled: *The Sacrament of Matrimony: a Dogmatic Study* will soon be available. The word "secular" is placed in quote marks because it is not the strict term dividing the states to be discussed here from the foregoing. A secular institute is a state of perfection and yet it is strictly a secular state.

of the early Church Fathers, the magisterium and theologians, before examining the considerations which presuppose this distinction.

The Distinction Between the Bishop and the Simple Priest

In addition to the office or function of deacon in the Church,[2] there was that of the presbyters, those who held certain positions of authority in the various Christian communities. In fact, this office was so well known and accepted that St. Luke, for example, does not even go into any explanation of it when speaking of them.[3] We are told that Paul himself appointed presbyters in the Churches which he founded.[4] And in Jerusalem we see that they had some share in the affairs of the Church although in subordination to the Apostles.[5] St. James likewise speaks of them as performing certain functions; i.e., anointing and forgiving sins.[6] In other sections of Scripture, through the use of other words by the inspired writers we know that they labored for the Christians,[7] and that they presided over the early Christians — in the Lord,[8] as Paul mentions in his Epistle to Timothy.[9] They also had the office of admonishing the early Christians,[10] and they were to be reverenced by the Churches by reason of the place which they occupied in them.

It is now almost certain and universally accepted that the Greek words *episcopos* and *presbyter* were designations of the same persons. The evidence for this is found in the Acts 20:17, 23; Titus 1:4, 7; 1 Tim. 3:2–7. Whether at this time those designated by the names *episcopos* and *presbyter* were bishops in the sense in which we use the word is not certain. Opinions concerning this question are still divided. Generally, however, it is denied. If 1 Tim. 4:14 seems to suggest that Timothy had been given the charisma of his office by prophecy and the imposition of hands of the presbyters, still this is not certain because we know that St. Paul mentions that He Himself had conferred the grace of the order upon Timothy. Moreover, the commission to Titus to appoint presbyters in the various places seems to indicate that these did not have the power to appoint such on their own.[11] Confirmation of this point might be found in the fact that St. Paul's praise of such as desire the office of *episcopos*[12] is more easily understood if it is the lower order of the priesthood that is in question. For certainly the whole tradition of the Church has looked askance at those who aspire to the prelacy.[13]

---

2 Cf. Acts 8:5–13; 26:40.
3 Cf. Acts 10:30.
4 Cf. Acts 14:22.
5 Cf. Acts 15:4, 6, 22, 23; 16:4; 21:18.
6 Cf. Jas. 5:14 ff.
7 Cf. 1 Thess. 5:12–13.
8 Cf. Rom. 12:8.
9 Cf. Jas. 6:17.
10 Cf. Acts 20:31; 1 Cor. 4:14.
11 Cf. Tit. 1:5.
12 Cf. 1 Tim. 3:1.
13 Cf. Holzmeister, Bib. 12 (1931), 41–69.

Other theologians, however, hold that these terms refer to those who possessed the episcopal office as it exists today. In their opinion, we can deduce from Scritpure that there were two orders — that of the *episcopoi-presbyteroi* (one order) and that of the deacons. It was only sometime later that the former of these orders was divided into the priests of the first rank and those of the second rank. However, as we ought to note, this is the opinion of theologians and not that of exegetes.[14]

What can be concluded with certainty is that the existence of bishops, such as we know them now, was an actuality in Apostolic times. There is no doubt that Timothy and Titus were bishops since they ordained, and carried out other episcopal functions.[15] Likewise they had authority over the presbyters since they were responsible for their sound doctrine and for sitting in judgment over them.[16] It is probable that the Apostles themselves kept that control of the Churches, sending their representatives who possessed episcopal authority to the various Churches to represent them. The *presbyteroi-episcopoi* in these localities, then, would assist them in their work.[17]

While it is true that the Fathers used the word *sacerdos* for the two personalities in the Church, the bishop and the priest, still from the very

---

[14] Cf. *The Distinction Between the Episcopate and the Presbyterate according to the Thomistic Opinion*, G. Dolan, C.M. (Washington, D. C.: Cath. U. of America Press, 1950), pp. 4–5.

[15] Cf. 1 Tim. 5:19–22; Tit. 1:5–7.

[16] Cf. 1 Tim. 1:3; 3:1–15; 4:11; 5:19; 6:2; 2 Tim. 4:2–5.

[17] Father C. Spicq, in his treatment of this question, mentions that the words were at one time used interchangeably, but with the passage of time there was a gradual adaptation and limitation of the term *episcopos*, this latter word being employed as time went one, even in the books of Scripture, to designate those priests who exercised the pastoral ministry in the local Churches (cf. Acts 2:28; Phil. 1:1). By the time of the pastorals *episcopos* had become a special or technical name or term for a special kind of presbyter, one who presided and in whom a special quality was sought. In this way there was a gradual reservation of the term to those who have what we today call the episcopal functions and duties. Thus even in these latter Scriptural works, we see that the *episcopos* is a presbyter, although not every presbyter is an *episcopos*, in the new meaning of that term. In other words, Father Spicq concludes, "the presbyter-episcopos has no quality essentially different from that of all other presbyters nor even in all likelihood a privileged dignity, and that is why the desire must be stimulated. But he does exercise a special function" (*Les Epîtres Pastorales* [Paris: 1947], pp. 84–93, *passim*).

For Father Spicq, the office of *episcopos* common to all presbyters earlier at Ephesus and Philippi is now reserved to one person especially qualified, and although all priests retain the authority previously exercised, there is but one who presides. His dignity is no greater than that of his fellow priests, but the duty he undertakes is more important or extensive and charged with greater responsibility than that of the presbyters as a whole. This function of presiding is not something which is entirely clear in Scripture, although it does seem that he was something of a *primus inter pares* — "the first among equals."

beginning they insisted upon a distinction between the two. St. Ignatius, for example, writing in the second century, says:

> for since you are subject to the bishop (episcopos) as to Jesus Christ, you seem to live not according to man but according to Jesus Christ who died for us, so that believing in His death you might escape death. It is necessary then that as often as you do something, you do it always under the guidance of the bishop, and that you be also subject to the presbyterate as to the apostles of Jesus Christ. . . . Let them reverence the deacons . . . even as the bishop, (episcopos) who is a type of the Father, and the presbyters the senate of God and the council of the Apostles.[18]

In the course of years, the word sacerdos came to refer to the priests of the second rank or order, although even to the time of the tenth century bishops were called sacerdos. Priests then came to be known by various names from this time on: priests of the second rank, second priest, priests of the second merit, and others.[19]

This distinction is rather clearly indicated in the official documents of the Church from the earliest times. St. Clement of Rome writes in his Letter to the Corinthians: "for they do not go astray who follow the commands of the Lord. Inasmuch as peculiar gifts have been bestowed upon the chief priest, a special place has been assigned to the priests and special duties are incumbent upon the Levites."[20]

In the "Ancient Statutes of the Church" we read of the presence of the following orders: bishop, priest, deacon, subdeacon, acolyte, exorcist, lector, porter, and another, that of psalmist or cantor, which, however, from the document does not appear to have the same status as the others mentioned. For all the others are conferred by the bishop, while this last one is given merely through a priest. The author of these statutes seems to have been Caesarius of Arles.[21]

The Council of Trent speaks of the orders of the Church beginning with the priesthood.[22] But the same Council does mention very explicitly that there is a distinction between bishops and priests, for the former, who have succeeded the apostles, belong in a special way to the hierarchy of the Church and have been placed by the Spirit to rule the Church and can perform many other functions over which the priests of the lower order have no power.[23] "If anyone says that in the Church a hierarchy has not been instituted by divine ordination which consists of bishops, priests

---

18 Epistle to the Trallians, 2, 1, PG 5, 676; 3, 1, PG 5, 677; 7, 2, PG 5, 680.

19 Cf. St. Leo the Great, Sermon 48, 1, PL 54, 298. Likewise the Epistle Si Instituta Ecclesiastica, PL 20, 554; St. Optatus of Milevia, Against the Schism of the Donatists, Bk. I, Chap. 13, PL 11, 910.

20 Denz. 42.

21 Cf. Denz. 150.

22 Cf. Denz. 958.

23 Cf. Denz. 960; also 966.

and ministers . . . A.S." And likewise in the following canon of this same Council: "If anyone says that the bishops are not superior to priests or that they do not have the power to confirm and ordain, or that the power which they have is common to them and to priests . . . A.S."

Pius XII, in the Apostolic Constitution *Sacramentum Ordinis*, also speaks of these orders: the episcopate, the priesthood, and the diaconate, each of which confers a *special grace* and *spiritual power*.

From these documents of the Church, it seems that we can very safely conclude that there is a distinction between the orders of the episcopate and of the priesthood as we know them today. Just exactly what that distinction is is *not* made clear in the documents which we have. For that reason, the dispute about the difference between the two orders still persists.

What can be gathered from Scripture and Tradition and the documents of the Church concerning the distinction between the two offices is: first, bishops are superior to priests in the power of orders and the power of jurisdiction; second, this hierarchy proceeds from divine law and ordination; third, priests cannot ordain, at least *ex officio*, that is to say, they are not in any way the ordinary ministers of the sacrament of Orders.

Outside of these things which are of faith, a theological problem is still much discussed in the schools, concerning the *precise* distinction between the episcopate and the priesthood. The problem rests on the different modes of viewing the episcopate. This can be considered *adequately*, as theologians say, or *inadequately*. Adequately considered, it would include all that we find in the order of the priesthood — the power to consecrate, the power to absolve — plus the ordinary power of confirming, of ordaining, and of governing. All theologians hold that the episcopate in this sense is an order and a sacramental one distinct from all others. Inadequately considered, the episcopate includes only those powers *added* to those proper to the priesthood, namely, the power to confirm, to ordain, and to govern. With this distinction in mind the following opinions are given by theologians:

1. The episcopate *inadequately* considered is not a sacrament distinct from that of the priesthood. This opinion was taught by all but a few from the twelfth to the sixteenth century and is today held by many Thomists and other theologians.[24] These authors teach that the episcopate, if we limit our understanding of it merely to the added powers which it

---

[24] Cf. P. Vermeer, *Bijdragen*, 13 (1952), 262–275; Charles Journet, "Vues récent sur le sacrement de l'ordre," in *Revue Thomiste*, 53 (1953), 91–108. Garrigou-Lagrange, O.P., *De Eucharistia*, p. 411, J. Beyer, S.J., "Nature et position de sacerdoce," in *Nouvelle Revue Théologique*, 76 (1954), 356–373, 469–480, and again in *Les Instituts séculiers* (Bruges: 1954), pp. 152–180.

gives to those of the priesthood, is not a sacramental order distinct from the latter. Rather, it is merely the extension of the priesthood, and, as they say, its perfect complement. It is an intrinsic modification of the presbyterate and therefore the complement of the greatest and supreme sacramental order. Only those orders which have a relationship with the Eucharist are sacramental.

2. The greater number of modern theologians teach that the episcopate even inadequately considered is a sacramental order distinct from that of the priesthood. They teach that it is not merely an extension of the priestly order but is a sacramental order in its own right, in somewhat the manner in which the priesthood itself is distinct from the diaconate. It is not true to say that only the orders which have a relationship with the Eucharist are sacramental. It is sufficient for them to produce grace and power.[25]

3. Still a third opinion which might be advanced — somewhat similar to that given immediately above — is this. The order of the episcopate even inadequately considered is a true sacramental order. While it is true that the orders are distinguished only by reason of their having a relationship to the Eucharist, still this relationship can be either direct or indirect. Any order, whether it be directly or indirectly ordered to the Eucharist, so long as it produces a spiritual power and grace ex opere operato, is a true sacramental order. That the episcopal consecration today confers both grace and power as sacramental effects can no longer be denied in the light of the Apostolic Constitution Sacramentum Ordinis. For this is specifically stated therein.[26]

While we admit that the distinction between the episcopate and the priesthood is not the same as that which exists between the diaconate and the priesthood, still such a distinction is not, or at least does not seem to be, necessary in order to constitute the episcopate a true sacramental order distinct from the priesthood itself. They are distinct sacramental orders because they confer a distinct grace and a distinct power. Thus the priesthood confers the powers of consecrating the Eucharist, and of absolving from sins those over whom one receives delegated or ordinary jurisdiction, and the grace necessary for the accomplishment of these duties. The episcopate, however, confers its own special grace and the ordinary powers proper to the bishop, that is the power of confirming, of ordaining, and of governing. This is most important in respect to

25 Cf. E. Boularand, S.J., "La consécration épiscopale, est — elle sacramentelle?" in Bull. litt. écclés., 54 (1953), 3–36.

26 Cf. AAS 40 (1948), 5–7; for tr. of this Apostolic Constitution, cf. Canon Law Digest, III, p. 396 ff.

something that will follow immediately, namely, the question of whether the priesthood is a state of perfection, or whether the priesthood establishes one in any state of perfection. For there have been some, particularly in recent years, who have insisted that the diocesan priesthood shares in the state of perfection which is proper to the bishop, namely, as we have seen, the *status perfectionis exercendae*. If we keep the above notions in mind concerning the distinction between the episcopate and the priesthood, I am sure that the opinion followed, will appear to be the more probable.[27]

The Priesthood and Perfection

In order to understand the problem which will be taken up in the following pages, we ought first of all to indicate the relationship between the priesthood and Christian perfection. In this connection, we should note that perfection is to be understood not as the state of perfection or as a juridically constituted external manner of life according to a given discipline, but rather in the sense of an *interior* perfection of Christian charity. In regard to this, from the whole of tradition and the unanimous teaching of the Fathers of the Church and of the documents issuing from her solemn magisterium, we have to conclude that the priest, by reason of his vocation and his calling, has a *more serious* obligation of striving after the interior perfection of charity, or of being perfect than does the simple religious.

While it is true that there are no explicit texts in Scripture concerning this precise problem, still there is no doubt that Christ did demand of his disciples a high degree of holiness of life. At the Last Supper, for example, we know that He spoke clearly to them concerning the holiness which He expected of them.[28] Their faith is to be a strong faith, and their confidence and trust in God lively. A strong love is to be shown by them in the manner in which they keep His commandments. They are required to abide in Christ in order that they might go forth and bear fruit. They are to be identified with Him in suffering, in patience and courage. Their love for one another should be extraordinary and their unity with Christ and the Father most intimate.

In their ministry, by reason of their contact with men, they are to let their light shine before them such that others might see their good works and give glory to the Father who is in heaven.[29] Moreover, they are to be the salt of the earth, the light of the world, giving to others the example of holiness which they themselves have received from Christ.[30] St. Paul,

---

[27] Cf. *Le Clergé diocésain*, A. Charue (Paris: Desclée, 1960), p. 89 ff., esp. p. 100.
[28] Cf. Jn. 14–17.   [29] Cf. Mt. 5:16.   [30] Cf. Mt. 5:13.

likewise, writes of the perfection of the priest in his epistle to Timothy. "But thou, O Man of God, flee these things; but pursue justice, godliness, faith, charity, patience, mildness . . . I charge thee in the sight of God . . . that thou keep the commandments without stain, blameless until the coming of our Lord Jesus Christ."[31]

The Fathers likewise insist upon the perfection of the priest. St. John Chrysostom's lengthy treatment constantly comes back to this. When there is question of choosing those who are to have the care of souls, only those should be selected who surpass all others in spiritual excellence.[32] The soul of the priest should shine as a light illuminating the world.[33] And the beauty of the soul of a priest should be in all respects so resplendent as to gladden and enlighten the souls of all who see him.[34]

St. Gregory the Great states that the holiness of the priest is not common to all but quite singular in degree. It should be a holiness which seeks only the things of Christ. He likewise insists that this more than average holiness and perfection should be developed even before the priesthood is conferred upon the candidate.[35]

St. Jerome, writing to Rusticus the monk, tells him to be perfect in the monastery so that he might be worthy of becoming a cleric. For those who are to fulfill this office must be holier and purer than those who have retired to the mountains.[36]

In a rather beautiful passage we find St. Peter Chyrsologus emphasizing the same note:

> Be you the priest and the sacrifice of God; do not lose that which has been given you by the authority of God. Clothe yourself with the garment of sanctity, gird yourself with the cincture of chastity; let Christ be the covering for your head; let the cross of Christ be the protection before your face; instil in your breast the sacrament of divine wisdom; constantly burn the incense of prayer, grasp the sword of the Spirit; let your heart be as it were an altar on which you may safely offer your body as a victim to God. Offer Him your faith for the chastisement of perfidy; offer Him your fasting that gluttony may cease; offer your chastity as a sacrifice that passion may die; place on the Altar your piety that impiety be put away; call upon mercy that avarice may be overcome; and that folly may disappear the immolation of sanctity is called for. In this way shall your body also be your victim if it has not been wounded by any dart of sin.[37]

He together with the others insists on the necessity of sanctity or holiness for anyone advancing to receive the order of the priesthood.

---

[31] 1 Tim. 6:11–14 passim.
[32] Cf. De Sacerdotio, 2–2, PG 48, 633.
[33] Ibid., cf. 6–4, 681.
[34] Ibid., cf. 3–14, 650.

[35] Cf. Dialogues, 4, 59, PL 77, 428.
[36] Cf. Letter 125, 17, PL 22, 1082.
[37] Sermon 180, PL 52, 500–501.

And this trend has been constantly repeated by all ascetical writers on this subject.

The Code of Canon Law demands of all clerics that they lead a holier life than the laity, and if this is true of those who have received merely the minor orders, a fortiori it is true of those who have received the priesthood.[38]

Moreover, the ordination ceremony is very explicit on this point; as one proceeds through the various orders, the obligation to seek and to be holy in life and manner of living is constantly reiterated. The bishop warns those who are about to receive the priesthood: "Truly, it must be with great fear that you ascend to so high a station; and care must be taken that heavenly wisdom, an irreproachable character, and long continued righteousness shall commend the candidates chosen for it." Later on, the ceremonial mentions that "the ministers of the Church should be perfect in faith and practice," in other words, that they should be well-grounded in the twofold love of God and of neighbor. In one of the admonitions, the bishop says to the ordinands: "Let your conduct be the outcome of a chaste and holy life. Consider what you do, imitate what you handle, and as you celebrate the Mysteries of the Lord's death, be earnest in ridding your members by mortification of all vices and lusts. Let your teaching be a spiritual remedy for God's people; let the fragrance of your lives be a delight to the Church of God, that both by preaching and by example you may build up the house of God, that is, the family of God, so that neither may he be condemned by the Lord for having promoted you to so sublime an office, nor you for taking it upon yourselves; but rather that He may reward us all." And, again, in the form of the sacrament itself: "Grant we implore Thee, almighty Father, to these Thy servants the dignity of the Priesthood; renew within them the spirit of holiness that they may keep the rank in the service which they have received from Thee, and by their conduct, may afford a pattern of holy living. May they be worthy fellow workers of Our Order, and may every kind of righteousness shine forth in them, so that hereafter giving a good account of the stewardship committed to them, they may obtain the reward of never ending bliss."

When the bishop clothes the priest with the chasuble he says, "Take the priestly vestment whereby charity is signified, for God is able to give thee an increase in charity and its perfect work." And somewhat later on in the ceremony the bishop invokes from God the fullness of His grace upon these His servants: "O God the source of all holiness, from whom are true consecration and fullness of blessing, pour down upon Thy serv-

---

[38] Cf. Canon 124.

ants whom we now call to the honor of the priesthood, the grace of Thy blessing, that by the gravity of their actions and the example of their lives, they may show themselves elders formed by the rule which Paul gave to Titus and to Timothy; that meditating on Thy law, day and night, they may believe what they read, teach what they believe, follow out their instructions in practice and give proof in themselves, and set the example of justice, fortitude, steadfastness, mercy, and all the other virtues, and by their admonition confirm others in the same and keep the gift of their ministry pure and undefiled." And when they receive the stole crossed in priestly fashion, the bishop says to them: "May the Lord clothe thee with the stole of innocence."

This teaching of the liturgy is a constant theme of the recent Popes when treating of the priesthood. Pius X makes it of obligation that bishops above all else should see to the development of the sanctity of their clergy.[39] Likewise in his *Haerent Animo*[40] he repeats a similar doctrine concerning the necessity of holiness in the life of the priest.

Pius XI, in his encyclical on the Catholic priesthood, also insists on the necessity of sanctity in one called to the priesthood:

> The priest therefore must approach as close as possible to the perfection of Him whose vicar he is, and render himself ever more and more pleasing to God, by the sanctity of his life and his deeds. . . . And surely every reason we have urged in showing the dignity of the Catholic Priesthood does but reinforce its obligation of singular holiness, for as the Angelic Doctor teaches "To fulfill the duties of Holy Orders common goodness does not suffice; but excelling goodness is required, that they who receive Orders and are thereby higher in rank may also be higher in holiness." . . . Cut from the forest beams fit for building; but do not place the weight of the building upon them at once. Delay many days until they are dried and made fit for the purpose; because if this precaution be omitted very soon they will break under the weight; or to use the short but clear expression of the Angelic Doctor: holiness must come before Holy Orders. . . . Hence the burden of Orders should be placed only on walls seasoned with sanctity freed from the damp of sins.[41]

This same teaching is repeated in the *Menti Nostrae* of Pius XII:

> According to the teaching of the Divine Master, the perfection of the Christian Life consists especially in the love of God and of one's neighbor, a love that is fervent, devoted, painstaking. . . . However, the priest is bound to do this by his very office. By its very nature every priestly action necessarily tends to this end, since the priest is called to this divine vocation, destined to it by his divine office, and confirmed by a divine grace.[42]

39 Cf. *E supremi*, ASS 36 (1903), 135–136.   41 AAS 28 (1936), 20–21.
40 Cf. ASS 41 (1908), 555–577.   42 AAS 42 (1950), 660–661.

The rest of this encyclical insists on the same qualities.

Perhaps no one more clearly than Pope John XXIII has pointed out this obligation. In his *Sacerdotii Nostri Primordia* we find the following passage:

> Therefore the cleric is not bound by divine law to the evangelical counsels of poverty, chastity, and obedience. Yet the man who would infer from this that clerics are less bound than the members of religious communities by the obligation of tending toward evangelical perfection is certainly misrepresenting the true meaning of this same Sovereign Pontiff [Pope Pius XII] who was so concerned with the holiness of the clergy and is contradicting the constant teaching of the Church on this subject. The truth is completely opposed to this unwise inference. For the proper performance of the priestly duties there is *required a greater inward holiness than even the state of perfection requires*. Even though the evangelical counsels are not made mandatory by the force of the clerical state itself for ecclesiastics so that they may be able to attain this sanctity of life, nevertheless for ecclesiastics as for all the faithful these same counsels constitute the surest way to attain the desired goal of Christian perfection. Furthermore, and this is a great comfort to Us, there are many priests today endowed with generous virtue, who although belonging to the diocesan clergy seek aid and support from pious associations approved by the authority of the Church in order that they may be able more easily and more readily to enter upon the way of perfection. They thus show that they understand this teaching.[43]

In treating of this question theologians usually advance three reasons for demanding a greater holiness for the priesthood than for the religious life. The first is taken *from the nature of priestly ordination*. Every duty or office demands the corresponding requisites necessary for it to be performed as it ought or in a fitting manner. The office of the priesthood, however, since it is the highest given to men by God, demands a holiness of life that is appropriate. Therefore, this office ought to be possessed by those who possess among their qualifications holiness of life.

A second reason is taken from the priest's duties toward the sacramental Body. The more holy the action exercised, the more holy ought the person exercising it be. Of all the actions, however, which can be performed by an individual even instrumentally speaking, none is more holy than the offering of the Sacrifice of the Mass. The person, therefore, entrusted with this action must exceed all others in holiness of life.

Still a third reason can be found by considering his duties toward the Mystical Body. He who is entrusted with the care of souls and the duty of leading them to holiness of life must himself possess that which he intends to give to others, for no one gives what he does not have. The

---

[43] NCWC trans., pp. 6–7.

priest, however, is one into whose keeping is entrusted the care of souls, seeking the holiness and the perfection of the Christian life. For this reason, then, the priest in order fittingly to perform his office must himself possess that which he intends to give to others.

St. Thomas himself notes: "Sacred Orders presupposes sanctity; whereas, the religious state is a means of reaching sanctity. Thus the weight of orders is to be placed on a framework or walls that are seasoned by sanctity; the weight of the religious life, however, seasons the walls, that is, men, by drawing out the damp of vice."[44] Some authors have insisted on the fact that the illuminative stage is the degree of charity fitting for the reception of Holy Orders, so that the priest already purified from sin may illuminate others. On the other hand, for the religious state it is sufficient that one be in the purgative stage. Because priestly ordination gives one something more noble than the religious profession — a share in the priesthood of Christ — this office is more sublime than that of the religious state and demands a corresponding degree of interior holiness. A cleric in sacred orders, other things being equal, would sin more grievously if he should do anything against sanctity than a religious who is not in sacred orders, although the religious is bound to observances to which those in sacred orders are not bound.[45]

It is not strictly necessary that the priest should have actually acquired this perfection. It is sufficient if this perfection should exist in his intention, in his resolution. This obligation of tending to perfection is not distinct from the obligation proper to his priestly obligations, any more than the obligation of a religious to tend to perfection differs from his obligation to observe his vows.[46]

The Priesthood and the State of Perfection

In recent years an old problem has been the subject of much discussion. It centers around the precise relationship between the diocesan priesthood and the states of perfection. Fundamentally it seems that we can reduce the positions of present-day authors to two. First, there is that of those who hold that the members of the diocesan priesthood are not in any state of perfection, neither the *status perfectionis acquirendae*, nor the *status perfectionis exercendae*; that is to say, they do not by reason of their ordination belong to either the state of perfection that is proper to religious or to that proper to bishops. The other opinion holds that diocesan

---

[44] II–II, Q. 189, a. 1, ad 3m.

[45] Cf. II–II, Q. 184, a. 8.

[46] Cf. Garrigou Lagrange, O.P., *The Priesthood and Perfection* (Westminster, Md.: Newman, 1955), p. 76 ff.

priests belong to the bishop's state of perfection in a kind of subordinate way, calling it the *status perfectionis exercendae seu servitii*. We will attempt to examine the variant opinions choosing that which seems to be the more probable in accordance with the reasons given.

The first opinion states that the priesthood, as such, is not to be considered as pertaining to the states of perfection, neither to that of the religious nor to that of the bishop.

As Father Dukehart, in a thesis attempting to support the second opinion which will be given shortly, admits: "those who take this view are clearly in the majority." To give the arguments proposed in defense of this position, it would be well to break the thesis down into two parts: (a) the secular or diocesan priest does not belong to the state of perfection of the religious; and (b) he does not pertain to the state of perfection proper to the bishop.

a) The diocesan priest does not belong to the state of perfection proper to the religious, that is, the *status perfectionis acquirendae*:

There is no doubt among authors on this point today, for the matter was more or less definitely settled by Pope Pius XII in his *Provida Mater Ecclesia*, the Constitution establishing the secular institutes, and again in the *Annus Sacer*. Therefore, we can propose this as a *certain teaching*. We will give merely the documents of the Church and theological arguments for this.

In *Provida Mater Ecclesia*, Pius XII wrote as follows:

> Nor was this all. Lest the public and solemn profession of holiness be frustrated and come to nothing, the Church with ever increasing strictness was willing to recognize the canonical state of perfection only in societies which were erected and governed by herself, that is, in religious institutes[47] whose general form and purpose she had approved by her Magisterium, after a slow and careful examination. . . . These requirements are laid down so strictly and absolutely in Canon Law that in no case, not even by way of exception, is the canonical state of perfection recognized, unless its profession is made in a religious institute approved by the Church. . . .
>
> . . . Hence in the first place, the public state of perfection was counted as one of the three principal ecclesiastical states, and in it alone the Church found the second order and grade of canonical persons.[48] Here is something surely worthy of attentive consideration; while the other two orders of canonical persons, namely, the clerics and the laity, are found in the Church by divine law, to which the ecclesiastical institution is superadded[49] inasmuch as the Church is established and organized as a hierarchical society; this class, namely, that of religious, intermediate between

---

[47] C. 488, 1°.   [48] C. 107.   [49] CC. 107–108, § 3.

clerics and the laity and capable of being participated in by both clerics and laity,[50] is entirely derived from the close and very special relationship which it has to the end of the Church, that is, to the efficacious pursuit of perfection by adequate means.[51]

The same Pope, in speaking to the International Congress of Religious Institutes held in Rome in 1950, reaffirmed this same doctrine:

It is against this truth to assert that the clerical state as such, as it proceeds from divine law, by its very nature, or at least in accordance with the demands of this nature, asks that the evangelical counsels be preserved or kept by those who belong to it, and for this reason can be called or ought to be called a state of evangelical perfection (acquirendae) to be acquired. The cleric is not bound, therefore, to observe by reason of divine right the evangelical counsels of poverty, chastity, and obedience; and especially is he not bound in the same way and for the same reason in which the obligation arises in a religious state in which these vows called public, are undertaken. This does not prohibit him, however, from privately and voluntarily undertaking these obligations. Likewise, that priests of the Latin rite are held to observe celibacy neither removes the difference between the clerical and the religious state nor pertains to it. The religious cleric, not insofar as he is a cleric but insofar as he is a religious, professes the state and the condition of evangelical perfection.

Moreover, the religious state is not restricted to either of the two groups which exist in the Church by Divine right, since both clerics and lay persons alike can become religious, and on the other hand, the clerical dignity lies open to religious and those who are not religious. One would therefore be mistaken in appraising the value of the foundations which Christ laid in building His Church if He should judge that the peculiar form of the secular clerical life as such was established and sanctioned by our Lord and redeemer and that the peculiar form of the regular clerical life, though it is to be considered good and worthy of approbation in itself, is still secondary and auxiliary in nature since it is not derived from Christ. Wherefore if we keep before our eyes the order established by Christ, neither of the two special forms of clerical life holds a prerogative of divine right since that law singles out neither form nor gives to either precedence over the other. What then, the difference is between these two forms, what their mutual relations are, what special task in working out the salvation of mankind has been assigned to each, all these details Christ left to be decided according to the needs and conditions of succeeding ages, or rather, to express Our mind more exactly, He left them to the definitive decisions of the Church herself.

Moreover, these clerics can, if they wish, enter or form secular institutes which we have also entered under the title of state of perfection, since they are also bound to the observance of the three counsels. But if they do this, they are in the state of perfection (acquirendae) by reason of the fact

---

[50] C. 107.
[51] Cf. AAS 39 (1947), 115–116. Canon Law Digest, III, pp. 135 ff. For the tr. used here, cf. Haley, op. cit., pp. 119–120.

that they are members of secular institutes, and not by reason of the fact that they are clerics.[52]

In this same allocution the Holy Father mentions that the reason one enters the religious state is not basically and fundamentally that he wishes to flee the world or that he is afraid of meeting the dangers which he has to encounter in the world as a secular cleric, but rather because he receives a *divine vocation* to this state which he wishes to combine with the clerical state. That is why no one is to try to deter one from entering the religious priesthood, if he feels called to it; nor should one force one into it if he does not feel called to it.

The theological reasoning behind this conclusion is rather simple. Those are said to be in the state of perfection (*acquirendae*) who bind themselves by vow to refrain from worldly affairs, which they might lawfully use, in order to give themselves more freely to God; that is to say, that only those are said to be in this state of perfection who profess publicly before the Church the observance of all three evangelical counsels. Through the reception of sacred orders, however, one does not in any way profess the evangelical counsels. This, as we know, is the teaching of tradition and of the magisterium of the Church as seen in the *Annus Sacer*. Therefore priestly ordination, as we know, does not *ipso facto* establish one in the state of one striving after perfection.[53]

In the discussion which follows this reasoning, St. Thomas mentions that by the reception of a sacred order, one receives the power to perform certain sacred acts in a divinely instituted office. For this reason, Holy Orders is not to be considered as placing one in any state, but rather in some office. By receiving this power he is not *ipso facto* bound to those things which are of perfection except to the extent that in the Western Church the reception of the subdiaconate includes the taking of the vow of chastity, which is one of the things that pertain to perfection. It is clear that he is not said to be placed in the state of perfection proper to those who undertake the observance of the evangelical counsels, even though an interior or inward perfection is required in order that one exercise such acts worthily.

It seems, however, that even though priestly ordination does not oblige one to make profession of obedience and poverty under vow still the practice of these is most highly recommended. Indeed that he must practice these acts of obedience and of poverty, together with the observance of perfect chastity, has been stated time and again by the Popes in their

---

[52] *Annus Sacer*, AAS 43 (1951), 26–36 passim. Cf. *Canon Law Digest*, III, p. 119 ff.

[53] Cf. II–II, Q. 184, a. 6.

encyclicals and other pronouncements on the priesthood. Thus Pius XI writes:

> But by its very nature as an active and courageous company, the Catholic Priesthood must have the spirit of discipline, or to use a more deeply Christian word, *obedience*. It is obedience which binds together all ranks into the harmony of the Church's hierarchy. . . . This obedience, priests promise to the bishop after Ordination, the holy oil still fresh on their hands. On the day of his consecration, the bishop in his turn swore obedience to the supreme visible Head of the Church, the successor of St. Peter, the Vicar of Jesus Christ.[54]

Likewise *poverty* is also very specially recommended to all priests:

> On the other hand, by sincere disinterestedness the priest can hope to win the hearts of all. For detachment from earthly goods, if inspired by lively faith, is always accompanied by tender compassion toward the unfortunate. Thus the priest becomes a veritable father of the poor. . . . Thus the Catholic Priest is freed from the bonds of a family and of self interest, the two chief bonds which could bind him too closely to earth.[55]

This same teaching is repeated also by Pius XII in the *Menti Nostrae*.

> In an age like ours in which the principle of authority is grievously disturbed, it is absolutely necessary that the priest, keeping in mind the precepts of faith, should consider and duly accept this same authority, not only as the bulwark of the social and religious order, but also as the foundation of his own personal sanctification. (They must preserve intact their fidelity to Christ and to the legitimate authority, established by Him) . . . to these you must also unite daily a detachment of your hearts from riches and from the things of the earth. Reverently take as your models those great saints of ancient and modern times who join this essential detachment from material goods to a profound trust in Divine Providence and a most priestly zeal. . . . Even priests who do not make a profession of poverty by a special vow must always be guided by the love of this virtue, a love that ought to show itself in the simplicity and modesty of their manner of life, in their living quarters, and in their generosity to the poor.[56]

b) Nor do diocesan priests belong to that state of perfection proper to the bishop, i.e., the state of perfection *exercendae* or *communicandae*.

While it is true that no papal documents nor any coming from the various congregations of the Church, have officially pronounced on this matter, nevertheless it seems according to some authors that they might be cited in favor of it inasmuch as they all regard the priesthood as a "secular" state. From this it seems that we might *suspect* that the priest-

---

[54] *The Popes and the Priesthood*, pp. 59–60.

[55] *Ibid.*, p. 58.

[56] AAS 42 (1950), 664–665. NCWC ed., pp. 8–10 *passim*. Cf. also *Sacerdotii nostri primordia* cited above.

hood as such is to be numbered among the secular states in the Church, and therefore, not to be considered a state of perfection in any sense of the phrase.[56a] We might indicate some passages from the writings of several recent Popes.

Pius XI:

it has been in fact, precisely in times which seemed least propitious, that the number of priestly vocations increased. This is clear from Catholic hagiography of the nineteenth century, a century rich in splendid names on the rolls of both secular and regular clergy.

Let them be persuaded that in no better way than by this work for an increase in the ranks of the secular and regular clergy can the Catholic laity really participate in the high dignity of the royal priesthood, which the Prince of the Apostles attributes to the whole body of the redeemed.[57]

And now, finally to you, dear Sons, Priests of the Most High, both secular and regular the world over, We address Our words.[58]

Pius XII:

For this reason We exhort all priests, both those of the diocesan clergy and those belonging to religious orders or congregations, to go forward, bound close together with bonds of fraternal charity, in union of strength and will toward the common goal: the good of the Church, personal sanctification and the sanctification of the faithful.[59]

Between the two hierarchical ranks is placed the religious life which, taking its origin from the Church, owes its whole purpose for being and its value to its strict relation with the end of the Church which is to lead all men to the acquisition of sanctity. Therefore, clergy and laity can enter this state, and religious and non-religious can aspire to the priesthood. It is an error in the appreciation of the bases on which Christ founded the Church to think that the particular condition of the secular clergy as secular has been established by Christ and that the regular clergy, although good and legitimate should be considered as secondary and auxiliary. Christ did not establish a form of double clergy. There is no preference for one or for the other. As to their roles in work for the salvation of souls, that is left to the needs of the moment and the decision of the Church. The ministry of both secular and regular clergy should be in collaboration with and under the direction of the bishops and particularly of the Pope. As to the state of perfection, those are bound to seek it who publicly make vows as religious, and it is not true that the clerical state as such, because it is of Divine law, exacts the profession of the evangelical counsels or demands the following of evangelical perfection. The cleric is not constrained to the counsels of poverty, chastity, and obedience by divine law, though he may make these engagements freely and privately.[60]

[56a] The argument is not too strong as can be seen from a note made above. A secular institute is a secular state and still a state of perfection.   [57] Cf. 1 Pet. 2:9.

[58] Ad Catholici Sacerdotii; cf. The Popes and the Priesthood, p. 69 ff., passim.

[59] Menti Nostrae, AAS 42 (1950), 682.

[60] Annus Sacer, AAS 43 (1951), 24–30; cf. Canon Law Digest, III, p. 119 ff.

In our day, therefore, the Church has the benefit of a great throng of ecclesiastics who are devoted both to the pursuit of perfection by the assistance of the evangelical counsels and to the fulfillment of the functions of the priesthood. This great body of men constitutes the clergy who are called religious, alongside those who are called *secular or diocesan*. Under the same supreme authority of the Roman Pontiff and the direction of their Bishops, these two groups thrive and flourish with a fraternal rivalry and a mutual assistance which is profitable to both.[61]

While it is true that we cannot deduce from this that the priesthood is not a state of perfection, or that it does not share in the state of perfection proper to the bishop, still from the meaning and use of the word "secular," it might be argued — not very cogently, I fear — that the priesthood is to be classed among the "secular" states rather than among the states so-called of perfection, at least, at the present time. There is a much stronger argument, however, which we shall now take up.

*   *   *

In the beginning of the theological discussion it would be well to give the theological reasoning for this opinion first, and then, afterward, a few added ideas might be presented.

Only those are said to be in the state of perfection *exercendae* or *communicandae* who are under the *perpetual* obligation, by consecration or (as St. Thomas says: under the obligation of a perpetual vow) to retain the care of souls. This, however, is true of bishops, since they have a perpetual obligation to that which is of perfection.

Parish priests, however, or, let us say, secular or diocesan priests, do not have this *perpetual* obligation of caring for souls *by reason of their ordination*. Rather, this is committed to them by their respective bishops and superiors.

Therefore, priests by reason of their ordination are not to be considered as belonging to the state of perfection *exercendae* or *communicandae*.[62]

According to Father Dukehart,[63] the *basic argument* of St. Thomas in excluding secular priests from the state of perfection proper to the bishop is that they lack permanence or stability in regard to three things. First, the priest does not have the chief or *principal* obligation in regard to caring for souls. This pertains rather to the bishop. Thus the Angelic

---

[61] *Sedes Sapientiae, AAS* 48 (1956), 355; cf. *Canon Law Digest*, IV, p. 169 ff.

[62] Cf. II–II, Q. 184, a. 6.

[63] Cf. *State of Perfection and the Secular Priest* (St. Meinrad, Ind.: Grail Publications, 1952), pp. 54–65.

Doctor writes: "Bishops have the chief care of the sheep of their diocese, while parish priests . . . exercise an inferior ministry under the bishops."[64] And again: "As parish priests have not the chief charge, but a certain ministry as committed to them by the bishop, so the pastoral offices does not belong to them in chief, nor are they bound to lay down their lives for the sheep, except insofar as they have a share in their charge. Hence, we should say that they have an *office pertaining to perfection*, rather than that they attain the state of perfection."[65]

Second, they seem to lack permanence in their remaining in the service of the diocese. For they are free to enter some religious order if they so choose. This provision remains today in Canon Law, with the stipulation, however, that for the *liceity* of their entering some religious community they must have consulted the bishop, who is free to detain them if the departure of the cleric, or priest in this case, would result in serious harm to souls and the harm could not otherwise be remedied. As we pointed out in discussing the conditions for licit entrance into religion, these two conditions must be found *together* before an Ordinary is justified in objecting to the entrance of one of his clerics (or priests) to a religious community. Usually a slight delay is sufficient to enable the bishop to meet the needs of the diocese. What should be noted, however, is that the bishop has the right to veto the proposal of the cleric or priest *not* because he is in a better position or state as a diocesan priest *but because serious harm may come to souls, and this harm cannot be in any way avoided*. Only when these two conditions are present, canonists teach, can the Ordinary forbid one of his priests to enter a religious community.

Third, diocesan priests do not have a vow or a permanent obligation with respect to the things which are of perfection. Thus Thomists in general today hold that St. Thomas, speaking of the bishop's having a perpetual vow meant that he has a perpetual obligation which is equivalent to his having a perpetual vow.

A *second* argument which St. Thomas uses in support of his thesis is that a secular or diocesan priest does not undertake any obligation *with a certain solemnity*. Father Dukehart states that he advances this merely to show the instability of the priest's status as pastor of souls. For he (St. Thomas) points out that only bishops receive their pastorate in a solemn manner (by episcopal consecration); whereas parish priests receive theirs merely by a commission or appointment.[66]

---

[64] II–II, Q. 184, a. 6, ad 2m.
[65] *Ibid.*, ad 3m.
[66] Cf. II–II, Q. 184, a. 7, ad 2m. Cf. C. Dukehart, S.S., *loc. cit.*

While Father Dukehart has pointed out the arguments used by St. Thomas, it seems that he has reversed the logical procedure of the arguments and, consequently, the importance which we are to attach to them. For the primary, and, therefore, the fundamental and basic reason why a bishop is in a state of perfection and a priest is not stems from the fact that the consecrations which they receive are distinct. The whole argument from stability follows upon this presupposition, and not vice versa. For without this consecration the bishop would in nowise be bound perpetually to care for the souls of his diocese.[66a]

Consequently, the whole force of the argument of the Angelic Doctor lies not in the priest's lacking stability, but rather in his lacking the episcopal consecration. As we have seen, then, the episcopate is a sacramental order distinct from that of the priesthood insofar as it confers upon the bishop ordinary powers of orders and of jurisdiction which are not proper to the priest. Thus, for example, he alone has the right ex officio, and perpetually of conferring sacred orders and of confirming, so that wherever and whenever he uses these powers, he does so validly. The consecration of the bishop, then, wedding him, as it does, to a See (even though only a titular one), gives him the perpetual obligation of caring for the souls of that diocese, and this he cannot lay aside except with the permission of the Holy See.

Just as a religious enters into his state of perfection by the religious profession, in such a way that without this profession he would not be in the state of perfection, so, too, the bishop enters into the state of perfection proper to bishops only through the episcopal consecration. Just as the religious profession makes one permanently stable in the pursuit after perfection, so, too, does the episcopal consecration make the bishop permanently obligated to exercise or communicate perfection in the diocese over which he is placed.

From this it follows that the priest, secular or regular, is not to be considered as pertaining to the state of perfection of the bishop, precisely because he does not have the episcopal consecration, which is the fundament and basis for his being in this state. Thus the solemnity which St. Thomas requires for one to be in the state of perfection is very determined. For the religious, it is the religious profession of public vows (or some equivalent); for the bishop, it is his episcopal consecration. Where either or these two is lacking the state of perfection, either acquirendae or exercendae, will not be found.[67]

[66a] See note 55, p. 111.

[67] Cf., e.g., Sylvius, Commentarium in St. Thom. Aquinatis, 4 ed. (Antwerp: 1693), in II–II, Q. 184, a. 6, Vol. III, p. 932; cf. also A. M. Henry, O.P., "Q'est-ce qu'un prêtre," in La Vie Spirituelle, 78 (1948), 191; J. De Guibert, Seminaire ou Novitiat

The *Second Opinion* states that the secular or diocesan priest is in a state of perfection, that of the bishops (*exercendae*), but in a subordinate manner, therefore, properly speaking (*servitii*). Thus Father Dukehart writes:

> Many call the state of the secular priests the *status perfectionis exercendae*. It is our intention to retain this terminology. The state of secular priests is a state of exercising or communicating perfection, a fact that was brought out by several writers. . . . Far from rejecting this point of view, we rather hold to it firmly and agree that secular priests are in the *status perfectionis exercendae*. Yet because this precise phrase has been used universally to indicate the state of perfection proper to bishops, it seems best to add an explanatory term and say that the state of priests is *perfectionis exercendae seu servitii*.[68]

After a lengthy treatment of Canon Law, the Fathers of the Church, and the nature of the priesthood, Father Dukehart in his well-organized work writes:

> This evidence (for his position) falls under two general headings — ecclesiastical discipline and the nature of the priesthood. Looking to the law we found that the present discipline as set forth in the new Code imposes upon the secular priests a permanent obligation to serve in the diocesan apostolate.[69] We discovered too that this has been the spirit of the law from the very beginning[70] except during one era extending from the eleventh to the sixteenth century. Looking to the nature of the priesthood, we saw that in the New Testament, the Roman Pontifical and the writings of many authors[71] the priest appears dedicated to service in the bishop's apostolic mission. An examination of the thought of the Fathers[72] revealed the same — that a secular priest is one permanently engaged in the apostolate of the diocese for which he is ordained.
>
> There is good evidence, therefore, for saying that the secular priest has a perpetual obligation assumed with a certain solemnity, to what pertains to perfection. And this is the same as saying that he is in a state of perfection. Thus we are brought back to the statement made at the beginning of the fourth chapter, considering the nature of a state of perfection as defined by theologians. It is evident that secular priests are in a state of perfection which may be called the *status perfectionis exercendae seu servitii*.[73] This opinion far from contradicting that of St. Thomas and the one given as the first opinion goes beyond it.[74]

In defending this position he is not at all novel or alone. It was held by John Gerson (1363–1429), a chancellor of the University of Paris, who

---

(Paris: 1938), pp. 107–108; W. Humphrey, *Elements of Religious Life* (New York: Benziger, 1903), pp. 17–18.

[68] *Op. cit.*, p. 91.
[69] Cf. Chap. 4.
[70] Cf. Chap. 5.
[71] Cf. Chap. 4.
[72] Cf. Chap. 5.
[73] *Op. cit.*, p. 138.
[74] *Ibid.*, p. 169.

vigorously opposed the claim of religious to their being in a state of perfection higher than that of parish priests. In fact, he claimed that "pastors were in a state of perfection, not only perfection to be acquired, but also perfection to be exercised, since to them belongs the obligation as well as the authority to lead souls to God according to the three hierarchical acts, which are to purge, to illumine, and to perfect."[75]

Another defender of this position is *Francis Suarez, S.J.*[76] While it is true that he often speaks of priests, whether they be pastors or not, as being in the state of perfection *inchoative,* or *aliquo modo,*[77] still from the overall picture of his writings, he seems to favor the opinion proposed immediately above, even though his reasons are a little different. He does not, like Gerson, place secular clerics in the state of perfection proper to religious that is *acquirendae* by their vow of chastity, but rather in that state which is proper to bishops, even though in the lowest grade of this state. This is true because their ordination introduces them into a very special and immutable condition or category of life, and because they are ordained for the sacrifice of the Mass, thereby acting as a mediator between God and the people, interceding in the name of the whole Church for the faithful.[78] He says that they are obliged, therefore, to certain exterior acts of virtue, as well as to merely interior ones, and that for this reason they must be said to be in some way in the state of perfection at least inchoatively.[79]

Citing the arguments of St. Thomas, he refutes them by saying that: first of all, no vow is required for the bishop to undertake the care of souls: then neither is it required for the priest; second, the free entry into religion which is permitted the priest and not the bishop does not prove that their obligation to care for souls is insufficient to constitute a state, but proves at most that this obligation is not altogether absolute. Thus he argues that a religious may pass from one order to another, which does not prove that he was not at first in a state of perfection, but only that his former state was less strict or less perfect; third, they may not simply resign their charge. For they are obliged to have their bishop's permission according to Church Law.[80] Moreover, he goes on

---

[75] De Statu Curatorum, Omnia Opera, II, p. 534; cf., also, his De Perfectione Cordis, III, p. 441; Sermo contra bullam mendicantium, II, pp. 436–437; Sermo de vita clericorum, II, p. 577.

[76] 1617.

[77] Cf. De Religione, tract. 7, Bk. I, Chap. 17, n. 4, Omnia Opera, XV, p. 85.

[78] Cf. ibid.

[79] Cf. ibid.

[80] We have already seen why they must have their bishop's permission; to avoid harm to the diocese, not because they are in a state of perfection as Suarez here very definitely implies.

to say even bishops can resign their Sees, and the Pope himself, provided, of course, it is done according to the proper procedure.[81] For these reasons he concludes:

> And so we said above that through this (ordination) the state of perfection of simple priests is, as it were, begun; now indeed we add that when a pastoral charge is added, a certain state of perfection somehow in its own grade is completed for these minor prelates. . . . For on account of the ministry of consecrating and offering the body of Christ, which they assume by priestly ordination, they are obligated to a loftier consecration to divine things and a greater purity of spirit. And on account of prelature, they are required to devote themselves to promoting the salvation of their fellow men. *And since by reason of their ordination they are perpetually held to both works,* it is not incongruous to say that they are in a state of perfection in the manner indicated, though in a lower or even the lowest grade of that kind, as was explained.[82]

And then he adds that Thomas and Cajetan do not disagree with him but rather insist upon another terminology.

Another defender of this position is *St. Robert Bellarmine* who merely states this position without giving any explanation.[82a] *Cardinal Manning,* in his *Eternal Priesthood,* likewise holds that priests are in a state of perfection, although it is not too certain what he means by this. He does use the idea that a priest is ordained to exercise perfection, not only to be perfect, but also to impress on others the perfection of our divine Lord.[83] *Cardinal Mercier* also implies this, although he will not say that a priest is in a canonical state of perfection. Thus he writes:

> Cooperators with your bishop, united in mind and will with his apostolate, you too, are in possession of this form of pastoral charity, which would inspire you, should it be necessary, to give your life for your flock and in which Catholic Tradition sees the superiority of the episcopacy shine forth brighter than every other state of life — you then have the right to consider yourselves, before God, as being associated with the highest state of perfection in the world.[84]

[81] He forgets, however, that when they resign, they are appointed to a titular see; whereas when a pastor resigns, he is not appointed to a titular parish.

[82] Cf. *ibid.,* p. 92.

[82a] *De Gemitu Columbae,* Bk. II, Chap. 5, *Opera Omnia,* VIII (Paris: Vives, 1872), p. 433.

[83] Cf. p. 44.

[84] *La Vie intérieure* (Paris: 1919), p. 204. In modern times, Canon Mahoney likewise espouses this theory in *The Secular Priesthood* (London: 1930), pp. 183, 179–180. For him the priest's "service of the diocese" is practically the canonical equivalent of the vow and the promise made formerly in England not to enter religious Orders and to serve on the mission, under the control of Bishops (*ibid.,* p. 180). C. Spicq, O.P., also endorses this theory. He writes of the secular or diocesan priest: "Wholly given over to God and to souls, he is assuredly in a state of perfection." "Spiritualité sacerdotale dans le Nouveau Testament," in *La Vie Spirituelle,* 78 (1947), 459.

Rather than undertake a complete refutation of this second opinion, we will merely take the summary which Father Dukehart has given of both the Thomistic opinion and his own and the comparison which he has made between the two. In the light of this summary, we shall merely point out certain things which will weaken, though not destroy, the strength of the arguments which he advances. Father Dukehart has summed up these positions in five points.

I. It is incorrect to attribute a state of perfection to priests by reason of their ordination, for sacred orders, as St. Thomas clearly points out, simply gives one the power to perform sacred *acts*: they do not place him in a state of perfection except insofar as ordination involves, in the Western Church, the vow of perfect chastity.

But here St. Thomas, Father Dukehart maintains, is obviously arguing that "ordination does not place one in the state of perfection *proper to religious*, that is of acquiring perfection, because it necessitates, merely the taking of one vow. We have said, however, that our position is that the priest is in the state of perfection proper to the bishop and not to the religious. Therefore, on this point we agree with him."[85]

Our own comment on this is that all today must agree on this point, because this is the mind of the Church and not merely of a theologian.

II. Even though priests exercise perfection, they lack *stability* in this, for they are free to forsake the care of souls and enter the state of perfection (religion).

Dom U. Beste, O.S.B., can also be cited in support of this opinion (cf. *Introductio in Codicem* [Collegeville, Minn.: St. John U. Press, 1938], p. 307 in relation to can. 437). Another most ardent devotee of this particular theory is Canon Eugene Masure, who treats it in several books (cf. *De l'eminente dignité du sacerdoce diocésain* [Lille: Bloud and Gay, 1938], Chap. 4, pp. 122–139 and esp. pp. 159–162; *Parish Priest*, tr. of *Prêtres Diocésains* [Chicago: Fides, 1955]; "La perfection exigée par le sacrifice de la Messe," in *La Vie Spirituelle*, 44 [1935], 114). Another author who can be cited for this theory is Pascal Parente (*The Ascetical Life* [St. Louis: B. Herder, 1944], p. 218). He likewise takes up the position from the notion of "state" showing that the priest is definitely in a state by reason of his receiving major orders — a state of service or ministry. For it involves a complete and permanent dedication of self in God's service, to which he is "dedicated and consecrated permanently and irrevocably" (op. cit., p. 220). And finally another author also is cited for this theory, M. J. Nicolas, O.P., who holds that the condition of priests has changed greatly since the days of St. Thomas. "Ordained under the title of the diocese it is difficult not to see in the bond which binds them to their bishop, whose cooperators they are, a link strong enough to constitute them in a state of life" ("Sacerdoce diocésain et vie réligieuse," in *Revue Thomiste*, 56 [1956], 180). However, we ought to note, that much as even Father Dukehart would like to, he cannot point to the use of the expression "state of perfection" in any of the above categories in the article of this author. He seems merely willing to go along with the opinion which is here mentioned. The arguments for it appear good, while those against it, today at least, appear inadequate (cf. Dukehart, op. cit., p. 88).

[85] *Op. cit.*, p. 171.

The author then points out, that this is no longer true. For secular priests are placed under the will of another, so that their entering an order is illicit unless the bishop gives his permission. Thus a priest's obligation to remain in the service of the local Church is fully characterized by that moral permanence necessary and sufficient for a true status or state. Absolute stability is not required for a state of perfection. Bishops can be relieved of their pastoral charge. Religious can be dispensed from their vows, and can desert the religious state at the expiration of temporary vows.[86]

In regard to this observation of Father Dukehart's, we might mention that the purpose of this requirement of Canon Law is to prevent there occurring any shortage of priests in a diocese which would cause harm to souls. Thus, the canon makes it *illicit* (not invalid as it does in the case of a bishop) for one in major orders to enter the religious life without having first consulted the bishop. The latter can veto the proposal only on condition that the withdrawal of the cleric in major orders would be harmful to the care of souls, and that this harm cannot be avoided in any other way. The Canon does not forbid a cleric to leave his diocese because he is in a state of perfection, or because he has a permanent obligation to care for souls, but merely to *safeguard* the *needs* of the diocese, and prevent the recurrence of what were once called *vagi*, or wandering clerics without any stable residence. Moreover, this obligation, as is evident, is *not at all essential* to their ordination or priestly consecration, for if it were it would also be part of the essence of the regular priesthood, which it obviously is not. It is something which is connected with their ordination, so that proper and fitting sustenance might be had by the individual, and that he might have some stable residence and means of livelihood.

The priesthood gives one the power of offering the Sacrifice of the Mass and of forgiving sins provided one receives the jurisdiction of the ordinary of the diocese or of his local prelate in some communities. The argument of St. Thomas is not one that limits the concept of priestly ordination at all, as Canon Masure holds, to the celebration of Mass. For it is the proper office of the priest to sacrifice. It is rather one which follows from the strict theological aspects of the priestly ordination as such, in contradistinction to the episcopal consecration, which establishes one in the state of perfection. Thus, regardless of who the individual in question is, whether he be regular or diocesan, once he receives episcopal consecration, he automatically is in the state of perfection proper to the bishop. This state of perfection is joined inti-

---

[86] *Op. cit.*, p. 172.

mately and essentially to the episcopal consecration itself and is not merely something annexed to it by reason of some determination on the part of the Church. In this it differs from priestly ordination, which these authors say, in the case of a regular does not establish one in the state of perfection proper to the bishop, but which, in the case of a diocesan priest does. Cannot the words of Pius XII in the *Annus Sacer* be quoted in refutation of this:

> It is an error in the appreciation of the bases on which Christ founded the Church to think that the particular condition of the clergy as secular has been established by Christ and that the regular clergy, although good and legitimate, should be considered as secondary and auxiliary. Christ did not establish a form of double clergy. There is no preference for one or the other. As to their roles in work for the salvation of the Church, this is left to the needs of the moment and the decision of the Church. The ministry of both regular and secular clergy should be in collaboration with and under the directions of the bishops and particularly of the Pope.[87]

It is *not* a question of state, but rather of the needs of the diocese, as a protection for the diocese, that prevents a diocesan priest from entering a religious order without first consulting a bishop. Canonists maintain that the bishop *cannot* veto such a proposal, unless such a move would harm the souls of the diocese, and unless this harm could not be in any other way avoided. Only the office of the bishop establishes one in the state of perfection *exercendae* or *communicandae*, because episcopal *consecration* by which he enters upon the office of the bishop, also, *ipso facto* establishes him in the state of perfection proper to the bishop.[88]

III. Bishops and religious may not be dispensed from the obligations they assume, except by the Holy Father himself; whereas priests may be exempted from the work of the diocese simply by obtaining leave from the bishop.

Regarding this statement Father Dukehart remarks:

> We answer in the first place that such permanence from which only the Holy Father can dispense is not clearly a requisite for a state of perfection. The bishops and religious Orders are *directly* under the Holy See. Hence

---

[87] *AAS* 43 (1951), 30. Cf. *Canon Law Digest*, III, p. 119 ff.

[88] So Creusen and Ellis, *Religious Men and Women in the Code*, 6 Engl. ed. (Milwaukee: Bruce, 1957), pp. 140–141: "But the Church affirms here the entire liberty of everyone to follow the call to a state of perfection and no one needs permission of a superior to do so. Still if the departure of a cleric who has received major orders deprives souls of help which is gravely needed and which cannot be supplied by others, the Ordinary is authorized to enjoin prohibition which divine law then imposes. How can this disposition of the law be interpreted or reconciled with the opinion of those who see in the regular clergy only a clergy of the second class on the fringe of the hierarchy and who consider the entrance of a secular priest or cleric into religion as a step downward or an act of cowardice?"

they must apply there for dispensation, for they have no other immediate superior in the Ecclesiastical hierarchy. The secular priest must apply to his immediate superior. In addition, while the priest's entry into religion removes his obligation to serve in the diocesan apostolate, he yet remains perpetually a mediator who communicates perfection to all the faithful, at least by offering the holy sacrifice of the Mass.[89]

Two things ought to be noted in refutation of this observation:

1. Again here, Father Dukehart seems to have misinterpreted the mind of St. Thomas. For the reason why neither religious nor bishops can depart from their posts is that they have, through a vow or consecration, established themselves permanently in the service of God. They cannot of themselves revoke this decision, unless this be sanctioned by the Holy See or the Local Ordinary, as the case may be. Thus a religious upon receiving a dispensation is dispensed from his vows and *ipso facto* ceases to remain in the state of perfection. A bishop, on the other hand, while being relieved of the care of his diocese is given a titular see, being wedded to *that* see just as he was to his residential see. Thus he does not in any way cease to be in the state of perfection proper to the bishop — this not because he retains a see, *but because his episcopal consecration is perpetual*. He receives the titular see *as a sign* of this perpetual obligation and of his "wedding" to some part of Christ's flock. Every sign because it denotes a relation demands a fundament.

2. There is implied here, as in the position of Father Suarez given above, that the priest is in a state of communicating perfection because he is obliged to offer up the Holy Sacrifice of the Mass and act as a mediator between God and men. Theologians, however, teach, that a priest who is without the care of souls is not obliged to offer the Sacrifice of the Mass except a few times a year, that is, on the more important feasts of the Church, and this obligation is one which he has by reason of the benefit (the order of the priesthood) conferred upon him.

> Some have said that a priest may lawfully refrain altogether from consecrating, unless he be bound to do so, and to give the sacraments to the people, by reason of his being entrusted with the care of souls.
> But this is quite unreasonable, because everyone is bound to use the grace entrusted to him when opportunity serves according to the words of the Apostle:[90] "We exhort you that you receive not the grace of God in vain." But the opportunity of offering sacrifice is considered not merely in relation to the faithful of Christ to whom the sacraments must be administered, but chiefly with regard to God to whom the sacrifice of this sacrament is offered by consecrating. Hence, it is not lawful for the priest, even though he has not the care of souls, to refrain altogether from celebrating; and he seems to be bound to celebrate at least on the chief festivals and especially on those days on which the faithful usually communicate.[91]

---

[89] *Op. cit.*, p. 172.   [90] 2 Cor. 6:1.   [91] III, Q. 82, a. 10.

This is far from the idea of Father Suarez and that of Father Dukehart and those who follow this second opinion. For to be obliged to offer the Sacrifice of the Mass on the chief festivals of the year does not seem to imply the perpetual obligation of acting as mediators between the faithful and God which they attribute to priestly ordination. While it is to be most highly recommended that they offer Sacrifice frequently, even daily, still this is not of obligation, *by reason of their priestly ordination*, as, for example, is true in the case of the bishop exercising perfection by reason of his episcopal consecration.

IV. While secular priests have the care of souls and exercise perfection, yet they are not in the state of exercising perfection, for they do not have the first or chief care of the flock.

In reference to this statement Father Dukehart writes:

> Leaving other obvious answers aside, we merely point out here that this would argue only to the fact that the state of bishops is more stable than that of priests, not that the office of priests lacks stability sufficient for a state. Besides what is to be said of auxiliary bishops? They too fall short of having the chief care over the flock.[92]

This argument advanced by St. Thomas as we saw in one of the objections is not to be considered apodictic. It is merely one in which he shows that an argument proposed against him is not entirely cogent. It is *not* to be considered the fundamental or basic argument, for this always remains the same, *the perpetual obligation which is received through episcopal consecration*. Thus the very basis for this stable and permanent obligation comes from the consecration, and as long as that is not removed, one remains in the state of perfection *exercendae*.

With respect to auxiliary bishops, the answer is clear: they have received episcopal consecration and are *ipso facto* in the state of perfection proper to such, and, as we know, retain the perpetual power of perfecting others (e.g., through the sacraments of Confirmation and Holy Orders which they always and everywhere administer validly).

V. One last assertion to be drawn from St. Thomas' explanation is this — that a vow is necessary for the stability of a state of perfection, and priests take no vow to care for souls.

Referring to this Father Dukehart again says:

> It is not clear, however, that St. Thomas requires a vow for a state of perfection. This was discussed in the first part of the third chapter, where St. Thomas' teaching was explained. Moreover, it should be remarked that bishops take no vow to care for souls. Again the new secular institute is officially designated as a canonical state of perfection by Pius XII, yet

---

[92] *Op. cit.*, p. 172.

vows, properly so called, do not seem to be required of a man or woman who enters one of these institutes. Solemn promises to observe the three evangelical counsels seem to be sufficient.[93]

In answer to this statement, we say that even though a vow is not required, still there must be some solemn promise to observe the counsels in the case of one entering a secular institute, and this must be *in intentione* perpetual even though one may later decide to revoke this decision. Moreover, once one recedes from this profession of the counsels, he is automatically outside the state of perfection. In this case, then, as well as in the case of a religious, the obligation comes *from the act of profession* and is not merely annexed to it; it flows out of it, for the vow of its very nature stabilizes one in some good, so that, without it, one might have a quasi stability but not one that is equivalent to such as is brought about by vow. In the case of a bishop, however, the obligation which is imposed by the very fact of his consecration is equivalent to a vow — as most authors admit, as we saw above.

Therefore, briefly summing up the arguments for the first opinion and against the second, we might merely say that the mind of St. Thomas is to include in the states of perfection those who assume the obligation of those things which are of perfection, through some profession or consecration, and this as essentially connected with itself, or at least flowing out of it as a proper property, so that, wherever you find the one you must find the other. Priestly ordination, however, of itself, does not necessarily establish one in the state of perfection *exercendae*, for then all priests, whether secular or regular, would automatically belong to the bishop's state of perfection — a situation which these authors have not sufficiently demonstrated. Such then, in brief is the substance of the theories proposed and the evaluation of them. The first opinion still seems to be the more probable and more cogent.

*   *   *

There are merely a few observations which the writer would like to make:

1. If it is true that the obedience and service of a diocese is sufficient to establish one in the state of perfection proper to the bishop, then why is not obedience to the Sovereign Pontiff, the bishop of bishops or the chief bishop in the Church of Christ, sufficient to establish the regular clergy[93a] in the state of perfection proper to the Pope? For by their ordination they enter, first of all, the service of the Vicar of Christ on earth,

---

[93] *Op. cit.*, p. 173. (We might note that secular institutes are not a canonical state of perfection as yet, but only juridical.)   [93a] Of pontifical institutes.

and that by a perpetual obligation — just as perpetual as that of the diocesan priest in regard to his own local ordinary. Since the Pope is surely no less a bishop than a local ordinary, then the regular clergy, by reason of their immediate service of the Pope their highest superior, are also in the state of perfection proper to the bishop of bishops, the state of perfection *exercendae*.[94]

2. While the author approves most heartily of the recent attempts made to ennoble and to describe the dignity and role of the diocesan priesthood, by attempting to "contemplate this state in the light of the episcopal state that dominates it and vivifies it with its grace and ties it to the apostles and to Christ directly, without the intermediary of any founder, in immediate union with the essential holiness of the Church," still he does not feel that the attempts have always been made in accordance with the demands of a strict and precise theology.[95] That one is ordained for the service of the diocese or under the title of poverty or of the common table, merely indicates that one has a stable livelihood, that one gives service to a diocese, or to a religious order, or to a religious community, and these, in turn, have the obligation of caring for the one ordained. Therefore, it does not seem to be in accordance with the mind of the Church that one should "not want to add anything else to the dignity of the priesthood."[96] Such an attitude would more or less give the impression that the religious state added to the dignity of the

---

[94] "And it often happens in missionary territories that all the clergy even including the bishop belong to the regular clergy of the Church. Let no one think this is an extraordinary or abnormal state of affairs to be regarded only as a temporary arrangement and that the administration should be handed over to the secular clergy as soon as possible. . . . Again the exemption of religious Orders is not contrary to the principles of the constitution given to the Church by God, nor does it in any way contradict the law that a priest owes obedience to his bishop. For according to Canon Law exempt religious are subject to the authority of the local bishop so far as the administration of the episcopal office and the well regulated care of souls require. But even putting aside this consideration, in the discussion of the past few decades concerning the question of exemption perhaps too little attention has been paid to the fact that exempt religious even by the prescriptions of Canon Law are always and everywhere subject to the authority of the Roman Pontiff as their supreme Moderator and that they owe obedience to him precisely in virtue of their religious vow of obedience. Indeed the Sovereign Pontiff possesses ordinary and immediate jurisdiction over each and every diocese and over the individual faithful just as he does over the universal Church. It is therefore clear that the primary law of God whereby the clergy and the laity are subject to the rule of the bishop is more than sufficiently observed as regards exempt religious, as it is clear that both branches of the clergy by reason of their parallel services conform to the will and precept of the Church" (*Annus Sacer*, AAS 43 [1951], 29–30); *Canon Law Digest, loc. cit.*

[95] Cf. *Parish Priest*, Eugene Masure, tr. Angeline Bouchard (Chicago: Fides, 1955), p. 236.

[96] Masure, *op. cit.*, p. 236.

priesthood is something which the Church more or less tolerates, rather than wholeheartedly approves and admires, as Pope John XXIII has explicitly stated.

It is a better thing to undertake something under vow than to undertake that same thing without a vow, as we have seen, because under vow the act becomes one of the virtue of religion, the highest of the moral virtues. The Church, however, strongly recommends poverty and obedience to priests; and, therefore, those who observe these practices under vow are doing a better work than one who does not do them under vow. Nor must we forget that these vows (in pontifical institutes) enter one, first of all, in the service of the Church, since the first and highest superior of all religious is the Sovereign Pontiff himself, who has the right to command religious even in virtue of their vow.

Nor does it seem right to say that there is any special spirituality for the diocesan priest that is *essentially* different from that of a religious priest. For the priesthood has a spirituality of its own, and the fact that one is or is not a member of a religious community would merely place the emphasis on one or other of the aspects of the spirituality of the priesthood. Just as two diocesan priests may take different routes in arriving at the fullness and perfection of their priestly spirituality, so too, do religious priests of different orders take different routes (a question again of emphasis) in attempting to reach the perfection of the same spirituality. Thus, while we very definitely agree that there is a distinction in vocations to the priesthood and to the religious life, the religious priest, *by reason of his priesthood*, has exactly the same vocation as the diocesan priest and is subject to the "same inward law of apostolic charity." This inward law of apostolic charity is not something proper to the diocesan priest, but rather pertains to the priesthood *as such*, regardless of how one may be called by God and the Church to exercise this apostolic charity. Once again, we must not forget the words of the Holy Father: "There are not two forms of clergy."

3. The conclusion reached by the Angelic Doctor concerning the relationship between the religious state and the priesthood still seems to be most acceptable, and to be preferred. Thus he states:

> When we compare things in the point of supereminence, we look not at that in which they agree, but at that in which they differ. Now in parish priests and archdeacons three things may be considered, their state, their order, and their office. It belongs to their state that they are seculars, to their order that they are priests or deacons, to their office that they have the care of souls committed to them.
>
> If we compare a diocesan priest with the religious priest, and both of them have the care of souls, then the religious will excell the diocesan

priest with regard to state because the religious state is higher than the secular state. But with regard to the other things, the office and the order, both will be equal. If the religious, however, does not have the care of souls, then it is evident that he is superior as regards state, equal as regards order, but inferior as regards office.

We must, therefore, consider which is the greater preeminence — that of state or that of office — and here it seems we should take note of two things: goodness and difficulty.

Goodness: From this viewpoint, the religious state surpasses the office of parish priest, because a religious pledges his whole life (by profession) to the quest of perfection, while the parish priest does not pledge his whole life to the care of souls, as a bishop does (by his consecration); nor does it belong to him principally to exercise the care of souls, as it does to the bishop, but only in certain particulars regarding the care of souls committed to his charge.

Whence we might compare the religious state to their office, as the universal is compared to the particular, and as a holocaust with a sacrifice, which is less than a holocaust. Hence it is said[97] "Clerics wishing to take monastic vows, through being desirous of a better life, must be allowed by their bishops the free entrance into the monastery."

This comparison, however, must be considered as regarding the genus of the deed, for as regards the charity of the doer, it happens sometimes that a deed which is of less account in its genus is of greater merit if it be done out of greater charity.

Difficulty: From this viewpoint, if we consider the difficulty of leading a good life in religion and that of caring for souls, we can say that it is more difficult to lead a good life, together with the exercise of the care of souls, on account of the dangers, although the religious life is more difficult as far as the genus of the deed is concerned, by reason of the strictness of religious observance.

From the point of view of one who has to live a deep spiritual life in the face of many dangers, his life is in a sense more difficult, and demands great virtue. Thus Chrysostom writes: "When the pilot is surrounded by the stormy sea and is able to bring the ship safely out of the tempest, then he deserves to be acknowledged by all as a perfect pilot . . . the monk, therefore, is not to be compared with one who, cast among the people . . . remains firm because the latter both in the calm and in the storm piloted himself to safety."[98] This proves nothing more, however, than that the state of one who has the care of souls is fraught with more danger than the monastic state; and to keep oneself innocent in face of a great peril is proof of greater virtue. On the other hand, it also indicates greatness of virtue if a man avoid dangers by entering religion. For this reason, then, we must make a distinction between that difficulty which arises from the arduousness of the deed and that which results from the outward obstacles encountered in the performance of a good work. That difficulty which arises from the arduousness of the deed adds to the perfection of virtue; but the difficulty

---

[97] In Gratian's decretals, No. XIX, Q. 1, Chap. 1, RF 1, 839.
[98] On the Priesthood, Chap. 6, PG 48, 683.

which results from outward obstacles *sometimes lessens* the perfection of virtue — for instance, when a man does not love virtue so much as to wish to avoid the obstacles to virtues; and sometimes it is a sign of more perfect virtue — for instance, when a person does not forsake virtue, although he is hindered in the practice of the virtue unawares, or by some unavoidable cause. *In the religious state there is greater difficulty from the arduousness of the deeds;* but for those who in any way at all live in the world, there is greater difficulty resulting from *obstacles to virtue* — which obstacles the religious has had the foresight to avoid.[99]

However, when we compare priests with simple religious, then it is evident that the pre-eminence of orders excels by way of dignity; since by holy orders a man is appointed to the most august ministry of serving Christ Himself in the sacrament of the altar. *For this requires a greater inward holiness than that required for the religious life.* Hence, other things being equal, a cleric who is in holy orders sins more grievously if he does something contrary to holiness, than a religious who is not in holy orders, although a religious who is not in orders is bound to regular observance to which a person in holy orders is not bound.[100]

When we ask which is the greater vocation there is no categorical answer. They are of different orders, as it were. It would be like trying to compare sound with color. It will always depend upon our approach to the problem.

4. We must admit that in the course of years, the diocesan priesthood has often been the victim of harmful calumny on the part of some and of underestimation on the part of others. Thus one author writes:

> But what of secular priests? There can be no doubt that even apart from their sublime dignity they are in a state which far surpasses that of the laity, because of the vow of chastity they have made, and in virtue of their holy ministry. This excellent state is to be positively approved for those who having talent and character are nevertheless hardly fitted for religious obedience or the community life, or do not give evidence of such a will as to justify the hope of a firm resolution to enter the religious state. But there seems to be no doubt that there will always be very many who will shrink from the additional self-denial demanded by the poverty and obedience required in the religious state, inasmuch as men are little inclined to such complete voluntary surrender of self.[101]

To this the author does *not* wish to subscribe. Rather, we ought to keep in mind the note which was sent to the Bishop of Namur by the Sacred Congregation of Extraordinary Ecclesiastical Affairs:

> When anyone says that a priest who wants to tend to perfection must become a religious or at least a member of a secular institute; and when

---

[99] II–II, Q. 184, a. 8, ad 6m.
[100] *Ibid.*
[101] *Religion and Ecclesiastical Vocation*, A. Vermeersch, tr. Jos. Kempf (St. Louis: Herder, 1930), p. 71.

anyone tells a young man who is hesitating to choose between the secular priesthood and entrance into a religious order that it is a question of generosity; when anyone declares that he who decides in favor of the secular clergy proves that he is not generous enough to give himself entirely to the service of God; or when anyone thinks that he cannot counsel a young man in this undecided state to enter the seminary rather than a religious institute, or when anyone goes so far as to say that the Church tolerates the secular clergy as a last resort, but that the ideal would be for all priests to be religious; that is a false understanding and erroneous application of the Holy Father's allocution of December 8, 1950, *Annus Sacer.*[102] The Bishops have the right to oppose propaganda for the recruitment of religious societies which is based on incorrect theoretical premises and capable of leading into error and which is, at the very least, lacking in practical loyalty; and they may establish just and strict limits for this propaganda by administrative decisions.[102a]

5. We would do better, in regard to the whole matter, to follow the advice and wisdom of Pius XII in the *Sedes Sapientiae:*

> For with the passage of time the union of the states of perfection with the *priestly dignity* and the apostolic office has become ever more frequent and thorough. . . . In our day, therefore, the Church has the benefit of a great throng of ecclesiastics who are devoted both to the pursuit of perfection by the assistance of the evangelical counsels, and to the fulfillment of the functions of the priesthood. This great body of men constitutes the clergy who are called religious alongside those who are called secular or diocesan. Under the same Supreme Pontiff and the direction of their bishops, these two groups thrive and flourish with a fraternal rivalry and a mutual assistance which is profitable to both. . . .
>
> This point must be kept in mind by all whose duty it is to bring together and test such vocations. They must, then, never compel a person in any way to embrace the religious or priestly state. They must not invite or admit one who gives no sure signs of the divine call. They should not advance to the clerical ministry one who shows that he has been called by God only to the religious life, or force into the secular priesthood one who has received this twofold vocation.[103]

The question of religious versus secular is one which comes from God, for it is He who sows the seed of vocation in the hearts of individuals; and some he calls to the secular or diocesan priesthood and others to the religious priesthood. It should not, therefore, be looked at in terms of greater or lesser generosity, but rather in terms of the divine call. Thus we have saints in both categories: St. Thomas, St. Bonaventure, St. Ignatius, etc.; the Curé of Ars, St. Joseph Cafasso, St. Joseph Cottolengo. Therefore,

---

[102] *Annus Sacer, AAS* 43 (1951), 26–36; cf. *Canon Law Digest, loc. cit.*
[102a] *The States of Perfection,* ed. G. Courtois, pp. 209–210.
[103] *AAS* 48 (1956), 357–359; cf. *Canon Law Digest,* IV, p. 169 ff.

we ought "to flourish with a fraternal rivalry and mutual assistance which is profitable to both."[104]

The Signs of a Priestly Vocation

In general, as was true in the case of the religious vocation, there are two signs which manifest a vocation to the priestly life: the right intention and fitness — which, of course, can be subdivided into intellectual, moral, physical, and family background. Each of these will be treated rather briefly, since in some respect they are like those seen above in connection with the religious vocation.

The Right Intention

With regard to the priesthood, this right intention will include three things. First, it demands that one have the *desire to serve Christ for the love of Christ.* Thus our Lord Himself asked Peter, "Simon, Son of John, lovest thou Me?" Second, it includes *love for the Church* — for her teaching, her liturgical life, her militant life, and her suffering life. And, third, it includes *love for mankind and for souls.* This includes, of course, interest and concern in their material needs and especially in their spiritual needs. But it does not exclude an inclination, even a strong inclination, for a quiet scholarly life or for services within the house of God itself, as is true, for example, of those who dedicate themselves to study or to the contemplative life. *Da mihi animas,* "Give me souls" was the cry of a St. John Bosco, and it is the cry of the priestly vocation, regardless of where this priesthood is to be exercised — in the cloister or outside. For the priest is ordained to offer sacrifice for men and for the needs of the Church, that is, of souls. Thus, *a desire to lead souls to God or to work for their salvation, through the work of the priesthood,* is the sign of the right intention.[105]

---

[104] This same conclusion has been very well established by Bishop Charue of Namur, *Le Clergé Diocésain* (Desclée: 1960), pp. 149–159.

[105] Concerning this "right intention" a doubt has been raised by some authors, as to whether a person who wishes to become a priest with the express intention of making sure of his own salvation, or as a sure means of securing his salvation has the right intention demanded by Canon Law. With respect to this, two answers have been given by authors:

In the negative: he does not have the right intention. This was the opinion of Canon Lahitton (*op. cit.,* n. 430). However, we ought to note that he was speaking of the secular or diocesan priesthood in this place.

In the affirmative: he does have the right intention. This is the opinion of Lehmkuhl, who says that it is sufficient for a vocation to the priesthood that one have his eye fixed purely and simply upon God's honor and his own salvation. This opinion

From this it is clear that we must be careful in setting up signs for the priesthood not to limit them to a phase of the priesthood or to a way or manner in which it is to be exercised. Rather, the signs of vocation should be looked at — in accordance with that which constitutes the essence of the vocation. What is to be determined is whether the person wishes to exercise the priestly ministry and whether he wishes to do this in some active apostolate or in some contemplative apostolate.

Wrong Intentions

Because papal documents have insisted upon one's having the right intention, we might indicate, at least very briefly, some of those reasons or motives which would constitute a wrong intention. First, there would be the desire to use the priesthood for material and personal gain and advantage. While it is true that this may not often occur, particularly in our country, still its possibility is not to be overlooked. Where such an intention is discovered, either it must be eradicated, or the person must be informed that such does not constitute a right intention and motive for entering the priesthood.

Another wrong intention would be the desire to enjoy in the priesthood an easy and carefree life. Sometimes, this could be present, particularly in younger persons, who see in the priesthood the lack of certain responsibilities — of family, for instance — which tie a person down. "Father can go here and there," etc. Thus, their attraction for the priesthood is natural, and not supernatural. While it is true that something of a natural motive is not entirely forbidden, particularly in the initial attraction, still the counselor must see in the person desirous of entering the seminary a motive which is basically and fundamentally, and not merely accidentally, supernatural.

Still a third wrong intention would be the desire to seek the priesthood for the honor and prestige which it brings. Often this, also, has an attraction for one leading him to enter the seminary; and again we can expect to find it among youth, more often than among older persons who seek admission.

---

seems to be in keeping with the notion of the priesthood and of sacrifice to which the priest is called. For as St. Thomas mentioned, the privilege of offering sacrifice must not be considered merely from the viewpoint of man's needs, but especially (principaliter) from the viewpoint of honor and reverence to God. For the finis cuius gratia, the ultimate end of the sacrifice of the Mass, is to give honor and glory to God, or to show Him reverence and respect for His being the Creator and Governor of all things. Man and the needs of man are merely the finis cui, a kind of intermediate or subordinate end, the one who profits by it. Cf. III, Q. 82, a. 10.

Fitness

The second sign of a priestly vocation is that of *fitness*, which as we said above, can be divided into several kinds — intellectual, moral, physical, and environmental, if you will.

By *intellectual fitness* we mean the qualities of mind that are necessary to exercise the priesthood. This will sometimes vary in given cases, particularly when there is question of exercising the priesthood in some religious order or congregation. Some institutes require a greater amount of intellectual talent than others by reason of the apostolate to which they are dedicated. The experience of each community and diocese usually indicates what this should be.

By *moral fitness* we mean the presence of that virtuous organism or life of soul that is required for the priestly life. This quality embraces not only the ability of preserving perpetual chastity, but it ought to include the presence — and to a rather marked degree — of the other virtues as well. Too often, perhaps, we limit our consideration of moral qualities merely to that of chastity, whereas, in reality, other virtues are very requisite for a true and promising priestly life. Thus humility and obedience must be present; self-control, kindness, generosity and unselfishness, prudence — at least in keeping with one's age — love of truth, frankness, and modesty — in a word, piety, that sort of piety which can be considered to be priestly.

Thus Pius XI gave the following advice to those charged with the formation of candidates for the priesthood:

As the Angelic Doctor teachers: "To fulfill the duties of Holy Orders, common goodness is not sufficient; but excelling goodness is required; that they who receive orders and are thereby higher in rank than the people may also be higher in holiness."[106]. . . Clerics must lead a life, both interior and exterior, more holy than the laity, and be an example to them by excelling in virtue and in good works.[107]. . . Make piety, purity, discipline, and study flourish in the seminary. . . . He must look to the priesthood solely from motives of consecrating himself to the service of God and the salvation of souls; he must likewise have, or at least strive earnestly to acquire, solid piety, perfect purity of life, and sufficient knowledge. . . . Whoever, on the other hand, urged on perhaps by ill-advised parents, looks to the priesthood as a means of temporal and earthly gains which he imagines and desires in it, as happened more often in the past; whoever has a special tendency to sensuality and after long trial has not proved he can conquer it; whoever has no aptitude for study and who will be unable to follow the prescribed courses with due satisfaction, all such cases show that they are not intended for the priesthood. . . . Hence do not fear to

---

[106] Supl. Q. 35, a. 1, ad 3m.   [107] Cf. Can. 124.

seem harsh if, in the virtue of your rights and fulfilling your duty, you require such positive proofs of worthiness before ordination. . . . Cut from the forest beams fit for the building; but do not place the weight of the building upon them at once. Delay many days until they are dried out and made fit for the purpose; because if this precaution be omitted, they will soon break under the weight, or to use the short but clear expression of the Angelic Doctor: Holiness must come before orders. Hence the burden of orders should be placed only on walls seasoned with sanctity, freed of the damp of sins.[108]

In general, regarding the moral qualities required for one desirous of entering the seminary, we can say that they are about the same as those required for one entering the religious life; and these have already been given above.[109] There is this one observation, however, that must be made. For the priesthood, whether diocesan or religious, greater and more perfect moral qualities must be exacted than for the religious life. For the priesthood, as we have seen, exacts greater holiness of life than does entrance into the religious life. This is the constant teaching of theologians and the Church. Thus, it seems very strange that anyone should feel that a person who is less generous would be suitable for the diocesan priesthood but not for the religious life. If he is less generous, then he is less virtuous, for virtue and generosity are proportionate. With respect to moral qualities, therefore, we must demand more of one seeking to enter the priesthood than of one seeking to enter the religious life. For holiness is in some way a prerequisite for ordination to the priesthood whereas it is not so for the religious life, in which one intends to strive for perfection. Thus St. Alphonsus requires positive goodness of character.[110]

By physical health we mean the ordinary strength of body necessary to fulfill the duties of the priesthood. And here it might be mentioned that one must be free from more or less pronounced nervous or functional disorders, which indicate basically a lack of proper balance in outlook and mentality and attitude toward certain aspects of life. An indication of the presence of these is the fact that one has to see a psychiatrist for constant and prolonged treatment (not periodical or occasional). If this is really necessary, then it is a sign, at least in the opinion of the writer, that the person is lacking in one of the requisites for a vocation, namely, mental balance, or normal attitudes toward the things of life.

By environmental fitness we refer especially to one's family background. This certainly must be healthy. Bishop Stockums, in his work Vocation to the Priesthood,[111] notes that the "parental home of a candidate must enjoy

---

108 Ad Catholici Sacerdotii, The Popes and the Priesthood, p. 51 ff. passim.
109 Cf. p. 229–242 ff., especially p. 235 ff...
110 Cf. Great Means of Salvation and Perfection, p. 493 ff.
111 St. Louis: B. Herder Bk. Co., 1942, p. 92.

a good reputation. For when the dignity of the priestly state is considered, it is fitting to demand that a family which hopes to place one of its sons at the altar of God should enjoy good repute in the community. The sound sense of the faithful would see it as incomprehensible, as a glaring discrepancy, if a candidate for the priesthood should come from a home which bears a reputation that is, at best, dubious." If this was ever true it is true today when so many homes know very little of the religious training and background necessary for the development of the seed of vocation.

In a recent address to the Bolivian Eucharistic Congress, Pius XII mentioned the role of the family in the development of the vocation to the priesthood:

> The re-Christianization of the family is through the Eucharist . . . and it seems a natural introduction to the problem you have studied these past few days. For it is from a family which has been strengthened, invigorated, and vivified and sanctified by the Eucharistic life that priestly vocations spring. There can be no doubt that it is through the sacrament of the altar that men come to a knowledge of Jesus Christ, gaining thereby a deep understanding of His mission and taking from it a desire to offer themselves to carry on the mission by means of the priesthood. Indeed a life of intense piety, sustained and fed in a special way by the heavenly bread, must be naturally conducive to an increase of priestly vocations.
>
> We can be equally sure that in the presence of the Lamb continually sanctified on the holy altar, souls which are dedicated to perpetual immolation may through their tears and heartfelt prayers obtain the graces necessary for dew to fall upon the dry earth and bring forth the flower of vocation.
>
> From a practical viewpoint, however, all these graces come to souls in an ordinary way, that is they come through a Christian home, a sound religious education, and through a spirit of piety which is always felt within the home. It frequently happens that all the best efforts of teachers go for naught if such family consideration is lacking, or even worse, if the family spirit is contrary. Truly this situation would be a grave one and would demonstrate a serious lack of the spirit of Faith.[112]

The Theology of the Interior Priestly Vocation

In general, we can say that the theology of the interior vocation to the priesthood follows along the lines of the theology of the religious vocation with, of course, some well defined differences. We might say that the priestly vocation also affects the virtue of religion and the act of devotion proper to it. The difference between this vocation and that of the religious life seems to lie in the fact that the first demands a desire to enter upon the acts of the ministry. Or, if you will, it is a state of life in which

---

112. *The Pope Speaks*, III (1957), 403.

one will possess the power for the sacred acts of the ministry of the altar. Unlike the religious vocation, the vocation to the priesthood does not demand the desire to mancipate oneself perpetually and entirely to the service of God, but, rather, it offers to God, as St. Thomas notes, one's labors, which is a sacrifice and not a holocaust. In other words, not all the actions of the priest partake or come under the shadow of the virtue of religion, merely by reason of his ordination, as the actions of the religious do, by reason of his profession. For the vow or promise made in the profession of the evangelical counsels bring all the acts of the person bringing them under the shadow or the embrace of the virtue of religion, while ordination does not do this. Thus, while every action of a priest ought to tend to perfection, since the priest is called to this by his divine vocation, still not every act of a priest must fall under the shadow of the virtue of religion. However, we must note that the excellence of the acts demanded by the priestly vocation is greater than the excellence of the acts demanded by the religious vocation, and thus in order to fulfill them perfectly, one needs greater interior holiness.

The vocation to the priesthood can usually be recognized by the fact that one wishes to work for the salvation of souls in and through the ministry of the altar, or in and through the acts of the priesthood. And this desire must be firm and persistent, in order to constitute the recta intentio required by the Church.

*   *   *

In conjunction with this notion, the author would merely like to indicate some lines of thought which could be developed into a priestly spirituality.

By reason of his closeness to Christ, to the Word Incarnate, which he has received through the sacramental character, the priest receives an abundance of grace necessary to fulfill the most sublime of actions. This grace is always increased in proportion as the disposition of the priest increases. He receives not only grace through the sacrament but the right to additional and more intensive or perfect graces necessary for a constantly increasing holiness in the performance of his duties. The sacramental grace of orders, through the proper use of the actual graces which are directed to the soul by God throughout the course of one's life, can and should become more perfect, more radicated in the soul as the years of the priesthood pass by.

Any analysis of the sacramental grace of the priesthood would reveal that there are three qualities which are affected in some special manner. Because he is called to a life of greater victimhood, in imitation of the victim whom he daily offers and consecrates, he is called to the perfection of *charity and of fortitude* — which latter has as its special act martyrdom, or the giving up of one's life for the sake of good. The priest, by reason of his calling, must become more and more like the Victim of Calvary, and consequently display in his life the virtue of *apostolic charity* and *love for souls,* as well as that of *fortitude,* particularly realized through its potential parts, *magnificence, magnanimity, patience,* and *perseverance.* To offer one's life for the flock, which is at least to some degree incumbent upon a priest entrusted with the care of souls, is an act of fortitude, even though it be commanded by charity. For this reason the life of the priest must be characterized by this note to such a degree that it is a continuous act of martyrdom, of giving up his life for God's people.

Because the priest is ordained also to guide souls, to forgive sins, and to give counsel and advice, another virtue affected by the grace given through this sacrament is that of *prudence.* That is why he is called presbyter, an elder, one noted for his prudence and discretion in ruling the people of God. Whether his mission is to continue and to share in the magisterium or teaching authority of the Church, by trying to invest and instill into society the spirit of Christ, trying to cover it with the spirit of Christ, or whether it is to guide souls chiefly through interior direction exercised either in the tribunal of penance or outside of it, the priest must always exercise prudence beyond that of other men. It is the grace of orders which supplies him with the grace needed for his role as a Catholic teacher or educator, safeguarding the spirit of Christ in his field, or as one dedicated and entrusted with the interior guidance of souls.

In the long years of his training before ordination, the priest-to-be should be exercised along these lines that he might develop the necessary automatic or natural habits and virtues which will assist him so greatly in his future ministry. The practice of charity, of fortitude, and its potential parts, of the integral parts of the virtue of prudence, that is, docility, understanding, memory, discovery, reasoning, foresight, circumspection, and caution — all these must be exercised in the formative seminary years, as well as in the early years of his priesthood.

SECTION 2. CONSECRATED CHASTITY, OR THE LIFE OF VIRGINITY IN THE WORLD

While there have been some who have questioned the existence of a life of dedicated chastity or virginity in the world as a vocation, and as a special mark of God's love for an individual and of the individual for

God, still, this has always been the repeated teaching of Scripture, of many of the early Fathers of the Church, and the magisterium. Since we have already seen a rather full scriptural analysis of this truth in connection with the vow of chastity, we will concentrate here on the historical and magisterial sources.

We might divide our historical consideration into the following points: (1) virginity as an ideal and the position of women in ancient civilization; (2) consecrated chastity in the thought of the Greek fathers; (3) and consecrated chastity in the thought of the Latin fathers.

Virginity as an Ideal and the Position of Women in Ancient Civilization

One of the things that seems to have astonished the early pagans concerning the conduct of the Christians, in addition, of course, to their fortitude in undergoing martyrdom for their faith, was *their self-control in sexual matters*. This produced a rather deep *admiration for those who practiced this continence*. And from that twofold attitude — astonishment and admiration — it seems that the pagan world was rather happy with this new institution.

There were in paganism virgin goddesses — Athena, Artemis, Vesta — and their veneration could have led to some ideal conception of virginity among pagans. Moreover, they did have their virgin priestesses, such as Pythia at Delphi and the Vestals at Rome. Thus chastity and purity did have a part in some forms of pagan worship. However, this was usually required only for a time, that is, during the time of their service, lasting oftentimes several years. But it does not seem to have been a permanent way of life. By the time Christianity appeared on the scene, however, this aspect of paganism had more or less disappeared or had been reduced to mere formalism without any real living or vital content.

In general, it can be said that in the time we are considering women were considered essentially as men's inferiors. And the more barbaric the mode of life the more were they mistreated by them. But the more civilized the society became, the more did woman come to the forefront of life. There was an emancipation of woman even in ancient civilization, but it was perhaps the lot of far fewer than it became later on and especially in our own day. It can be seen first in Greece, especially at Athens. Then after some centuries we find it also in Rome. By the first centuries of the Christian era the evolution seems to have been more or less universal in Latin countries as well as in Greek. This liberation however, does not seem to have reached to the sphere of sex itself, and consequently on this score woman was still humiliated, subjected, and degraded. Because of this fact, it may be asked whether or not the enthusiasm with which the Christian message was greeted by the women of these centuries arose from their desire for a liberation far more complete and more perfect than that offered them on a purely secular level. At any rate, they did seem to take to it.

Again another impetus toward the practice of celibacy and virginity was the advent of several dual theories which explained the world and man by the action and rivalry of two opposing principles, that of good and of evil. Practically all of them agreed in placing sexuality in the realm of evil and condemning it unconditionally. Consequently, in theory at least, these served to preach a rather severe ascesis based on continence. These theories soon penetrated the Christian movement taking definitive shape in the rigoristic heresy of the Encratites, which condemned marriage and made continence a condition of salvation.

While these "assists and preparations" in the very heart of pagan society might have contributed *something* of a psychological background for the spread of the Christian ideal of virginity, just how much or to what extent they did so is something that has not been and perhaps may never be determined. At any rate, it can be stated that the obstacles to be surmounted by Christianity on this score were at least equal to the favorable conditions that it encountered.

Consecrated Chastity in the Thought of the Greek Fathers

It can be stated without reservation that *the doctrine of Christian virginity reached its fullest development in Patristic literature* where, with the teaching on martyrdom, we find perhaps one of the most comprehensive declarations on this state of life that we have ever had. In fact, it seems that we can also say that this development regarding the state of life known as virginity was also responsible for giving us some of our greatest insights into the mystery of sex and into that institution which St. Paul referred to as the *Magnum Sacramentum* — Christian marriage.

The practice of virginity from the very beginnings of Christianity is amply testified to in the accounts of the martyrdoms of the virgin saints. They were said to have died in defense of the faith and also in defense of their virginity, or to be more specific, in defense of *their marriage to Christ*. Often this expression is explicitly stated — they were *already betrothed to Christ*. The various acts which recount the martyrdoms of these virgins at least testify to a tradition and to the excellence in which such a spiritual or heavenly marriage was held by the early Church.[113] This

---

[113] Cf. *Acta Sanctorum*, Jan. II, ed. 16, 43, p. 352 ff.

is fully borne out from an examination of some of the principal Greek Fathers.

Origen, as we know, attempted to obtain chastity by mutilating himself, which, though wrong as he readily admitted later on, still shows the veneration in which he held this state. An immaculate body, that especially is a living sacrifice that is pleasing to God.[114] Frequently in enumerating the hierarchy of those in the Church he would place the virgins immediately after the martyrs giving, therefore, a definite priority to this practice.[115] When speaking of the betrothal of virgin martyrs we find before Origen's time the other writers placing the emphasis on their union with Christ. It was to Him that the virgin was betrothed and if she underwent martyrdom for the faith it was for her the occasion of entrance into the bridal chamber and she went forth to meet her Bridegroom, Christ the Lord, in glory. But when we come to Origen's treatment of virginity we find that he treats of it independently of martyrdom for the most part. It is no longer merely the virgin in her virgin body who is united mystically to Christ. Rather, two spiritual notions appear in his exposition: the Word and the soul. He preferred to speak of the spiritual side of man, as though virginity were merely a reflection of something far more important. Whereas the Latin Fathers, as we shall see, remained faithful to the earlier terminology extolling the marriage of the virgin with Christ, Origen preferred to speak of the union of the soul with the Word. And after some time this manner of speaking was accepted into Western literature, and this especially so in connection with the medieval mystical writers.

The entire commentary of Origen on the Song of Songs is at bottom nothing more than a treatise on the perfection of virginity taken in its widest sense, and on perfect chastity. In this book of Scripture he sees, on the one hand, the nuptials of Christ and the Church and, on the other, that of the Word and the human soul, or what has been called by later mystical theology the mystical or spiritual marriage of the perfect soul and God. There are in his concept of virginity two notions which are new in relation to the previous tradition. First, this marriage which before seems to have been especially achieved by martyrdom could be achieved even here on earth as a result of a deep and profound spiritual martyrdom, or asceticism and purification. The second idea that he seems to stress is that virginity is an angelic life on earth. Virgins and the continent are, like the angels in heaven, vowed to a life of praise and their task is to sing angelic

---

[114] Cf. In Rom., 9, 1, PG 14, 1205 A.
[115] Cf. Homil. II in Jesu Nav., 1, PG 12, 834; In Rom., 1, 1, PG 1205 A.

hymns among men.[116] It was for this reason that some have objected to Origen's concept of virginity since he failed to take into consideration sufficiently the fact that virginity as we conceive it is specifically *human* and is not an "angelic virtue" at all. However, when understood correctly it seems that this expression can be justified in the light of our Lord's statement that in heaven they shall neither marry nor be given in marriage. Since the Virgin and the celibate are already, as it were, living the life of the blessed *by way of anticipation,* they too are like the angels.[117]

Another of the early Greek writers on this subject, *Methodius of Olympus,* gives us a new approach to the subject. In his first discourse he presents virginity as the crown of Christ's work; it is the completion of the moral progress brought to man by the redemption of the world. In the second discourse he teaches that the union of man and woman given to us in Genesis is to be understood primarily and principally as an image of the union of Christ and the Church. This is the end toward which it should *always* move here on earth. In the fourth discourse he launches a new conception which was to become classical. It is a further development of the theology just mentioned. He attempts to show how *virginal purity is the means par excellence of regaining the lost immortality of our first parents.* Borrowing from Origen he shows that virginity of soul and body practiced with zeal and perseverance has its place in the Holy of Holies, on the altar of the temple, before the Ark of the Covenant and that it is the *highest degree of perfection* to be attained *in this world.* In the sixth discourse, Methodius shows that it is the pure virgins, now brides of the Word, who follow Him wherever He goes and who alone are able to sing the hymn spoken of by John in the Apocalypse. In the seventh discourse, he likens the brides of the Word to the bride of the Song of Songs whose adornments delight Christ because they resemble the Church, the perfect bride, as they also resemble the immaculate and virgin flesh of the Lord. He ends his eleven discourses with a wonderful hymn to Christ sung by the virgins in honor of the Bridegroom and of the Church, his chosen bride.

We are presented with a wider perspective, it would seem, by this author. Virginity, by renouncing the things of the flesh which is defiled by sin, becomes in some sense the restoration of the first state of man and woman before the Fall, a state in which the union of man and woman was given an *essentially transcendent orientation,* that is, toward Christ and the Church. This typology was the loftiest aspect of this union. By

---

[116] Cf. "Le Prêtre et la Louange divine," in *La Maison Dieu,* no. 21 (1950), p. 7 ff.
[117] Mt. 22:30.

breaking what raised it up, by defiling himself with sin man became incapable of making a reality of this figure which was only partially set right by the sacrament. God, although making marriage holy in the new dispensation, nonetheless kept the restoration of the primitive purity of this union for another kind of marriage — that of those who are called to lay aside the primitive symbol now tarnished by sin and come directly to the marriage of heaven without passing by way of the earthly figure. It is this concept of virginity that seems to be the leitmotif of all the doctrinal developments of virginity which we find in the early Fathers.

Gregory of Nyssa, another of the Greek Fathers, also took up the question of virginity and its excellence in comparison with marriage. He also teaches that the practice of virginity is an art and a faculty of the more divine life. It disposes those who live in the flesh to be like incorporeal beings. If the way to reach our goal is the restoration of the primitive state of the image of God now hidden under the stains of the flesh, then our task is to become again now what the first man was at the beginning of his life.[118] He holds that if man had originally cleaved to God from the first moment of his being immediately he would have achieved his perfection. Time, the succession of generations, and sex, would have been spared him. His development would have been that of an angel. In reality his was an animal development. God foresaw that man would sin and created him in a state which already bore something of its mark, of which sexuality is the chief character. When we are all united with Christ and have rejected the old man completely, this condition will disappear. In Christ there is neither man nor woman.[119]

For Gregory, virginity was the first stage on the road of return to paradise and marriage was the last stage on the way which removed us from the life of paradise; it served to fix us more and more in the present life.[120] In fact, Gregory went even further. He thought that the original plan for the propagation of man was not through the union of the sexes but rather through some mysterious method like the angelic method of propagation, a method, however, which he does not explain. Nonetheless we must be careful not to attribute to Gregory the conclusion that marriage was evil. This he explicitly denies as do all of the Greek Fathers.

Still another of the Greek Fathers, St. John Chrysostom, also felt much the same concerning virginity and marriage as did Gregory of Nyssa. He, too, held that virginity would have been kept in the state of innocence

---

118 Cf. De Virginitate, 5 and 12, PG 46, 348 B and 373 C.

119 Cf. Gregoire de Nysse, La Création de L'homme, with introduction by J. Laplace, no. 55, Sources Chrétienne, 6.

120 Cf. De Virginitate, Chap. 12, PG, 376 A.

and that humanity would have been propagated without sin and by some other than the normal means of propagation.[121] It might be mentioned here that John Chrysostom recommended virginity more often and gave it higher praise than any other Father of the Church.

Among the other Greek Fathers mention is also made of virginity, but in general most of them give no more than a series of counsels, under other forms and other ideas, in regard to what we have already seen to be the main thought of the foregoing authors — the soul's union with the Word, the angelic life, etc.[122]

In conclusion: a study of the Greek Fathers would disclose that their teaching on marriage and virginity does not at all serve to oppose the two states to each other; rather, the two states overlap. Virginity goes all the way along a road on which marriage stops half way. Virginity is situated along the same line of life as marriage, though farther on and transcends the earthly state of the magnum sacramentum. It attains directly what several of the Fathers predicated of Christ and the Church — the actual substance of the eternal marriage — and is merely a formulation of the eschatological theology of the betrothal of the soul with the Word. True marriage, for them,[123] is the marriage of virgins, and that of our earthly kind is merely a counterpart of this in the temporal and material order.

Consecrated Chastity in the Thought of the Latin Fathers

In the thought of the Fathers of the West we note trends very similar to those which appear in that of the Greek Fathers. The monastic life and its precursor, the life of individual or very small groups of ascetics living apart from one another, demanded that the members live vowed celibacy. Around the year 360 a small little work entitled The Life of St. Antony began to meet with success in the West. It appeared to be just what thousands of fervent Western Christians were longing for, a safe plan free from illusions for arriving at the heights of Christian perfection. St. Athanasius by his stay in Rome (A.D. 339) put many of these persons, men and women, in contact with the success of the Pachomian communities and the regular life led by widows and virgins dwelling in Egypt. Stories and accounts such as those related by Athanasius when he was in Rome aroused the enthusiasm of Marcella whose studious and mortified

---

[121] Cf. De Virginitate, PG 48, 543.

[122] Cf. Basil of Ancyra, De Virginitate, PG 30, 669 ff.; St. Gregory of Naz., Oratio XXXVII, PG 36, 281, and Poemata, PG 37, 521 ff.; St. Cyril of Alexandria, Sermo Adversus Eunuchos, PG 77, 1105 ff.; St. Athanasius, Epist. ad Arnoun, PG 26, 1173–1174.

[123] And this seems to be very much in keeping with the words of Christ cited in the twenty-second chapter of Matthew.

life gave rise to a little group of women of culture enamored of the spiritual life and exegesis under the tutelage of St. Jerome. She was the soul of the group and Jerome its oracle, its guide especially in matters of exegesis. And one of the things which he emphasizes in the practice of asceticism was that of chastity which he placed in a position of pre-eminent honor.

The last years of the fourth century saw a change in the interior structure of the Church. We know that virginity began to have not only a place of honor, but a kind of code or form of life with rights and privileges that became increasingly more evident. It was more and more favored with the attention and guidance of the Latin bishops, no doubt spurred on by St. Athanasius during his stay in the Holy City. It was already a state of life, but now it gave rise to a very definite cenobiticism, which also favored a more clearly defined teaching regarding virginity. We might attempt to trace the development in the early centuries by giving the thought of some of the early Latin Fathers.

In his apology addressed to the Emperor Hadrian (about 155) we find St. Justin exalting chastity and recognizing it as the typical expression of Christ's sublime moral teaching. He is rather vociferous in his praise of the manner in which it seems to transform souls. For this reason he makes it a point to refer to men and women, Christians from birth, who have kept their virginity intact for sixty or seventy years, admiring the strength of this morality which involves restraint both exterior and interior, even in regard to thoughts and desires. He indicates how wonderfully this practice has changed those who formerly were slaves to their senses into models of continence and witnesses to the mercy of Christ and the power of His grace.[124]

Thus Justin shows that the cult of chastity caused a great gulf between Christian morals and those practiced by the pagans of that day. It provided a striking contrast to incest which was excused by the misconduct of the gods and which was denounced in no uncertain terms even by Minucius Felix himself.[125] It appears that Justin referred to the practice of chastity as a witness or argument in favor of the power and authenticity of the Gospel of Christ. If the Gospel could move men and women to the practice of perpetual celibacy and virginity, then it certainly must be a genuine thing.

Toward the middle of the third century, St. Cyprian wrote a treatise on the life of virginity, consisting mostly of practical directives for it.[126] He

---

124 Cf. Apologia, 1, 15, PG 6, 349.
125 Cf. Octavius, XXXI, 5, ed. J. Martin, Flor. Patristicum, p. 72.
126 Cf. De Habitu Virginum, PL 4, 452 ff.

was *obliged* to write it, in this sense, that he had to correct certain disorders which had crept in among those leading the life. He greeted them as "the most noble part of the whole assembly of Christ," but he also deplored the scandals of which some of them were guilty.[127] He felt that many of these disorders were a result of lack of instruction concerning the responsibilities which the state of virginity entailed. These he intended to point out. And in so doing he gives us a picture of what that life demanded at the time in the eyes of the Church. Modesty, poverty, abstension from provocative finery, avoidance of public places such as baths, and worldly meetings: these were the points of common discipline that perseverance in the state of virginity required with great exactitude.[128] Cyprian seemed to have borrowed from Tertullian the idea of virginity implying a *personal gift to Christ and to God*: "Those who have dedicated themselves to Christ have vowed themselves to God both their flesh and their mind."[129] But he did not emphasize the precise nature of this consecration. Rather, his work *De Habitu Virginum* seems to dwell on his attachment to the Church, the source from which sprang his special concern for virgins. It was for this reason that he considered them to be the most noble part of the flock of Christ (the Church), the flowers whose seeds the Church carries in her womb, the jewels with which her spiritual grace decks herself.[130] Yet it must be stated that in his writings these ideas were still in their embryonic stage and waited the development which they would see in later authors. Suffice it to say that in Cyprian's time the predominant concern in regard to virginity was a moral one.

Perhaps no one more than St. *Ambrose* brought out the excellence and dignity of the state of virginity dedicated to God. From the time of Cyprian on, the practice had continued to increase, and the discipline governing the institution had taken on an official character symbolized by the veiling, the *velatio*, as it was called. This was the solemn conferring of a veil by a bishop or by the Pope, and gave rise to an expressive liturgy and rite the elements of which were the result of long-standing experience. However, what is worthy of note is that Ambrose derived his ideas on this institution not from his predecessors among the Latin Fathers but rather from the East.

He preached frequently on this topic in his diocese of Milan, urging many of the young girls of the city to embrace this way of life and also urging their parents not to prevent those who wished from entering upon it since it was most pleasing to God. Most of his ideas are contained in his *De Virginibus*. There he teaches that the great dignity of Christian

---

[127] Cf. cols. 455, 468.
[128] *Ibid.*, col. 470.

[129] *Ibid.*, cols. 477–478.
[130] *Ibid.*, col. 450.

chastity and its particular requirements are derived from a fundamental privilege: that virgins are the *brides of the Word made flesh*. This title formed the justification and the reward of the martyrdom of the young Agnes. Christian virginity assumes its true proportions in the Mother of God and in the Church, the bride of Christ. Ambrose was among the first to extol and defend the absolute and perpetual integrity of the Mother of God and it was he who exalted the fruitful virginity of the Church, the source which communicates an identical privilege to Christian virgins. Children of a virgin-mother, they are mothers in their turn and their fruitfulness surpasses the fruitfulness of the union of men and women. This idea was merely thrown out, so to speak, in passing by Ambrose only to be taken up and treated at greater length by St. Augustine.

In the psalms and in the Canticle of Canticles we find many images which attempt to portray and to foreshadow the union of the soul with God or with Christ. These Ambrose made use of in order to give expression to the spiritual realities of the highest order experienced by those who dedicate their lives exclusively to Christ through the practice of perpetual virginity. We must be careful, however, not to attribute to Ambrose any denigration of the lives of married people or of the institution of marriage itself. But he did attempt to give to virginity its rightful place of excellence superior to that of marriage, in the Church.[131]

However, even though Ambrose did more than any of the preceding Latin Fathers to produce a theology of virginity, he did not succeed in attaining a definitive synthesis which would satisfy later tradition. Such a synthesis required a much more speculative genius than Ambrose.

Perhaps no other of the Latin Fathers proved to be more *controversial* in regard to virginity and continence than St. *Jerome*. There is no denying his position in regard to the excellence and superiority of virginity over marriage. But those who read him sometimes wonder whether or not he does not hold marriage to be an evil in itself. It can be said that there are two cardinal principles in Jerome's spiritual direction: *renunciation*, total and absolute; and *virginity*, or perfect continence. So far as the second principle is concerned, we must attempt to understand his insistence on chastity to avoid misunderstanding the man. First of all, it can be stated that Jerome's teaching in regard to virginity and chastity is in perfect conformity with the traditional teaching of the other Fathers. Second, Jerome, we must remember, was forced to defend this teaching against very strong and persuasive opposition. And Jerome was a strong character in everything he did and said or wrote, not excepting his works

---

[131] Cf. *De Virginibus*, Chap. 7, PL 16, 272.

on virginity. His teaching concerning virginity might be summed up in the following ideas.

The primary point, one that we have already seen, is that *virginity allows one to give oneself to the full service of God.* This he bases on St. Paul's famous text to the Corinthians,[132] from which he draws his definition of a virgin: "one who thinks about the things of the Lord, that she may be holy in body and in spirit since it avails nothing to have virginal flesh and be married in thought."[133] It is this difference that sets off a virgin serving the Lord from a married woman. The former is able to follow a regime of prayer and fasting and is not called upon to devote her time to vanity and adornment to please her husband. Nor are her thoughts taken up with the care of a household. Thus she is free to serve the Lord with singleness of mind and an undivided love.[134]

But Jerome insists over and over again that the *life of virginity is not of precept; it is of counsel.* It is beyond the ordinary powers of human nature to live a life of angelic purity and can only be done at the invitation of and with the power of Christ. Thus he says:

> What is demanded is commanded. What is commanded must necessarily be done and if it is not done it is punished. But after all that is an empty sort of command whose fulfillment rests on our free choice. Moreover, if the Lord had commanded virginity, by the same token He would have condemned marriage and removed the very seed plot out of which virginity springs. If He had cut off the root how could He have expected the fruit? . . . Do not wonder that set as we are amidst the delights of the flesh and the allurements of vices, an angelic life is not required but only recommended. When a counsel is given it is a matter of free acceptance. But if it is a command then it is a matter of required service.[135]

In the course of this letter he mentions also that the master of the race in which all Christians run puts up a reward or prize, and He invites all Christians to run holding in His hand the prize of virginity. . . . He does not say that we must run willing or not, but whoever is willing and able may run and be victorious.[136]

Another point of Jerome's teaching is that the real value of virginity in the eyes of God is that it is *freely chosen.* The greater love that Christ gives to those who choose this way of life comes from their having *willingly surrendered what was not demanded* of them. Such a surrender is a great grace since it offers up what is not commanded and is not satisfied with surrendering or rendering only what is required and no

---

[132] Cf. 1 Cor. 7:32–34.
[133] *Adversus Jovinianum,* I, 13, *PL* 23, 241–242.
[134] Cf. *ibid.,* I, 13, *PL* 23, 240.
[135] *Ibid.,* I, 12, *PL* 23, 237–238.
[136] Cf. *ibid.,* I, 12, *PL* 23, 238.

more. Christ lovingly takes these to His heart since they have made themselves as they are for the sake of the kingdom of God. By their offering they have become pure temples of God, and being unstained in mind and body they are in truth a clean and whole burnt offering made to God.[137]

The motive that he presents for this choice is the love of God, the love of Christ. Happy that conscience and heart in whom there is no other love than that of Jesus Christ! For it is He who is wisdom and chastity, patience and justice, and all the virtues.[138] It is through the practice of virginity that one follows closely in the footsteps of Christ and gives herself to the highest of all loves.[139]

To this primary motive Jerome adds another: this state is a great gift made possible for women by Mary. In ancient days continence was found only in men and Eve continued to bear children in her sorrow. But now because of the Mother of God the gift of virginity is made possible for women.[140] Thus the following of Christ and His Mother made up the fundamental motive and it is to these that there is dedicated the first fruits of virginity in both sexes.[141]

In all this Jerome's teaching on virginity does not differ from that of the other Fathers. What gives it the appearance of difference is his manner of speaking concerning Christian marriage. His thought on this might, and actually does, for some, leave his readers with the impression that he considers marriage to be an evil, or almost an evil, or, at least, that there is nothing good about it. He denies explicitly, of course that he ever held that there was anything evil in this institution: "We do not follow the teaching of Marcion or that of the Manichaeans on this point or disparage marriage."[142]

Thus his teaching is quite clear and orthodox. He merely places marriage in a subordinate position, which the whole of Christian Tradition likewise does. Virginity is the great Christian ideal. It is the perfect following of Christ, but for all its superiority it does not make marriage an evil. Indeed if it were not a good what greatness or grandeur would there be for one to renounce it?[143] There is merely question here of a good and something that is better, like silver and gold. Silver is good

---

[137] Cf. ibid.
[138] Cf. Letter 130, 19, PL 22, 1123.
[139] Cf. Letter 22, 17, PL 22, 405.
[140] Cf. Letter 22, 21, PL 22, 408.
[141] Cf. Letter 48, 21, PL 22, 519; Letter 22, 18, PL 22, 405.
[142] Adversus Jov. I, 3, PL 23, 223.
[143] Cf. I, 40, PL 23, 282.

but gold is better.[144] And in confirmation of this he notes that the Church while accepting marriage subordinates it to virginity and widowhood. If married men are indignant with this approach then let them vent their anger not on him but rather on Scripture which teaches this openly.[145]

In his Epistles marriage certainly does not receive the marvelous treatment which we find being presented today. Yet there is a reason for this. Jerome was considering marriage as it existed in his day, and very often it was a rather sordid affair, particularly in the Roman society with which he was acquainted. Quite naturally, then, he would hold this up to ridicule and say that it was much better for one not to expose oneself to such an institution. As for the work against Jovinian which has received much criticism for its disparagement of marriage, we must attempt to understand the reasons behind what he wrote. He mentions them at the outset of this work: "His whole answer rests on the well-founded suspicion that Jovinian upholds marriage so strongly in order to disparage virginity. Because when the lesser is equated with the greater, the lower profits by the comparison and the higher suffers."[146] To St. Jerome such a situation was not only Christianity without the Cross, but the struggle of gluttony and lust to overthrow the Cross; and his reaction was characteristic of his temperament.[147]

At the very beginning of the fifth century St. Augustine devoted one of the first of his great works to the subject of virginity. In this work De Sancta Virginitate, he repeats many of the ideas already given by his master Ambrose, submitting them, however, to deeper investigation and giving them enduring form. In the very center of his thought he points out the *spiritual motherhood* of the virgin.[148] Sanctity is the principle that makes this practice fruitful. Mary and the Church represent its perfect types. For each of these perfect virgins sanctity forms their true relationship with Christ, a relationship so close that it cannot be compared with even physical generation. Consecrated virgins, as the Gospel says, should be the *mothers of Christ* by begetting Him spiritually by their faith and docility to His Word.[149] In another sense these are also brides of Christ by reason of their consecration to Him.[150]

Augustine is also clear in pointing out that virginity *in itself* is without

---

[144] Cf. *Letter 22, 18; Letter 50, 5, PL 22,* 405, 516.
[145] Cf. *Letter 48, 2, PL 22,* 494–495.
[146] *Ibid.,* 20, *PL 22,* 509.
[147] Cf. I, 3, *PL 23,* 223–224. Cf., on this whole teaching of St. Jerome, "St. Jerome as a Spiritual Director," E. P. Burke, C.S.P., in *A Monument to St. Jerome,* ed. by F. X. Murphy, C.Ss.R. (New York: Sheed and Ward, 1952), pp. 143–170.
[148] Cf. *De Sancta Virginitate,* 3, 5, 6, 7, *PL 40,* 397 ff.
[149] Cf. *De Sancta Virginitate,* 2, 3, *PL 40,* 397 ff.
[150] *Ibid.,* 8, 11, 12, *PL 40,* 400 ff.

any special dignity. In fact, *in itself* it is *not* superior to marriage. On the contrary, it is less perfect inasmuch as the love of those who are married is stable and fixed in one another, whereas that of the unmarried person not consecrated to God is ever seeking its object. Thus it is the consecration that fixes one's heart on and in God. No other love could be more sublime than this.[151]

The teaching of Augustine is especially remarkable for its practicality and understandableness. He recommends an attitude of *gratitude* to God for having given this gift, since consecrated virginity has no better title to nobility than its *supernatural origin*. In his eyes it is impossible to dissociate virginity from *humility* which is the fundamental discipline summing up the whole monastic asceticism. To it belongs the art of forming the virgin of God on the model of the Christ of the Gospels and of making her a true *bride of the Word*.[152]

When Augustine discovered these depths of virginity and celibacy for himself and for posterity we find that very quickly monasteries began to spring up all over Africa. The impulse seems to have come from him and then spread outward to other towns. It was thus that the dream which had haunted him since his conversion of restoring the primitive community of Jerusalem where the faithful lived in common and persevered in the breaking of bread was once again to be realized as a concrete reality. His own episcopal town of Hippo was the seat of three monasteries for men, and one for women over which his own sister ruled.

From all this it is clear that it is the *unanimous* teaching of the Fathers of the Church that virginity consecrated to God is superior to the state of marriage even though this latter be a sacrament of the Church. While it must be acknowledged that the sacramentality of Christian marriage was not understood in the precise sacramental language which we have today, still this does not interfere with our conclusion. The Fathers were acquainted with Christian marriage as such, and nonetheless considered chastity dedicated to God as a state far superior to it. It would perhaps, in our own day, be most wise for teachers and preachers to point this out *occasionally* to the faithful, indicating to them the reasons given in the preceding discussion as the reasons which have been advanced by those who are considered to be faithful witnesses not to a personal opinion, but rather to the teaching of our Lord and His Church.

Moreover, this teaching on the excellence or superiority of virginity over marriage has also been *extended to the state of widowhood*. Suffice it to quote the clear thought of Augustine on this matter:

[151] *Ibid.*, II, col. 401.   [152] Cf. *De Sancta Virginitate*, 31–41, PL 40, 412–421.

For while either one is in error (to make nuptials equal to virginity, or to condemn marriage as an evil) these two errors in their over eagerness to avoid each other attack from opposite extremes since they have refused to cling to the middle position of truth in which both from reason and from authority of the Holy Scriptures, we find that marriage is not sinful, yet we do not make it equal to the blessing either of virginal or even widowed continence.[153]

The Magisterium and Virginity

Coming to another of the sources, we find that the Church herself has not issued a large number of documents bearing on this question. Most often in her official councils it was treated in connection with many other subjects. Nonetheless it has been the subject of a solemn definition in the Council of Trent as we have already seen in treating of the counsel of chastity.

The Council of Saragossa in Spain in 380 attended by two bishops from France fixed forty as the age for the admission of consecrated virgins. The Liber Pontificalis attributed a similar measure to St. Leo I. These directives were followed by the Councils of Arles and Narbonne in 506. In Africa, however, at the Council of Hippo (393) presided over by Bishop Aurelius (Augustine was there) the Fathers authorized the consecration of virgins from the age of twenty-five on. Four hundred years later this age was considered traditional by the Council of Frankfort.

Outside the monastic framework, consecrated virginity tended to disappear. The Church recommended to virgins in general the common life understood in a rather wide sense, but for a long time did not wish to strictly impose the monastic life even on those who were consecrated by public rite. It left them free in the world though honored as befitted their state. This situation, however, became more and more rare until in many places they were no longer recognized by the law of the Church. They were never generally restored as a legal institution, and later still were prohibited.[154] Finally, the Second Council of the Lateran under Innocent II suppressed these domestic virgins.[155] From this date on they were obliged to live under the same roof, with their own chapel, refectory, and dormitory. This in itself is evidence of the sublimity and excellence with which the Church has always held this institution.

It seems that the subject of the superiority of virginity and celibacy over marriage was not challenged to the extent that it drew any great number of statements and declarations from the magisterium — until

---

[153] De Sancta Virginitate, 19, PL 40, 405.
[154] Council of Carthage III, c. 13, a. 397, Mansi, 3, 885 Council of Orleans V (a. 549), c. 19, Mansi, 9, 133; Council of Paris V (a. 614), c. 12–13, Mansi, 10, 542.
[155] (A. 1139) Mansi, 21, 532.

rather recently. With the reign of Pius XII, however, this topic was the subject of several pronouncements. Here we shall limit ourselves merely to the encyclical *Sacra Virginitas*. Only sections of it will be quoted here:

> . . . Innumerable is the multitude of those who from the beginning of the Church until our time have offered their chastity to God. Some have preserved their virginity unspoiled, others, after the death of their spouse, have consecrated to God their remaining years in the unmarried state and still others repenting their sins have chosen to lead a life of perfect chastity; all of them are at one in this common oblation, that is, for the love of God to abstain for the rest of their lives from sexual pleasure. May then what the Fathers of the Church preached about the glory and merit of virginity be an invitation, a help, a source of strength, to those who have made the sacrifice to persevere with constancy, and not take back or claim for themselves even the smallest part of the holocaust they have laid on the altar of God.
>
> And while this perfect chastity is the subject of one of the three vows which constitute the religious state, and is also required by the Latin Church of clerics in major orders and demanded from members of Secular Institutes, *it also flourishes among many lay people in the full sense*; men and women who are not constituted in a public state of perfection and yet *by private promise or vow completely abstain from marriage and sexual pleasures in order to serve their neighbor more freely and to be united with God more easily and more closely.*[156]

> Holy virginity and that perfect chastity which is consecrated to the service of God are without doubt among the most precious treasures which the Founder of the Church has left in heritage to the society which He has established. . . . However, since there are some who *straying from the right path* in this matter so exalt marriage as to rank it ahead of virginity and thus depreciate chastity consecrated to God and clerical celibacy, Our apostolic duty demands that We now in a particular manner declare and uphold the Church's teaching on the sublime gift of virginity and so defend Catholic truth against these errors.[157]

> By these words the divine Master is speaking not of bodily impediments to marriage *but of a resolution freely made to abstain all one's life* from marriage and sexual pleasure. For in likening those who of their own free will have determined to renounce these pleasures to those who by nature or the violence of men are forced to do so, is not the Divine Redeemer teaching us that *chastity to be really perfect must be perpetual?*[158]

> Here it must be added as the Fathers and Doctors of the Church have clearly taught that virginity is not a Christian virtue *unless we embrace it for the Kingdom of heaven*, that is, unless we take up this way of life precisely *to be able to devote ourselves more freely to divine things, to attain heaven more surely and with skillful efforts to lead others more*

---

[156] AAS 46 (1954), 160–161.
[157] The Pontiff then goes on to quote Mt. 19:10–12; AAS 46 (1954), 161, 163.
[158] *Ibid.*, p. 164.

readily to the Kingdom of heaven. For they are not to renounce marriage as though it were something despicable; rather they are to renounce it because virginity is something beautiful and holy.[159]

This then is the primary purpose, this the central idea of Christian virginity: to aim only at the divine, to turn thereto the whole mind and soul; to want to please God in everything, to think of Him continually, to consecrate body and soul completely to Him.[160]

Moreover, the Fathers of the Church considered this obligation of perfect chastity as a kind of spiritual marriage in which the soul is united or wedded to Christ; so that some go so far as to compare the breaking of the vow with adultery. Thus St. Athanasius writes that the Catholic Church has been accustomed to call those who have the virtue of virginity "Spouses of Christ." And St. Ambrose writing succinctly of the consecrated virgin says, "she is a virgin who is married to God." In fact as is clear from the writings of this same Doctor of Milan, as early as the fourth century the rite of consecration of a virgin was very like the rite the Church uses in our day in the marriage blessing. . . . It is nothing else but love of Him that sweetly constrains the virgin to consecrate her body and soul entirely to her Divine Redeemer. . . . Certainly it is the love of Christ that urges a virgin to retire behind convent walls and remain there all her life in order to contemplate and love the heavenly Spouse more easily and without hindrance; certainly it is the same love that strongly inspires her to spend her life and strength in works of mercy for the sake of her neighbor.[161]

From our Lord's words referred to above it has already been implied that this complete renunciation of marriage frees men from its grave duties and obligations. Writing by divine inspiration the Apostle of the Gentiles proposes the reasons for this freedom in these words: "I would have you be without solicitude." "He that is with a wife is divided." Here, it must be noted that the Apostle is not reproving men because they are concerned about their wives, nor does he reprehend wives because they seek to please their husbands, rather he is asserting clearly that their hearts are divided between the love of their spouse, and beset by gnawing cares and so by reason of the duties of their married state they can hardly be free to contemplate the divine.[162]

It is easy to see why persons who desire to consecrate themselves to God's service embrace the state of virginity as a liberation in order to be more entirely at God's disposition and devoted to the good of their neighbor.[163]

There is yet another reason why souls desirous of a total consecration to the service of God and neighbor embrace the state of virginity. It is . . . the numerous advantages for advancement in the spiritual life which derive from complete renouncement of all sexual pleasure. It is not to be thought that such pleasure when it arises from lawful marriage is reprehensible in itself. On the contrary the chaste use of marriage is ennobled and sanc-

[159] Ibid.
[160] Ibid., p. 165.
[161] Ibid., p. 166.

[162] Ibid., p. 168.
[163] Ibid., p. 168.

tified by a special sacrament as the Fathers themselves have clearly remarked. . . . (But) as the Angelic Doctor has it, the use of marriage keeps
the soul from the full abandonment to the service of God.[164]

The Holy Father then goes on to delineate the various fruits of virginity:
these are the various works of mercy — corporal and spiritual — which
those living this life undertake for Christ. In so doing *they do not abdi-*
cate their paternity or maternity but rather increase it immensely, be-
getting not for an earthly and transitory life but for the heavenly and
eternal one. Also, prayer offered for others and the trials willingly endured
for their sake which are other perfect forms of charity toward one's
neighbor would also be included among its fruits. Another fruit is
that of *faith and sanctity.*[165]
In another section he speaks of virginity as being an *angelic virtue,*
something proper to the angelic life, that is, to that life which we shall
one day live in heaven.

> Virginity fully deserves the name of *angelic virtue* which St. Cyprian
> writing to virgins affirms. What we are to be, you have already com-
> menced to be. *You already possess in this world the glory of the resurrec-*
> *tion;* you pass through the world without suffering its contagion. In pre-
> serving virgin chastity you are the *equals of the angels of God.*
> To virginity is awarded the *tribute of the highest beauty;* it is because
> its example is captivating. And besides by their perfect chastity do not all
> these men and women give a striking proof that the mastery of the spirit
> over the body is the *result of the divine assistance* and the sign of proven
> virtue?[166]

> Worthy of special consideration is the reflection that the most delicate
> fruit of virginity is this that virgins *make tangible as it were, the perfect*
> *virginity of their mother the Church and the sanctity of her intimate union*
> *with Christ.* In the ceremony of the consecration of virgins the consecrat-
> ing prelate prays God that there may exist more noble souls who disdain
> the marriage which consists in bodily union of man and woman but desire
> the mystery it enshrines, who reject its practice while loving its mystic
> significance.[167]

> The greatest glory of virgins is to be the living image of the perfect
> integrity of the union between the Church and her divine Spouse.[168]

Again in another part of the encyclical the Holy Father returns to the
question of the excellence of celibacy and chastity over marriage and
states that it was *necessary to issue this encyclical because of recent*
attacks on this traditional doctrine of the Church. These errors were

---

[164] *Ibid.*, p. 169.
[165] Cf. *ibid.*, pp. 170–172.
[166] *Ibid.*, pp. 172–173.

[167] *Ibid.*, p. 173.
[168] *Ibid.*

briefly: (1) perpetual chastity would do harm to one's balance and nervous system and therefore harm one's personality; (2) the grace of the sacrament of marriage which is conferred ex opere operato renders the use of marriage so holy as to make it a fitter instrument than virginity for uniting souls to God, for marriage is a sacrament whereas virginity is not; (3) the mutual help which is sought in Christian marriage is a more effective aid in striving for personal sanctity than the solitude of the heart, as they term it, of virgins and celibates. Of the first two ideas, he says: "We denounce this doctrine as a dangerous error." For while the sacrament does grant grace, still the purpose of marriage was not to make the employment of marriage per se a more fitting or perfect instrument for uniting the souls of husband and wife with God by the bonds of charity. Even the Apostle teaches that they have the right of abstaining for a time in order to give greater freedom to the soul that wishes to give itself over to the thought of spiritual things. As for the third objection, those who have perpetual chastity receive from God, the Giver of all heavenly gifts, something spiritual which far exceeds the mutual help which married persons can confer on each other. Their personality suffers no harm or loss, but gains immensely.[169] Yet he is quick to add:

> It must be clearly stated that because virginity should be esteemed as something more perfect than marriage, it does not follow that it is necessary for Christian perfection. Holiness of life can really be attained even without chastity that is consecrated to God. Moreover, it is not something that is of precept. It is of counsel. Hence it demands first a free choice and supernatural help and grace from God.[170]

> To sow the seeds of perfect purity and to arouse a desire for virginity has always belonged to the function of the priesthood. . . . We trust that those educators of youth who have succumbed to errors in this matter will repudiate them as soon as they are detected and will consequently strive seriously both to correct them and to do what they can to provide every help for the youth entrusted to their care who feel themselves called by divine grace to aspire to the priesthood or to embrace the religious life, in order that they may be able to reach their goal.[171]

> Moreover, as the obligation of Our Apostolic Office demands We urge fathers and mothers willingly to offer to the service of God those of their children who are called to it. But if this be a source of sorrow, trouble or regret, let them seriously meditate upon the admonition which Ambrose gave to the mothers of Milan: "The majority of young women whom I knew wanted to be virgins, but were forbidden to leave by their mothers. . . . If your daughters want to love a man the laws allow them to choose whom they will. But those who have a right to choose a man, have they no right to choose God?". . .

---

[169] Cf. ibid., pp. 175–177.   [170] Ibid., p. 179.   [171] Ibid., pp. 178, 179.

Let parents consider what a great honor it is to see their son elevated to the priesthood or their daughter consecrate her virginity to her Divine Spouse.[172]

In these passages we are once more given to understand that the teaching of the early Fathers which we have examined is also the official teaching of the magisterium of the Church.

*   *   *

As we mentioned, when treating of the Fathers' teaching on marriage and virginity, Paul explicitly taught that widows also were considered to be in a state superior to that of those who are married, if they had decided to remain unmarried for the future in order to give themselves more freely to God. This teaching was strongly recalled by Pius XII in an address which he gave to the world Union of Family Organizations on September 16, 1957. The pertinent extracts are as follows:

It is noticeable that the very word "widow" produces in those who hear it a sadness and even a sort of aversion, and so some widows refuse to bear this name and do everything possible to make people forget their condition. They give the excuse that widowhood is a humiliating thing and gives rise to pity, and places them in a position of inferiority which they wish to escape and even forget. Many regard this as a normal reaction, but — let us speak plainly — it is hardly a Christian reaction. Doubtless it reveals a more or less instinctive apprehension in the face of suffering, but it also betrays ignorance of profound realities. . . .

Although the Church does not condemn remarriage she shows her predilection for souls who wish to remain faithful to their spouse and to the perfect symbolism of the sacrament of marriage. She rejoices when she sees the spiritual riches being cultivated which are proper to this state. The first of these, it seems to Us, is a strong conviction that far from destroying the bonds of human and supernatural love which are contracted in marriage, death can perfect them and strengthen them. . . .

When one of the spouses loosed from his mortal bonds enters into the divine intimacy God frees him from every weakness and all the dregs of selfishness. He also invites the one who is left on earth to enter into a more pure and spiritual state of mind. Since one of the spouses has consummated his sacrifice should not the other be willing to detach herself more from the world and to renounce the intense but fleeting joys of sensible affection which bound the husband to the home and monopolized her heart and energies? . . .

The sacrament of marriage, symbol of Christ's redeeming love for the Church, applies to the husband and wife the reality of this love. It transfigures them; it renders the husband similar to Christ who delivers himself to save mankind and the wife is similar to the redeemed Church which accepts its part in the sacrifice of Christ. Widowhood thus becomes in some manner the natural outcome of this mutual consecration. It repre-

[172] Ibid., p. 190.

sents the present life of the Church Militant deprived of the vision of its heavenly spouse but still unfailingly united with Him, walking with Him in faith and hope, living on that love which sustains it in all its trials and eagerly awaiting the final fulfillment of the promises that were made in the beginning. Such is the greatness of Christian widowhood *when it is lived as a prolongation of the graces of matrimony and as a preparation for their flowering in the light of God.*

How wrong it would be to take advantage of widowhood to free oneself from the reserve and prudence proper to single women, and to abandon oneself to the vanities of an easy and superficial life. . . . She whose companion has been called back to God should realize *the urgent necessity of cultivating her spiritual life,* if she wishes to preserve her interior peace and face all her tasks unflinchingly. She should not let a single day go by without devoting some time to meditation, a few privileged moments when she will feel closer to the Lord and to the husband who continues to watch over her and her home. In her family or professional relations or with her friends she will introduce *the distinctive note that characterizes her apostolate: the testimony of her faithfulness to a beloved memory,* and of her having found in this faithfulness and the renunciations it involves, a more profound, more stable, more luminous happiness than that which she had to renounce.[173]

It would be difficult to find anything, even among the writings of the Fathers of the Church, expressing the reasons which should lead one who has lost her husband (and this same idea would be true of one who has lost his wife) through death to remain as she is since such a life is better than that of remarriage.

The *theological reason* that might be advanced to show that dedicated virginity is superior to marriage is very simple. Whatever unites us more perfectly and more immediately (objectively speaking, of course) to our last end is, simply speaking, more excellent. Consecrated virginity, however, because it frees us from the cares and distractions of the married state, more easily enables us to be united with God, our last end. Consequently, this form of life is, objectively speaking, more excellent than, and superior to, the married state.

Marriage truly sanctifies all that is corporal, all that is material. Indeed it can be said that it plunges the whole of the bodily and carnal life of man into Christ. It is a most profound form of earthly sanctification such that we can say in the communion of love or charity and human love existing between two persons even the most instinctive bodily actions of man are sanctified, and are virtuous. But because the activity involved in marriage evokes the highest possibility of which the human body is capable, laying bare the vital corporal foundations or roots of our human personality, it requires a most arduous and intense asceticism to bring all

---

[173] *The Pope Speaks,* 4 (1957), 288–289, passim.

its details into holiness. The division which is felt within the human personality because of concupiscence is deeply felt even in Christian marriage. There is something that is not always wholly given to God, as Pius XII has pointed out.[174]

Virginity, on the other hand, transcends this division. This does not mean, of course, that concupiscence is not present in a person who has consecrated his or her life to God. What we mean is that concupiscence is symbolically and objectively, as it were, transcended, even though subjectively it will probably be experienced and felt. Virginity implies that as far as we can we renounce the very sources of this division within our personality. What the married man or woman must attain gradually through the grace of God — the spiritualization of the flesh — the virgin or celibate accomplishes in one act of the will by entering upon his or her state of life. Virginity must constantly be seen as a preference in love. It is the rejection of or the turning away from one form of charity, only to assume a higher one that is the total form as it were, directed immediately to Christ Himself. It is the state of a soul by way of anticipation sharing in the risen life where the immediate presence of the Triune God is experienced, filling the soul with intense joy in the presence of its spouse. It is the state of those who share in the life of the 144,000 of the Apocalypse standing around the throne of the Lamb in an attitude of eternal worship and praise.

Virginity is without meaning if it does not denote a love for a Person, or if it does not involve a personal love. By the free and irrevocable decision to reserve from all men the personal mystery of oneself and open this only to Christ, the virgin or celibate becomes wedded to Christ in an intimacy that in inexplicable and independent of sentiment or feelings.

Those Who Should Be Advised to Follow This Vocation

As a general rule, consecrated virginity can be advised, in something of the way in which the religious life can be advised. That is to say, it can be proposed as a counsel of the Lord, and, therefore, as worthy of consideration. For this reason then, it is always permitted to exhort others to this state, in a more or less general way, because it is possible, it is

---

174 "Even though marriage is a true sacrament, one of the seven sources of grace instituted by Christ Himself, and even though it involves a mutual offering of one spouse to the other and cements a real union of lives and destinies, still there remains something that is held back, something that is not actually given or at least something that is not wholly given. Only virgin souls can make that offering of self that for other loving souls is an unattainable goal." "The Nursing Sister," address, of April 25, 1957, in The States of Perfection, ed. G. Courtois, p. 288.

permitted (even counseled by Christ and the Church), and it is better.

One must be careful, however, in setting forth this advice or in urging others to embrace this way of life. And the reason is rather obvious: there are some who have received this gift and others who have not received it. That is why the Holy Father mentioned in the course of the encyclical that each one should

> study his own strength, whether he can fulfill the precepts of virginal chastity. For of itself, it is attractive to all. But one's forces must be taken into consideration, for the words of the Lord are, as it were, an exhortation stirring on His soldiers to the prize of purity. For virginity is a difficult virtue; that one be able to embrace it there is needed not only a strong and declared determination of completely abstaining from marriage; but also a constant vigilance and struggle to contain and dominate the rebellious movements of the body and soul, a flight from the importunings of the world, a struggle to conquer the wiles of Satan. For the root and flower of virginity is a crucified life.
>
> Prior to entering upon this most difficult path, all who, by experience, know that they are too weak in spirit should humbly heed this warning of Paul the Apostle, "If they do not contain themselves let them marry." For many the burden of perpetual continence is a heavier one than they should be persuaded to shoulder. And so priests who are under grave obligation of helping young people who declare they are drawn by some movement of soul to the priesthood or to enter religious life must urge them to ponder the matter thoroughly, lest they enter upon a way of life which they cannot hope to follow sturdily and happily to its end. They should prudently examine the fitness of candidates, even obtaining, as often as is proper, the opinion of experts; and then if serious doubt remains, especially if it is based on experience, they should make use of their authority to make candidates cease from seeking a state of perfect chastity; nor should these latter ever be admitted to Holy Orders or to religious profession.[174a]

This way of life, whether inside the cloister or in the seminary or in the world, should not be advised except to one who has proved himself and is solidly virtuous, instructed in the spiritual life and accustomed to prayer. This is especially true when there is question of living this life in the world without the aids afforded by a community or institute. Moreover, even when one is permitted to make this promise, it should be merely for a time at first, and then only after probation and assurance that one can lead this life, perpetually.

In proposing this vocation as one of the states of life one might use the words of the Holy Father himself when he writes:

> We urge fathers and mothers willingly to offer to the service of God those of their children who are called to it. But if this be a source of

---

[174a] The States of Perfection, ed. G. Courtois, p. 241.

trouble, sorrow or regret, let them seriously meditate upon the admonition which Ambrose gave to the mothers of Milan: "The majority of the young women whom I knew wanted to be virgins were forbidden to leave by their mothers. If your daughters want to love a man, the law, allows them the right to choose whom they will. But those who have a right to choose a man, have they no right to choose God?"[175]

SECTION 3. THE STATE OF CHRISTIAN MATRIMONY

Coming to the last of the states of life, we have Christian matrimony. Today, by reason of the heavy emphasis on marriage courses in high schools and colleges, students often are left with the practical feeling that marriage is to be put on a par with the other states of life in the Church. However, this is false as the foregoing treatment has shown. Among all the states of life, marriage, although it is a sacramental state, occupies the lowest place with the exception, however, if it is actually considered to be a state, of the single (nondedicated) life in the world. For all its real beauty, therefore, such as has been pointed out by modern writers, marriage is less excellent than the states we have treated and, therefore, is placed here, in the last place.

Because this work is chiefly concerned with the places and purposes and excellences of the various walks of life, it is of these alone that we shall treat, leaving the other particulars to the sacramental treatment of this state of life. [176]

The Sanctity of Married Life

While there have been those in the history of the Church who considered the married state to be evil, still it is the teaching of the Church that this state is holy and represents in some manner the union of Christ with the Church. That marriage is something holy and sanctifying is clearly set forth in Scripture, the writings of the Fathers, and the documents of the Church, and can be shown from reasons of fittingness.

In his Epistle to the Corinthians, in the same passage in which he writes about virginity, St. Paul also indicates the goodness and the excellence of marriage. Thus he writes: "I wish you were all in the same state as myself; but each of us has his own gift from God, one to live in this way and another in that."[177] Thus it is evident that the married state can be counted among the gifts of God, even though it is not to be counted as excellent as the state of Paul. And again, the same Apostle writes: "Not

---

[175] De Virginibus, Bk. I, Chap. 10, PL 16, 205.

[176] A fuller treatment of these ideas and many others will shortly appear in The Sacrament of Matrimony: a Dogmatic Study.

[177] 1 Cor. 7:7.

that thou commit sin if thou marriest."[178] Thus he clearly indicates that matrimony is not to be considered as an evil. And again Paul writes that "a man is well advised to give his ward in marriage."[179] And finally, of one who does not remarry after the death of her husband, he says that she is "more blessed if she remains as she is,"[180] thus indicating that she is blessed even though she does remarry.

While the goodness of marriage is clearly attested to in 1 Corinthians, its sanctity is brought out most clearly in the famous Ephesian passage.[181] The sanctity of married life is indicated in the prototype to which it is likened or referred, namely, the Mystical Body, or the union of Christ and the Church and the fruitfulness of this union. Marriage, or the union of husband and wife, is part of the mystery of salvation which includes, as we know, in the mind of Paul redemption in Christ, and through His death and resurrection, our adoption as sons, and our sanctification in the Spirit. It includes the mystery of the rejection of the Jews and the choice of the Gentiles. It includes the summing up of all things visible and invisible in Christ. And it ends with the final return of all this which is the fulfillment of Christ to God who fills everything. Then Christ is to return to the bosom of the Trinity so that we end where we began, with God who is all in all. This whole is for the praise of His glory.

Matrimony is associated by Paul with this mystery of salvation, since it symbolizes in a special way something of the mystery of Christ — His union, His fruitful union with the Church. Marriage for Paul is not just a sign or symbol of the Mystical Body — the Whole Christ, the "two in one" since through baptism we become, as it were, members of His body, flesh of His flesh, and bone of His bone, as Eve was of Adam. No, marriage is the type of which the Mystical Body is the prototype. Marriage was intended to portray the Mystery of the Mystical Body. Thus, in a sense, we can say that Christian marriage re-creates the union of Christ with His Church, somewhat as the Mass re-creates, as it were, and reenacts daily the single Sacrifice of Calvary. When God became man He bound Himself by the conditions of our humanity, the essential condition of which is, in the present state, at least, contingency — the property of existing only at a particular moment in time. Now Christ is the Church which is flesh of His flesh and bone of His bone having been born of His side on Calvary. The reincarnation of Christ has to be realized anew in every generation and it is in marriage that this union is realized. By baptism Christ is united with the individual soul.

---

[178] 1 Cor. 7:28.
[179] 1 Cor. 7:38.
[180] 1 Cor. 7:60.
[181] Cf. Ephes. 5:23 ff.

By marriage He is united with a new being, the mode of being which we call the Mystical Body, so that we can say that through marriage the Church in microcosm is produced.

The union of matrimony gives concrete and visible expression to the realism of the Church's union with Christ. It does not produce this union, of course, since this is prior to it and independent of it. The mystery of the Incarnation, God becoming man in the unity of one person, is continued in the Mystical Body where God and man become one mystical person. Marriage, or the marriage between two Christians, is a visible sign, a sacrament or symbol of this mystery — God's union with men in the mystical person which we call the *Totus Christus*. In this union the husband plays the role of Christ and the wife plays the role of the Church, and their Christian union portrays the union of Christ and the Church who form one mystical person.

That this mystery produces grace *ex opere operato* is not at all indicated in the text. However, this is, in a sense, something that naturally follows upon the union. For from the fact that the union does imply and present its difficulties, and that family society in order that it might be what it ought must depend upon the help of God, we must conclude that graces are probably given the members bound to one another to realize this goal. But this is not laid up to the mystery as such or to the union or the sign. Rather, it is a consequence of it in the Scripture text being referred to; it is not something that is immediately signified.

Doctrinally from Scripture, we would deduce the following: (1) the union of man and wife in marriage is a sensible sign which reflects or re-presents the great mystery hidden for ages and now revealed — the plan of Christ's union with the Church, God's union with man, or the mystical marriage of God with His people; (2) neither from the text nor the context, however, can we say that Paul indicates that grace is automatically produced by this union. This is merely implied in the context.

The early Fathers, even in extolling the excellence and the superiority of virginity over matrimony, have always considered marriage as something good and holy, sanctifying, as we have seen above in treating of consecrated virginity. Thus, St. John Chrysostom writes: "Marriage is a legitimate thing, this I confess. . . . Virginity is a good thing; and to this I also consent. And I confess that this latter is better than the former. And if you wish to know how much better, as much as heaven is better than the earth, as much as the angels are better than men. Indeed if I could say anything stronger, I would add more."[182]

Likewise, St. Augustine writing on holy virginity says:

---

[182] *In Genesem*, 5, Hom., 21, 4, PG 53, 180: *In Matt. Hom.*, 43, 5, PG 57, 464 ff.

I advise virginity; still far from censuring marriage as being bad I praise it. . . . Now between counsel and prohibition, there lies an abyss as deep as between liberty and necessity. A friend who counsels leaves his friend free to follow another view.

When I advise virginity I pass no censure on marriage nor do I blame one who resists my counsels. I admire indeed the generous athlete who rushes on in the career of virginity but have no fault to find with him who does not enter that career, for blame is allowed only in reference to a really bad act. But how can it attach to Christians whose only reproach is that they confine themselves within a more modest sphere and dare not aim at the highest efforts of virtue. I shall not praise the vigor and the energy of his courage, but neither will I allow myself to cast blame on timid reserve. . . . I do not oppose marriage which I hold to be holy and lawful.

Marriage is good since it keeps man to his duty and hinders him from falling into sin. Therefore, do not condemn it because it is fruitful of happy results. . . . It saves us from profaning the holy temple, our bodies; it supports the weak and strengthens their steps. But support of that kind is of no use to the strong and the robust man. Far from being necessary for him, its sole effect is to scatter in his way a thousand obstacles which slacken his progress while lessening his merit and glory.[183]

These are merely a few isolated passages. A more thorough analysis would strengthen our position. For the manner of speaking of the Fathers clearly shows that they considered the institution to be holy and to be reverenced in the Church. It had to be celebrated before a minister or representative of the Church. The ceremony and institution was regulated in accordance with ecclesiastical laws. And it conferred in some way the grace of the divine assistance on those who entered it.

While it is true that some of the earlier documents of the Church do not bring out the sacramentality and the sanctity of the married state as strongly as the later documents, still they do indicate quite clearly that it is not to be considered as an evil, but as a good form of life, according to which man and woman can work out their eternal salvation.[184]

While the Fourth Lateran Council[185] and the Council of Florence[186] clearly indicate the sacramentality of marriage, still it remained for the Council of Trent to bring out something of the *sanctity* of this way of life:

But the grace which was to perfect that natural love and indissoluble union and was to sanctify those united in marriage, Christ Himself, in-

---

[183] De S. Virginitate, Chaps. 8–10, passim, PL 40, 400–401.

[184] Cf. The Council of Braga (II) in 561; Denz. 241; also the profession of faith prescribed for Durand of Osca, in the year 1208, Denz. 424.

[185] Cf. Denz. 430.

[186] Cf. Denz. 695, 702.

stitutor and perfector of the venerable sacraments merited for us by His Passion. The Apostle Paul intimates this when he writes: "Husbands love your wives as Christ loved the Church and delivered Himself up for it"[187] immediately adding: "This is a great sacrament; but I speak in Christ and in the Church."

Since, therefore, matrimony in the law of the gospel is, because of the grace given through Christ, superior to the marriage unions of earlier times, our holy Fathers, the Councils, and the tradition of the universal Church have always rightly taught that matrimony should be included among the sacraments of the New Law. Contrary to this teaching, evil foolish men of our day not only entertain wrong notions about this holy sacrament but in their usual way . . . they spread many ideas that are foreign to the understanding of the Catholic Church and to a long approved custom dating back to the apostolic times.[188]

But it is above all the pontiffs of the social era who have time and again pointed out the sanctity that is inherent in Christian marriage. In 1880, Pope Leo XIII, in his encyclical *Arcanum Divinae Sapientiae,* wrote:

They [the Holy Fathers, the Councils and Tradition of the universal Church] teach too that Christ brought it about that husband and wife, sheltered and strengthened by the heavenly grace which His merits produced may attain sanctity in the marriage itself. And in their union, a union marvelously conformed to the pattern of His own mystical marriage with the Church, Christ brought to perfection a love that is natural; and by divine charity He made a stronger union of the naturally indivisible society of husband and wife. . . . A further consideration is that as a consequence, matrimony is a sacrament because it is a sacred sign and produces grace and reflects the mystical marriage of Christ with the Church. The image and likeness of this marriage are found in the bond of the perfect union which joins together a man and a woman, and this is nothing more than matrimony itself. Thus it is evident that among Christians every marriage is by its very nature and essence a sacrament. And nothing is more repugnant to the truth than to say that the sacrament is a kind of embellishment of the contract, a property extrinsic to and flowing from it, and that the sacrament can be distinguished and separated from the contract by the will of men.[189]

In this particular encyclical it is quite evident that the marriage union among Christians is something that is, by its very nature, holy, since it is sacramental and, therefore, contains and gives grace, those graces necessary for the fulfillment of this life in the Church.

This teaching of Leo XIII was repeated even more strongly by Pius XI in the encyclical *Casti Connubii:*

Christ the Lord in raising the matrimony of His faithful to the dignity of a sacrament of the New Law made it a sign and source of that peculiar

---

[187] Ephes. 5:25.   [188] Denz. 969–970.   [189] Denz. 1893–1894, *passim.*

internal grace which perfects natural love and confirms an indissoluble union, and sanctifies both man and wife. Therefore when the faithful give their sincere matrimonial consent they open up for themselves a vast treasure of sacramental grace from which they draw the supernatural strength to fulfill the duties of their state with fidelity, holiness, perseverance until they die. If men do not place any obstacle in the way, this sacrament increases for them the permanent grace source of their supernatural life, sanctifying grace; and it gives them special additional gifts, good inspirations and seeds of grace, at the same time augmenting and perfecting their natural faculties. Thus husband and wife can have more than an abstract appreciation of all that pertains to the goals and duties of their married state; they can have an internal realization, a firm accomplishment of it; and finally this sacrament gives them the right to ask for and receive the help of actual grace as often as they need it to fulfill the duties of their state . . . the faithful once joined by marriage can never be deprived of the help and abiding force of the sacrament. These parties not fettered but adorned by the golden bond of the sacrament, not hampered but assisted should strive with all their might to the end that their wedlock not only through the power and symbolism of the sacrament but also through their spirit and manner of life may be and may remain always the living image of that most fruitful union of Christ with the Church which is to be reverenced as the sacred token of most perfect love.

To the natural sacredness of marriage as an institution created by God, there must be added that new element of dignity which comes from the sacrament, by which Christian marriage is so ennobled and raised to such a level that it appeared to the Apostle as a great Sacrament honorable in every way. This religious character of marriage, its sublime signification of grace and the union between Christ and the Church evidently requires that those about to marry should show a holy reverence for it and zealously endeavor to make their marriage approach as closely as possible to the archtype of Christ and the Church[190]

The *theological explanation* for the holiness of marriage comes from its sacramentality. For a sacrament by definition is something that *ex opere operato* contains and produces the grace which it signifies. Matrimony, however, is a sacrament of the Church, instituted by Christ. Therefore, matrimony contains and produces the grace which it signifies — the holiness and grace helps necessary to accomplish the duties of one's state.

The object of this sacrament is to conform one to the passion of Christ, as is true of all the sacraments of the Church. In the case of matrimony, it does not conform the one who receives it to the passion of Christ with regard to the punishment or suffering involved in this action, but rather *with respect to the charity that was involved in the passion,* through which charity He suffered joining to Himself the Church as Spouse. It

---

[190] Denz. 2237. Other passages from the pronouncements of Pius XII might also be cited, but these will be given in the work soon to be published mentioned above.

was this that led St. Paul to insist that husbands love their wives as Christ loved the Church. It was love which motivated Christ to undergo the passion and death of the Cross; and it is also love which ought to motivate the relations between husband and wife through this sacrament, a love, however, that is not merely natural but of the supernatural order as was Christ's — the love of charity. However, for all its excellence, the love of this surrender involved in marriage cannot measure up to that which is shown through one's giving up oneself directly to Christ. For in the one case there is a going to Christ through an intermediary; there is a union of oneself with Christ or with the Church through some intermediary. Whereas in the other case, in the case of complete dedication through religious profession or through the vow of virginity, one goes immediately to Christ and unites oneself immediately to Him without going through any intermediary. And this, of course, is a more direct union with Him, one that indicates the attempt and the effort to live here on earth the life of the blessed in heaven where there will be neither marriage nor giving in marriage.

The Place or Role of Marriage in the Church

In the division of the sacraments we find that some are ordained toward the welfare of the individual and others toward the common good or welfare of the Church. Matrimony falls among the latter sacraments, since it is a social sacrament in and through which the Church is propagated corporally. In this sense it is opposed to the other social sacrament of the Church, Holy Orders, which has as its aim to spiritually propagate the Church.[191] Thus St. Augustine has written: "all these are blessings because of which marriage is a blessing: offspring, conjugal faith, and the sacrament. . . . By conjugal faith care is taken that there be no union outside the marriage bond with another . . . by offspring, that children be begotten in love and nourished with kindness and brought up religiously; but by the sacrament, that the marriage be not broken. . . . This is as it were the law of Marriage, whereby the fruitfulness of nature is adorned and the depravity of incontinence is controlled."

> Thus the child holds the first place among the blessings of matrimony. Clearly the Creator of the human race Himself, who because of His kindness wishes to use men as helpers in procreating life, taught this in paradise when He instituted marriage saying to our first parents, "increase and multiply."
> Indeed Christian parents should realize that they are not called merely to propagate and preserve the human race, on earth, nor even to pro-

---

191 Council of Florence, Denz. 695.

create men who worship the true God in any way, but to give children
to the Church of God, to procreate fellow citizens of the saints and members of the household of God, so that the number of worshippers of God
and our Savior may be constantly increased.[192]

Another purpose for which matrimony exists is the mutual interior
formation of husband and wife, or what Pope Pius XI called the

> constant zeal for bringing one another to perfection in the true sense, as
> the Roman Catechism teaches. This can be said to be the very first reason
> and purpose of matrimony, if matrimony be not accepted too narrowly
> as instituted for the proper procreation and education of children, but
> more broadly as the mutual participation in all life and as companionship
> and association.
>
> That is why the love in matrimony does not and was not meant to rest
> only on a carnal inclination which very quickly disappears, nor on pleasing
> words only, but also on the innermost affection of the heart, one that is
> proved by external deeds, since the proof of love is the manifestation of
> deeds. These deeds or works in the life of the home not only include mutual
> assistance but also aim at making the two persons engaged in this way of
> life help each other to form and to perfect the interior man more fully,
> so that through their partnership in life they may advance in the virtues
> more and more and may grow especially in true love toward God and
> their neighbors. Manifestly, the most perfect example of holiness is to be
> found in the Lord, and all, in whatever condition and on whatever honor-
> able way of life they have entered with God's help, should also arrive at
> the highest degree of Christian perfection as is proved by the example
> of many saints.[193]

Another of the purposes of the sacrament of matrimony is to represent
constantly in the world of creatures the union of Christ with the Church.
In this sense we know that a Christian husband and wife have as part
of their mission in the Church to represent before men the union of
Christ with the Church and the love which Christ manifested for the
Church, together with the devotion and subjection which the Church
shows to Christ. Christian matrimony, as well as virginity has this role
in the Church, but each in its own special way — matrimony insofar as
the Church is fruitful in producing children, and virginity insofar as the
Church is immaculate and spotless and the bride without spot of Christ
the Lord. St. Thomas has brought this out quite well:

> Every sensible thing the Church uses has a spiritual significance. And
> since a corporal thing fails to represent adequately something spiritual, one
> spiritual reality may sometimes be represented by several sensible signs.

---

[192] Cf. *Casti Connubii*, AAS 22 (1930), 542. This primary purpose of marriage has
been the object of many recent pronouncements. Cf. *AAS* 36 (1944), 103 (*Canon
Law Digest*, III, p. 401 ff.); 43 (1951), 84; 48 (1956), 469.
[193] *Casti Connubii*, Denz. 2232.

The spiritual marriage of Christ and the Church is fruitful; for by it sons of God are given birth. And it is also pure and immaculate; for as the Epistle to the Ephesians reads "Christ also loved the Church and delivered Himself up for it . . . that He might present to Himself a glorious Church, not having spot or wrinkle or any such thing.". . . For which reason St. Paul writes "For I have espoused you to one husband, that I may present you as a chaste virgin to Christ."[194]

Now bodily fruitfulness and virginity or integrity of the flesh are incompatible. Therefore two different signs are needed to represent the spiritual marriage of Christ with the Church, one to image its fruitfulness, and the other to reflect its perfect purity or integrity.

Since on earth marriage represents the fruitfulness of the spiritual relationship between Christ and His Church, another symbol is needed to typify its integrity; this occurs in the veiling of virgins as the ceremony clearly indicates. And for this reason the Bishop alone to whom the care of the Church has been entrusted receives their vows.[195]

In this I think that we can also see the superiority of virginity over matrimony, for although each of them includes in its very makeup both purity or innocence and fruitfulness, each does not visibly show both of these elements. The institution of virginity shows visibly the immaculateness and integrity and purity of the union of Christ with the Church and only invisibly, but really, the fruitfulness of that union. Matrimony, on the other hand, shows visibly the fruitfulness of that union, and only invisibly, through the practice of marital chastity, the integrity or purity of that union. Visible integrity with spiritual fruitfulness is more excellent than spiritual integrity with material or corporal fruitfulness since the former imitates more perfectly the life of the angels and the blessed in heaven, or we might say, the last end or the very purpose for which man was created. Thus, as we know, the aim of the whole economy of grace is to effect the perfect union of the soul with Christ, or the spiritual marriage of the soul with Christ, and this is more perfectly and more directly effected in and through the institution of virginity.

The Theology of the Interior Vocation to Marriage

Although some have questioned the use of the term "vocation" in reference to marriage, feeling that this term ought to be reserved to the higher states of life, still it seems that we can accept this expression. Thus Pius XII writing in the Sedes Sapientiae writes: "Inasmuch as God is the principal author of every state of life and of every natural and supernatural disposition, a real vocation to any state of life must be called in a sense, divine. If this be so, how much more so must one call the

---

[194] 2 Cor. 11:2.   [195] IV Sent., Dist. 38, 2. 1, a. 5.

religious and priestly vocation *divine*, since it is invested with a sublime dignity and adorned with so many natural and supernatural gifts."[196]

We can say, then, that Divine Providence does mark out some for this state as He destines others for those other states which we have examined. Thus the term *vocation*, even *divine vocation*, can be applied, at least in a broad sense, also to Christian matrimony.

Granted this, the vocation to the married state also in some way affects the virtue of religion, insofar as Christians are to see in it a way of working out their salvation, a way of uniting themselves more closely with God and of contributing to the growth of the Church. However, the act of devotion elicited in entering this state, *objectively* speaking, does not have to be as intense as that elicited by one entering a state in which he dedicates himself entirely to God. For Christian marriage of its very nature demands that the two persons have duties toward each other as well as toward God. For this reason St. Paul mentions that those who embrace this walk of life are solicitous for the needs of one another as well as for those of God. There is the concomitant possibility that there will be a divided love, as Pius XII has taught so clearly:

> Hence, however, it must be noted that the Apostle is not reproving men because they are concerned about their wives . . . rather is he asserting clearly that their hearts are divided between love of God and love of their spouses and beset by gnawing cares; and so by reason of the duties of their married state, they can hardly be free to contemplate the divine. For the duty of the married life to which they are bound clearly demands [this]. For spouses are to be bound to each other by mutual bonds, both in joy and in sorrow.[197]

The vocation of the married does not demand of them the holocaustal act which the religious life demands, nor does it demand as sacrificial an act as does that of the priesthood. In the case of those who enter upon the state of matrimony, the *act of devotion* is *sacrificial*, that is, at least so far as the *objective* requirements of the vocation are concerned; whereas in the case of religious, it is *holocaustal*; and in the case of those who enter the priesthood, it is more sacrificial. In the case of those who undertake a life of perpetual dedicated chastity, it would be holocaustal at least in this one area.

It is, of course, possible that the intensity of the virtue of religion of two persons entering upon the married state might be greater than that of many entering upon the religious state or the priesthood; but the act of devotion made by those entering upon this way of life (matrimony),

---

[196] *AAS* 48 (1956), 357–358; cf. *Canon Law Digest*, loc. cit.
[197] *Sacra Virginitas*, *AAS* 46 (1954), 168.

objectively speaking, does not have to be as great as that made by those entering upon the other states of life. Here we might make a distinction between an "appreciative" intensity and one that is sensible. Thus, for example, a mother is required to love God more than her own child "appreciatively," even though "sensibly" her love for her child will often-times be more pronounced than her love for God. So, too, the religious profession, or the act of entering upon a life of perpetual chastity, is the sign of an "appreciative" love for God, and is a more intense act of devotion, not sensibly but volitionally, than that made by two persons entering the sacrament of matrimony.

As a conclusion to our discussion of this idea of the "vocation" to marriage, it may be said that marriage is a vocation if "vocation" be taken in a broad sense, that is, as designating any stable provision of Divine Providence for His creatures in working out their salvation. That it is a "special vocation" does not seem to suit the sense of this term, for usually this refers to one of the more excellent, or so-called "higher," states or walks of life — the religious life, the observance of the counsels in a secular institute, the observance of perpetual chastity under vow or prom-ise, or the priesthood. Nor does it seem that we can call marriage a "vocation of counsel," from the words of our Lord or from those of St. Paul. Suarez, indeed, states that in the strict sense of the term marriage is not of counsel, for the only thing that is of counsel in the writings of the Apostle is the state of celibacy. "If they cannot contain themselves, let them marry and again I say this by way of concession; I am not im-posing a rule upon you. I wish you were all in the same state as myself."[198]

The Signs of This Vocation

In general the signs of a vocation to marriage are about the same as they are for any vocation. However, the one sign that is required is

[198] 1 Cor. 7:9, 6–7. With regard to the sacramental grace of marriage, we ought to note that it is something which is given initially in and through the marriage ceremony and continues to grow and develop throughout the years of this union. Thus those who have entered upon this state have the right and title in the sacramental grace or the peculiar bent of sanctifying grace which they have received in the sacrament, to demand of God the actual graces needed to correspond with the demands of their state. On this score Pius XI has written:

". . . If doing all that lies within their power they cooperate diligently, they will be able with ease to bear the burdens of their state and to fulfill their duties; by such a sacrament they will be strengthened, sanctified, and, in a manner, consecrated. For . . . just as by Baptism and Holy Orders a man is set aside and assisted either for the duties of the Christian life or for the priestly ministry and is never deprived of their sacramental aid, so quite in the same manner (although not by a sacramental character) the faithful, once they are joined by marriage ties, can never be deprived of the help and the binding force of the sacrament (Casti Connubii, AAS 22 (1930) 555.

that one desire marriage, that there be present the firm will to enter upon this way of life, from proper and virtuous motivation. In this it differs from the other states which demand a firm resolution or proposal toward another way of life. This is, in general, the one sign that indicates the presence of a "vocation" to the state of marriage. The other qualities must be present; health, physical and mental, as well as moral and intellectual qualities, insofar as these are required by this state.

We should note that marriage is not obligatory for any individual. For while it is necessary for the human race, it is not of obligation for any particular member of the human race. St. Alphonsus teaches that a person who frequently falls into sins against chastity would be obliged to marry if he would not take any other means of avoiding a relapse. However, one should be very careful in advising marriage to one who commits sins of this sort, since it is not the cure for all such sins. Sin results from bad inclinations or vicious inclinations and the state of marriage does not *ipso facto* remove these. There is no one, provided he wills sincerely, who cannot effect a cure for these faults by the use of salutary remedies. For who is there, the same saint says, who has not under his hands the powerful arm of prayer with which every passion can be conquered?[199]

For this reason, youth must be counseled that there is a remote and a proximate preparation for marriage. The remote preparation consists in keeping the commandments, leading a life of virtue during the period of childhood and adolescence. The virtuous person, experience shows, has a much better chance of living a happy married life than one who has not lived a life of virtue prior to entering upon this state. As one is before entering marriage, so is he likely to be during it. Since his vocation will demand of him a virtuous life and virtuous care of those entrusted to him by Divine Providence, he himself must possess the virtues and must exercise them throughout his entire life; and the perfect criteria of this is his having lived and observed them *before* entering upon this state.

The *proximate* preparation demands the choosing of a good partner. In so deliberating, those who are planning on marriage should keep before their minds the thought, first, of God and of the true religion of Christ, then of themselves, of their partner, of the children to come, as also of home and civil society, for which wedlock is the fountainhead. Let them diligently pray for divine help so that they will make their choice in accordance with Christian prudence, not led by the blind and unchecked impulse of lust, not by any desire of wealth, or other base influence, but

---

[199] Cf. *Theologia Moralis*, III, tr. 2, n. 209.

by a true and noble love and by a sincere affection toward the future partner; and let them strive for the ends for which this state was constituted by God. Lastly, let them not fail to ask the prudent advice of their parents, with regard to the partner; and let them regard this advice seriously, in order that by their mature knowledge and experience of human affairs, they may guard against a harmful mistake, and on the threshold of matrimony may receive more abundantly the divine blessing of the commandment "Honor thy father and thy mother" which is the first commandment with a promise: "that it may be well with thee and thou mayest be long-lived upon the earth."[200]

*   *   *

APPENDIX. THE RELIGIOUS PROFESSION:
WHY NOT A SACRAMENT?

So often when mention is made of the excellence of the religious life over the state of matrimony, the question arises as to the nonsacramental status of the religious profession. If it is a more excellent way of life than that of marriage, then why was it not elevated to the dignity of a sacrament?

The reason, perhaps, for this misunderstanding comes from the lack of knowledge concerning the various sacramental graces, and the reasons for which the sacraments of the Church were instituted under the present economy of grace. Basically they are two, according to St. Thomas: (1) to perfect men in those things which pertain to the worship of God through the rite of the Christian religion; and (2) to act as a remedy against those defects brought about by sin.[1]

The sacraments were instituted by Christ in order to present man with the various remedies as well as with the various graces of orientation, which he would need in order to live out the fullness of his Christian life which so closely parallels his natural life — and the needs which this latter entails. Each of the sacraments gives a special grace which in some way is linked up and connected with the various positions or functions which one occupies or performs as a result of having received a given sacrament. The position occupied or function performed in the Church will determine the special grace received through it, that is, a certain extension

---

[200] *Casti Connubii*, America Press ed., pp. 37–38.
[1] Cf. III, Q. 65, a. 1.

of grace, together with a certain intensity of that grace, proportionate to the role to be played and the responsibility to be shouldered in the Mystical Body. Each sacrament, we might say, gives a certain share or measure of the fullness of grace proper to Christ our Head, which as we know was perfect, both by way of extension and by way of intensity. It is, so to speak, a channel through which a share or portion of the grace possessed fully at its source is given partially to those who approach more or less closely to receive it.

According to the teaching of many theologians, a teaching which St. Thomas merely proposes as given in his day (though he himself does not seem to be very enthusiastic over it), each of the sacraments has a special though not exclusive relationship with one or other of the virtues. Thus Baptism is closely linked up with faith, since it is the *sacramentum fidei*; Confirmation with the virtue of fortitude, since it is the *sacramentum roboris*; the Holy Eucharist, with charity, since it is the *sacramentum seu vinculum caritatis*; Penance, with the virtue of justice (penance), since it is the *sacramentum compunctionis*; Extreme Unction with hope, since it is the *sacramentum spei*; Holy Orders with prudence, since it is the *sacramentum gubernationis* and Matrimony with temperance, since it is the *sacramentum unionis maritalis seu procreationis*.

Each of these sacraments, then, gives a grace which has directly a twofold purpose; to perfect or to enable one to perform the requirements demanded by the reception of the sacrament, and to heal the wounds which would interfere or act as obstacles to the virtuous fulfillment of the duties required. The sacramental economy is something very much of the earth, such that it would not have been instituted by God had man not fallen into sin.[2] In fact we can say that when God bypasses, so to speak, the sacramental economy, He is acting in a way in which He would have acted had man not fallen into sin, that is, by Himself directly infusing into the soul the graces man would need to unite himself more perfectly with Him. For the fact that these graces should be infused through some sensible ceremony indicates a weakness on the part of man, and not a perfection, according to St. Thomas.

In the phenomenon of the religious vocation, and especially that of the religious profession, God chooses to act as He would have acted in the state of innocence, that is, without the instrumentality of sensible ceremony. For when one makes a profession of vows, the grace is given not through any sensible element used in such a ceremony, but rather directly by God Himself working in the interior of the soul. By the grace or call of religious vocation, and especially by the grace and the act of religious

---

[2] Cf. III, Q. 61, a. 2.

profession, a soul is taken up by God in a most special way, and the state into which the person is assumed is of heaven, heavenly, rather than of earth, earthly. Therefore it is a sign and figure, not only of the perfection and the harmony and the life of the state of innocence, but even more, of the life of the blessed; for it is of these that our Lord Himself has said, "they are as the angels in heaven." The religious state, or the life of dedicated virginity, denotes in its overall implications an *eschatological* state, one that is not of earth, but rather is an anticipation of the life which the soul is to lead in the Beatific Vision when it shall be united with God alone. It is a living while still on earth or *in via*, of the life of the resurrected, or it is the life of those living in the triumphant resurrection of the flesh. That is why such a person bears witness to this faith of the Church in the resurrection.

It is for this reason, then — because of the *perfection* of the way of life which is signified by consecrated or dedicated chastity — that it seems more *fitting* that no sacrament be instituted for it, for it is an event in and through which *something proper to eternity*, to our first meeting with Christ in heaven *takes place* by way of anticipation here on earth. By calling a person to this life God calls him to share in something of the perfection and the perfect grace of the other life, the life beyond the grave which is a life without sacraments, since no cure or remedy is needed by man in this state.

In short, it is the *very signification and meaning* of dedicated or consecrated chastity both on the part of the man and the woman that precludes any necessity for a sacramental sign and so consequently a sacrament. In the case of a man, voluntary celibacy practiced for the sake of the kingdom of God denotes perfect death to the world. It is a second baptism, one that goes further than the first baptism, since figuratively he leaves the world and is no longer numbered among its members. In the case of the woman there is this reality present and also another, that of her *direct and immediate marriage with Christ*. Both of these are *eschatological states* demanding no sacramental sign or sacrament. Indeed in the early Church, especially in the case of virgins, no public ceremony was undergone by those wishing to lead this life. It was strictly a matter of an *internal desire or promise made to God*. It was *visible* to others insofar as they saw by acts that this person was not interested in marriage, etc. But no external or public ceremony was had. Thus virginity or celibacy has always been considered to be primarily an internal thing, a firm purpose on the part of the person called by God to dedicate his or her life to Him alone. The ceremony was instituted for many reasons of fittingness, for regulatory purposes, and for the edification of the people of God.

Even today one can make a *private vow* of perpetual chastity outside of any of the so-called "states of perfection." And this private vow also places him or her in a way of life superior to marriage.

Indeed, in a sense it would be unfitting for there to be a sacramental sign because then the *heavenly nature* of this vocation and way of life would be somewhat diminished and it would be brought into the realm of earthly states and realities, at least so far as its essential element is concerned — the firm purpose of the will to abstain from all venereal pleasure for the sake of the kingdom of God. The Angelic Doctor indicates this line of thought himself when he writes in the Fourth Book of the *Sentences*:

> In the consecration of virgins as in the anointing of kings and in other blessings of this sort grace is given unless there be some impediment on the part of the recipient. *These ceremonies are not called sacraments*, however, because *they have not been instituted to cure the disease of sin* as the other sacraments have.[3]

This is not so strange as we first might think it to be. Something similar can be found in the life of the Mother of God. So far as we know she did not receive Baptism (although some theologians teach that perhaps she did, but this can be questioned) nor Confirmation, nor Extreme Unction, nor Penance, because she received something far more excellent or had no need for them (her divine maternity and Immaculate Conception, and her perfect sinlessness throughout her entire life). There is such a thing as one's being called out of the ordinary ways of humanity by a special invitation of God and given grace directly, outside a visible channel. In this sense we might say that such a person is above the sacramental system in this one particular, not because of any deficiency in the system, but rather by reason of the excellence and eschatological meaning and dignity of the vocation or gift which God Himself has bestowed. Thus, in our case, one is singled out by God and given another task in the Church to be a sign or symbol which will present visibly before men the bride of Christ not *in via* but *in termino*, in heaven, where there is no marrying nor giving in marriage, and where there is no sacramental system.

It is for this reason that we have two ceremonies and two vocations in the Church: one indicating the union of Christ with the Church *in via* and another indicating the union of Christ with the Church *in termino*. The condition of the first is of time and is mutable, as it were, open to increase in progeny, etc. The condition of the second is of eternity, immutable, and the person might be said to share, mysteriously, of course, in the *nunc stans* of God Himself.

---

[3] Dist. 38, q. 1, a. 5, ad 2.

The Graces of Marriage and Those of Celibacy or Virginity

In order to help us understand the excellence of the grace of the religious profession, and its superiority over the grace which is given through the sacrament of marriage, it might be helpful to compare them according to sacramental terminology. While it is true the religious profession is not a sacrament, still in its overall makeup it presents almost a perfect parallel to the sacramental process of Matrimony. For this reason, a comparison between the two will serve to bring out the differences and the similarities between them. Before giving this schematic comparison, however, it would be best to indicate the meaning of some of the terms which will be used. In the sacramental process, we find three elements, the *sacramentum tantum*, which is the external or visible sacramental rite; the *res et sacramentum*, which is a reality, having merely one relationship in the case of some sacraments, and two in other sacraments; and finally, the *res tantum*, which is the grace of the sacrament. We might picture this sacramental process in the following schema, and then apply it to the problem at hand.

Sacramental Process

Sacramentum Tantum (that which signifies):
The external rite of a sacrament, the matter and form, joined together signifying something, some effect.

Res et Sacramentum (that which is signified and that which signifies) can be considered as:
Character: in those sacraments which impress a character; as such the *res et sacramentum* is a remote disposition for grace. In Matrimony, the *res et sacramentum* is not a character, but a *bond* as we shall see.

Res et Sacramentum: proximate disposition for grace or the *res tantum*, which is given in the sacrament.

Res Tantum (that which is signified):
The habitual grace of the virtues and the gifts: this is, sanctifying grace perfecting the essence of the soul, and the virtues and the gifts perfecting the various faculties.

The special help of the sacrament: this is a certain special help or effect which in the genus of material causality is the *res et sacramentum* considered as a proximate disposition for grace. In the genus of formal causality this disposition is the special effect of the sacrament and becomes with the presence of grace a *formed* disposition, permanently healing the defect against which it is given. It is also a special strength, which one or more virtues enjoy to enable the person to carry out the duties entailed by the sacrament.

Applying this to the sacrament of matrimony and the religious profession, or vow of chastity, we have the following schema:

The Sacrament of Matrimony	*Religious Profession* or *The Promise of Chastity to God*
The expressed consent of two baptized persons (the *Sacramentum Tantum*) representing the mutual interchange of promises on the part of Christ and the Church in reference to a fruitful union (a mystical oneness *in via*)	The expressed promise of chastity representing an eschatological state — for the man death to the world, for the woman death to the world and marriage with Christ in reference to His pure and immaculate union with the Church — (a mystical oneness *in termino*)
↓	↓
Brings about	Brings about
↓	↓
The *Res et Sacramentum* or bond which:	A *moral* bond which:
1. As a *bond* links the two persons to one another in something of the way in which Christ and the earthly Church are linked to each other. In this sense the *Res et Sacramentum* is a *remote disposition* for the grace of the sacrament.	1. As a *moral bond* or link existing between the soul and God unites them in a most intimate way such that their union represents that of the *blessed* soul with God in heaven. In this sense, the bond acts as a *remote* disposition for the grace proper to this way of life.
2. As a proximate *disposition*, prepares the soul *immediately* for the grace of the sacrament.	2. As an *immediate* or *proximate disposition*, prepares the soul immediately for the grace proper to this state or way of life.
↓	↓
This leads in	This leads in
↓	↓
The *Res Tantum* or the sacramental grace of marriage. This includes three elements as we saw above:	The grace of state or that grace proper to religious life or dedicated chastity. This includes likewise three elements:

1. The modification of sanctifying grace and of the infused virtues such as they are needed in carrying out the demands of the married state.[4]

1. The modification of sanctifying grace and of the infused virtues such as they are needed to carry out the specific duties or demands of this way of life — the spiritual marriage or radical baptism which this promise is a sign of.

2. The healing of the wounds of sin that might prove to be obstacles to the full flowering of this union.[5]

2. The healing of the wounds of sin that might prove to be obstacles to this union and prevent one from realizing its full flowering.

3. A concomitant effect which is a title to all the actual graces appropriate to this way of life.[6]

3. A concomitant effect which is a title to the actual graces appropriate to this state.

It is through the res tantum and all that it implies that the bond of union is kept intact and virtuous and that the holy union of the two persons is enabled to increase during the years of their married life.

It is through this grace of state and all that it implies that the bond which is established by the promise — the soul's complete and total dedication to God either through mystical death or through mystical death and marriage as the case might be — is kept intact and virtuous and that the union of the two — God and the soul — is enabled to increase during the years of this way of life.

The grace infused into the soul by reason of the promise of dedicated chastity is superior to that which is given through the sacrament of matrimony since it elevates one to a higher state of life and of union with Christ than does the sacrament of matrimony. For in the first instance one enters into immediate union with Him, whereas in the latter one enters into only mediate union with him through another human being who represents in the institution of Christian marriage Christ Himself.

Thus perfect chastity is a better figure of the union of Christ and the Church, for there the union is entirely spiritual. Christian marriage, on the other hand, symbolizes a union of two persons that is partly spiritual and partly material.

The sacramental grace of matrimony is one that modifies or orientates the life of sanctifying grace given through the sacrament, to enable it to

---

[4] Cf. Sacramental Process above.   [5] Cf. ibid.   [6] Cf. ibid.

produce in the life of those entering this state the virtuous image of the fruitful union of Christ with the Church. Along with this grace there is given infallibly the title or the right to the actual graces necessary to fulfill the functions of this life.

The grace which is given to one through the voluntary assumption of the state of celibacy or virginity modifies or orientates the life of grace in such a way that it is enabled to perform the duties required by this way of life. Thus chastity, for example, will have more ample chance for exercise. In the case of matrimony the virtue of temperance is permanently modified in so far as the concupiscible faculty is healed in a radical manner, in a manner which reaches the very root of the disturbance, and in so far as the virtue of temperance is strengthened to meet the demands of conjugal life. In a similar way in regard to the grace given to one at the time of profession or promise of chastity made to God, the virtue of religion and the virtue(s) of virginity, (liberality, and obedience) are permanently modified, both insofar as the difficulty which one will experience in rendering to God holocaustal subjection is concerned, and insofar as these virtues are strengthened to meet the demands of this new state. (This is to be understood not in an exclusive sense, that is, that only these virtues are affected, but rather in a precise sense.) Indeed, as St. Thomas mentions, in the case of one who has resolved to lead a life of perpetual chastity, there is no longer question of exercising the virtue of chastity; from that moment on there is question of exercising a special and different virtue — that of virginity.[7]

Just as the sacramental grace of matrimony can be increased or nourished and strengthened by the faithful performance of the duties of this state, so too, in the case of voluntary virginity or celibacy, the special grace of this way of life is also strengthened and increased through fidelity to the duties which it entails, duties which are demanded so frequently and in such a holocaustal way.

The internal bond set up in matrimony is temporal of its very nature, insofar as it represents the marriage of Christ with the Church according to its fruitfulness which is, as we know, something of time. The internal bond established by the promise of chastity, on the other hand, since it represents the immaculateness and purity of Christ's union with the Church is something that is de se perpetual, eternal, seen and realized in its full implications only in eternity. For this aspect of Christ's union with the Church — its immaculateness and purity — is something not only of time but something that will continue for all eternity; in fact, it would seem to reach its full meaning and beauty only there.

---

[7] Cf. II–II, Q. 152, a. 3.

In all this talk about the superiority of virginity or celibacy over marriage we must be most careful not to form the judgment either in ourselves or in others that married love is a snare or a trap. It is not an absolution that is given for faults of the senses. It is rather God's elevation of all those acts which will spring from marriage, including those of the flesh which are right and necessary for building life insofar as they are performed with the intention of carrying out in some way the divine plan. For those who are not called to the high vocation of loving God *directly* and *alone*, the way to this love of God will usually be found through the love of a creature who represents Christ or His Church. The force behind this kind of intermediate love, if you will, is also charity, the same charity by which we love God.

Consecrated chastity, however, has as one of its first missions to keep before the eyes of the world that there is a reality or a world of realities which lies far beyond the present one. It is a perpetual commitment by means of which one takes his or her place as a visible witness to the underlying power and truth of all Christianity — no human creature can possibly satisfy man. Only God has this right and this power. Consequently, chastity dedicated to Christ is a kind of constant "historization" or "enfleshment" of a truth expressed so long ago and so admirably by the great St. Augustine: "Our hearts have been made for Thee, O Lord, and they will not rest until they rest in Thee."[8]

---

[8] *Confessions*, I, 1. PL 32, 661.

In concluding this work we might mention that it has been our aim merely to give some understanding of the theology of vocation in its many aspects — exterior, that is to say, the exterior arrangements of the various states of life; and interior, that is to say, the interior effects which they have on the various virtues of the soul. But for all the information which may have been given in the course of these pages, there is need for information of a higher order, through that wisdom which has been very fittingly described in Scripture. It was this wisdom which Solomon asked for when he wrote:

> Wisdom I ask of thee, the same wisdom that dwells so near thy throne. . . . For it is from me that sons and daughters of thine must seek for redress . . . thou hast bidden me raise to thee temple and altar, upon the holy mountain where thou dwellest, model of that holy tabernacle made long ago, whose pattern was of thy own devising. Wisdom was with thee then, privy to all thy designs, she who stood by thee at the world's creation and knows thy whole will, the whole tenor of thy commandments. Let her be thy envoy still out of thy heavenly sanctuary, send her out upon thy errand to be at my side too, and share my labors. How else shall thy will be made clear to me. For her no secret is too dark. So shall my task be accomplished as thou wouldst have it be. . . . Ever since the world began, wisdom was the salve they used, that have won thy favor.[9]

---

[9] Wisd. 9:4–19 passim.

Index

Abdication of fatherhood or motherhood, and virginity, 137

Abnegation of will, by obedience, 146

Absolute, desire for, in contemplative, 61

Act of contemplation, effects of, 60

Action, result of contemplation, 162; spirituality of, 40, 73

Active and contemplative lives, 39 ff; compared, 69 ff; division of life into, 41 ff; harmonization of, 48; practical observations on, 78 ff

Active life, 64 ff; compared with contemplation, 69 ff; meaning of, 43; purposes of, 167

Active religious, contemplation of, 52

Actual graces, vocation and, 204 f

Adaptation, 171; of work to temperament, 82

Adolescence, usual age for vocation, 202

Alphonsus, St., on obligation of following vocation, 210; on signs of religious vocation, 229; special internal grace required for vocation, 187 ff; vocation theory of, 180 ff

Ambrose, St., on virginity, 309 f

Analysis of vocation, biblical, 13 ff; see also Vocation

Angelic life, virginity as, 304 f, 306; see also Virginity

Annunciation, vocation and, 8

Annus Sacer, on evangelical counsels, 115

Anselm, St., on teaching of youth, 155

Anthropocentric spirituality, 171 n

Antonomastically, members of religious communities called religious, 112

Apostolate, gradual introduction to, 169 n; medical, 156 ff; of widowhood, 321

Apostolates, of teaching and preaching, 153; variety of, and perfection, 80

Apostolic vocation, born of charity, 84

Aptitudes, correct use of, 82

Aquinas, St. Thomas, 4; act of contemplation, 59; causes of vocation, 203; on degrees of poverty, 168; on diocesan priesthood and state of perfection, 275; on divine election, 195; on divine vocation, 182 ff; division of vocation for, 22; division of theology, 5; on episcopate as state of perfection, 255; on excellence of religious vocation, 251; on excellence of vow, 151; on intensity and extension of grace, 197; on interior holiness of priest, 272; on obligation of following vocation, 214 f; on poverty, 121; pre-eminence of contemplative life over active, 70 f, 73; relation of active to contemplative lives, 84; special internal grace required for vocation, 187; on state of perfection, 111 n; on transferring from one institute to another, 249 n; on virginity, 125

Aquirendae, status perfectionis, 110

Arintero, John, on difference of vocations, 85

Assimilation to God, vocation and, 19

Attraction, relation of, to vocation to secular institute, 107

"Attraction" theory, 179 ff

Augustine, St., on profane study and prayer, 57; on purpose of theology, 3; on reconciliation of two lives, 42; on study, 156; on virginity, 313

Austerity, and excellence of religious community, 168

Authority, of God in religious obedience, 141; role of, in vocation, 18

Balance, emotional, in priestly and religious vocations, 298; required in contemplative, 61

Beauty of Church, difference of grades and, 89

347

175; on obligation of following vocation, 207 f
Vigor of vocation, measurement of, 245
Virgin, image of, 318; as image of
Church, 130; as mother of Christ,
310
Virginity, as act of faith, hope, and love,
131; as angelic virtue, 133; as angelic
way of life, 306, 311, 318; apostolate
and, 159; charisma of N.T., 131; and
Christian perfection, 319; as codified
way of life, 308; consecrated, in world,
as vocation, 301 ff; dedicated, eschatological state, 338; dedicated, who should
be advised to lead this life, 322; difficulties in, 138; dignity of source, 310;
donation of body to Christ, 199; earliest form of asceticism, 117; equal to
marriage to Christ, 303; as eschatological, 133; as eschatological state demanding no sacramental sign, 338; free
choice of, 311; and free choice and
grace, 319; fruitfulness of, 132, 313;
fruits of, 318; gift of God, 133, 138,
312, 314, 323; gift of, manifestation
of God's love, 138; gift of person to
God, 309; graces of, compared with
those of marriage, 340 ff; highest degree of perfection, 305; indissolubility
of, 228; as marriage with Christ, 317;
means to regain immortality, 305; and
motherhood, 313; motives for, 127 ff,
312, 316; and nervous system or personality, 319; personal love for Christ,
322; positive aims of, 139 f; really perfect, perpetual, 316; sign of all-embracing love, 141; specific kind of chastity,
125; superiority of, over marriage,
126 ff, 132, 313, 326 f, 322; symbolism
of 331 f, 342; transcends division of
heart, 322; as true marriage, 132; vocation of, a gift, 126; way in paganism,
302; as witness to power of Gospel,
308
Virgins, consecrated, living at home
(domestic), 315; veiling of, in early
Church, 309
Virtue of religion, and marriage, 333;
priestly vocation and, 299 f; in religious
vocations, 113
Virtues, proportionate growth in, 91; relationship of, with sacraments, 337;
role of, in vocation, 204
Vision, Christ's, as end of teaching, 154

Visions, and charismatic gift of prophecy,
32
Vocation, assimilation to God, 19; basic,
Christian, 20 ff; Bible and, 13; causes
of awareness of, 203 f; communication
of God's grace, 11; complete notion
of, 184; definition of, 6; determined
by God, 7; a dialogue, 9; discernment
of, time of, 246 ff; division of, 18 ff;
election of God and, 13; elements of,
in Bible, 14; elements of, today, 17,
184, 192; external, 174; fundamental
theological principle of, 7; genesis of,
202; grace of, obscure but real, 9;
gradual growth of, 193; how made
known, 14 ff; image of God and, 19 n;
includes preparation by God, 192; loss
of, 245; to marriage, 332 f; to marriage, gift from God, 324; to marriage,
signs of, 324; means of nourishing,
242 ff; modification of grace-life and,
11; in natural order, 18 ff; religious,
nature of, 195 ff; not of human making, 18; not immediately perceptible,
201; obligation of following, 207 ff;
ordinary and extraordinary, 175, 219;
place of study of, 6; possible to lose,
201; predestination and, 7; presentation
of, by recruiter, 222; problem of, 1 ff;
problem of temporary, 223, 228 and
n; purpose of, 10; in relation to theology, 5; religious, defined, 201; religious,
signs of, 228 ff; religious, theories of,
173 ff; a reserved thing, 14; rewards
of, 16; role of authority in, 18; to
secular institute, 107; in a sense divine,
192; signs of, 175, 181, 182, 190;
signs of contemplative, 60 ff; signs of,
to priesthood, 295 ff; special gift, 176;
special grace, 108 f; special internal,
nature of, 195 ff; special, theories of,
177 ff; supernaturality of, 9; study of,
proper to many disciplines, 2; in supernatural order, 20 ff; as total commitment, 16; usual age for, 202; virtue of
religion and, 196 f
Vocational counselor, see Counselor
Vocations, fostering of, 242 ff; parental
interference with, 137; a theology of,
4
Vow, and bishop's obligation to flock,
257; counsels and, 149; definition of,
151; excellence of works done under,
150; of obedience, 141 ff; of religion,